CHAUCER AND HIS FRENCH CONTEMPORARIES
Natural Music in the Fourteenth Century

Chaucer and His French Contemporaries

Natural Music in the Fourteenth Century

JAMES I. WIMSATT

UNIVERSITY OF TORONTO PRESS
Toronto Buffalo London

© University of Toronto Press 1991
Toronto Buffalo London
Printed in Canada
Paperback edition 1993

ISBN 0-8020-2742-3 (cloth)
ISBN 0-8020-7189-9 (paper)

Printed on acid-free paper

Canadian Cataloguing in Publication Data
Wimsatt, James I.
Chaucer and his French contemporaries

Includes index.
ISBN 0-8020-2742-3 (bound)
ISBN 0-8020-7189-9 (pbk.)

1. Chaucer, Geoffrey, d. 1400 – Style.
2. Chaucer, Geoffrey, d. 1400 – Knowledge –
Literature.   3. English poetry – French influences.
4. French poetry – To 1500 – History and criticism.
I. Title.

PR1940.W55 1991 821'.1 C91-094466-0

Publication of this book is made possible by a grant from the
National Endowment for the Humanities.

To my family

Contents

Preface

Of the several stories of the relationship of Chaucer's writings to literary traditions – to classical Latin, to Christian Latin, to Italian, to Old French, and to Middle French – scholars have treated the connection to Middle French the least fully and with the least understanding of the norms of the literature. Yet a good case can be made that the contemporary French poets exerted the most important, because the most basic, influence on Chaucer. Part of the problem has been that modern scholarly specialization has fractured the bond between poetry and music. Chaucerians have not connected the powerful demonstrable influence that Guillaume de Machaut and the poets of his tradition exerted on Chaucer with the fact that Machaut's lyrics set to music are 'amongst the most elegant' artworks of the Middle Ages.[1] The relationship between Chaucer and his French contemporaries has been seen as a product of historical circumstance rather than aesthetic communion. In this book I aim to show the integral connection of two high poetic arts and to demonstrate how Chaucer's poetry derives major values from the Middle French formes fixes lyrics, which are all in origin musical forms, and from the longer poems that are closely related to the lyrics. Critics have given the narrative values of Chaucer's work sufficient attention; Chaucer is above all a story-teller, they claim. Yet literature began with lyric, and so did Chaucer. I hope to illuminate the essential lyric values in his work that originate in the French poetic mode.

I began reading Middle French poetry a quarter-century ago as a student. I was trying to find out exactly what Chaucer added to his French sources to produce the marvellous elegy *The Book of the Duchess*. At the outset I confronted a paradox. The articles of George Kittredge in particular showed that there was relatively little in the poem that had not been touched by the Middle French originals,[2] yet the evaluations of scholars asserted the poverty of the French work. Virtually everyone thought it precious, arid, vapid, and the like. In attempting to account for the seeming transformation of dross to gold, I wrote a doctoral dissertation and then a book that centred on the development of the long French love poem up to the *Book of the Duchess*. In the process I found out that the poem Chaucer had produced from the foreign materials was certainly original, but that those materials had unrecognized aesthetic qualities which entered intrinsically into his poem. My book *Chaucer and the French Love Poets* (1968) treated primarily features of narrative structure in the French works. It did not deal systematically with Chaucer's continuing relationships to the contemporary French writers, nor with what I have come to recognize as the essential aesthetic feature of the Middle French mode, its lyric nature. It is these that provide the focus of the present book.

Happily, other scholars have also been developing a taste for Middle French poetry in recent decades. Their work provides both support for my judgments and aid for my analyses. Daniel Poirion's *Le Poète et le prince* (1965) has been crucial, providing a perceptive, encyclopaedic study of the Middle French forms and the cultural milieu that produced the work.[3] More recently Douglas Kelly's comprehensive work on the mode, *Medieval Imagination*, has shown the valuable contribution of rhetoric to the French poets' work.[4] In particular, musicologists and specialists in literature have been concentrating their attention on Machaut, the leading figure in the tradition. Symptomatic of the burgeoning interest in the great poet-composer's work are the two major symposia which observed the six hundredth anniversary of his death in 1977, and several recent critical books on his poetry.[5]

Chaucerians, however, have not been generally affected by the new enthusiasm of Romance scholars for these writers. Impressive evidence of Chaucer's use of their work continues to be presented, but it is chronically minimized or ignored. Though the formes fixes lyrics are the foundation and base of the French mode, these especially are denigrated, as in this faint praise by an estimable Chaucer scholar:

In a very real sense ... late medieval lyrics are more a manifestation of manners, broadly taken, than of literary inspiration ... and perhaps they should be thought of as versified conversation rather than poetry. They aim at truth and pleasantness, though more often at the latter. Generally speaking, they are essentially affable works, their platitudes keyed to reinforcing social and ethical norms, their language suitably decorous. Their goal more often than not is enjoyment at the level of recreation, refreshment – the kind of unchallenging satisfactions associated today with the popular arts.[6]

From such a comment one would hardly suspect that the work in question supplies a primary element in Chaucer's poetry from the *Book of the Duchess* through the *Legend of Good Women* and is still important in the *Canterbury Tales.*

The scholarly treatment of *Troilus and Criseyde* has been particularly egregious in its neglect of the Middle French relationship. A major point of this book is that the influence of the Machaut tradition on Chaucer reached its apogee in the *Troilus.* Yet two important recent studies by eminent scholars that focus in their entirety on Chaucer's poetic materials for *Troilus* – one of them is even called *Chaucer and the Poets* – do not once mention Machaut.[7] Since the extent and nature of the influence obviously has not been apparent to many people, and since *Troilus* is Chaucer's most important complete poem, let me anticipate later discussions by suggesting briefly where the effect of the French poetry is found in the work.

Boccaccio foremost, then Guido delle Colonne and Benoît de Sainte-Maure, Boethius and Dante, Vergil and Statius, Ovid and Jean de Meun – all of these had a major effect on *Troilus.* Chaucer not only responded to their language and used it, but he understood and absorbed the great and diverse artistry of these poets, displaying it metamorphosed in his magnificent poem. If we allow for the vast contribution of these great writers, there seems to be no room for the Middle French poets to have an effect. The fact is, however, that much of their influence enters on another level. For instance, while the 'Canticus Troili' (book I 400–20), which Troilus sings to himself after seeing Criseyde in the temple, is 'a fairly close rendering of Petrarch's Sonnet 88,'[8] the sonnet is not the only work in the background. There is also the source of the narrative context, the *Filostrato.* Furthermore, apropos of my argument, there is the matter of lyric type, which obviously is not derived from Petrarch. The very length of the piece betrays the generic difference. Chaucer could have easily made the fourteen lines of the Italian into two rime royal stanzas of seven lines, but he chose instead to make a virtual ballade. The Middle French ballade, the favourite lyric type of the fourteenth-century French poets and of Chaucer, is a three-stanza form, its stanzas typically tied together in a logical chain. Conformably, the English poet expanded Petrarch's sonnet to three stanzas of seven lines each, and gave it a discursive development characteristic of the ballade. It is of fundamental significance that the rime royal versification of *Troilus* derives from the most popular of the French ballade stanzas, thus making the ballade potentially present throughout the work. Its form comes to the fore not only in the 'Canticus Troili' but also in numerous other passages in the poem; typically, Chaucer expanded kernels of narrative detail, often Boccaccio's, into well-formed lyric expositions that match or approximate ballade form.

The presence of contemporary French poetry in *Troilus* is not always hidden behind texts like Boccaccio's story or Petrarch's sonnet. There are in places substantial direct borrowings of phraseology from Machaut, which together with notable influences on characterization and incident manifest the French presence in *Troilus*. The most extensive passage drawn directly from the French is one of the most crucial in the poem, Antigone's song, primarily inspired by several lays of Machaut. In this song we find unalloyed the lyric component of the formes fixes mode, which affects the whole of Chaucer's version of the narrative and differentiates it radically from Boccaccio's. The fact that Antigone is singing (even if only in the reader's mind) is significant, for music figures importantly in the mode. It was in the work of talented musical composers like Adam de la Halle and Jean Lescurel that the mode first gained its identity and vitality, and even when its poets came to use the metrical forms without musical accompaniment the verse retained musical properties, as I will discuss in succeeding chapters.

Conditions in the world of scholarship are in some ways quite auspicious for demonstrating the contribution of the French lyric mode to Chaucer's 'makynge.' The historicist proclivities of today's scholars should help here. Even before the renewed emphasis on history, Daniel Poirion perceived that the cultural context provided by the court is essential to an appreciation of Middle French poetry; that is, we need to understand its audience and its function, which assuredly went beyond providing recreation. Whoever wishes to understand what contemporary French poetry meant to Chaucer must look to historical factors attendant on its production and performance.

A related development in Chaucer studies, the growing interest in literary context – broad matters of intertextuality – also should help. While curiosity about Chaucer's Middle French connections has remained moderate, there has been a notable increase in this decade in the number and quality of publications on Chaucer's Italian affiliations. One can enumerate editions, studies, and translations by Piero Boitani, Nicholas Havely, Howard Schless, Barry Windeatt, David Wallace, and Donald Howard.[9] These works are generally marked by a much more sophisticated view and treatment of source material than has tradition- ally been the case. David Wallace's study of Chaucer and the early Boccaccio, for instance, deals broadly with many facets of the relation- ship in order to present the larger picture of 'Chaucer's development as a European poet,' and thereby shows how Boccaccio and other Italian poets drew on the French tradition. Such work, then, both prepares the way for broader and more penetrating treatments of source relationships and invites us to view the matter in continent-wide perspective, whereby one may see the usual precedence of the French work through most of the fourteenth century.

On the other hand, contemporary criticism has focused more on nar- rative than on lyric, with the result that narrative values especially today are the centre of critical attention. This situation favours work on Boc- caccio, whose main strength is in his narrative, but it tends to skew analyses of Chaucer's writings. Lyric elements are basic in all of his work before the *Canterbury Tales*, yet the preoccupation of critics with narrative and the linear progress of discourse has led them to neglect the lyric aspects – the ruminative and emotive expression and the mus- ical features that are so important to his verse. It is precisely these elements in Chaucer's work that the Middle French poetry inspired. My initial task, then, is to focus attention on aspects of Chaucer that have been accepted unanalytically as incidental or as somehow inherent in the narratives or the poet's personality.

My ultimate goal is to show the essential lyric qualities that Chaucer's poetry derived from the French work and to analyse his literary rela- tionships to the various poets. Most of this book is built on a chrono- logical plan, which suits my aim of presenting the main facts of Chaucer's relationships to his French contemporaries in the most accessible form. Before undertaking this historical narrative, however, I describe in the first chapter the Middle French lyric mode – the mode of 'natural music' – using Machaut's and Deschamps' explicit statements about it and a selective analysis of Machaut's practice. The remaining chapters treat, in order, (2) Jean de le Mote, whose evident importance for the mode and for Chaucer has not been previously recognized; (3–5) Guillaume de Machaut, the main name in Middle French poetry and by far the most important contemporary French influence on Chaucer; (6) Jean Froissart, a major poet as well as a chronicler, whose career provides a near counterpart to Chaucer's; (7) Oton de Granson, probably Chaucer's best friend among the prominent poets and the highest ranking of them; (8) Eustache Deschamps, whose work is rich in materials important for this study, but whose effect on Chaucer's work has been consistently overrated; and (9) the status of the poetic tradition in France and England in 1400, the year Chaucer died. My narrative of the development of the French mode and its effects on Chaucer's poetry extends almost exactly over one century, beginning in the reigns of Philippe le Bel and Edward II at the outset of the fourteenth century and concluding with the *Cent ballades*, the deaths of Granson and Chaucer, and the decline of Froissart and Deschamps at century's end. Much of what I present here makes explicit and synthesizes the results of my research and publications over the past twenty years on Chaucer's French relationships.[10] The debts I have incurred in the development of this book, then, are various and extensive, and the following list is by no means exhaustive. I am grateful to the Guggenheim Foundation for a fellowship in 1981–2, to the National Endowment for the Humanities and the National Humanities Center respectively for a fellowship and for a fine study environment and facilities in 1987–8, and to the University of Texas University Research Institute for its matching support in both years. For advice, encouragement, and assistance of various kinds I am deeply indebted to Morton Bloomfield, Derek Brewer, William Calin, John Hurt Fisher, John Fleming, Donald Howard, Robert Kaske, Robert Lumiansky, Russell Peck, and D.W. Robertson Jr. For reading and making valuable suggestions on some or all of the manuscript, I particularly thank Rebecca Beal, Rita Copeland, Lawrence Earp, William Kibler, David Wallace, Mary Ann Wimsatt, and the readers for the University of Toronto Press who made numerous very helpful suggestions and emendations.

I am grateful to the following for permission to quote from editions of Chaucer's and Machaut's verse: Houghton-Mifflin Company, publishers of *The Riverside Chaucer*, Third Edition (copyright 1987); the University of Georgia Press, publishers of *Le Jugement du roy de Behaigne and Remede de Fortune* (copyright 1989); and Nigel Wilkins, editor of *La Louange des dames* (copyright 1972). For permission to use parts of previously published articles of mine (cited in note 10 above), I also thank the editors and publishers of *Mediaeval Studies, Medium Aevum,* and *Yearbook of English Studies*. Finally, a word about the relationship of this book to Charles Muscatine's magnificent *Chaucer and the French Tradition*. Muscatine's approach and chronological focus are quite different from mine. Our studies, then, are complementary. I would wish this book, not to be measured against his, but to stand on the shelf beside his as another valuable demonstration of the permeation of Chaucer's work with French cultural influence.

CHAUCER AND HIS FRENCH CONTEMPORARIES
Natural Music in the Fourteenth Century

CHAPTER ONE

Natural Music in Middle French Verse and Chaucer

At the conclusion of W.B. Yeats's well-known lyric, *Sailing to Byzantium*, the aged speaker, having left behind the 'dying generations' of the natural world, pictures himself 'out of nature' and arriving at the 'holy city of Byzantium.' Once there, he declares, he will not take his 'bodily form from any natural thing,' but will assume a form like that of a bird made by goldsmiths from hammered gold and enamelling – such a bird as serves 'to keep a drowsy Emperor awake' or to sing 'To lords and ladies of Byzantium / Of what is past, or passing, or to come.' As Yeats presents it, the artistry that fashions his golden bird and its song has much more in common with the poetic process of Chaucer's French contemporaries (designed to please fourteenth-century lords and ladies) than with the Romantic art of Yeats himself; indeed, the bird and the song provide an excellent image for Middle French poetry, which I follow Eustache Deschamps in identifying as 'natural music.' In explaining natural music and its uses, this chapter provides a theoretical introduction to the subsequent historical survey of Chaucer's relationships to Middle French poetry.

The golden bird represents the poet 'out of nature' that Yeats's speaker wishes to become, whose lyric is constant and immortal though its subject is the world of mutability. Yeats thus sets up an intriguing distinction between the form and manner of the verse on the one hand and its subject-matter on the other. It is not so much that the poetic process makes the world of change immortal, but rather that mutability is made to subserve the 'artifice of eternity.' In the *Prologue* to his poetry, Guillaume de Machaut sets up a distinction between manner and matter that is ultimately quite similar to that which Yeats makes between the immortal bird and the mortal subject it celebrates.

As the fully matured statement of the premier French poet and musical composer of the fourteenth century who more than anyone else established the mode, the *Prologue* is particularly important.[1] At its beginning the goddess Nature presents to the poet the skills needed for verse composition (Scens, Musique, and Rhetorique), and then the God of Love appears, bringing Machaut appropriate subject-matter (Dous Penser, Plaisance, and Esperance). The first gifts bear on the manner of the poetry and the second on the matter; these do not necessarily accord:

Et s'on fait de triste matiere
Si est joieuse la maniere
Dou fait; car ja bien ne fera
Ne gaiement ne chantera
Li cuers qui est pleins de tristesse,
Pour ce qu'il het et fuit leesse.[2]   (V, 43–8)

And even though one writes about a sad subject, still the manner of the poem will be joyful; never will the heart which is full of sadness compose well or sing gaily, because it hates and flees joy.

Even when Machaut's lover protests his sincerity, stating that in his sadness he must be truthful and write a sad song, we understand that the poet differs from his fictional counterpart.[3] The poet's verse and the bird's song, their gaiety immutable, find their subject in the mutable fortunes of the mortal world. However sad the subject, the poem will express joy.

Whether the 'matiere' is happy or sad, Machaut states, when it is taken into the poem it becomes joyful. He thereby severs a connection between his own feelings and the feelings he represents within the poem. He also manifests no aim of stimulating the represented feelings in the audience. His stated object instead is to praise and please ladies (*Prologue* III, 24; V, 17–18, 177–8), and to reveal and glorify the benefits and honours that reside in Love.[4]

As with the song that the golden bird sings to a Byzantine court audience, Machaut's poems performed before the French courts find their subject-matter in the world of change – of happiness, apprehension, and sadness – but they purvey pure joy (gaudium), a quality of heaven, of a timeless sphere like Yeats's other-worldly Byzantium. It would not do, nevertheless, to speak of a strict division between the immutable and the mutable, since for both Yeats and Machaut the mutable subject becomes an integral part of the immortal songs. There is a difference between the poets' conceptions in that Machaut is more willing to rationalize his conception in Scholastic fashion than is the Romantic Yeats. For the latter the song of the golden bird represents an ineffable ideal poetry; it cannot be described. But Machaut is specific: for him the poem is characterized by gaudium and produced by Scens, Rhetorique, and Musique (*Prologue*, ballade I). Scens 'informs' the imagination ('engin'), and Rhetorique instructs in 'versifying' and 'metrifying,' but Musique is the particular bearer of Joy. Machaut was the leading French musical composer of his time. When he speaks of 'musique,' however, he does not mean simply what we call music. In the *Art de dictier* Eustache Deschamps, Machaut's disciple and celebrant, refers to both the accompanying melody of a poem and the sound system of a poem's words as 'music'. The sounds of the words he designates 'natural music.' Machaut composed many lyrics without supplying notation, and it seems clear that he, like Deschamps, thought of all such works as musical.[5]

'Natural music' as defined by Deschamps characterizes succinctly the distinctive quality of Middle French verse which exerted a major influence on Chaucer and through him on the English literary tradition. For the purposes of this study it is necessary to explore the significance of the term 'natural music' at some length, but first I want to consider two other terms that I also call upon frequently, 'lyric' and 'lyrical.'

LYRIC AND LYRICAL

In his essay 'Lyrik und lyrisch,' Emil Staiger generalizes that no 'law of genre' is possible for the noun 'lyric'/'lyrik' since the poems that have been identified as lyrics are too diverse. By contrast, he continues, the adjective 'lyric(al)'/'lyrische,' when applied to literature, has a relatively unambiguous significance. The explanation that he offers for the apparent discrepancy is that the adjective 'lyric(al)' is not related to the noun 'lyric' as the adjective 'iron'/'eisern' is related to the noun 'iron'/'eisen.' Unlike the latter pair, in which the adjective implies the noun (an iron bar must be made of iron), the lyric poem does not have to be lyrical, and, inversely, lyrical characteristics are not found in lyric poems alone. Thus, epigrammatic poems, though commonly called lyrics, often are not lyrical, while the term is readily applicable to many literary texts like dramas and novels that are clearly not lyrics.[6]

Staiger is discussing the accepted usage of 'lyrische' as applied to literature of every age. When I apply the noun 'lyric' and the adjective 'lyric(al)' to Middle French poetry here, I also use the terms in a non-specialized way, in line with accepted usage among literary critics. The discrepancy between the adjective and the noun presents the same difficulty for the description of Middle French poetry as for literature in general. In the main the poems, long and short, are highly 'lyrical' by almost anyone's definition; at the same time, a significant number of them conform to lyric versification, and are always called 'lyrics,' but are not lyric(al) in nature: political complaints, narratives of various kinds, humorous and bizarre pieces, witty dialogues.

'Lyric' and 'lyrical' are nearly indispensable terms for this discussion of Middle French verse. While they are not medieval terms, criteria originating in medieval tradition support the category 'lyric poem,' if not the less specific adjective. Modern criteria for a lyric poem accord with explicit and implicit distinctions that the French poets and their scribes make in the rubrics, in their discussions of form, and in the way in which they organize their manuscripts. Most of the Middle French 'lyrics' are distinguished by set forms, called formes fixes, and are labelled ballade, rondeau, virelay, lay, and chant royal (with other five-stanza forms). Poems in such forms are commonly grouped together in the manuscripts. Also logically classed as lyrics are other short poems of varying versification that are mixed in with the formes fixes in manuscript under headings like 'complaint,' 'prayer,' or such. Length is indicative but not controlling. Some rondeaux are only eight lines long, and some lays have as many as five hundred lines. At the same time, even when the content or length of some works does not exclude them from the category of lyrics, I do not so classify them if they have no fixed form and are never grouped with other lyrics in the manuscripts.

As applied to Middle French poetry in this study, therefore, the noun 'lyric' is based on distinctions that the medieval poets and scribes saw as significant. While it does not predicate a set of invariable characteristics, it does provide a firm division between lyrics and non-lyrics; there is no question of a half-lyric or a near lyric. The adjective lyric(al), by contrast, as used here and commonly in literary discussions, allows all manner of degree; it is clear that Middle French court poetry in general is lyrical, but there are degrees in its lyricality, and many of the long poems are more lyrical than some works with the forms of lyrics. Notwithstanding, the adjective is closely related to the noun since the qualities designated by 'lyric(al)' are those most characteristic of lyric poetry.

In the great body of modern critical writing on the subject, there is a certain basic agreement about these qualities. Some of the recent discussions may clarify what I signify by the adjective.

The well-regarded *Handbook to Literature* provides a starting-point. In defining the lyric poem, the *Handbook* essentially characterizes lyricality. The lyric, it states, is a 'brief subjective poem strongly marked by imagination, melody, and emotion, and creating a single, unified impression.'[7] Like most such definitions this one presents problems of vagueness ('marked by imagination,' 'unified impression'), but it also identifies specific characteristics, thereby providing a useful list for discussion of lyricality: brevity, subjectivity, emotion, and melody.

Brevity is perhaps the most frequently cited trait of lyric, but in the main short length is a symptom of a more basic and essential characteristic, that which Northrop Frye identifies as 'discontinuity,' a term I use frequently in this book. In Frye's vision of literature as a territory in which the different genres have varying degrees of dominance, he sees the 'lyrical area' as one in which the 'sense of the discontinuous increases.' In lyrical verse, he says, lines and stanzas keep interrupting, leading the reader away 'from an ordinary experience in space or time, or rather from a verbal mimesis of it.' Instead of a continuing narrative, the lyric provides a meditation or a discourse revolving around an occasion, either public, like a funeral, or private, 'like drinking or lovemaking.'[8] In Middle French poetry discontinuity is manifested most obviously in lines of set length, distinguished by complex rhymes and gathered in firm stanza units; these provide divisions for a lyric discourse that is very light on narrative, in long poems as well as short ones, focusing on such occasions as the impending separation of lovers or the lady's acceptance of her suitor.

The traits of subjectivity and emotion (more precisely, subjective point of view and emotive content) are closely related. In Roman Jakobson's view, for instance, the lyric poem is 'oriented toward the first person' and 'intimately linked with the emotive function,' typically representing the first-person speaker's feelings.[9] Jonathan Culler reminds us, though, that one ought not to think of the lyric utterance as primarily a realistic expression of feeling. 'The methodological heritage of the New Criticism encourages us to focus above all on the complexities of the speaker's attitude' revealed in the poem. But that focus can lead to denigration of works of more self-conscious rhetoric, as those marked by the figure of apostrophe, which usually seem overwrought if read as naturalistic utterance.[10] The stricture certainly applies to Middle French lyric, which is both rhetorical and conventional. Such poetry often becomes, in Jakobson's terms, 'poetry of the second person,' which is addressed pointedly to another, and 'is either supplicatory or exhortative.'[11]

W.R. Johnson's study of classical and modern lyric classifies lyric poems more sharply according to the object of the first-person speaker's discourse. Johnson sets up two main categories, 'the I–You poem, in which the poet addresses or pretends to address his thought and feelings to another person,' and the 'meditative poem, in which the poet talks to himself or to no one in particular or, sometimes, calls on, apostrophizes, inanimate or nonhuman entities, abstractions, or the dead.'[12] In Johnson's scheme, the I–You poem is characteristic of classical verse, while the meditative type has come increasingly to dominate nineteenth- and twentieth-century lyric. Johnson clearly prefers, or at least finds healthier, the I–You type, made up of 'lyrical discourse ... the process by means of which the lyric poet describes (and so evokes) an emotion or complex cluster of emotions while simultaneously submitting that evocative description to dialectical scrutiny, to deliberation, to argumentation' (p. 197). In the modern meditative lyric, by contrast, the sense of audience within the poem is lost.

Though he does say that Shakespeare, Donne, and Herbert are among the 'masters of lyrical deliberation' (I–You poetry), Johnson is little concerned with verse written between classical Latin times and the nineteenth century. He passes over medieval lyric in a paragraph, suggesting that it began 'in what Sir Thomas Browne calls "that vulgar and Taverne Musick, which makes one man merry, another sad," and that reminds him of "the sensible fit of that Harmony, which intellectually sounds in the eares of God" ' (p. 5). The second part of the quotation represents a thoroughly medieval attitude, suggesting a formal concern that looks to transcendental experience, while the first part is less authentic, evoking the spurious association of tavern and church that modern imagination has ascribed to the Goliards. On balance, the I–You / meditative distinction is quite enlightening for Johnson's study of classical and modern poetry, but it has little to contribute to a definition of lyrics such as Machaut or Chaucer wrote. 'Alas!' says Machaut, beginning a meditative type, 'I have failed in my very sweet desire, / Because Fortune is contrary to me,' and then 'Alas!' in an I–You type opening, 'I so much desire the time when I will see you, my very sweet one ... that it seems to me ... a hundred years since I saw your bright face.'[13] Subjective, emotive expression characterizes both poems, and the effect seems much the same whether or not the addressee is specified.

The features of discontinuity and emotive subjective presentation characterize most Middle French court poetry, but they do not primarily account for its particular character and value. The discontinuity of the poems, resulting mainly from the non-narrative nature of the content, is disguised and counteracted by long clauses and artful transitions. Similarly, the emotions of the speaker are not a strong force in the work. While the emotional commitment of the speaker in a lyric like Yeats's *Sailing to Byzantium*, expressed through a highly original mythology, is a major factor in its effectiveness, for Middle French poems hyperbolic expressions of feeling are matters of convention. The speakers who suffer and rejoice in relentless superlatives are counters that serve the more distinctive values of the French work. These values are manifested primarily in its sound system, what the *Handbook* calls its melody. In Middle French verse, unlike most Romantic and modern lyric, discontinuity, subjectivity, and expression of emotion subserve this melody – this poetic music.

A usual characterization of the lyric emphasizes the importance of sound and refers to its musicality, as in the *Handbook*. A longer definition will note further that the lyre is responsible for the word, and remark that Greek and other primitive poetry was originally performed to the accompaniment of a harp. Some see this early connection of lyric with music as inorganic, and the divorce of music from lyric as a natural historical development, but almost all probing discussions find continuing significance in the association. For Northrop Frye, once a practising music critic, the originary association of lyric with music has two integral consequences: it leads the verse away from ordinary language, from 'sense into sound, from reason into rhyme, from syntax into echo, assonance, refrain, even nonsense syllables.' Another consequence is that 'the words do not resonate against the things they describe, but against other words and sounds.'[14] In another formulation Tilottama Rajan, asserting the 'monologic' tendencies of lyric in contrast to other literary genres, speaks of the conventions that 'ask us to respond to poetry on the level of sound rather than content and as song rather than language.' These conventions 'allow the poem to unfold in a timeless and transcendental space.' The consequence for Rajan is that 'lyric, because of its proximity to song, is associated with a logocentrism that mutes the difference between language and what it signifies, whereas drama makes explicit the dialogic nature of language.'[15] Both Frye and Rajan suggest that meaning in lyric is more or less expendable. The German critic Emil Staiger also indicates that lyrical verse may sacrifice sense for sound.

Such poetry is markedly 'musikalisch,' he states, 'so much so that often the sense of the words seems less important than their sound. We understand lyrically in a direct manner, without the grammatical, logical, or perceptual relationships having to be clear.'[16]

The rhythmic sound patterns of lyric poetry assuredly are musical. And in the Middle French lyric more than in almost any body of poetry the sound system is dominant, making the term 'music' appropriate. This does not mean, however, that verbal sense is made either unclear or irrelevant, as the critics' statements might suggest. Rather, as John Stevens says of Dante's conception of lyric, 'It is not that the "sound must seem an echo to the *sense*" but something more physical – "the sense must seem an echo to the *sound*." '[17] Middle French poetry conforms to this conception; it does not sacrifice sense to sound, but rather puts the sense in service to the sound. After treating somewhat cursorily modern insight into the relation of sound to sense in poetry, I will try to show just how this may be true through a discussion of Deschamps' conception of 'natural music.'

Recent treatments of lyric have tended to concentrate on aspects of point of view and subject-matter rather than the sound,[18] which is often dismissed with vague commentary on the music of the verse. When modern theorists do write about sound, the assumption is that the phonetics of a work ideally reinforces the sense, usually mimetically or expressively. Paul de Man finds Rilke most successful when 'the play of sound seems mimetically to overcome contingency ... as sound reinforces and determines meaning.'[19] Northrop Frye similarly finds mimesis, 'imitative harmony,' in the sound of a poem by Wyatt.[20] Likewise, in the essay 'Linguistics and Poetics,' Jakobson argues against 'phonetic isolationism,' stating that 'any conspicuous similarity in sound is evaluated in respect to similarity and / or dissimilarity in meaning.'[21]

In these treatments of the relation of sound and sense, the implicit model is one that is inherent in structural descriptions of language. Analysis begins with the phonemes, significant units of sound, progresses to the morphemes, the clusters of phonemes that make bases and affixes of words, and then builds to the syntactical ordering of morphemes in sentences. This structural level is made to correlate with lexical meanings to convey the sense of an utterance. Such a model seems to accord very well with one's intuitive experience with everyday use of language. One has a meaning to convey, so one builds up sentences that will express this meaning; whatever the details of the construction of the sentences, the structure will subserve the content.

Literature, however, involves a specialized use of language. In Jakobson's useful schematization of the factors of verbal communication, the 'poetic' function of language focuses on the message itself, this notably in contrast to the 'referential' or 'denotative' function.[22] Not that the 'poetic' function supersedes the 'referential'; in literature the poetic simply is emphasized. Umberto Eco, making use of Jakobson's analysis, notes that 'Insofar as the aesthetic text has a self-focussing quality ... its structural arrangement becomes one of the contents that it conveys.'[23] A use of language that focuses on the phonetic aspect of the message, then, will add to the contentual meaning.

The analysis appears unexceptionable; where Middle French poetry calls the analysis into question is in the tacit or expressed assumption that in successful poetry the added phonetic meaning is somehow designed to reinforce the semantic meaning and is successful in so far as it does: 'The sound must seem an echo to the sense.' Jakobson seems of two minds on the subject. One of his well-known analyses clearly illustrates this assumption that mimesis is the major consideration for effective phonetics. To illustrate how sound functions poetically as an adjunct to the sense, he cites the slogan of Dwight Eisenhower's election campaign, 'I like Ike.' He finds that 'both cola of the trisyllabic formula "I like / Ike" rhyme with each other, and the second of the two rhyming words is fully included in the first one (echo rhyme), / layk / – / ayk /, a paronomastic image of a feeling which totally envelops its object. Both cola alliterate with each other, and the first of the two alliterating words is included in the second: / ay / – / ayk /, a paronomastic image of the loving subject enveloped by the beloved object. The secondary, poetic, function of this campaign slogan reinforces its impressiveness and efficacy.'[24] Jakobson describes what we might call a phonetic embrace, a synesthetic hug. Common phonetic analyses of poetry will stress comparable mimetic and expressive effects: the onomatopoeia of 'whine' or 'giggle,' or the expressive effects of a 'gloomy' series of back vowels or of an 'angry' collection of consonant clusters, and so on. Such analyses applied to verse perhaps overemphasize local and limited effects of particular phraseology. The regular sound patterns that carry through a poem typically have much more important values that are formal rather than mimetic or expressive; this applies especially to Middle French 'natural music.'

Ideas that Jakobson expresses when he is talking about the semiotics of art suggest bases for a more global analysis of the sounds in a text, and are much more applicable to Middle French verse (and probably to verse in general). Here he does not allege expressive or mimetic values. Quoting approvingly Gerard Manley Hopkins' statement that 'The artificial part of poetry, perhaps we shall be right to say all artifice, reduces itself to the principle of parallelism,' Jakobson explains that as a feature of all artifice, parallelism 'is the referral of a semiotic fact to an equivalent fact inside the same context'; the effect is self-referential. He sees this principle as relevant not only to poetry; of music he states that 'In the musical art the correspondences of elements that are recognized, in a given convention, as mutually equivalent or in opposition to each other, constitute the principal, if not the only, semiotic value.' He finds support in Stravinsky's repeated claim that 'music is dominated by the principle of similarity,' and in Schönberg's statement that 'to compose is to cast a glance upon the theme's future.'[25]

The principle of parallelism in sound dominates the Middle French formes fixes lyrics, which have stanzas of set length, mostly uniform line lengths and caesura, complex rhyme schemes with the same rhyme sounds used throughout the poem, and refrains of one or more lines for each stanza. In the terms of Jakobson's semiotic analysis, it seems quite appropriate to refer to these works as musical.[26] The medieval conception of music as a form of mathematics makes the idea even more apt and meaningful, for in this view the semantic content of the poetry can be seen as itself contributing to the music through abstraction and repetition, and the referentiality of both expression and content can be seen not only in modern terms as reflexive parallelism, but also in a medieval view as forming a symbolic entity that looks outward to a spiritual realm where weight, number, and measure reveal divine beauty.

NATURAL MUSIC

As Deschamps describes 'natural music' in the *Art de dictier* (*Art of Writing Poetry*), it is simply the sound of the words of poetry. From his description, then, one gathers that all poetry has natural music, but of course poetry for Deschamps was primarily the Middle French form in which sound is privileged above other features. Other poetic modes do not similarly foreground sound. Especially since the eighteenth century, literary theorists, including the poets themselves, have treated the phonetics of verse as ancillary and subservient to the semantics. There is therefore particular appropriateness in reserving the label 'natural music' in this study for the Middle French type and for describing Chaucer's verse in the same mode. Though only Chaucer's shorter poems may be seen as natural music unadulterated, almost all of his poetry partakes of it, especially that in stanzas. There is only an apparent paradox in the fact that much natural music never had musical accompaniment. In the fourteenth century lyric texts lacking music became the rule, and, as we have seen, common usage in literary discussion warrants our talking about lyric texts as musical in themselves.

Deschamps' classification of poetry as a branch of music was not new. In his thirteenth-century *Parisiana Poetria*, John of Garland presented rhythmic poetry as a species of music, and the definitions in two French treatises that followed Deschamps' work show that his idea remained current through Middle French times.[27] It was more common to view poetry as rhetoric. The Provençal *Leys d'Amors* (1342), like Deschamps, prefaces its classification of poetry with a consideration of the Seven Arts, but it places poetry under Rhetoric, not Music.[28] And Dante's title for his treatise on poetics, *De vulgari eloquentia*, clearly allies vernacular verse with rhetoric,[29] though, as we will discuss, music figures prominently in his definition of 'poesis.' The same alliance with rhetoric is found in the several late medieval French manuals for poets which Langlois appropriately calls 'Arts of the Second Rhetoric.'[30] Yet, whichever rubric for poetry was used, rhetoric or music, all of these medieval treatments of poetics place primary emphasis on the repetitive sound patterns, the quality that certainly motivated both Deschamps and John of Garland to identify poetry as music.

Deschamps' *Art de dictier* is poorly organized and fragmentary, and the thinking behind it often seems pedestrian, but the treatment of vernacular verse as 'natural music' has both originality and considerable descriptive power, particularly for Middle French poetry. In Deschamps' usage, accompanying melody – what we commonly call music – is 'artificial music,' while the words of a poem – the text – make 'natural music.'[31] Of themselves, poetic texts are musical and able to stand alone: 'Each of these two [types of music] is pleasant to hear by itself. The one may be sung without word with voice and art; likewise, the words of the poems may often be spoken in many places where they are willingly heard, where the melody of the artificial music would not always be appropriate, as between lords and ladies aside and in private; or natural music may be said and spoken from the mouth of a single person, or some book of these pleasant things read before someone who is sick, and in similar cases where the song performed would be out of place because of its loudness.'[32]

Certain scholars have seen in Deschamps' 'natural music' his excuse for not composing music for his lyrics as the poets conventionally had done. Numerous others have recognized it as more than a convenient excuse, but their conclusions often differ: some see him as asserting the independence of poetry from music, others posit a close alliance between the two.[33] The last view, I believe, is the accurate one; Deschamps is not rationalizing his personal inability, nor is he making poetry a separate art. He means just what he says; drawing on traditional ideas, supported by no less an authority than Dante, he is claiming that poetry – text by itself – is a kind of music.[34] This conceptual alliance of poetry and music provides an important key to understanding Middle French verse, especially in the light of the common medieval conception of music by medieval theoreticians.

According to their theory, music was an expression of mathematical ordering. Its abstract numerical quality generated Saint Augustine's influential statement, 'Musica est scientia bene modulandi' / 'Music is the science of good measurement.' It was the most exact of the mathematical sciences and therefore a principle of creation, for God's mode of action was seen as mathematical, based in the biblical text, 'Thou hast ordered all things in measure and number and weight' (Wisdom of Solomon 11:20). Music worked by cosmic principles, and was inherent in the perfectly harmonious movement of the heavenly bodies. Its source was in the empyrean, and angels were the consummate musicians. An important consequence of a mathematical conception of music is that mimetic or expressive properties were not attributed to music. It was only in the Renaissance that it generally was seen as directly representing ideas and embodying emotion.[35] John Stevens notes of song since the Renaissance that 'when the words [of a song] express a mood, refer to an object, make a plea, we expect the composer to match them,' but he doubts that 'Machaut's songs ever embody such a relationship.'[36] This is at least relatively true for the whole mode, and it applies to both the natural and the artificial music – that is, to the sounds of the text as well as to the melody.

That the principle of a non-mimetic, non-expressive relationship of the sounds to the verbal meaning applies to the phonetics of the poetic text as well as to any musical notation provided for the text is a main tenet of this study. Musical presentation was especially important in the genesis of the main formes fixes (ballade, rondeau, virelay), since they originated as dance lyrics, and it had permanent effect on certain aspects of the versification. But while the major French poets after Machaut did not compose music for their works, and Machaut himself supplied no accompanying music for the greater part of his lyrics, the concept of music as number continued to rule the poetry.

Deschamps speaks of the powers of music to refresh the weary,[37] and Machaut declares in his *Prologue*, citing the examples of David and Orpheus, that music has power to make men joyful, appease the wrath of God, and to move even inanimate objects (85–146); it is clear that they saw it as a powerful emotive force. Nevertheless, they do not suggest that music is directly representational in conveying either mimetic or expressive significance.[38] For them, music's power lay in its mathematical ordering, which had a harmonizing effect on the vital spirits; its measure and proportion were internalized in the hearers and resulted in their calming and healing.[39] This comes through in Machaut's discussion of music in his *Prologue*. Consonant with his description of the 'matere' of love poetry, he emphasizes the characteristic gaudium of music. Like Amour, it is inherently joyful: 'Music is a science which encourages laughing and singing and dancing. It doesn't care for melancholy or for the man who broods on trivial matters ... Wherever [Music] is, she brings joy' (85–91). The effect does not result from a lilting melody or a spirited rhythm, but rather because 'everything about [music] is more exactly proportioned than in any other science' / 'Tous ses fais plus a point mesure / Que ne fait nulle autre mesure' (99–100).[40]

Music assuredly was seen as suitable for entertainment indoors and out, but it was not seen as mere pastime. Its basis in number and proportion made it particularly suitable to prayers addressed to God, and characteristic of heavenly beings and heaven itself. Machaut speaks with admiration of the central role of music in the Mass. 'Is there anything more worthy,' he asks, 'than to praise God ... and His sweet mother ... by singing?' He goes on to comment that the angels, saints, and archangels praise God in Heaven by their singing, which affirms that 'Music is in Paradise' (101–25). The perfection of number, expressed in music, thus brings us close to the divine.

The mathematical nature of music and its consequent non-referential character indicate why Machaut and his contemporaries did not think it imperative to make the words comprehensible in their complex polyphonic arrangements, why in their music they did not evoke physical phenomena – the rushing of the wind, the clashing of armies, the calm of sunset – and why there was no attempt to imitate or stir the passions. To quote John Stevens once more (this time discussing a Machaut complainte), 'It is unnecessary to make any cross-reference between the poem and the melody except *metrically* ... There is no *referential* relationship between the two. Neither the mood, nor the ideas ... nor the concepts of particular words, are the subject of musical attention.'[41]

With such understanding of music in mind, we may summarize the nature of the verse Deschamps calls 'natural music.' As with melody, the sounds of the text are to be conceived in mathematical and abstract, as opposed to expressive and naturalistic, terms. The most prominent aspects of the verse and the verbal sound will be its regular divisions of pause, line, and stanza, and its regular phonetic repetitions, especially those of rhyme and refrain. The number of syllables per line will be absolutely consistent, the caesura very regular, and the complex rhymes the same in each uniform stanza. The formal, mathematical quality of the versification will be abetted grammatically by a syntax whose phrases and clauses fit unobtrusively into line and hemistich, and semantically by highly conventional imagery and diction. The meanings carried by the words – by the sentences of the text – will tend to abstraction and frequently will be repetitive. In this fashion both syntax and sense become an adjunct to the patterns of the sound. Roger Dragonetti describes similarly the semantics of the Old French chanson; the lyric fiction, he says, should lack 'all traces of individuality, that thereby the sensibility of the listeners may be drawn by exclusive attention to the play of figures, of rhythm, and of song.'[42]

NATURAL MUSIC IN FRENCH AND ENGLISH LYRIC POEMS

The highly formal fourteenth-century French lyrics, representatives par excellence of Deschamps' 'natural music,' have not appealed to modern tastes. However, the negative judgment of our time is based on norms that the medieval French writers would hardly have understood. Exactly what they were working for, well expressed in the term 'natural music,' can be approached by looking at a rather extreme example. Machaut's ballade 'Douce dame, vo maniere jolie' has a particularly strong sound system. In addition to the requisites of the standard ballade form – three stanzas with the same rhymes repeated throughout the poem, each stanza concluding with a refrain line – it employs an important special effect, called 'équivoque et retrograde,' whereby each line begins with the sounds (in this case two full syllables) that ended the previous line:

Douce dame, vo maniere jolie
Lie en amours mon cuer et mon desir
Desiramment, si que, sans tricherie,

Chierie adès en serez, sans partir.
Partir vaut miex que d'autre souvenir   5
Venir peüst en moy, qui en ardure
Durement vif et humblement l'endure.

Dure à moy seul, de tous biens assevie,
Vie d'onneur plaisant à maintenir
Tenir m'estuet dou tout en vo baillie   10
Liement, et, pour joie desservir,
Servir vous vueil et mes maus conjoïr.
Joïr n'espoir, helas! et sans laidure
Durement vif et humblement l'endure.

Dur espoir ay, puis qu'Amours ne m'aïe.   15
Aïe à vous me convient requerir;
Querir ne l'os, pour ce qu'à m'anemie
Mie ne doy ma dolour descouvrir.
Couvrir en moy l'aim miex jusqu'au morir.
Morir me plaist, et, combien que me dure,   20
Durement vif et humblement l'endure.[43]

Sweet lady, your pretty ways bind in love my heart and my desire desiringly, so that you will always be held dear for them without trickery, completely. [Even] parting is worth more than the thought of another can produce in me, who while burning live painfully and endure it humbly.

Hard to me alone, lady replete with all good, I must lead a life of honour happily, pleasant to maintain, wholly in your power, and to merit joy I wish to serve you and with you to take pleasure in my sufferings. I have no hope of having joy, alas! and without offending, I live painfully and endure it humbly.

A hard hope I have, since Love does not help me. I must ask help of you. But I dare not ask it, since I must not reveal my trouble to my enemy. I prefer to hide it in me until death. It pleases me to die, and, whatever the difficulty, I live painfully and endure it humbly.

The seven-line stanza form used here, known in English as rime royal, is Chaucer's favourite. The retrograde arrangement, though, is not Chaucerian; as a matter of fact, it is hardly typical of its author, being the only ballade of Machaut – Chaucer's main French model – that uses the retrograde device.

Though it is in a sense atypical, I use the work as an example because the additional sound repetition emphasizes the phonetic qualities that constitute 'natural music.' In the *Art de dictier* Deschamps states that the retrograde/équivoque device makes 'the strongest ballades possible to compose' / 'les plus fors balades qui se puissent faire.'[44] His phraseology suggests, correctly I think, that the sound repetitions at the beginning of the line fit in with and intensify in so far as is possible the other formal elements of the work. We might first consider the nature of this device and its contribution to the form of the lyric, and afterwards deal more generally with the rhymes to which the repetitions are closely attached.

In Deschamps' usage, neither 'équivoque' nor 'retrograde' has its Modern French meaning. 'Retrograde' for him means simply the immediate repetition of sounds, and 'équivoque' means using the repeated sounds to produce a different sense; thus, '-lie' at the end of the first line is the ending of 'jolie,' but in the second line it is a verb meaning to tie or bind; 'desir' in the second line is a noun, and in the following line it is the first element of an adverb. For the relationship between the repeated elements to be 'équivoque,' at the least there must be a change in the part of speech; beyond this requirement the connection of sense to meaning in the rhymed sounds is entirely arbitrary. Thus, between the repeated sounds there is often no accord in the meanings, as in 'bail*lie*' (10, power) and '*lie*ment' (11, gaily). Or the sense may even be opposed, as 'tri*cherie*' (3, trickery) to '*cherie*' (4, dear), with the opposition having no special significance. The arbitrary relationship strictly accords with the aims of 'natural music' as I have described it, in which no direct bond between the sound and the sense is cultivated. The echoing of sounds with no stable connection to the meaning serves to subordinate the semantic to the phonetic aspects of the language, the phonetic being in itself more distinctive in this poetry.

The retrograde repetitions, of course, also reinforce the line divisions, the rhymes, and the refrains which are the essential and constant features of phonetic repetition in the ballades. By virtue of their relatively abstract meanings, the rhyme elements in these poems also help to make the phonetic independent of the semantic. For confirmation we can refer to the lyric at hand. Two of its three rhymes, *-ie* and *-ir*, are simply grammatical endings, marking mainly nouns and infinitives, and in no case carrying lexical meanings. Only the third rhyme, *-dure*, sometimes acts as a stem. As a result, with most of the lines – seventeen out of twenty-one – the rhyme falls on a grammatical suffix, so that although we might assume that the rhyme will emphasize major words and point up meanings, the effect instead is to distract us from the important lexical elements and draw our attention to the sound pattern – the music. To make this point clear, we might look at a stanza of a Middle English lyric from the famous Harley 2253 manuscript (from the fourteenth century), for which the principles of versification are quite different from the French.[45] The individual lines make heavy use of alliteration, and the stanzas have in addition a uniform rhyme scheme:

Ichot a burde in boure bright	I know / maiden / bower
That sully semly is on sight	exceedingly comely
Menskful maiden of might,	noble / power [over us]
Feir and free to fonde.	beautiful / enjoy
In all this wurchliche won	splendid world
A burde of blod and of bon	
Never yete I nuste non	knew
Lussomore in londe.[46]	more lovely

Just as with the French ballade, the subject-matter here is the narrator's love for his lady. The English lover in this particular work is in a happier state than the Frenchman of the previous poem, but in both traditions the lovers run the gamut of emotion; they suffer, they praise the lady, and they live in bliss with about the same frequency and to the same degree.

Yet the versification of the two traditions is radically different. In this English lyric almost every important word – the nouns, adjectives, and verbs that carry major lexical meaning – is pointed up either by alliteration or by rhyme. Since the alliteration consistently falls on the first letter of the stems, and the rhymes are mostly parts of monosyllabic stems, they serve to emphasize the semantic content and to bind the phonetic systems of the verse to the meaning. In the French poem, by contrast, there is little to help bring out the important lexical elements. There are comparably drastic differences in other aspects of the versification, in the matter of syllable count, and in the use of caesura. The lines of the French poem have exactly ten syllables to the line, and the caesura falls regularly after the fourth syllable (occasionally after the sixth, the standard alternative); the units of syntax are made to conform to the sound system. With 'Ichot a burde' there is a flexibility that accommodates clauses and phrases of varying lengths; in this lyric, as is typical, there is no regular caesura and the number of syllables in the line varies from six to nine.

The English poem has a certain tumbling rhythm that would allow us to speak of its music, but not as readily as with the French work; and indeed it seems likely that the Middle English alliterative lyrics trace their ancestry to prose.[47] But the Romance lyric had always been musical, both in its traditional accompaniment of 'artificial' music, and in the text's being considered musical of its very nature, as Dante testifies in *De vulgari eloquentia.*

In his unfinished treatise Dante deals at length only with the canzone form, but his discussion of the stanza applies well to the stanzas of the Italian ballata or the French ballade.[48] Dante says that the stanza is the basic unit of the canzone and has 'a capacity for the whole art'; that is, if we know how to make the stanza, we know how to make the poem. He defines a stanza as 'the combination of lines and syllables within the limits of a determined melody and in harmonic relation,'[49] or, as another translation has it, 'a stanza has a fixed music and numerical proportion, being a bounded structure of lines and syllables.'[50]

Whichever translation one follows, it is obvious that Dante considers melody and numerical proportion the important aspects of the structure. This is made more explicit in his further description of the stanza. He says that the stanza can have a single melodic line throughout, without repetitions, or it can have a pivot, a diesis, with repeated melodic parts lying on either side, or on both sides of the pivot. The 'division of the melody,' then, is a crucial matter.[51] With the French ballade the same definition applies; what the French do fits into Dante's prescriptions, though with less freedom of variation. The French stanzaic melody is always divided by a diesis, and the first part, the 'front,' contains two exactly symmetrical sections, while the second part, the 'cauda,' almost always constitutes a single section. Thus, the front of a rime royal ballade (such as 'Douce dame, vo maniere jolie') set to music has a text rhyming *ab* twice, with each *ab* having the same melody, and the cauda *bcc* has a single separate melody. The diesis, obviously, occurs at the end of line 4.

Dante assumes that a lyric text will accommodate a potential musical setting, but he says that melody is not essential to the form. To support this assertion, he notes that while a text may be called a canzone, the music cannot. The canzone proper therefore consists of 'harmonized words for a musical setting,'[52] with the musical notation not itself required to fulfil the form. Deschamps' treatment of the Middle French lyrics accords well with such an assumption. There are various specific ways in which the text and melody of French fixed forms conform to each other and to Dante's description. In the case of the rime royal ballade with musical setting, isosyllabic and rhyming ababbcc, there are certain matters in which the musical notation and the structure of the text will be made to fit each other. The two *ab* sections will exactly match each other in melody, line structure, and rhyme, while the unduplicated bcc section will have a different, unrepeated melody. If the lyric lacks notation, the musical structure will still be present, implicit in the versification, marked especially by the rhyme.

Rhyme is a very prominent feature in the Romance lyric, and both Dante and Deschamps illustrate and discuss its use in detail. The rhymes of a stanza, according to Dante, contribute particularly to 'the sweetness of a whole unit in harmony.' His phraseology suggests that rhymed poetry possesses an independent musicality. Dante is precise about the proper use of rhyme, even beyond what has to do with the musical setting. Especially he recommends two additional conditions that rime royal, the favourite stanza of both Machaut and Chaucer, fulfils particularly well. One is the connection of the two parts of the stanza, the front and the cauda, which is effected by having 'the first line of the last part ... rhyme with the last line of the first part.' This results, Dante says, in a 'rather beautiful concatenation of the stanza itself.' In rime royal, accordingly, the last line of the front, *abab*, rhymes with the first line of the cauda, *bcc*. Dante further states that 'the endings of the last lines will be arranged more beautifully if they fall into silence with a rhyme.'[53] Thus, he praises the effect of ending a stanza with two rhyming lines, as happens in rime royal.

Dante is not discussing ballade stanzas like rime royal, however. For him, the supreme lyric form was the canzone, the Italian version of the French grand chant courtois. Like the canzone and the Provençal canso in their linguistic habitats, the chanson reigned as the pre-eminent poetic form in France through most of the thirteenth century. In contrast to the ballade, the chanson had no set number of stanzas (there were commonly five or six), and there was no refrain. The fourteenth-century chant royal, which was not given a refrain till after mid-century, is the direct descendant of the grand chant; in the Middle French period it and all the related five-stanza formes fixes found their homes in the puy and seldom were accorded musical accompaniment.

The absence of the repetitive refrain made the chanson text markedly less 'musical' than the ballade, which became the reigning form at the Middle French courts after about 1300. The ballade and the related rondeau and virelay had originated in the thirteenth century as dance forms, and through mid-century were commonly set and sung to music.[54] Ironically, the musical nature of the forms led to a decline in musical accompaniment for them, for the polyphonic musical settings which Machaut and others came to give them made the works unsuitable for dancing, and their difficulty ultimately discouraged all but very skilled composers from providing notation.

While the ballade form underwent an evolution throughout the fourteenth century, the development of the form in the latter part of the fourteenth century did not have important effect (except in connection with the envoy) on Chaucer, who modelled most of his lyrics and his stanzaic verse on the ballades of Machaut, which were mainly composed between 1340 and 1365. (I will elaborate upon this point in the next chapter.) To suggest the close relationship, and to illustrate further the 'musical' traits of the verse of the two poets, we might compare a stanza of the Machaut ballade 'Toute ensement' with a stanza of Chaucer's lyric *To Rosemounde*. Machaut's stanza, eight lines of decasyllables except for a seven-syllable fifth line, with an *ababccdd* rhyme scheme, is one of three that he most favours, and on occasion he sets it to music. I quote the first of the three uniform stanzas:

Tout ensement com le monde enlumine
Li biaus solaus, quant il rent sa clarté
Et que ses rais la froidure decline
Et fait venir les biens a meürté,
  Einsi le haut bien parfait
De ma dame vaint tout vice et deffait:
Par tout resplent sa vaillance et habunde
Mais de son bien, certes, c'est tout le monde.[55]

Just as the fair sun lights up the world when it shines, and as its rays lessen the cold and make things ripen, even so the great perfect good of my lady overcomes all vice and defeats it: her excellence shines and abounds everywhere, and as for her virtue, indeed, it's the whole world.

Like 'Tout ensement,' *To Rosemounde* is a ballade with stanzas of eight lines, but they are all uniformly decasyllabic. Chaucer employs the 'Monk's Tale' rhyme scheme that both he and Machaut often used. The first stanza illustrates:

Madame, ye ben of al beaute shryne
As fer as cercled is the mapamounde,

For as the cristal glorious ye shyne,
And lyke ruby ben your chekes rounde.
Therwith ye ben so mery and so jocounde
That at a revel whan that I see you daunce,
It is an oynement unto my wounde,
Thogh ye to me ne do no daliaunce.

We may think of the 'natural music' of these texts as having two aspects: that which relates it to the 'artificial music' which is a potential component of both, and that which is independent of melody. As regards the first, though no music was composed for either of these poems, both have an 'underlying musical structure'[56] stemming ultimately from the ballade's origins as a dance form. The prosodic structure is closely related to the potential musical form. The conventional musical organization of the stanza may be described as I I II.[57] Each I is usually two lines long, the two I's together forming the frons: the II is the remainder of the stanza, the cauda or tail. This organization of the melody conforms to the structure of metre and rhyme in the verbal text. The musical measures reflect the dependable regularity of the syllable count, and the music further conforms closely both to caesura and to line divisions. Thus, Machaut's music regularly observes caesura at the fourth syllable with rests and/or melismas,[58] and it consistently sets off the rhymes at line ends with notes of extended duration and sometimes with preceding melismas and following rests.[59]

The ballade stanzas of Machaut and Chaucer quoted above both display the potential musical form, though Chaucer's not quite as strictly as Machaut's. With both poems the first four lines form a frons (I I) rhyming *abab*, and the last four a cauda (II). Both lyrics, furthermore, have a completely regular syllable count, thereby facilitating the conformity of musical measure.[60] In the matter of caesura, however, while Machaut's poem comes close to absolute regularity, Chaucer's does not, particularly in the stanza quoted. In all but two of the twenty-four lines of 'Tout ensement' caesura occurs between the fourth and fifth syllables. *To Rosemounde*, by contrast, has nine variant caesuras. These occur in bunches, though, making for regularity; from line 8 to line 19 the caesura occurs consistently at the standard position, syllable 4.[61]

Of course, all facets of the poetry's sound patterns, not only those that originate in the practices of the musical composers, are relevant to what Deschamps calls 'natural music.' Particularly important are the phonetic qualities of the words and the rhymes, major subjects of the

Art de dictier. After the introduction on the Seven Arts, in which he fixes verse in the classification of natural music, Deschamps proceeds to an analysis of the sound values of letters – mutes, liquids, vowels, demi-vowels, and so on – suggesting his high sensitivity to the phonetic quality. He employs the remainder of the treatise for a discussion of the various lyric types.

In his relatively unsystematic characterization of the lyric types, rhyme is the feature of versification that Deschamps refers to most frequently,[62] and an oral reading of Machaut's and Chaucer's poems suggests how important the rhyme sounds are for this kind of verse. Comparing the two poems, one may be impressed by Chaucer's command of rhyme in the face of his (generally valid) complaint about the scarcity of rhyme in English.[63] His rhyme sounds are more complex than Machaut's and he manages with fewer of them; the French poem uses four rhyme sounds, the English but three for a ballade of the same length. The French has an approximate alternation of masculine and feminine rhymes[64] with some use of 'rime consonant,' vowel only, or vowel and consonant. All of Chaucer's rhymes, being feminine, extend over two syllables; furthermore, and quite important to the effect, all of his include a nasal [n]. Machaut's poem utilizes a large number of nasals and sibilants, but his graceful, understated refrain has an effect entirely different from the repeated o's and e's in open monosyllables in Chaucer's 'Though ye to me ne do no daliaunce.'[65]

In the jaunty staccato of its refrain, as well as in some other aspects of the sounds of *To Rosemounde*, we may find a minor but marked expressive element that is not present in 'Tout ensement' and is foreign to the 'natural music' of the mode. Machaut's poem exemplifies this music. The sounds have little discernible expressive relationship to the sense of the words. The images and the diction are strictly conventional, their commonplace nature reducing their prominence *vis-à-vis* the sound. In the stanza quoted, for example, the well-worn images of light express the triumph of good. The lady is like the sun which overcomes the cold and ripens things; her goodness shines out and defeats all vice. Machaut's diction is likewise quite predictable; there is not a word in the stanza, indeed in the whole ballade, that surprises us. At the same time there are repetitions of the usual words that are almost incantatory. In accord with the poem's categorical praise and exaggerated comparisons, all three stanzas begin with *tout* or *tant* or both, leading in each case to conjunctions *com*, *quant*, and/or *que*; and then *tout* sounds again in the refrain lines. *Bien* in the refrain has four counterparts in the rest of the text; and in stanza 3 the simple possessive *son*, referring to the lady's various conventional qualities (onneur, douceur, pris, etc.), occurs six times in two series before its final utterance in the refrain. This repetition of almost empty words – words which because of their predictability or grammatical status carry minimal lexical meaning – contributes to a privileging of sound values over the sense.

Comparable promotion of sound over meaning may be found in the rhymes in 'Tout ensement.' Most of the rhyming elements have negligible semantic content. The *-é* rhyme ending is a grammatical marker of either a noun or a past participle, and *-ait* is a grammatical suffix of a noun, a verb, or an adjective. The other two rhyme endings of the poem, *-ine* and *-onde*, are often part of the stem (m*onde*), but they too serve as markers of verbs (dec*line*). The rhyme, then, tends to focus on abstract grammatical meaning rather than on the lexical meaning carried in the stems of the words.

In the relationship of the sounds to the meaning of the text, this poem is typical of the formes fixes lyrics. Although rhyme is a prominent feature, it often carries more abstract grammatical meanings, thereby working together with the strong rhythmic patterns to make a music of the text with which the verbal meanings are consonant and not competitive. The diction and images – conventional, unobtrusive, and often abstract – make the sense handmaid to the sound. To repeat John Stevens' words about Dante's conception, 'It is not that the "sound must seem an echo to the *sense*" but something more physical – "the sense must seem an echo to the *sound*." '[66]

The sound patterns of Chaucer's *To Rosemounde*, it must be granted, are not always so neutral in relation to the sense as one would expect in a forme fixe poem. The metrics, as already noted, are generally regular. The language too conforms in large part to the type. There is a predictable recurrence of 'so,' 'as,' and 'al,' characteristic of the conventional hyperboles and similes of the poetry; one also finds predictable words and images, like 'beaute,' 'shyne,' and 'mery'; 'cristal,' 'ruby,' 'wound.' At the same time there is humour in the staccato effect of the refrain, already discussed, and in some quaint diction and images, underlined by rhymes on stem syllables: the bookish reference to the 'mapam*ounde*'; the lady 'so joc*ounde*' with her childish 'chekes r*ounde*' and 'semy voys that ye so smal out twy*ne*,' and in the next stanza, the hapless lover like a 'pyk walwed in galaunty*ne*.' In this case the sounds are expressive in that they emphasize the humorous content of the words. Through them Chaucer plays with the conventions of the poem in praise of the lady.

Chaucer does not habitually reflect his meaning in the sounds, either mimetically or expressively – though he does more than Machaut, as *To Rosemounde* suggests.[67] Furthermore, though we may find humour in the rhymes of *To Rosemounde*, the intensive use of the devices of sound characteristic of Middle French poetry is not of itself humorous, either intentionally or unintentionally. Chaucer himself often uses exceptional sound effects without a humorous edge or other significant semantic implications. *Womanly Noblesse* provides a good example. Again, the first stanza illustrates:

> So hath myn herte caught in remembraunce
> Your beaute hoole and stidefast governaunce,
> Your vertues al and yowre hie noblesse,
> That you to serve is set al my plesaunce,
> So wel me liketh your womanly contenaunce,
> Your fresshe fetures and your comlynesse,
> That whiles I live, myn herte to his maystresse
> You hath ful chose in trewe perseveraunce
> Never to chaunge, for no maner distresse.

The other two stanzas comparably utilize the same two rhyme sounds, both characteristically French suffixes, both extended, both incorporating sibilants. There are, then, twenty-seven consecutive line endings of -*aunce*, -*esse*, plus four more of -*aunce* in the envoy. Yet the ludicrous effect that seems guaranteed by such extravagance does not materialize. The sense, while serving the sound, is not subverted by it. Though there is a certain light tone in the poem that is implicit in the mode, it is not a comic piece like *To Rosemounde*. The poem's diction includes only the predictable words: 'herte,' 'beaute,' 'noblesse,' 'trewe,' etc., and it is filled with forty first- and second-person pronouns. Such elements acting with the versification produce an effective piece of 'natural music.'

To Rosemounde and *Womanly Noblesse* surpass the usual rhyming effect of the French ballade, yet they hardly go beyond the rhyme effects of the typical French lay and virelay, whose lengthy stanzas of short lines regularly have but two or three rhyme sounds, themselves often phonetically interrelated. It is perhaps no happenstance, then, that both of these ballades of Chaucer, with their complex rhymes, find probable originals in virelays of Machaut. The virelay is the second type of lyric that Deschamps exemplifies in the *Art de dictier*. The form of the virelay (also called chanson baladée) normally requires three stanzas with an extended refrain of three to seven lines that opens and closes the poem and is also repeated between stanzas. The refrain and first stanza of Machaut's 'Dame, le doulz souvenir,' which, like *Womanly Noblesse* deals with the lover's sweet memory of his lady, illustrate the form:

Refrain: *Dame, le doulz souvenir*
           Qu'ay nuit et jour
           De vo parfaite douçour
           Que tant desir
           Me fait en joie languir
             Et en dolour.

Stanza 1:   Car quant je puis bien penser
           Par doucement ramembrer
             Et à loisir
           Qu'il n'a en vous point d'amer
           Fors tout doulz a savourer,
             Et qu', au plaisir
           De tous, des dames tenir
             Vous oy la flour
           Et des bonnes la millour,
             Pas ne m'aïr;
           Car en moy joie gringnour
             Ne puet venir.

Refrain: *Dame, le doulz souvenir, etc.*[68]

Lady, the sweet remembrance that I have night and day of your perfect sweetness, which I desire so much, makes me languish in joy and in sorrow.

    For since I can well ponder by sweetly remembering at my ease that there is nothing bitter about you, but all is sweet to savour, and that, as all are pleased to say, you hold the flower of womanhood and are the best of the good, then I have no vexation; for greater joy could not come into me.

    Lady, the sweet remembrance, etc.

As is common in Machaut's virelays, there are two rhyme sounds in the refrain with a third added in the stanzas, all phonetically related: *-ir,*

-our, -er. Womanly Noblesse has longer lines than most virelays, but it is probably as close as Chaucer gets in a whole poem to virelay form. It has but two rhyme sounds, closely related; its stanzas open with an *aabaab* rhyme scheme typical of Machaut's virelays; and its first two lines are virtually repeated at the end of the poem, as is the case with the multi-line virelay refrain which appears at beginning and end (as well as between stanzas).

Anelida's complaint in *Anelida and Arcite* (211–350) is the other work by Chaucer that displays significant affinities to virelay metrics, especially by virtue of internal rhymes in two of the stanzas (272–80, 333–41). These represent especially impressive technical achievements, again belying the scarcity of rhyme in English. We might look at six lines of the first of these stanzas, divided medially to point up the rhyme:

My swete fo,	why do ye so,	for shame?
And thenke ye	that furthered be	your name
To love a newe,	and ben untrewe?	Nay!
And putte yow	in sclaunder now	and blame,
And do to me	adversite	and grame,
That love yow most –	God, wel thou wost –	alwey? (272–7)

When the lines are cut off at the rhyme sounds, which provides a reasonable alternative format, each stanza produces twenty-seven short lines with an *aabccb*, etc., rhyme scheme:

My swete fo
Why do ye so,
 For shame?
And thenke ye
That furthered be
 Your name ...

The Machaut virelay quoted is very much like this; other virelays are even more like it.

Such a sequence also resembles stanzas of short lines found in the lays; however, the lay form features numerous varieties and mixtures of rhyme schemes and line lengths. To judge by his extant work, Chaucer never tried to compose anything like a lay, which Deschamps accurately calls 'une chose longue et malaisiée a faire et trouver' / 'a long and difficult thing to make and create.' The song of Antigone in *Troilus* derives materials from Machaut's lays,[69] and it has something of the typical lay length, but its versification bears little relationship to the form.

Another type that has minimal relevance to Chaucer's practice is the complaint (though one might suppose otherwise, since manuscript rubrics consistently identify several of his pieces by that label), and he makes use of the language of several Machaut pieces called 'complaintes.' But even though the complaint is often mentioned in contemporary lists of lyric types, unlike the French types we have been discussing it has virtually no history as a musical form[70] and never achieved a standard versification of its own. Deschamps does not mention it in the *Art de dictier*. Machaut, like other poets, attaches the label 'complainte' to works of various metrics. Nevertheless, his frequent use of a sixteen-line stanza with an *aaabaaabbbbabbba* rhyme scheme in poems he calls complaintes perhaps constitutes an attempt to identify this verse form with the type. In Chaucer's poetry the rhyme scheme is found in two stanzas in Anelida's complaint (256–71, 317–32).[71] But such other 'complaints' as *Complaint of Venus*, *Complaint to His Lady*, and *Complaint to His Purse*, have stanzas related to the ballade. There are also no poems by Chaucer in the five-stanza forms particularly popular in the puys: chanson royale, pastourelle, and serventois.[72] In the *Art de dictier* Deschamps mentions such forms only in conjunction with a discussion of puy presentation, giving one example (with the mistaken label 'balade' in both manuscripts).[73] With Chaucer the statement in the *Legend of Good Women* (F 423; G 411), crediting him only with ballades, rondeaux, and virelays among the various types, agrees rather closely with the extant evidence.

By a large margin the ballade was the most common of the French formes fixes in the fourteenth century; it was a staple for all purposes. As a consequence, in his *Art* Deschamps gives more examples of the ballade form than of any other.[74] With Chaucer too, to judge from his extant work, the ballade was much the favoured form, and its contribution to the metrics and rhetoric of his stanzaic work can hardly be overestimated. Nine of his short poems carry over into English the ballade versification complete, utilizing characteristic stanza forms, repeated rhymes, and refrains; two of these are triple ballades.[75] Six more of his shorter poems incorporate a total of thirteen formally defined three-stanza units that have approximate ballade metrics.[76] The only other forme fixe that Chaucer takes over into English complete is the rondeau, which in the *Art de dictier* Deschamps exemplifies in both the

eight-line form favoured by Machaut and the thirteen-line form that
Chaucer employs in two extant pieces.[77] Ballade, rondeau, and virelay
are closely related forms.

Chaucer's stanzaic poems, long and short, commonly use the most
popular ballade stanzas. Of the fifteen lyrics that comprise or incorporate
ballades or near ballades, nine use rime royal (ababbcc) and three the
'Monk's Tale' stanza (ababbcbc). Rime royal similarly was Machaut's
favorite ballade stanza; of his 265 ballades, 138 are in rime royal. Machaut
also used the Monk's stanza (for 7 poems), but Deschamps was its champion, writing 495 ballades that use it; it was also Granson's favourite (24
poems). There are larger implications of ballade versification for Chaucer's stanzaic works. In the light of his great debt to Machaut, his familiarity with the other French writers, and his metrical practice in the
short poems, it is hardly daring to infer that the stanzaic form of his
longer pieces in rime royal and the Monk's stanza – which include the
Parliament of Fowls, *Troilus and Criseyde*, and five of the *Canterbury Tales*
– develop from French ballade usage. Rather, it is surprising that there
has not been more general agreement that these stanzas of Chaucer
originate in the ballade.[78] For the versification of Chaucer's stanzaic
works only the 'Clerk's Envoy,' the terza rima in *Complaint to His Lady*
(23–39), and the tail-rhyme of the 'Tale of Sir Topas' lack antecedents
in the formes fixes; and of these the 'Clerk's Envoy', with its repeated
rhymes in -*ence* and -*aille*, is clearly related to them.

NATURAL MUSIC IN MACHAUT'S 'REMEDE' AND CHAUCER'S 'TROILUS'

The consummate representative of natural music among longer Middle
French poems is Machaut's *Remede de Fortune*, and the most important
English poem that has a substantial element of natural music is Chaucer's
Troilus and Criseyde, though it is generally identified as epic and/or
romance rather than lyric. These two long poems will serve here to
exemplify natural music in extended verse. Both integrate lyric forms,
and despite their narratives both have fundamental lyricality: to varying
degrees they display the discontinuity, subjectivity, and emotive content
that is characteristic of lyric, these features assisting the metrics, grammatical structure, and conventional content in creating impressive natural music.

Remede de Fortune can be seen as the archetypal poem among Middle
French dits amoureux. It is a mirror of court life, and it incorporates an

art of poetry and an art of love. The narrative upon which it builds this threefold summa is quite simple. The lover is the central figure and narrator. As is proper, he is a poet who spends his time writing lyrics in his lady's honour. The story gains its initial impetus from a lay of his, complete with music, which fortuitously and anonymously comes into the lady's hands. She has him read it and afterwards inquires who wrote it. Torn by emotion, unable either to acknowledge the work or to lie to her, he leaves abruptly and goes off to the Parc de Hesdin where he makes a long formal complaint against Amour and Fortune. Responding to the complaint, Lady Esperance appears and proceeds to console him with Boethian wisdom and two songs. Her long presentation, which is the central component of the poem, sufficiently encourages him that he returns to the lady's chateau. There he joins the carole the lady is participating in, and subsequently confesses his love; after careful questioning, she accepts him into her service. They participate together in the activities of the castle – Mass, dinner, musical entertainment, games – but fear of scandal keeps her from giving him any sign of favour. The poem ends with Amant in a state of suspended animation.

This uncomplicated story, typical of the mode, provides a basis for extensive lyric development, formal and informal. Lyric discontinuity is evident throughout. There are nine independent intercalated lyrics which interrupt the octosyllabic couplets, including the lover's lay and complaint, and the chant royal and ballade of Esperance. As Ernest Hoepffner has noted, the lyrics taken together embody a tableau of the principal types, one example of each, presented in order through the poem from the most to the least metrically complex. According to Hoepffner, Machaut's purpose was to act as a literary legislator for the time by setting up models of the types for others to follow.[79] This seems clear, but there is much more to the poem's lyric nature. In addition to the set pieces, the narrative provides a series of occasions for lyric development in discrete (discontinuous) passages of the couplets themselves. Indeed, in presenting in first-person narrative a typical lover's career, from uncommitted youth to acceptance by the lady to separation from her, it forms a cycle of the typical situations. One after another of them is suited to lyric development: the young man is assigned a lady by Amour; he praises her as his exemplar and guide; powerless to declare his love, he writes poems about his longing; he stands mute and embarrassed in her presence; despairing of Love's help, he complains against Fortune; he looks forward to Death, makes his will, is saved by Hope, resolves to declare himself, hesitates before her, at length makes his declaration; she tests him, then accepts him; he rejoices in Love, imagines that she is fickle, is reassured by her; yet, at the end, he still must endure separation. Each stage provides a lyric moment.

In addition to its full set of lyric forms and its cycle of lyric situations, a third dimension of the *Remede* as poetic lesson-book is provided by the Boethian dialogue of Lady Esperance and the lover (1608–2892). The presentation of Esperance is the core of the Art of Love of the *Remede*. Esperance treats extensively the problems that Fortune presents to the lover and she expatiates on the mysterious beneficence of the God of Love. In the course of the discussion, she develops many of the commonplaces of the love poetry: the least gift of the lady is worth more than the lover can merit; since the lady has all virtues she must have pity; the lover's confusion before the lady has shown him to her as true lover; and so on.

Much of the language derives from the *Roman de la Rose*, but the love affair is far from that of the *Roman*. The lover is shy and restrained, not importunate; his overt aim is to honour and serve the lady, not to get her to bed; he abides by Bien Celer (Hide Well) in order to avert slander against the lady, not to conceal misbehaviour. That Esperance's Art of Love finds its model in the Boethian discourse of Reason in the *Roman de la Rose*, rather than from the Ovidian lecture of the God of Love, is an index of the change in sensibility between the poems. The poetic locus of action is another major indicator of the difference. The Amant of Guillaume de Lorris operates in a cosmic garden of procreation; his ultimate aim is copulation. Machaut's lover moves in a castle and park so close to reality that it can be located on the map; his ultimate aim coincides with that of the poet – to honour the lady.

Love poems of all times claim to present real experiences of the speakers, but in this matter they obviously vary. Middle French poems were often written for patrons and about their experiences. The question of the relation to reality is explicitly broached in the *Remede* by the identification of the locale as Hesdin, site of the great palace and park that Jean le Bon frequented. If the place has a real location, then are the main figures simply ideals, or are they meant to represent real people? Because the lady is the centre about which this poem and all the poetry turns, her identity perhaps is the key. Machaut concludes his general *Prologue* by emphasizing the centrality of the lady in his oeuvre:

Or pri a Dieu qu'il me doint grace
De faire chose qui bien plaise

Aus dames; car, par saint Nichaise,
A mon pooir, quanque diray,
A l'onneur d'elles le feray.[80]

Now I pray to God that he give me grace to write something pleasing to ladies; for by Saint Nicaise, as far as possible, whatever I say, I say for their honour.

The poet is to produce poems founded on the honour and praise of women. To accomplish this purpose he will embody in his depictions the admirable qualities of women. But where in his experience will the poet find his model, the counterpart to this exemplary lady? Will he find it in the pretty attendant with whom he carries on a more or less serious flirtation (Chaucer found his wife among Queen Philippa's damsels)? In the lady who presides (queen, princess, duchess)? Or in the idea of woman abstracted from the characteristic virtues of all the court ladies whom he knows and has heard about?

It seems clear that the abstracted idea of woman provides the characterization of the beloved lady of the poems; the descriptions are consistently of ideals that no actual lady would have fulfilled on all counts. At the same time, through an acrostic or a pun the poet sometimes lets us know that there is a real lady to whom the poem is directed and whom the idealized depiction more or less indirectly compliments. This actual person obviously might be anyone whom the poet fancies, but such evidence as we have suggests that in the case of the fourteenth-century poets the patroness most often is the poem's object: Bonne of Luxembourg, Blanche of Lancaster, Isabelle of York, Marguerite of Flanders, Anne of Bohemia, Isabelle of Bavaria. To increase the 'louange des dames' the court poet writes about an ideal while honouring a grand lady. He typically has no thought of soliciting the lady's love in any milieu but that of the narrative, in which the usual Amant counterpart of the poet is at once more naïve and worthier than the writer is known to be. The conventions are so well established, the representation so idealized and stylized, that there is little chance of anyone's taking offence. There are, of course, no rigid rules about the real-life reference of a poem. At times, for instance, the first-person narrator of a lyric or dit is meant to represent a nobleman on whose behalf the poet composes his poem, as in Machaut's 'Complainte VI.' In that work an acrostic reveals that it was written for Pierre, King of Cyprus, and addressed (in all likelihood) to Marguerite of Flanders.[81] The basic intention would have been political instead of amorous, to gain the powerful lady's help for Pierre's crusade. Thus, while Marguerite doubtless was meant to see the lover's extreme expressions of distress as arising from a gentle heart like Pierre's, she was not expected to respond directly to him as suitor or lover, nor would she have thought of doing so.

In presenting Bonne of Luxembourg in the guise of the ideal lady,[82] the *Remede* is quite in line with the custom of the Middle French mode. With the musical notation of seven fully developed lyrics, it also recapitulates the mode's history as it is bound up with notation. Even as regards narrative the work is allied with lyric, for the simple love stories that underlie the lyric genre are the genesis of the narratives of *Remede de Fortune* and dits amoureux like it. The longer narratives grow out of the conventional stories that the short poems predicate. Later dits with no formal lyric insertions and no music still participate in the line of development. Besides the conventional stories and rhetorical figures, they retain much of the 'natural music' of the regular metrics, the complex rhymes with heavy word-play, the repetitive diction, and the predictable narrative and exempla, all of which give them a euphonious and abstract character that may be called 'musical.' Almost any passage in the couplets of *Remede*, where there is neither music nor fixed form, shows these characteristics just as formal pieces do. We might instance the passage in which Amant describes the effects of his first sight of the lady, which anticipates the experiences of Chaucer's Black Knight and of Troilus:

Ainssi fist Amours par son art
Qui maint franc cuer doucement art
Que, quant premiers ma dame vi,
Sa grant biauté mon cuer ravi.
Et quant de s'amour fui espris,
Jonnes estoie et desapris,
S'avoie bien mestier d'aprendre,
Quant tel fait vouloie entreprendre.
Que dis je? Ains l'avoie entrepris,
Qu'ains conseil ne congié n'en pris
Fors a mon cuer et a ses yeus,
Qui en riant m'ont en maint lieus
Prié que par amours l'amasse
Si doucement, que je n'osasse
Leur veul refuser, ne peüsse.
Et mes cuers vouloit que je fusse
Touz siens, et je aussi le vouloie,

Et pour ce a eulz me conseilloie.
Si qu'ainssi fui, se Dieus me gart,
Pris par Doulz Ris et Douz Regart.
Et certainement, se je eüsse
Tant de bien en moy que je fusse
Aussi sages com Salemons,
Et fust miens quites tout li mons,
Et aussi preus comme Alixandres
Ou comme Hector, qui gaire mandres
Ne fu de li quant a valour,
Et sc'eüsse autretant d'onnour
Comme ot Godefroy de Buyllon,
Et la biauté qu'ot Absolon,
Et de Job la grant pasciensce,
L'estableté et la constance
Et de Judich et de Socratés,
Qui en .i. point estoit adés,
Car pour gaaingne ne pour perte
Ne se mouvoit, tant fust aperte,
Et avec ce l'umilité
Que Hester ot, et la loyauté
De Abraham, a verité dire
Ne peüsse je pas sousfire
Pour dame amer de tel affaire.
Mais Amours le me firent faire
Qui m'i donnerent liegement,
Quant je la vi premierement;
Si que siens sans riens retenir
Sui, quoy qu'il m'en doie avenir,
Et serai, tant com je vivray,
Ne jamais autre amour n'avray.   (87–134)

Thus Love, by her skill, which gently enflames many a noble heart, caused my
lady's great beauty to carry away my heart when first I saw her. When I was
kindled by her love, I was young and inexperienced, and I had much to learn
if I wished to embark upon such a course. What am I saying? I had already
embarked upon it, having asked advice and leave only of my heart and her
eyes,which often laughingly bid me so sweetly to love her that I dared not and
could not refuse their wish. My heart wanted me to be hers entirely, and I too
wanted it, and therefore I heeded their advice. Thus, God help me, I was captured

by Sweet Laughter and Sweet Looks. Yet truly, if I were so gifted as to be as wise as Solomon, and if all the world were completely mine, and I were as valiant as Alexander or as Hector (who was scarcely less brave than he) and if I had as much honour as Godfrey of Bouillon, and the beauty of Absalon, and Job's great patience, and the steadfastness and constancy of Judith and of Socrates, who always held to one position, because he would not change it for loss or for gain, no matter how great; and if I had in addition the humility of Esther and the faithfulness of Abraham, in truth I would still not be worthy to love a lady of such rank. But Love made me do it, who made me her liege man when first I saw her; so I am hers without reserve, come what may, and will be hers as long as I live, nor shall I ever love another.[83]

The content here is reflective, descriptive, and hyperbolic, much more characteristic of lyric than of narrative. What is more, the passage fits together rhetorically and metrically as the lover's unified statement of the permanent effects of his first sight of the lady. It begins and ends with his declaring that Amour permanently changed him when she showed him the lady ('Ainssi fist Amours ... quant premiers ma dame vi' [87–9]; 'Mais Amours le me firent faire ... Quant je la vi premierement' [128–30]), and in between he develops the themes of her worth and his unworthiness. In the versification the rhymes are particularly notable; almost all are extended to more than one syllable ('aprendre' / 'entreprendre'; 'Alixandres' / 'gaires mandres,' etc.) with an occasional cleverness ('Dieus me gart' / 'Douz Regart'). The heavily subordinated and co-ordinated syntax fits easily into the line units, with numerous enjambments that do little violence to them. The filiation of this passage to the sung lyric that is its ancestor, and its compatibility with such lyrics, is manifest. It is a fine example of 'natural music,' as is the comparable passage in the *Book of the Duchess* (1052–87). *Remede de Fortune* and the other dits amoureux in the same line of development are virtually made up of such passages.

Despite its alliances with the long narrative forms of epic and romance, Chaucer's *Troilus and Criseyde* partakes of the highly lyric dit amoureux. According to my analysis, *Troilus* has fifty-six developed lyric passages, amounting to 1,532 lines (of 8,238) essentially non-narrative, which might, with moderate alteration, be made into separate lyrics closely related to the formes fixes.[84] In the rime royal stanza form, in their diction and imagery, in their rhetorical orientation and logical development, and often in their very length, most of these passages are fine examples of natural music. Much of the remainder of the poem also shows filiations with the French. To call *Troilus* a collection of 'lyric clusters' or a 'sonnet sequence'[85] is hyperbolic but hardly perverse, as may be illustrated by setting a ballade of Machaut beside a passage from the opening of Chaucer's poem.

Machaut's 'Plourez, dames' is quite typical of his ballades, and yet it has claims to special status as a work that Machaut particularly prized and that was well known both to his French successors and to Chaucer. Probably composed in the 1350s when Machaut was near the peak of his creative powers, it is one of but two lyrics that he esteemed so highly as to put it in three places in the complete manuscripts of his poetry: in his collection of lyrics without music, the *Louange des dames*; among the 'balades notées' with music; and as an intercalated lyric in the late long *Voir-Dit*. Chaucer made use of this ballade most notably in the *Complaint of Mars*, and Deschamps clearly considered it a Machaut trademark.[86] Its subject is thoroughly conventional; like scores of formes fixes lyrics, it is concerned with the lover's prospective death. Because the generic lover was absolutely dependent on the lady and Amour, many occasions could threaten his life: the lady's refusal, his inability to see her or go to her, a prospective separation, her betrayal of him, malicious gossip about either of them, her death. In 'Plourez, dames' the situation is not specified; the audience is told only that the speaker expects to die soon, though it is possible that help will materialize. The work as a whole is a request to ladies for their tears and prayers. In conformity with ballade form, the poem has three stanzas, each employing the same rhymes and terminating with the same refrain. The first stanza shows its form, rhetorical approach, and general content:

Plourez, dames, plourez vostre servant,
Qui toudis ay mis mon cuer et m'entente,
Corps et penser et desir en servant
L'onneur de vous que Diex gart et augmente.
    Vestez vous de noir pour my,
Car j'ay cuer teint et viaire paly,
Et si me voy de mort en aventure,
Se Diex et vous ne me prenez en cure.[87]

Weep, ladies, weep for your servant, who has always put his heart and purpose, body and thought and desire into serving your honour; may God increase and augment it. Dress in black for me, for I have a stricken heart and a visage grown pale, and I see that I will die if God and you do not take care of me.

In the two stanzas that complete the ballade the lover makes his will, leaving his heart to the ladies' protection, his flesh to the worms, and his possessions to the poor; but finally he suggests that since the ladies are so replete with good, they may still save him.

Conventional generic elements are found in all aspects of the representation in 'Plourez, dames.' The characters prominent in the poem are the standard narrator-lover, the collective ladies of understanding whom he addresses, and a deity who is both the God of Love and the Christian deity. The filiations of the poem to Christian prayer are obvious. The imagery comes from the familiar iconography of death and dying: weeping mourners, black garments, a will or testament, a death bed, prayers for the dying. The diction is highly conventional and repetitive, thereby creating parallel patterns of sound and meaning. There is an unusual degree of repetition of the personal pronouns; the first-person singular occurs twenty-one times in its various cases in the poem, the second-person plural fifteen times. The lexical patterning is also served by the repetition of nouns and verbs drawn from the poetic world of Amour: Dieus (seven times), plourez–plourant, servant, mis–met, cuer (four times), mort, parti–departi, and priez–depri. The restricted lexicon that results from convention and repetition compares in its statistical limitation to the phonetic design made up by consonant-vowel combinations or to the simple syntactic combinations that compose a grammatical pattern. In this way, representational elements make up an abstractable formal pattern congruent with that of the phonetic and grammatical schemes.

As in all Middle French lyrics, the pattern of sound is a notable feature.[88] Repetitions demanded by the ballade form include the use of the refrain and of the same rhyme sounds in the three stanzas. In 'Plourez, dames' each of the four rhymes appears six times. As was considered desirable, there is an alternation of masculine and feminine rhymes.[89] Many of the rhymes are extended; that is, they involve at least two syllables, as with rhymes throughout on -ente and -ure. The identical rhymes on 'servant' in the first stanza and 'depri' in the third stanza are both extended and équivoque. The rhyme is prolonged to three syllables in 'ce parti' and 'departi' in the second stanza. In addition to these phonetic matters involving the standard form of the ballade, Machaut makes further discreet uses of sound patterning throughout the poem. One notable aspect of this appears in the recurrence of the initial labials p-, v-, and m-. Together with an impressive number of verbs and nouns in the poem that begin with one of these labials ('plourez,' 'priez,' 'vestez,' 'vers,' 'viaire paly,' 'mis,' 'mort,' etc.) are found many of the form words ('vostre,' 'vous,' 'vo,' 'pour my,' 'me voy,' etc.). The labials also participate with other sounds in the substantial unobtrusive alliteration ('Mon cuer vous lais et met en vo commant').

A major aspect of Machaut's lyrics is the fitting of the syntactic units to the metrical divisions of line and stanza in his verse, the apparent ease of the conformity obscuring an impressive grammatical variety and complexity. Sentences of all lengths occur in Machaut's ballades, but long sentences are much more common. His eight-line stanza usually is made up of two extended sentences, with the length achieved by liberal compounding and subordinating of clauses. In 'Plourez, dames' each stanza has two complete sentences. In the first and third stanzas we find a typical structure, with the opening sentence ending at line 4, coincident with a break in the rhyme scheme and the underlying musical form.[90] As might be expected when long sentences are employed in verse, enjambments are not infrequent; in this poem there are six. At the same time, in Machaut's ballades the enjambment never involves unusual grammatical disjunctions, such as separation of preposition from object or adjective from noun. He avoids these assiduously.

In building his long sentences Machaut employs a multiplicity of syntactic structures. Thus, while convention and repetition conduce to uniformity in the diction, commonly an element of great variety, the patterns of syntax, by nature much more limited, are quite varied. The result is that image, lexicon, and syntax have comparable degrees of patterning and variety. The poem at hand makes use of many kinds of co-ordinating and compounding. At the same time, there is nothing fatiguing or awkward about the sentences. One does not stumble over them in reading, nor does one need to hear them repeated in order to comprehend them. For all of the apparent intricacy of syntax, Machaut's sentences have a smoothness and elegance that provides the major precedent for the ease of Chaucer's verse.

'Plourez, dames' offers a specific precedent for certain passages in Chaucer's poetry. One of these is the final tern of the complaint section of 'Complaint of Mars' (281–98) in which Mars asks knights, ladies, and lovers for their pity. Another is Criseyde's 'testament' (IV 771–91) when she concludes that she will naturally die when she parts from Troilus. In both of these three-stanza set pieces the images also centre on mourning and death; black clothes, holy tears, request for pity, and bequeathal of heart specifically evoke Machaut's lyric. But I want to concentrate here on comparing 'Plourez, dames' with four stanzas of *Troilus*, where the congruencies are less specific and the important generic relationships stand out more clearly. The passage in question follows the three stanzas that open the poem, in which the narrator announces his subject (the 'double sorwe of Troilus'), invokes the Fury, and acknowledges his inadequacies. He then petitions lovers, as Machaut had petitioned ladies, with a series of imperatives, ending with a statement that equates his act of composition with prayer:

> But ye loveres, that bathen in gladnesse,
> If any drope of pite in yow be,
> Remembreth yow on passed hevynesse
> That ye han felt, and on the adversite
> Of othere folk, and thenketh how that ye
> Han felt that Love dorste yow displese,
> Or ye han wonne hym with to grete an ese.
>
> And preieth for hem that ben in the cas
> Of Troilus, as ye may after here,
> That Love hem brynge in hevene to solas.
> And ek for me preieth to God so dere
> That I have myght to shewe in som manere
> Swych peyne and wo as Loves folk endure,
> In Troilus unsely aventure.
>
> And biddeth ek for hem that ben despeired
> In love, that nevere nyl recovered be,
> And ek for hem that falsly ben apeired
> Thorugh wikked tonges, be it he or she;
> Thus biddeth God, for his benignite,
> So graunte hem soone out of this world to pace,
> That ben despeired out of Loves grace.
>
> And biddeth ek for hem that ben at ese,
> That God hem graunte ay good perseveraunce,
> And sende hem myght hire ladies so to plese
> That it to Love be worship and plesaunce.
> For so hope I my sowle best avaunce,
> To prey for hem that Loves servauntz be,
> And write hire wo, and lyve in charite,
>
> And for to have of hem compassioun,
> As though I were hire owne brother dere. (I 22–51)

It is remarkable that although they occupy a dominant place in the crucial introductory stanzas of the poem, these thirty lines contribute nothing to the exposition or the narrative. Their role is purely lyric. The passage is a self-contained set piece that keynotes lyric themes which run through the poem right to the Dantean conclusion, and which are enunciated repeatedly by all the main characters as well as by the narrator.

Like Machaut's ballade, the passage represents a type of love lyric common in Middle French verse, the prayer; more particularly, both examples are petitions expressed in quasi-Christian terms and forms, and addressed to initiates of love, asking them to assist lovers in their need and distress. Of course there are formal differences between the two; Chaucer's stanzas do not have a refrain or a consistent repetition of rhymes. At the same time the origin of Chaucer's rime royal stanza is found in Machaut's ballade practice, and analysis of the imagery, diction, and syntax shows further basic affinities.

Chaucer's imagery and the figures invoked in the passage are standard fare in the French lyrics: in the world called up some few of the lovers find contentment, are pleasing to their ladies, enjoy heaven's solace, bask in happiness; most of them are enduring pain and woe, and they despair and suffer because of wicked tongues and long to leave the world; all of them are servants of Love, in need of prayers for grace, which will give them the strength to persevere in their calling. The narrator who refers to this world of Amour and who speaks on behalf of lovers is another relatively common figure in the lyrics. His deity seems both pagan and Christian; he mentions prayers to 'God' three times, but he also names 'Love' as a presiding power five times. The diction is again remarkably repetitive: 'ye' and 'yow' echo through the first stanza, 'hem' and 'hire' in the last three. Forms of 'love' occur seven times, and forms of 'pray' and 'bid' six times. None of the words are unusual; 'plese', 'ese', 'despeyred', and 'wo' are all repeated, and fortified by 'pleseaunce', 'pite', 'peyne', 'apeyred', 'grace', 'adversite', etc.

The standard imagery and repetitive conventional diction again make it appropriate to speak of a pattern that matches the abstract design of the phonetics and the grammar. Though there is no refrain or consistent repetition of rhyme, the rime royal versification as Chaucer practises it here produces a marked phonetic configuration. The three rhyme endings that he intertwines in each stanza are predominantly extended rhymes, and two rhyme sounds of the first stanza (*-ese*, *-e*) are repeated in the third and the fourth. The anaphoral *ands* and *thats* that begin almost half the lines, and the seven imperative *-eth* inflections that regularly recur, reinforce the repetitive effects of the rhymes. Producing an effect comparable to the alliterating labials in 'Plourez, dames,' Chaucer uses numerous labial plosive p's and b's in important words and phrases like 'bathen,' 'drop of pite,' and 'despeired'.

Chaucer's complex, flowing syntax is vital in the effect of the passage. Three of the four stanzas are made up of two sentences, the other of one.[91] Following Machaut's practice, all three sentence-endings within the stanzas come at the conclusion of lines in the middle of the stanzas, two of them at the metrical (and musical) hinge – that is, at the close of the *abab* section. The smoothness of the sentences masks impressive complexity. If we take the single sentence that makes up stanza 4, for instance, we find the sense flowing easily from the subject ('ye loveres') and a modifying clause ('that bathen ...'), to a conditional clause ('If ony drop'), and thence to the two main verbs ('remembreth ... and thenketh'), the first possessing a double object with complex modifiers ('Passed hevynesse ... and ... the adversite'), and the second leading to a con-cluding chain of three clauses. Undoubtedly, Chaucer learned much about building such sentences in emulating Machaut, whether con-sciously or not. The use of enjambment is symptomatic of the syntactical affinity: in Chaucer's four stanzas there are eight cases of enjambment, proportionately equivalent to the six of 'Plourez, dames.' By comparison, the other generally less skilful French lyric poets use briefer sentences with more end-stopping, while Boccaccio's *Il Filostrato* employs a more paratactic syntax with more enjambment, conducive to a brisk narrative pace.

As I have said, these four stanzas keynote the pervasive lyric element of the poem. They serve to blend the conventional features of an ideal-ized world of Amour into the epic setting. The primary poetic values in the passage are those characteristic of works like 'Plourez, dames,' that is, of natural music. Representational features participate in the abstract patterning of the poem much as do phonetic and syntactic elements. In sum, Machaut's lyrics and dits provided Chaucer with a model of natural music which the English poet employed in all of his lyrics and much of his stanzaic work, *Troilus* most notably. In *Troilus*, of course, much goes beyond the Machauvian mode – the Troy story, the machinations of Pandarus, the trappings of heroic verse. Yet the French contribution is never submerged. It remains prominent in the ballade stanza that Chau-cer uses, in the large number of set pieces which with little alteration could be made into formes fixes lyrics, and in the character, dialogue, and behaviour of the lovers.

CHAPTER TWO

Poetry in the English Court before Poitiers (1356): Jean de le Mote

When Chaucer began court service in London in the late 1350s, the mode of French poetry that was in the ascendancy was thoroughly lyric in origin and spirit. Its typical subject was love, and its typical forms were those known as the formes fixes – the ballade, rondeau, virelay, chant royal, and the lay. The mode also was manifested in the longer dits amoureux, which are characterized by emotiveness and discontinuity, and for the most part are analysable as strings of lyric passages. By far the most important writer in the mode was Guillaume de Machaut (c. 1300–77). Though he did not originate the lyric forms or the dits, he so influenced their development and consolidated their dominant position that the whole body of Middle French court poetry is well identified as the 'Machaut tradition.'[1]

Before 1356 the full weight of Machaut's influence had yet to be felt in England, though another seminal figure in the formes fixes development, Jean de le Mote, seems to have been a major presence in the English court. It is le Mote who provides the ultimate focus for this chapter. Poetry such as his helped prepare for the cultural 'invasion' of London by French nobility beginning in 1356, the year that Jean II of France, captured at Poitiers, arrived in England. The presence of Jean's entourage and later that of his sons – especially the Duke of Berry – guaranteed that Machaut's work and style would become known in England while the French poet was still in his artistic prime. Young Chaucer was to become so imbued with the Machaut tradition of poetry, and so familiar with its materials, techniques, and purposes, that it provided a lyric matrix for much of his verse for thirty years. The poems that most obviously derive from the mode are the short works in ballade and rondeau form; the work whose language is most extensively drawn from the French verse is the *Book of the Duchess*. But the influence attains its greatest importance in *Troilus and Criseyde*.

The evidence is plentiful that the Machaut tradition was seminal in Chaucer's poetic career and constitutive in his verse. Given the historical timing of his arrival at court, the impact of the poetic fashion on him was predictable. In the world the boy entered this poetry was part of a vital literary tradition, providing him instruments and materials for developed poetic expression. It had, moreover, all the allure that popularity among the most successful and glamorous courtiers of Western Europe, notably those of England, could give it. To Chaucer in the late 1350s the ever triumphant Edward III could have appeared as nothing less than a new King Arthur (an image that Edward cultivated), the Black Prince a reincarnation of Gawain, the other leaders great heroes of comparable mythic status. The artistic expressions associated with their courts would inevitably have been invested with that aura of romance.

Since the poetry was a product of the French-speaking courts, the circumstances in which it was composed and performed are crucial to an appreciation of it. Its subject-matter has little to do with the great social and political developments of the time; instead, embedded in an idealized picture of knights and ladies is a treatment of the private life of the nobility, especially the refined relationships between the sexes, and their cultural avocations and aspirations. Because the work had a continuing restricted association with the royal courts of France and England, its audience was never large. The number of true aficionados could not have exceeded a few hundred, the total potential audience a few thousand. It was coterie art, moulded to the taste of an initiated nobility and their courtly followers.[2]

The formes fixes lyrics had become established in the courts in the half-century before Chaucer's arrival, developing from before the beginning of the fourteenth century, when the Middle French period is said to begin. As we have seen, the new forms reflected older trouvère types, but with structural modifications, increased prescriptiveness, and new favourites. The chant royal, with five stanzas and envoy, was descended from the Old French chanson and Provençal canso, but the chant and related five-stanza forms like the serventois were more current in the civic puys than in the courts. At court other forms came to the forefront whose musical aspect is especially prominent: the ballade, rondeau, and virelay. Unlike the chanson, these types originated as dance songs and had refrains.[3]

Because of such origins, French love poetry became even more musical than it had been in the previous centuries. By contrast, the Middle English lyrics of the time have no such musical affiliations, either in their origin or in their characteristically having musical accompaniment. The best secular English lyrics extant from the early fourteenth century are those of the Harley manuscript, which use an alliterative-accentual form that has its roots in English alliterative prose.[4] One would assume that the few such poems that acquired refrains, like 'Blow, Northern Wynd,' were provided with musical accompaniment, but it is remarkable that no music has survived for these or for any other English lyric of the first half of the century.[5] One might speculate that the prose origins of the English lyric metrics, in combination with the new developments in music and verse in France, made composers favour the French types, resulting in a decline in musical composition for English vernacular lyrics, especially in the courts. Such speculation from negative evidence assuredly is uncertain; nevertheless, the new French music and poetry obviously prevailed in the royal courts in England, as in France.

Though history often has been conceived all too narrowly in terms of the deeds of kings, in the case of Middle French court poetry the patronage by the royal families may properly be emphasized as the most consistent factor contributing to its flowering. Jean II (le Bon) of France and Edward III of England, with their immediate families, are at the centre of the fourteenth-century development; it began with their immediate forebears and continued to thrive after them among their numerous children. The royal names consistently are connected with the poets. Even the prime forerunner of the formes fixes writers, Adam de la Halle of Arras, who seems an urban uncourtly figure, served the French royal family; in 1307 we even find him (or at least a musician of his name) enlisted for the coronation of Edward II, father of Edward III.[6] The later poets had strong continuing ties with royalty. The most eminent figure in the early tradition, Philippe de Vitry, before becoming Bishop of Meaux was secretary and adviser to Philippe VI, and also enjoyed a close relationship with Philippe's son, Jean le Bon.[7]

Guillaume de Machaut had a close personal relationship with numerous royal figures: Jean of Luxembourg, the king of Bohemia (and the son of Dante's hero, Emperor Henry VII), his daughter Bonne and her husband Jean le Bon, their sons Charles V, Jean, Duke of Berry,

Philippe, Duke of Burgundy, and others. And the later prominent Middle French poets continued to enjoy comparable connections with the highest nobility. For almost a decade Froissart was secretary to Queen Philippa in England, and after she died he enjoyed the patronage of Duke Wenceslas of Brabant, the brother of Bonne and of Emperor Charles IV.[8] Eustache Deschamps was particularly proud of his intimacy with members of the French royal house, especially Charles VI and his brother Louis of Orléans, whom he long served. Oton de Granson found his main royal patrons in Edward III and Richard II of England; later in life he perhaps became close to Isabelle, queen of Charles VI. The major poets of the early fifteenth century, Christine de Pisan and Alain Chartier, also wrote their verse for royal audiences. These poets had considerable status, quite beyond that of minstrels. Beginning with Vitry and Machaut, they typically served as royal secretaries at the outset of their careers, then were appointed to important positions or sinecures later. They certainly wrote to please their patrons, but without overt servility.

Throughout Middle French times, then, the chief formes fixes poets composed for royalty, and of course the prisoner-poet Charles d'Orléans was himself of the royal house. Only the last prominent poet in the line, François Villon, had no close connection to the rulers of France or England, and even he could claim Charles d'Orléans as a sometime patron. Chaucer, of course, was comparable to the French poets in that he was in the personal service of the royal family including Edward III till 1374, and thereafter had a string of appointments from the monarchs. He differed from them in progressively widening his social and poetic horizons beyond the court and the Middle French tradition. He did not abandon either the court or the poetry; he simply developed broader associations and interests.

EDWARD III AS 'NEW ARTHUR' AND PATRON OF THE ARTS

Beginning in the 1320s, Jean de le Mote, whom a contemporary classes with Vitry and Machaut among musician-poets, likewise spent a career serving the highest nobility. He was poet at the court of Guillaume of Hainault, where Edward III met his future queen, Guillaume's daughter Philippa. Le Mote later belonged to the court in England after Edward became king in 1327 at age fifteen.

For a while Edward as king submitted to the tutelage of his mother Isabella and her lover Mortimer, but then he came into his own. Mortimer was dispatched without lengthy ceremony and Isabella silenced with a generous pension. After Edward consolidated his authority, and success in battle came his way at Sluys and elsewhere, he could on occasion relax and play the games of kings at home. His was not a grim court. In the 1330s and 1340s he was like the boyish Arthur in *Sir Gawain and the Green Knight*, with a lovely queen and a court full of young knights and ladies. A constant succession of tournaments and games, featuring processions, costuming, and banquets, diverted them;[9] the entertainments also performed an essential function in uniting Edward's supporters. It is no accident that the report of the tournament which he held at Windsor in early 1344 sounds like a romance, for policy as well as vanity encouraged Edward to present himself as a new Arthur, as his grandfather Edward I had done,[10] and the chroniclers conspired in the illusion.

Adam of Murimuth's description of the tournament at Windsor states that for three days the king and nineteen knights 'held the lists against all coming from without,' with the king bearing away 'the favours among those within.' On the following Thursday, 'the Lord King made a great supper at which he began his Round Table, and received the oaths of certain earls and barons and knights whom he wished to be of the said Round Table ... and he fixed the day for holding the Round Table in the same place [Windsor] on the feast of Pentecost next after ... He also ordained that there should be made in the same place a most noble house, in which the Round Table could be held at the term appointed.' There were to be three hundred knights, just as Arthur 'quondam rex Angliae' had presumably ordained it. At the feast Philippa and all her children were in attendance, along with the queen mother, her memory of Mortimer necessarily suppressed. There were 'rich foods and plenty of delightful libations to the satiety of all'; 'among the knights and ladies there was no lack of ring-dances intermingled with embraces and kisses.' The minstrels ('histriones') made excellent music ('summa melodia') and were given clothing, gold, and silver.[11] Some of the ring dances ('tripudia' or 'choreae') probably were virelays, sung in series without instrumental accompaniment.

Evidently an ambitious start was made on the building for the Round Table (not to be confused with Henry III's Round Tower at Windsor), which was to be two hundred feet in diameter,[12] but it was not ready for the feast of the Round Table apparently held in 1345 at Windsor; and by 1356 the project had been abandoned. Edward, however, by no means abandoned his pose and illusions of chivalric glory. The apocryphal story of the Countess of Salisbury's garter aside, romance and policy still lay behind his founding of the Order of the Garter in 1348 following the great victories at Crécy and Calais. And the Arthurian connection continued; one report declares that by creating the order 'he renewid the Round Table and the name of Arthure.' The chroniclers also associate the great feast held in 1358 after Poitiers with a renewing of the Round Table.[13] If the reports are to be credited, the kings of France were anxiously emulous of Edward's showy strategies; Thomas of Walsingham says that Philippe of Valois also set about building a Round Table in the 1340s,[14] and Jean la Bon later ordained an Order of the Star to match Edward's Garter.

If he was lucky, Geoffrey Chaucer was at Windsor for the 1358 celebration of Edward's last great success. Chaucer had begun his service with Prince Lionel's family near the height of the king's career. The poet Jean de le Mote perhaps was still active in the late 1350s. His name is hardly known today, but sufficient records and enough of his verse survive to suggest that before Poitiers he would have been much better known in England than Guillaume de Machaut. Such a possibility has not been recognized. The excellent preservation of Machaut's oeuvre, combined with the finished grace of his art and his powerful direct influence on subsequent poets, have led to his being treated implicitly as the sole beginning of the Middle French lyric tradition in France and England.[15] Poirion properly labels it the 'Machaut tradition,' for he is the central and dominating figure. At the same time, he had precursors and contemporaries who both influenced him and had continuing independent effect on the formes fixes tradition. In England the influence of Machaut, a Champenois, probably was slight before King Jean arrived after his capture at the Battle of Poitiers;[16] before that time the chief influence on the development of Middle French poetry there must have come from Flanders, Hainault, and northwest France.

In the thirteenth century, and continuing through the fourteenth, poetry flourished in those regions; geographical proximity made travel and trade with England common. Moreover, Edward III had special reasons for encouraging contact: not only was his wife a daughter of the house of Hainault, but after he undertook war with France in 1337 he needed friends; throughout the four decades of the Hundred Years' War that preceded his death he courted alliances with the Low Countries, and he frequently travelled there, sometimes for the purposes of battle. Important associations with literary men from the area were a natural consequence. Froissart is the best known of the poets to come to England from the Low Countries, but Jean de le Mote had been associated with

Edward's court decades before Froissart's advent in London. Because le Mote exerted an identifiable specific influence on both Machaut and Chaucer and made an important broad contribution to the mode, his literary career provides a convenient framework for talking about the development of Middle French poetry in England before Machaut's influence became dominant. His works further provide a basis for discussing specific literary developments that are important to succeeding poets and to Chaucer: the evolution of the poem with intercalated lyrics, relevant to all of Chaucer's long poems before the *Canterbury Tales*; the progress of the ballade form, which had an impact on all of Chaucer's stanzaic verse; and the growing importance of literary exempla in the poetry, which conditioned much of Chaucer's use of mythological material.

Since there is a record that le Mote was at work in the chancellery of Hainault in 1327,[17] it is likely that Edward first met the poet in Hainault when he came there with Isabella and Mortimer; the three had first left Edward II for Paris and had then been forced to leave the French court. At that time young Edward became betrothed to Philippa, who was two years younger than he; according to Froissart, he chose her for love from among the four daughters of the count.[18] Even though political considerations would have been primary, genuine romantic love seems entirely probable. Their ages (fifteen and thirteen) seem ideal for a medieval courtship; Edward's was an ardent and chivalrous disposition; and Philippa was an estimable courtly lady, always much admired. He might well have composed love poetry for her in the fixed forms, or had some poet like le Mote write it for him. In the light of his family's predispositions, the customs of the two courts, and the character of the prince, either would have been possible.

The evidence of Edward's cultural sophistication and his patronage of the arts is substantial, though it has sometimes been ignored.[19] His taste for poetry and music probably were developed through his mother and his wife, both of whom were closely related to French royalty. His father Edward II may have had little serious interest in the arts, though the chroniclers record, with some disapproval, that he busied himself about minstrels and masques, and there exists a French verse lament that he is supposed to have written.[20] Queen Isabella's literary interests ran deeper. Among the books that she possessed at her death were works dealing with all three romance 'matters' – those of Charlemagne, Arthur, and the Trojan War.[21] Mortimer perhaps also was inclined to romance literature; at least his holding a 'Round Table' celebration at Bedford in

1328, in accord with a family tradition, may indicate a penchant for old stories as well as his unbounded ambition.[22] Queen Philippa, whose family was especially cultivated,[23] was no doubt the most important continuing influence on the culture of the king and court, but his intellectual interests were also stimulated by his English associates. Richard de Bury, the author of *Philobiblon*, called by one modern scholar 'the first great European humanist'[24] and by another 'the greatest patron of his day and the greatest bibliophile of medieval Europe,'[25] was for many years Edward's chief minister and counsellor, and perhaps had been his tutor. Bury gathered around him distinguished scholars; among those who served as his chaplains were Thomas Bradwardine and Walter Burley. Henry of Lancaster was another intellectually active friend and counsellor of Edward; the powerful and wealthy father of John of Gaunt's Blanche, the author of the *Livre de seyntz medecines*,[26] he was himself a patron and associate of learned men.

From the beginning of Edward's reign, his court provided a home to men of letters, poets, and entertainers. Jean de le Mote seems to have been to a degree all three, and records indicate that he had a continuing, if not a constant, association with Edward from the 1320s or 1330s into and perhaps through the 1350s. We have already noted the record of 1327 that places le Mote in Hainault. At Antwerp in 1338 Edward granted to 'John de la Mote of Ghent' – in all probability the poet – a pension of twenty pounds a year or its equivalent in land.[27] In 1339 le Mote composed a long elegy, *Le Regret Guillaume*, on the death of William of Hainault, directed to his daughter Queen Philippa.[28] A possible relative of his, Isabelle de la Mote, is recorded as a damsel of Philippa's chamber in 1337 and is probably the same Isabelle mentioned in Edward's record in 1361.[29] In 1340 the poet was in Europe, probably Paris; in that year he completed two long poems, *Le Parfait du paon* and *La Voie d'enfer et de paradis* for Simon of Lille, goldsmith to Philippe VI. Nevertheless, he had probably already visited England, and he was to cross the Channel shortly for a more permanent stay. A record recently brought to light fixes him in England in 1343, when he was paid for entertaining the king at Eltham.[30] Later, a complex exchange of ballades across the Channel and a motet by Vitry indicate that he had gotten well settled with Edward.[31] Evidence suggests, then, that Jean de le Mote had a place of favour in the English court for many years, and there are further indications that he exerted a major influence on the poetic fashions to which Chaucer was exposed when he entered court life. Le Mote may well have been the first prominent court poet Chaucer met.

That le Mote was prominent in Continental literary circles is clear. The abusive poems written to and about him by the great Philippe de Vitry and his cohort Jean Campion, discussed below, provide compelling evidence of his status; they attack him with a violence reserved for celebrities. On the positive side Gilles li Muisis, writing in 1350, places le Mote in third place in the ranks of contemporary poets, after Vitry and Machaut:

> Or y rest Jehans de le Mote
> Qui bien le lettre et le notte
> Troève, et fait de moult biaus dis,
> Dont maint signeur a resbaudis,
> Si k'a honneur en est venus
> Et des milleurs faiseurs tenus.[32]

Now there remains Jean de le Mote, who composes both words and music well, making very lovely poems, from which many lords take pleasure, so that he has come to honour because of them and is accounted among the best poets.

Though li Muisis praises le Mote for musical as well as poetic composition, none of his music has come down to us. The poems that are extant, three long works and several ballades, doubtless represent but a fraction of his oeuvre; in particular we seem to be missing a large body of love poems as well as the music. What is left shows him as a poet of originality, sensitive to literary trends and pioneering their development in significant ways; at the same time, his long works tend to be rigid in structure and often fail to sustain the modern reader's interest.

Especially since Froissart and Chaucer followed in his wake in the royal court, the question of le Mote's social status is an interesting one. Another poet of the time with attachments to the Valenciennes court, who also wrote an elegiac poem for William of Hainault, was Jean de Condé. His description of his activities as court poet does not fit in with what we can reconstruct of le Mote's career or of the other formes fixes poets from Machaut on. Jean says of himself:

> Si sui des menestrex el conte,
> Car biaus mos trueve et les reconte,
> Dis et contes, et lons et cours,
> En mesons, en sales, en cours
> Des grans seigneurs, vers cui je vois,

Et haut et bas oient ma vois.
De mal à fere les repren
Et à bien fere leur apren;
De ce jour et nuit les sermon,
On ne demande autre sermon
En plusours liex où je parole.[33]

I am counted among the minstrels to the court, and I compose good poems and recite them, dits and stories, both long and short, in homes, in halls, and in courts of great lords where I go. Both high and low hear my voice. I warn them against doing evil and teach them to do well. Night and day I talk to them on this topic. In the several places where I speak they don't ask for any other kind of discourse.

Like his father Watriquet, Jean de Condé composed moral allegories and narratives, and on occasion racier stories. Among their extant works are none of the lyric formes fixes. The passage suggests that the nobility maintained the Condés and others like them more on a par with the servants than with the squires. By contrast, the prominent composers of formes fixes verse and music at the time enjoyed more elevated positions, Vitry being a royal secretary and then a bishop, and Machaut a secretary to kings and then a cathedral Canon.

Le Mote's social status must have been more like that of Machaut than that of the Condés. The 1327 record of him, when he surely was quite young, shows his being paid for copying some documents. He had the skills of a 'clerc,' then, with duties that would set him apart from the minstrel class, men like Brisebarre of Douay who could not read or write.[34] He was able to mix with members of the court on something like equal footing. The twenty-pound annuity that the king assigned to Jean in 1337 confirms that he was a man of standing. It is 50 per cent more than the annuity of twenty marks granted to Chaucer in 1367. Of Jean's three long works, two are of particular concern here as representative of the narrative poem with intercalated lyrics. The third is of less interest to us: La Voie d'enfer et de paradis[35] is a moral allegory that is comparable to works by the Condés, and even more like the Pèlèrinages of Guillaume de Deguilleville. Of mild interest to the Chaucerian is the fact that the Voie employs throughout the same twelve-line stanza of octosyllabics (aabaabbbabba) which Deguilleville uses for the ABC poem that Chaucer translates.[36]

TWO TYPES OF LONG POEM WITH INTERCALATED LYRICS

The evolution of the long French love poem with intercalated lyrics is quite significant for all of Chaucer's early long works, and notably for *Troilus and Criseyde*, which may be analysed as a work with many lyric set pieces interspersed.[37] Le Mote's two long works other than the *Voie* are integral in the development of such poems, and they illustrate the two primary types before Chaucer. In the first kind, by far the older, the function of the lyrics is to provide diversion and commentary that are not integral to the narrative; they interrupt the main story, to which they are lightly attached. Well-known examples of this sort are the romance of *Guillaume de Dole* (1210), *Cléomadès* (1280), and fourteenth-century poems like the *Roman de Fauvel* (1316)[38] and Froissart's *Meliador* (after 1360). Le Mote's Alexander romance, *Le Parfait du paon* (1340), with its digressive set of ballades, also represents this type. In the second kind, which developed in the fourteenth century, the interspersed lyrics came to perform a more essential function, representing integral high points in the stories. The narratives in these poems, instead of providing the dominant interest, are important vehicles for lyric expression. Nicole de Margival's *Dit de la Panthère d'Amours* (c. 1310) and Jehan Acart de Hesdin's *Prise amoureuse* (1332) are precursors of this later type, with le Mote's *Regret Guillaume* (1339) a full-blown examplar. A discussion of his *Parfait* and *Regret* will illustrate the two directions of the development, and will point up the aspects that are relevant to Chaucer's art.[39]

The Alexander romances to which the *Parfait du paon* provides a late sequel go back to the beginnings of romance in the mid-twelfth century; all of such romances were written in unequal laisses of twelve-syllable lines (whence 'Alexandrines'). Le Mote's poem is a sequel to the *Restor du paon* (before 1338) by the Picard Brisebarre le Court,[40] which in turn continues the story of *Voeux du paon* (c 1310) by the Lorraine poet Jacques du Longuyon.[41] Jacques' poem has a prominent place in literary history, in part because of its pioneering of both the plot motif of a 'vowing' competition and the set piece celebrating the Nine Worthies, and in part because of its distinctive and interesting treatment of its subject-matter whereby ceremonial activities within the court acquired a new prominence.[42] After the *Voeux*, the narratives of several prominent poems were made to turn about a series of vows made by great leaders to a festive fowl, either an actual bird prepared for a feast or an artificial one. In Jacques' work Alexander and several other characters swear before a peacock that they will accomplish certain grand exploits. Predictably, the remainder of the story deals with the carrying out of the vows.

As the Round Table celebrations show, the barriers between romance and life in fourteenth-century England were not inviolate. Jacques wrote the *Voeux* at the inspiration and command of Thiébaut, Bishop of Liège, who was related by marriage to Edward I and held several benefices in England.[43] And the subsequent narrative tradition was closely associated with the English monarchy; 'vowings' with crucial historical consequences were imputed to both Edward I and Edward III.[44] The second influential motif of the work, the literary tradition of the Nine Worthies, also is manifested importantly in French and English verse, in both brief and developed lists of exempla, and even in a set of marvellous female *preuses*, a subject developed below.[45]

The continuators of Jacques' *Voeux* helped assure his impact on late medieval narrative. In extending the story, Brisebarre in the *Restor du paon* and le Mote in *Parfait du paon* enter fully into the courtly spirit of Jacques' romance. The *Restor* tells of the restoration in gold of the original peacock; the style of the poem features rich description and much polite dialogue between the characters. In the further continuation in le Mote's *Parfait* there is a new series of vows, made to the golden peacock, and a new grand battle in which the vows are fulfilled.[46] The most valuable parts of the *Parfait*, from the standpoint of both literary interest and the preoccupations of this study, are the interludes in the court in which the subject of love dominates and a game framework controls. The ritual vowing, and the subsequent working out of the vows, of course is game-like; and even more fully participating in the ludic aspect of the *Parfait*'s narrative is the series of debates on questions of love and the poetic contest involving eight ballades, of which two are 'crowned,' as at a meeting of a puy. These are of great interest for the development of the lyric tradition, and especially for circumstances of composition and performance, all evidence of which is invaluable.

The games take place in the 'chambre amoureuse' of the palace belonging to Alexander's courteous Indian enemy, Melidus. When, early in the narrative, three of the six peers of Alexander are captured in battle, they find themselves in this chamber entertained by Melidus' four lovely daughters. To pass the time profitably Saigremore, one of the daughters, poses questions of love to the three peers in turn: Which suffers more in love, amie or amans? (487–8). Which is better for the lover, obtaining mercy when he asks for it or being put off with some hope of obtaining it eventually? (561–3). What three virtues are best for a lover to possess?

(612–14). Each peer answers one of the questions at length, and Saigremore diplomatically explains the mistakes of each.[47]

The day after this informal Court of Love, Alexander and his peers take advantage of a truce to visit Melidus' court and the 'prisoners.' When Alexander enters the 'chambre amoureuse' where they are held, the ladies tell him that he must converse and debate with them, or at least present a ballade. Though Alexander protests his lack of skill, they insist, and he initiates a series of eight ballades; after he recites his poem, the three captive peers and the four demoiselles present their verse in turn (1052–1369). If a meeting of a puy is here imitated, as it must be in part, the episode has historical value for understanding how the 'concours' were conducted.[48] And since le Mote was in the first place a court poet, and was writing for one of the king's functionaries who lived next door to the king,[49] one may also deduce from these interludes something about the literary practices of the nobility. They suggest notably that poetic competitions of a more or less spontaneous sort, involving questions of love, were an actual pastime of courtiers, and that ladies both composed lyrics and acted as judges in such games. In other words, love poetry was a game that all could play.[50]

The salient point about the *Parfait* for the present discussion is that the work represents the kind of long poem that incorporates digressive short lyrics. While the poetic contest that introduces the lyrics is made integral to the narrative, the texts of the eight ballades which make up the contest, and which are presented in full, are extrinsic; they constitute agreeable interruptions to a complex story with other concerns.[51] On the other hand, with le Mote's *Regret Guillaume* we find a poem in which the simple narrative acts mainly as a framework for lyric expressions; the body of the work is a connected series of complaints and ballades.[52] To a modern reader the work seems too repetitive, but it was very influential, not only in the development of the long poem, but also for the poetic use of mythology and for the effect it had on the ballade form. Specific echoes in Machaut's and Chaucer's work substantiate the general influence.

The main body of the *Regret* is taken up with the laments of thirty personified ladies for the death of William, prefaced by an introductory frame story. In contrast to the personifications in the *Roman de la Rose*, the ladies are not individually described and their allegorical natures are hardly distinguished. Moreover, while each nominally represents a separate virtue of Count William, their complaints usually go beyond the limitations of the personified virtues and become generalized laments appropriate to close personal associates of William. None of the personified figures interact as abstractions; they behave independently very much as court attendants at the count's funeral. Furthermore, the exempla most of them adduce are presented in such detail as to provide complex human analogues to William's situation rather than simple lessons about the qualities in question.

Le Mote prefaces the dream vision that occupies most of the *Regret* with a ninety-six-line statement that constitutes the most important antecedent of Machaut's Prologue, his art of poetry. Le Mote petitions God and Nature for the requisite faculties to celebrate properly the deeds of the 'high prince' (Count William), with the petition providing a brief analysis of the poesy.[53] Following the preface the frame-story begins; while it was plainly modelled on the *Roman de la Rose*, the frame provided an independent model for Chaucer's *Book of the Duchess*, and probably Machaut's *Jugement du roy de Behaigne*. As in the *Rose* the narrator gets up in his dreams, goes off into the lovely countryside where the birds sing 'amoureusement' (123) so that the wood is gladdened by their 'joli chant' (128), and he at length finds himself greeted by a lovely female personification at a wicket-gate in a wall. But in these parallels to the *Rose* the imitation applies more to style than to substance. The story is not of young love, and the narrator is not the generic Amant of Guillaume de Lorris. From the beginning of the dream he is primarily the practising poet. Successively he is involved in writing a lyric for a puy (100–4), offering to compose consolatory works (282–3), collecting poetic material (295–302), and – following the dream – putting it into new rhymes at the command of the queen (4564–73).

The wall at which the narrator arrives surrounds a most beautiful castle. Initially drawn to the place by the sound of gay music, he hears only loud complaining when he arrives. The lady who responds to his knocking, Debonnairté, cannot allow him to enter the castle proper; she says it now has no use for minstrelsy. But she does let him come through the gate and gaze through a small window into the room where thirty ladies are making 'grant doel.' She identifies the prince for whom they lament as William, Count of Hainault, Holland, and of Zeeland, and Lord of Frisia (338–41). Then she introduces the ladies, each of whom represents a noble virtue that the count possessed: Humelité, Proecce, Largece, Hardemens, and so on down to Gentilesce, Poissance, and the 'mistress of all others,' Perfection. While the narrator watches at the 'petit trou,' the ladies in turn make formal laments, ending invariably with a ballade.

Repeatedly they speak of the dead count as brother, father, master, and especially as 'ami.' A number of the twenty-eight exempla they adduce put the lady who speaks in the position of bereft beloved, as in the lament of Largece, who cites Aeneas' sudden departure from Dido, and Dido's subsequent suicide as analogous to William's death and its consequences for her. As his leaving pierced Dido with a sword, so it happened with her:

Ciers amis, teille est ma dolours:
Quant je vic que vous me lariés,
Si dolente en fui et si griés
C'onques fame ne puet plus iestre
Pour çou me repus en cest iestre,
Car, voir, je sui au monde morte.
Je n'ai mais castiel, tour ne porte,
Ne retour ù je puisse entrer.
Lasse, quant je l'en vic aler,
L'espée de dolour feri
En men coer et morte quaÿ.   (900–10)

Dear love, my sorrow is like Dido's: When I saw that you would leave me, I was as sorrowful and grieved as ever any lady was. Because of this I have hidden myself here, for indeed I am dead to the world. No longer do I have castle, tower, gate, or refuge which I can enter. Alas, when I saw him go from here, the sword of sorrow struck my heart and I fell dead.

The complaint works on an allegorical level: when William dies, Generosity itself dies. But the human application is also valid: the death of the flower of knighthood, William, bereaves all ladies. Like the *Book of Duchess*, le Mote's *Regret* is a dream vision, an elegy, and a poem of fin' amors.

Since Machaut's borrowings show that he knew the *Regret*, we may talk with some confidence of its effects on the development of the long poem. It stands in contrast to most previous long love poems, whether or not with formally distinct lyric insertions. Before the *Regret*, the dit amoureux generally was characterized by complex narratives or allegorical tableaux to which the lyric elements were ancillary. In the *Roman de la Rose*, to take the prime example, elements like the description of the carole and the narrator's complaints, which could make separable lyric pieces, are well subordinated to the allegorical story, whose prime interest is philosophical and psychological. In the *Regret*, by contrast, the descriptive and emotive elements come to the fore, with the main narrative clearly in their service. The story of the narrator's visit to the castle has little point except in giving each of the thirty ladies a chance to eulogize Guillaume. The same relationship of the narrative to the discursive is found in all of Machaut's dits. He learned from the *Regret* how to make the lyric content predominate and to feature lyric insertions in a slight narrative, though he was too good an artist to adopt Jean's mechanical patterns.[54]

In addition to its importance in the development of the long poem, the *Regret*, together with later works by le Mote, also plays a crucial part in the two other developments to be considered here: the evolution of the ballade form and the use of classical exempla, both matters of substantial importance for Chaucer. As already discussed, the ballade not only was Chaucer's favourite form for his lyrics, but it also provided the main precedent for his two favourite stanza forms, rime royal and the 'Monk's Tale' stanza, and the process of its development is directly relevant to much of his work.

THE DEVELOPMENT OF THE BALLADE IN THE FOURTEENTH CENTURY

The ballade contest of the *Parfait du paon* provides valuable insight into the fourteenth-century conception of the lyric. The discussion among the judges before they grant the awards offers particularly significant testimony about what the authors strove for and what the audience appreciated in the lyrics. We find that the judges do not choose the winners on the basis of charm or emotive effect, but rather for niceties of technique, aptness of phrase, and appropriateness of diction. Aristé, a peer of Alexander and one of the judges, briefly summarizes the performance of each contestant before giving the main prize to Clarete:

Vez ci la balade Dan Clin le combatant
Qui est bonne et bien faicte, ne la vois deprisant,
Mez ci ou secont ver a il .i. faus ronmant
Et en la Tholomer que vez ci ensuivant
Une redicte en sens y est, je vous creant.
En l'Aymon .i. genoul, alés le bien lisant;
Ce n'est riens qui ne va les vices espluchant.
La balade Alixandre que leüsmez devant

Elle est de vicez nette et va moult bien servant,
Mes il ne reva point tres hautement parlant,
Mes c'est celle des honmes ou m'iroie acordant.
Vez ci Deromadaire qui un poi va vantant,
Et Saigremore dist qu'elle a nouvel amant,
Li mot ne sont pas haut mes il sont bien plaisant.
Et Preamuse aussi en ce ver ci devant
A .i. [parler] pour nient qui mal i va seant,
Si qu'a verité dire, par les dix d'Abilant,
S'on donnoit pour honneur, royaume, ou terre grant
Si le doit bien avoir Clarete au cuer sachant.   (1410–28)

Here is the ballade of Dan Clin the warrior, which is good and well made; do not undervalue it. But here in the second stanza there is a false rhyme. And I aver that in the next poem by Tholomer there is a needless repetition. In Aymon's there is a grammatical error, go ahead and read it; there is nothing which hides the faults. Alexander's ballade, which we read earlier, is grammatically correct and serves well, except that it is not sufficiently elevated. However, of the men's ballades, it is the one I prefer. Now [among the women's poems] Deromadaire's is a little boastful. And Saigremore says that she has a new friend; her words are not elevated but they are pleasant. And Preamuse in the first stanza has a phrase that adds nothing and fits in badly, so that to tell the truth, by the god of Abilant, if one gave a price for honour, either realm or great lands, Clarete with her wise heart ought to have it.[55]

Even Alexander is fair game for criticism here; the poem of the king of kings is not elevated enough. Aristé's judgments put an emphasis on correctness in grammar and rhyme, decorum, and felicity of expression – matters of particular concern for Middle French natural music. He is more specific about defects than about merits, so that his praise of the triumphant Clarete seems vague: she has a wise heart. Nevertheless, the comment is probably well considered; it corroborates Alexander's statement after her recitation that she has 'un cuer ou science est plus enracinee' (1376, 'a heart in which wisdom is most deeply rooted'). In the final analysis it is the capacity of the heart that makes the best poem. The emphasis on technical matters on the one hand and on the heart of exceptional capacities on the other may strike the modern critic as too mechanical at one extreme and too vague at the other, but it is nevertheless quite in line with Dante's contrasting commentary on love poetry in De vulgari eloquentia and Purgatorio.

The medieval judges perhaps had a livelier concern for technical details than most critics today, but a modern critic looking at the ballades of the *Parfait* in comparison with other ballades of the time, especially the other ballades of le Mote himself, will be more conscious of historical developments than the fictional judges were. The common label 'forme fixe' suggests that the lyric had a set of invariable formulas in the Middle French period, but their fixity was relative. While the amorous subject-matter, the characteristic diction, and the three-stanza form with refrain remained reasonably constant through the century, there were important and continuing developments in the versification, as there were in the employment of literary exempla. We will take up the latter subject after dealing with the matter of ballade metrics. For the purposes of this analysis it will be convenient to posit early, middle, and late forms, all exemplified in the work of le Mote, who was a prime innovator.

A ballade of Nicole de Margival in the *Panthère d'Amours* is typical of the form at the very beginning of the century: brief, light, with a minimum of developed metaphor, personification, and allusion. In most ways the second stanza is typical of the poem and the type:

J'ai mis ja sans dessevrer
Cuer et corps en sa bailie,
Car bele est a regarder,
Cortoise et bien ensaignie,
Et trop plus que je ne die
  Plaine de valour;
  S'en merci Amour (2303–9)

I have placed my body and heart in her governance forever, with no separation, for she is beautiful to see, courteous and well-bred, and more virtuous than I can say; for which I thank Amour.

Like this work of Nicole, with its short stanzas of short lines with mixed lengths, the ballades in the *Parfait du paon* have forms mostly characteristic of the early century.

Six of the eight ballades in the contest are in seven-syllable and shorter lines; four have mixed line lengths; and three have two-line refrains. Clarete's crowned ballade and one other are the most substantial; in their full rime royal versification they look forward to works of the middle period, though in content the poems still have the lightness that marks the earlier works. The first stanza of Clarete's perhaps suggests

their quality. The sense and sound flow easily and gracefully, unen-
cumbered by allusion, complex metaphor, or multiple personifications;
before the refrain line, there is but one end-stop and no internal punctuation. The refrain is particularly effective in its sequence of cognates
of 'amer':

Tres gracieuse sui des biens d'amer
S'en lo Amours de cuer tres humlement,
Qui m'a a bon et bel fait assener
Par tel maniere et par itel couvent
Que quiconques verroit no maintieng gent
Veïr porroit tout en une assemblee
Amours, amé, amant, amie, amee.   (1349–55)

I am most favoured with the benefits of loving, and I praise Love humbly from
my heart, who has assigned me a good and handsome man in such manner
and by such covenant that whoever may see our way of life may see wholly
joined Love, loved one, lover, lady-love, beloved.

The word-play in the refrain, involving five stops succeeding an unin-
terrupted cadence in the first six verses, has an original effect unusual
in the lyrics; but in most respects the stanza and ballade are typical.

While le Mote's *Regret Guillaume* was composed earlier than the *Parfait*, in form the ballades that conclude its thirty complaints were considerably in advance of most ballades in the contest; they exhibit fully
the verse characteristics of the ballades of Machaut and others in the
middle period. Indeed, as a body they exerted the most powerful force
in the transition of the ballade form.[56] They were composed but seven
years after the *Prise amoureuse* (1332), whose nine intercalated ballades
still represent the early stages of the form.[57] But in contrast to those
lyrics and the works of all previous poets, the ballades of the *Regret*
have isometric lines, mostly descasyllabic, use seven- and eight-line
stanzas, and have single-line refrains.[58] All in all, the changes add substantially to the length and symmetry of the stanza, facilitating rhetorical
development and grammatical parallelisms.

In practice the originality in metrical form of these ballades is partially
vitiated by le Mote's rigid adherence to a uniform rhetorical pattern,
which makes the lyrics tiresome as a group if not always individually.
One of the more compelling ballades, subsequently echoed by Machaut,
illustrates the pattern. In the first two stanzas the personification who

speaks, Plaisance, declares that she will never be happy again because the loss of the count has robbed her of her own intrinsic nature; and in the third stanza she expresses the hope that William's heir will restore the realm, and her true personality in the process. Rhetorically, the three stanzas illustrate the 'enchaînement logique' characteristic of the type:[59]

> Coers de marbre, couronnés d'aÿmant,
> N'est point si durs, selonc m'entencion,
> Que li cuers est qui, de voloir engrant,
> Ama jadis men frere et men baron,
> S'en li n'en a grief tribulation,
> Car tant qu'en my jamais n'arai leecce,
> *Plaisance euc non, or ai à non Tristrece.*
>
> Cascuns sieut dire que j'estoie, à vivant
> De men cier fil, en grant audition,
> Et m'apielloit dame en tous biens faisant.
> Tant me portoit de domination.
> Or ai pierdu fief et possession
> Et par l'acort de grevainne Destrece,
> *Plaisance euc non, or ai à non Tristrece.*
>
> Or n'ai ge riens qui me voist confortant
> Que li pensers seulement au bouton
> Qui demorra sur le rosier croissant.
> S'il s'espanist par voie de raison,
> Ravoir porai encore men droit non;
> S'il ne le fait, je n'i voi autre adrece;
> *Plaisance euc non, or ai à non Tristrece.*   (2953–73)

A heart of marble, crowned with adamant, I think, is not at all as hard as the heart of the person who once loved my brother and husband ardently if he does not feel grievous affliction, for I have so much that I will never have joy. My name used to be Pleasure, now it is Sadness.

Everyone can attest that while my dear son lived I was a trusted companion, and that he called me lady while performing all good things; so much did he grant me dominance. Now I have lost my fief and my property, and with the assent of harsh Distress, whereas my name used to be Pleasure, now it is Sadness.

Now I have nothing to comfort me except the thought of the bud which is growing on the rosebush. If it blossoms in the way of reason, I will be able to have once more my true name, but if it doesn't I see no recourse. My name used to be Pleasure, now it is Sadness.

The rime royal stanza of this ballade is the most commonly used in the *Regret* and was the favourite form of Machaut.[60] The second most frequent ballade stanza in the poem is the Monk's stanza, with its eight lines rhyming *ababbcbC*, which became the favourite of Froissart and Granson.[61] Both stanzas seems to have been little used before le Mote. In versification, then, the ballades of the *Regret* look forward to the later French poets. So do they to Chaucer, since le Mote's two favourite stanzas here become Chaucer's favourites to the exclusion of almost all others.

Significantly, Machaut echoes the first line of this work in the refrain of one of his last lyrics, his only chant royal that has a refrain – a two-line refrain at that. Each of the five stanzas and the envoy conclude:

Cuer de marbre, couronné d'aÿmant,
Ourlé de fer, à la pointe asserée.[62]

Heart of marble, crowned with adamant, edged with iron, with steel at the point.

In this manifest elaboration of le Mote's image we see Machaut, writing in the 1360s, still influenced by the *Regret*; his work showed traces of le Mote's elegy throughout his career.[63] As I have mentioned, Chaucer also knew the *Regret*; and Froissart certainly would have been familiar with it, if for no other reason than his association with Queen Philippa. Its importance goes far beyond its attractions as a poem.

Some other lyrics of le Mote's which have survived separately indicate that he was a leader in a further development in the ballade form, which did not touch Machaut but which left its mark on Froissart, Deschamps, and later French poets, and perhaps on Chaucer. This involved using still longer, more substantial stanzas. While Machaut exploited the seven- and eight-line decasyllabic ballade,[64] by the 1350s ballade strophes of ten lines and longer, generally decasyllabic, were being used by other writers. Le Mote was probably important in introducing or popularizing that stanza too, adapting it from the lengthier puy forms like the chant royal, serventois, and pastourelle.[65] He uses the long stanzas in three of the four identified extant poems of his from after 1340, found in a series of six ballades in a late medieval manuscript miscellany.[66] These works are all identified by author, le Mote being the composer of the first two, the fourth, and the sixth; Philippe de Vitry of the third; and Jean Campion of the fifth. The third and fourth, and the fifth and sixth, form pairs, each pair constituting an unfriendly exchange across the Channel.

The attack by Vitry[67] and the response by le Mote, the third and fourth poems, provide the focus of the six-ballade set; the exchange thus involves the major poet writing for the French court before Machaut, and evidently the major poet of the English court before Froissart and Chaucer. Vitry's ballade attacks le Mote's extravagant use of names in his poetry, which the first two ballades in the set illustrate, and he also impugns his loyalty. Philippe had perhaps sponsored le Mote in Paris, and now is displeased to see him serving in England. If Vitry – an intimate of French kings – had indeed favoured le Mote with his friendship and wisdom, then the sharpness of the attack and the mildness of the ensuing response are understandable.

In the opening stanza Vitry envisions le Mote as a renegade in flight from France, tool and victim of the English. He then imagines that le Mote's spirit, having fled to a Dantean inferno, will be assigned to the circle of traitors at the bottom of hell.[68] In the final stanza he derogates le Mote's poetic achievement. In a series of allusions to the spring of the Muses, created by the hoof of Pegasus, he deplores particularly his irresponsible use of literary allusion:

> Certes, Jehan, la fons Cirree
> Ne te congnoit, ne li lieux vers
> Ou maint la vois Calioppe.
> Car amoureus diz fais couvers
> De nons divers.
> Dont aucuns enfes scet user
> Com tu, qui ne vaulz une mite
> A Pegasus faire voler,
> En Albion de Dieu maldite.[69]   (19–27)

Indeed, Jean, the fountain of Cirrha [Hippocrene] does not know you, nor the green place where the voice of Calliope stays. For you fill your love poems with bizarre names. Any child can write like you, who cannot in any way make Pegasus fly in Albion cursed by God.

It is interesting that Vitry employs the ballade form here for the purposes of invective, a use to which he frequently put the motet.[70] The stanza, consisting of nine lines, octosyllabic except for a short fifth line, is what we might expect of a poet of Vitry's vintage, in that it is more characteristic of the early than the late form and suitable for musical setting.

The ten-line stanza of le Mote's response, longer than was usually set to music, allows him space for developing several themes. Jean begins the poem with high praise for his attacker, then makes a firm but moderate defence of his own behaviour and writings. His is a reply such as one might anticipate from a former disciple to his master, hoping to calm the waters, and the poem evidently became widely known, for Deschamps later would imitate its opening lines in ballades to both Machaut and to Chaucer.

> O Victriens, mondains dieu d'armonie.
> Filz Musicans et per a Orpheus,
> Supernasor de la fontaine Helye,
> Doctores vrays, en ce pratique Anglus,
> Plus clers véans et plus agus qu'Argus,
> Angles en chant, cesse en toy le lyon!
> Ne fais de moy Hugo s'en Albion
> Suis. Onques n'oy ailleurs vent ne volee.
> Ne je ne sui point de la nacion
> *De terre en grec Gaulle de Dieu amee.*   (1–10)

O man of Vitry, worldly god of harmony, son of Music and peer of Orpheus, greater Naso of the fountain of Helicon, true doctor, Aulus Gellius among writers, more clear-sighted and acute than Argus, angel in song, restrain the lion in you! Do not make Hugo of me because I am in Albion. I never had inspiration or flight elsewhere. And I in no way belong to the nation of the land in Greek called Gaul, loved by God.

In what follows le Mote blames the 'reports of Eolus' (Rumour) for causing Vitry to attack him, and in a claim that could be appropriate to a churchman says that he serves the cause of good against evil in England. Promising to answer any accusations of treason made against him with the vocal powers of Echo, he concludes with the plea:

> Sy te suppli, ne banny mon bon nom
> *De terre en Grec Gaulle de Dieu amee.*   (29–30)

So I entreat you, do not banish my good name from the land in Greek called Gaul, loved by God.

The refrain line neatly undercuts the bitter refrain of Vitry's poem which impugns England. But for all of le Mote's diplomacy, it does not seem that his soft answer turned away the bishop's wrath, for in a motet Philippe renewed the attack, presenting his object – no doubt le Mote again – as a 'sad brute' who, fancying himself a poet, feeds the English with flattery.[71]

A second French writer, Jean Campion, followed up Vitry's attack; his ballade and the response to it by le Mote provide the last two in the six-ballade series. Campion, a cleric of Tournai and later of Bruges,[72] in a territory not directly under the French king, does not concern himself with le Mote's loyalty, but he is mightily offended by his deficiency in poetic skill. It may be in a spirit of mimicry that he employs the ten-line stanza of le Mote's poem, just as his extravagant three-line refrain of proper names represents an implicit comment on Jean's use of names. In the first stanza he refers to Vitry's ballade and asserts that while le Mote imagines himself to have drunk from the fountain of Helicon, he is much mistaken; none of the Nine Muses ever took him there. Vitry had consigned le Mote to hell for his treason to France; Campion says that he deserves hell for his use of names:

> Espoir, Caron en Phlegeton l'esprise,
> Ou Athleto en Lethés l'eut attrait,
> Ou en Cochite ou Thesipone est prise,
> Pour lui mectre el point qu'elle Athamas lait,
> Quant en ses dis noms de Bretesque mait
> Qui n'ont congneu poete en Meonie,
> En Manthe, en Peligne, en Verone né,
> *Ne Flactus, Clyo, Euterpe, Uranie,*
> *Thersicore, Erato, Melponmené,*
> *Thalye, Calliope et Polimnie.*[73]   (11–20)

Perhaps Charon will burn him in Phlegethon, or Allecto will have drawn him into Lethe, or into Cocytus where Thesiphone is held, to put him into the situation of Athamas, since he [le Mote] put into his poems bizarre names unknown to poets in Maeonia, Mantua, Peligni, or in Verona, or to Flaccus, Clio,

Euterpe, Urania, Terpsichore, Erato, Melpomene, Thalia, Calliope, and Polhymnia.[74]

Campion invokes the major Latin poets to support his attack on le Mote's practice. At the same time, by filling his poem with classical names he parodies the fault he is criticizing.

Le Mote helped establish the ballade stanza of ten and more decasyllabic lines, just as he earlier pioneered the seven- and eight-line isometric stanzas. The longer stanzas are less suitable for musical accompaniment, and ballades using them were not composed until the ballade form became less dependent on notation. Though le Mote himself was a musician, and there is plentiful indication that the ballades of the *Regret* were sung,[75] there is no hint that his responses to Vitry and Campion were set to music. Like Machaut, the musical composer le Mote was probably a leader in writing lyrics without music.

By the 1350s the province of the ballade had greatly expanded over what it had been at the beginning of the century, and it had become possible to weave complex argument and allusion into single poems. A fine, if extreme, illustration of the later ballade's potential weight and complexity may be seen in a work that probably originated the theme of the Nine Female Worthies.[76] Found in the most important manuscript anthology extant of fourteenth-century French lyrics, which has particular relevance to mid-century England and may even contain French poems by Chaucer, this ballade may have been composed by le Mote.[77] The numerous heroines, heroes, and historians referred to in the poem are authentic, but the assumption implicit in the poem that there is an established tradition of the 'Neuf Preuses' perhaps masks its status as the author's original invention:

Se la puissant royne Semiramis
Et Lampheto cheut a Penthesilee,
Ypolite, Menalippe, Themaris,
Deïphele, Sinope – dont Pompee
Troguë, Eusabé, Orose, Justin,
Ont maint fait d'armes escript et maint hustin,
Tant qu'elles sont aux neuf preux comparees –
Renesquissoient toutes et assamblees
Fussent ensamble pour moy nuire et grever,
A champ n'a ville, en terre ne en mer

Ne doubteroye eulz ne tout leur povoir,
Tant que je peusse ma dame en aide avoir.

Si conquist Aise Lanpheto par son pris
En toute Eroppe, Semiramis clamee
De tout le monde fu dame empereis,
Rommains vanqui Theuta mainte journee,
Thebes conquirent Deiphile et Argin,
Cirain de Perse mist Themaris a fin,
Sinope aussi conquist maintes contrees,
Ypolitë et Menalippe armees
Contre Herculés, champ le firent vuidier,
Penthesilee refist moult mes penser;
Pas n'oseroient moy courcier n'esmouvoir,
Tant que je peusse ma dame en aide avoir.

Car tant est grande, puissant, noble, gentilz,
Sage, vaillant, et par tout renomee
Qu'il n'est roy n'autre qu'il ne li soit sougis.
David mesmes, Josué, Machabee,
Julle Cezar, Hector, Alexandrin,
Godeffroy, Charles, et Artus, sens declin
Le serviro[ie]nt et toutes les contrees
Qu'onques ils tindrent, neiz les mons et valees
S'inclinero[ie]nt. Ou puet on donc trouver
Force qui puist soy vers moy comparer,
Ne que je deusse doubter a dire voir,
Tant que je peusse ma dame en aide avoir?

If the powerful Semiramis and Lampedo, along with Penthesilea, Menalippe, Hippolyta, Thamyris, Deïpyle, and Sinope [Antiope] – of whom Pompeius Trogus, Eusebius, Orosius, and Justin have written many a feat of arms and many a combat, so that they are compared to the Nine Worthies – were all reborn and gathered together to injure and trouble me, in neither city nor country, on land nor water, would I fear them, or all their power, as long as I could have my lady to help me.

Lampedo conquered Asia and all Europe by her valour, Semiramis was recognized as lady and empress by all the world, Teuta prevailed over the Romans many a day, Deïpyle conquered Thebes and Argos, Thamyris brought Cyrus of Persia to his end, Sinope too conquered many countries, Hippolyta and Menalippe stood against Hercules and made him flee the field, Penthesilea restored

... [?] But they would not dare anger or incite me as long as I could have my lady to help me.

For she is so great, powerful, noble, gentle, wise, valiant, and renowned in all lands that there is no king or other person who would not be subject to her. Even David, Joshua, Maccabaeus, Julius Caesar, Hector, Alexander, Godfrey (of Boulogne), Charlemagne, and Arthur, and all the countries they ever held, undoubtedly would serve her; even the mountains and valleys would bow to her. Where, then, might one find power which can compare to mine, or which I ought to fear in truth, as long as I have my lady to help me?

Conventional lyric praise of the lady and celebration of her inspirational force here provide occasion for enumeration of the feats of each of the Female Worthies, and for references by name to four historians and all the Male Worthies, about the maximum load of literary allusion that a ballade might bear.

Except that under Deschamps' influence the ballade was to acquire an optional envoy,[78] after le Mote the form stopped developing. With precedents like 'Se la puissant royne Semiramis,' ballade stanzas of nine, ten, and even fourteen decasyllabic lines gained currency alongside those of seven and eight lines, and extensive literary allusion became common. At the same time, many poets eschewed length and learning in favour of a less freighted effect. Machaut never used the lengthier stanza in ballades with or without music, and Froissart seldom did. Chaucer left no works in English in the longer ballade stanzas or anything like them.[79] Nevertheless, the stanza evidently was current in London by the 1350s, and most of the French ballades identified in manuscript by the initials 'Ch,' which could be Chaucer's, use the ten-line stanzas.[80]

The extensive use of literary exempla, which became a feature of the ballade at much the same time as the longer stanza came into fashion was part of a broader development that involved both the lyric and the dit amoureux; its effects pervade the work of all of the important fourteenth-century French poets, and it contributes in basic ways to Chaucer's use of literary allusion and exemplary narrative. Again Jean de la Mote seems to have been in the forefront of this development, both in popularizing the use and in the imaginative manner in which he handled them.

MEDIEVALISM AND HUMANISM IN MIDDLE FRENCH EXEMPLA

The longer stanzas of the ballade no doubt answered the desire of certain poets to put more substance in their lyrics. The use of literary examples became a particularly important source of this substance. Until Jean de le Mote's *Regret Guillaume* (1339), however, literary allusion was rare and generally brief in the long dits amoureux and virtually non-existent in ballade, rondeau, and virelay. For the dits there had been an obvious model for developed exempla in the stories of Narcissus and Pygmalion in the *Roman de la Rose*; however, a passing mention of David and Orpheus by Jehan Acart in the *Prise amoureuse* and brief series of non-pareils in Machaut's earlier dits, largely drawn from Nine Worthies, are much what one finds before le Mote exploited the possibilities.[81]

Le Mote presents a series of rather elaborate exempla in the formal complaints of the *Regret*. It seems that he had recourse to illustrative stories in order to vary the thirty laments by personified ladies. The first two of the thirty who complain adduce no literary examples, but each of the last twenty-eight presents an exemplum, including an extended application, that typically takes up more than half of the lament. These are drawn from a broad variety of literature: classical Latin narrative, the Bible, medieval romance, and the novella; and some evidently are original with him.[82] Most significantly original is his application of these exemplary narratives to essentially lyric purposes. In models such as the *Roman de la Rose* and the *Voeux du paon*, the Ovidian stories and the examples of the Nine Worthies serve to elaborate and illustrate the main narrative; in the *Regret* they subserve the individual expressions of grief and the lyric elegiac purpose of the whole.

The exempla of the *Regret* were very influential on Middle French poetry, perhaps most importantly on the exempla in Guillaume de Machaut's *Jugement dou roy de Navarre*,[83] a long dit amoureux which represents the poet's first use of extended exempla and is a major model for Chaucer's plan in the *Legend of Good Women*. In *Navarre*, as in the *Regret*, a series of female virtues, attendant on a central figure, support their presentations with elaborated exempla; three of Machaut's five stories are identical to le Mote's.[84] After *Navarre* Machaut extended his use of exempla, notably in several important long poems, including the *Dit de la fonteinne amoureuse*, *Confort d'ami*, and *Voir-Dit*. Especially through such poems, *Regret* exercised powerful influence on the subsequent practice of Middle French poets of frequent, diverse, and often extended literary allusion. But Machaut perhaps was more like Vitry in rejecting for the most part one influential aspect of le Mote's literary allusions, his practice of creating new stories and names with pseudo-classical credentials.

Nineteen of le Mote's stories have readily identifiable sources in classical legend, the Bible, and medieval story, but nine are not easily identified and some if not all of these no doubt are his own fictions. For instance, Hardemens tells a story of lovers called Tarse and Flore, who contrive to meet secretly despite their parents' prohibition; but Flore accidentally falls on his own sword while chasing a spy, and when he dies Tarse drowns herself. There are obvious parallels to Pyramus and Thisbe, and reminiscences of Fleur and Blanchefleur, and the names seem possible for an authentic legend, but the story evidently is le Mote's fabrication.[85] With such stories, and with a great number of comparable pseudo-allusions in his lyrics, le Mote made a good medieval use of literary legends, appropriating them as raw material rather than treating them as sacrosanct and immutable. Instead of carefully repeating a narrative as Ovid or an author of a medieval romance presented it, he freely mixed together elements from the whole tradition of narrative; he made up new stories to suit his purposes, and he improvised names to lend authenticity to his fabrications. Most medieval writers would not have been fazed by the liberties le Mote takes, but evidently Vitry and his follower Campion were very bothered. Their criticisms nevertheless did not deter others from following le Mote's lead. As we will see in Froissart's work, fabrication of exempla from Ovidian raw material is a major feature of his dits amoureux. And Chaucer makes numerous puzzling allusions which probably reflect a similar lack of concern for fidelity to canonical texts.

After the *Regret* we find le Mote extending his use of exempla to the lyrics, perhaps imitating the practice of Vitry in his motets.[86] Once the practice was established by those poets, the use of literary allusion became very popular in the later fourteenth-century formes fixes, especially in the ballades. But the model that le Mote was providing was entirely too free-wheeling for Vitry and Campion. The influence of Vitry's friend Petrarch perhaps may be discerned in their attitude towards le Mote's classical reference, which is very like the attitude of later Humanists towards medieval writers. They felt that he simply did not show sufficient knowledge of and respect for the Latin texts. As we have seen, Vitry derided his 'amoureus diz ... couvers de noms divers' / 'love poems filled with bizarre names' as childish, and Campion speaks of his 'noms bretesques' / 'foolish [Bretonesque] names' unknown to Homer, Virgil, Ovid, Catullus, or Horace. For Campion, the test obviously was whether the usage of classical poets warranted le Mote's names.

In the manuscript set of six ballades, the first two poems are obviously meant to illustrate what Vitry objected to. But while they do effectively illustrate le Mote's unrestrained practice, one may feel that it is not wholly to his discredit. Both ballades are love poems with an unhappy female narrator who refers by name to a large number of literary personages, with the particular allusions often obscure; and both poems use two-line refrains composed of a list of names. The opening stanza of the first poem illustrates the use made throughout of unfamiliar though intriguing references:

Cupido, qui mist Dyane et Jespee
Ou grief palagre en mer comme divesses,
Après ce que chascune fut trouvee
Lez Clopheüs sacrifiant ses messes,
Se venga bien du deduit Clopheüs
Quant lapider le fist par Oleüs.
Sur hault mer, helas! Que de nuisanches!
Et nonpourquant vers moy n'orent pesanches
Ne tant com j'ay n'orent ains fais horribles
Delf, Orius, Narcissus, ne Constanches,
Cridus, Pias, Lilions, ne Curibles.[87]

Cupid, who placed Dyane and Jespée in the sad waves of the sea as goddesses, after he found them beside Clopheus sacrificing his masses, avenged himself well for the pleasure of Clopheus when he had Eolus stone him. On the high seas, alas! What troubles! And nevertheless in comparison with mine they had no burdens, nor such horrible sufferings as mine never came to Delf, Orius, Narcissus, Constance, Cridus, Pias, Lilions, or Curibles.

The speaker proceeds in the next stanza to allude to the problems of each figure mentioned in the refrain, but except for Narcissus the stories seem strange, just as that of Cupid and Clopheus is not readily recognizable despite all the circumstantial detail supplied.[88]

In the multitude of ostensible allusions to classical figures in the two poems there surely is some element of fresh invention or creative misunderstanding on le Mote's part. For instance, in the first poem four 'hostesses' are ascribed to Acheron: 'Trible, Gibel, Cerbere, et Cohoemee' (25). To call Cerberus, if the reference is to the dog, a hostess is surely far-fetched and tends to confirm a suspicion that the other more obscure names are pure fabrications. Still, one cannot be certain how much he makes up. In the second ballade the ten names of the refrain, while not all well known, prove to be identifiable. And while in this poem le Mote seems inexact in some of his references to the Pyramus legend and the death of Helen,[89] the concluding stanza and refrain show that he is not wantonly careless in his more elaborate allusions:

Lasse, Avicene, ou sont voz medecines?
Je suis avec Dido a compagnie!
Ovide, ou sont remedes femenines?
Dieu de Nature, ou est voye de vie?
Phebus, en qui plaisance est herbergie,
Puisque Venus ne me veult secours faire,
Viengne Atropos moy tribler et deffaire,
Si qu'a mes maulx ne soit mais comparee
Ras, Tysbe, Helainne, Elye, Lucidaire,
Flore, Yde, Edee, Asse, ne Tholomee. (20–30)

Alas, Avicenna, where are your medicines? Dido and I are alike! Ovid, where are your remedies for women? God of Nature, where is the true way of life? Phebus, in whom pleasure finds his home, since Venus does not want to help me, let Atropos come to torment and undo me so that my ills may never be compared to those of Pyramus, Thisbe, Helen, Elyos, Lucidaire, Florida, Ydorus, Edea, Aristé, or Tholomer.

The references in the first eight lines and the first three names of the refrain are clear and straightforward, and if my understanding of the last seven names in the refrain is correct, they all may be found in the Alexander romances of Brisebarre and le Mote.

In these poems, no doubt the multiplication of proper names becomes tiresome, and the rhetorical structure is over-simple, but the imaginative mixture of myth and imagination also has interesting aspects, though Vitry finds it grotesque. In the motet already referred to, probably subsequent to the ballade exchanges,[90] he asks God to close the mouth of 'that fantastic'; it seems that le Mote's artistic taste in his French verse is as offensive to the bishop as his services to the English are:

Phi millies ad te, triste pecus,
cauda monstrum, quod in Francum decus
linguam scribis quam nescis promere!
Quid? Mugitum pro melo vomere
quod musicus horret ebmelicum!
Non puduit carmen chimericum

palam dare quod Flaccus versibus
primis dampnat. Ve! qui tot fecibus
Danos pascis, olei venditor,
mendacii puplici conditor ...   (Triplum, 1–10)

Fie! a thousand times on you, sad brute, monsters' member, for your writing in
the tongue of the Franks, their glory, what you don't know how to express!
What! To vomit unmelodious bellowing instead of song, which makes Music
shudder! He has not blushed to present openly what Horace damns in his first
verses. Woe! you who feed the English with so many feces, vendor of oil [flat-
terer], maker of public lies ...

The reference to Horace is to his attack in the *Art of Poetry* (1–13) on
painters and poets who fashion monsters by joining human heads to
animal parts; that is, they ignore decorum. Le Mote's use of the lovely
French language for his grotesque purposes deeply offends Vitry.

In his ballade response to Vitry, le Mote shows himself too medieval
to comprehend the spirit of the criticism. He defends himself by stating
that he 'never put a name in story or lyric which would not have served
any place' (27–8). He defends his use of names as effective, whether or
not they have exact precedents. Less tactful in his answer to Campion,
he suggests that there are many stories of which his antagonist is ignorant. 'Do you know all the romances in the world, and all the names?'
he asks (10–11). His last stanza of that poem, a puzzle for anyone, introduces several phony stories for Campion to puzzle over. The mocking
reference to the winds in the first line continues a recurrent subject from
the previous poems:

Tu qui tous vens yes congnoissans,
Congnois tu le Mur Graciien,
Le roc ou Phebus est regnans,
Et tous les clans de cel engien
Et de Cerberus le Mairien?
Nennil, certes! Mais d'Aridant
Congnoistras au fons la jus,
Car la te menront galopant
Tribles, Florons, et Cerberus.

You who know all the Winds, do you know the Wall of the Graces, the rock
where Phebus reigns, and all the noises of that device, and of Cerberus of the

Sea? No indeed! But you will learn to its very bottom the pit of Aridant [hell?], for there Trible, Floron, and Cerberus will lead you galloping.

In all of his four poems in the series, and here especially, le Mote mixes in new stories and new names as if they had equal status with standard legends like Paris' rape of Helen or Aeneas' desertion of Dido.[91] He suggests by his questions that Campion is too dull to understand how the underlying theory of creativity operates.

The attitude towards allusion that Mote expresses and exemplifies is evident in much of the French poetry that came after him. His fondness for evoking and retelling the traditional stories and his freedom in improvising on them and in creating factitious analogues find parallels particularly in the work of Froissart and Deschamps. The former is fond of dressing up new stories and strange names in the garb of tradition, and the latter's myriad allusions create difficulties for the commentator that are not attributable primarily to the poet's ignorance. At times Chaucer too shows something like le Mote's penchant for allusion and cavalier attitude towards known authorities. Though perhaps more interested than the other poets in the facts and details of traditional literature, he is hardly submissive to them. He has puzzled generations of scholars with such names as Lollius, Trophee, and Agathon. When in the *Book of the Duchess* he readily adopts Froissart's Enclimpostair, and has Alcyone die within three days of learning of Seys's death instead of giving her the Ovidian metamorphosis into a bird, and conversely in the 'Prologue' to the *Legend of Good Women* attributes to Alceste a metamorphosis into a daisy that is not sanctioned by previous literature, no doubt it is a matter of choice rather than confusion. He is displaying a spirit of creative assimilation like that Jean de la Mote had shown previously – perhaps was still showing when Chaucer arrived in the English courts.

Le Mote was an innovator of the first magnitude, and his contribution to the French lyric mode is manifold. His ballade forms in the *Regret Guillaume* probably supplied the main model for Machaut's seven- and eight-line stanzas, and for those of his successors, including Chaucer; and his later ballades helped establish a ten-line and longer ballade stanza as an alternative for the non-musicians like Froissart and Deschamps. His twenty-eight narrative exempla inspired Machaut's use of exempla in the *Jugement dou roy de Navarre*, which in turn became a model for the *Legend of Good Women* and for the incorporation of classical exempla in French dits amoureux; and his use of allusion in the ballades fostered a practice of reference to actual and imagined narrative, especially of a classical stamp. More broadly, le Mote was probably a crucial figure in establishing the ascendancy at court of the tradition of the lyric poet-musician. With his *Regret*, the long poem takes on a thoroughly lyric character, featuring lyric themes, subordination of narrative to the themes, and incorporation of formes fixes lyrics as an important element of the works. His later ballades similarly subordinate narrative allusion to lyric theme, and they expand the ballade form to allow for lengthier, often weightier, thematic development, and for the introduction of more complex learned references, often of a pretended authenticity. We might also recall the unique poetic contest that le Mote inserts in the *Parfait du paon*, which shows, and perhaps stimulated, the spirit of the puys in the poetic compositions of the courts.

All of the French poets discussed in this book, and Chaucer himself, whose poetry is our ultimate interest, were affected by developments in French poetry before, and aside from, Guillaume de Machaut. The leader in these in the Low Countries and England was Jean de la Mote. As important as his influence was on literary history, however, the work of le Mote that remains extant falls far short of Machaut's in quality as well as quantity. Le Mote was a figure of great significance, but there is no doubt that Machaut was the most important poet of the Middle French period, and in the next three chapters we will focus on his crucial contribution to Chaucer's art.

CHAPTER THREE

Chaucer and Machaut:
Man, Poet, Persona

In the theoretical introductory chapter on 'natural music,' the poetry of Guillaume de Machaut logically provided the main illustrative materials. His verse compositions, long and short, established the norm for the court mode through most of the Middle French period. And since he was the greatest of the poet-musicians, we might well expect to find the most impressive and authentic display of natural music in his work. At the same time, the earlier discussion of various lyrics of his and of *Remede de Fortune* was oriented towards explanation of the mode, in no way supplying the systematic treatment of his influence on Chaucer that this book is intended to provide for him and all of the French contemporaries. A discussion of the various aspects of Machaut's relationship occupies the next quarter and more of this book.

Machaut was a great artist: without conceit he himself knew it, his French colleagues and patrons knew it, and Chaucer knew it. The preservation of his verse and music in magnificent manuscripts, the dissemination of his work throughout Europe, and his decisive influence on subsequent generations of writers and composers testify to his greatness. Chaucer's initial experiences in hearing Machaut's work read and performed, perhaps by minstrels who came from France with King Jean, must have constituted a revelation to him of the power of poetry. As his own artistry developed subsequently, it stands in important ways closer to Machaut than it does to any writer of whatever century or country. Much of this closeness has to do with the poets' taking part in a common court culture, and much with the genius that both possessed.

CHAUCER AND MACHAUT AT REIMS AND CALAIS

Born about 1300, Machaut was some forty years older than Chaucer; but he lived so long that when he died in 1377 Chaucer was well into his thirties. By birth he was a Champenois, and after about 1340 he lived in Champagne as a canon at the cathedral of Reims. Through his young adulthood he served as secretary to Jean of Luxembourg, King of Bohemia, and afterwards maintained his royal connections. The marriage of Jean's daughter Bonne to Jean le Bon of France led to Machaut's coming to know and being favoured by some of the highest-ranking men in Europe: King Jean himself, Charles II (le Mauvais) of Navarre, Charles V of France, and the Dukes of Berry and Burgundy.[1] We might compare Chaucer's relationship to important men: Lionel of Clarence, John of Gaunt, and three successive English kings.

There were numerous times in his travels in France when Chaucer could have met Machaut. On two occasions we know that the poets were in close proximity to each other – in 1359–60 when Chaucer was taken prisoner during the siege of Reims, and in 1360 at Calais when the terms of the Treaty of Brétigny were being executed. In both cases poems of Machaut speak of his own presence, while official documents tell of Chaucer's.

The first document records the ransoming of Chaucer by King Edward. Chaucer's military service involved a less than triumphant English campaign; it was not like the dazzling successes of Crécy and Poitiers, and things were to get worse for England. The young poet began to learn early and at first hand that though Edward was alive, Arthur was dead, which may explain why, while earlier writers in England celebrated the new Arthur, the only appearance of Arthur in Chaucer's works is in the Wife of Bath's comic romance. French fortunes were changing; they were no doubt fortunate that Jean le Bon was held captive in England and never led them in battle after Poitiers, for his son Charles le Sage wisely decided to stay behind fortifications and fight a war of attrition, and his strategy proved quite effective. Of course, there were disadvantages for the French; their 'success' in defensive warfare had no glory, and it was vexing to live in a city like Reims under siege, with all the citizenry put under arms. One of the disgruntled was the sexagenarian Machaut, as his complaint 'A toi, Hanri' fully attests.

The poem places a reluctant Machaut in arms at the city gate in the very time that Chaucer was taken prisoner. It is hardly possible that the old poet helped to capture the young one, but it is conceivable that

Chaucer met him in Reims after being taken. One could fancy that Chaucer had already been so impressed by Machaut's verse and widening reputation as to strongly desire a meeting, that as a prisoner he was accorded adequate freedom to seek out the great man, and that Machaut was able and disposed to entertain an admirer. Given such circumstances, one might proceed to imagine Machaut's giving the young captive a treat by reading to him his new complaint addressed to 'Hanri,' which has the earnestness of the veteran literary man fallen on hard times. It is seasoned with a sardonic humour involving the poet himself that Chaucer would have readily appreciated. And there are indications that he came to know the poem, for it is in certain respects the closest model extant for Chaucer's *Complaint to His Purse*.[2] It is also one of the few works in French or English to provide a real antecedent for the decasyllabic couplets of the *Canterbury Tales.*

Aside from its relationship to Chaucer's writings, 'A toi, Hanri' ('Complainte III') is well worth quoting in full for the multiple insight it offers into the life of the poet, into the conditions in France when Chaucer was campaigning, and into the way lyric poetry and life could on occasion intersect in the fourteenth century. Though the mode of complaint is conventional, by virtue of its tone and biographical detail the poem has a stronger personal flavour than any other of Machaut's works. With sustained irony the poet presents a varied bill of grievances. He first laments the loss of his horses and dogs, perhaps casualties of the war effort, then bemoans in succession his potential role as reluctant warrior, the unjust taxes of pope and king, the unfriendly behaviour of his colleagues, and the neglect of his patrons:

A toi, Hanri, dous amis, me complain
Pour ce que mais ne queur ne mont ne plain,
Car à pié sui, sans cheval et sans selle,
Et si n'ay mais Esmeraude ne Belle,   5
Ne Lancelot, dont petit me deduit,
Quant la joie ay perdu de tel deduit.
Aguillonnez sui de mes anemis
Qui en mon cuer ont meinte peinnes mis.
Asservis sui, qui m'est chose trop ville,
Car il m'estuet mettre aus murs de la ville;   10
Et si vuet on que je veille à la porte
Et qu'en mon dos la cote de fer porte;
Ou il convient qu'ailleurs demourer voise

Et laissier Reins, dont petit me renvoise.
Encore y a chose qui m'est po belle,   15
C'est maletoste et subcide et gabelle,
Foible monnoie et imposition
Et dou pape la visitation.
Or faut paier pour .viij. ans les trentismes
Et sans delay pour le roy .iij. disismes.   20
Et li dyable porront de ce finer;
On porroit bien une mine miner.
Mieus me vauroit ailleurs estre .j. porchier
Que moy veoir einsi vif escorchier.
Et vraiement l'Eglise est si destruite   25
Que je ne pris sa franchise une truite.
Et se dit on que li rois d'Engleterre
Vient le seurplus de ma substance querre.
Malades sui et s'ay po de monnoie,
Et mes freres, dont plus assez m'anoie.   30
Après je doubt que ne soie en oubli
De mon droit dieu terrien qu'oncques n'oubli,
Eins le regret souvent en souspirant.
Mais ce qui plus va mon mal empirant,
C'est ce que bien à mon borgne oueil parçoy   35
Qu'à court de roy chascuns y est pour soy,
Car il n'est homs qui tant à moy aconte
Que de mes maus face samblant ne conte.
Mais j'aim la fleur de toute creature
Et grant doubte ay qu'elle n'ait de moy cure.   40
Fortune m'est dure, amere et diverse,
Qui ma cherrette einsi trebuche et verse.
Pour ce m'en vois demourer en l'Empire,
A cuer dolent qui tendrement souspire,
Qu'en ce païs trop me gaste et essil.   45
Las! or seray en l'Empire en essil,
Car je voy bien qu'estre convient comme un
Prestres et lais, et en main de commun.
Mais j'aim trop mieus franchise et po d'avoir
Que grant richesse et servitute avoir.   50
Or pense, amis, ay je assez de meschiés?
Foy que tu dois Amour, qui est mes chiés,
Pleure avec moy et complain ma dolour

Cuevre de plours ta face et ta coulour
Et di à tous qu'einsi, sans nul meffait,   55
Vois en essil, car je n'ay riens meffait,
Et que ja mais ne feray chant ne lay.
'A Dieu' te di, car toute joie lay.[3]

To you, Henry, sweet friend, I complain, because no longer do I ride over mountain and plain, but I am afoot, without horse or saddle, and I don't have Emerald or Belle any more, nor Lancelot, which provides me little pleasure, losing the joy of such pastime. I am brought to my knees by my enemies, who have given my heart many pains. I am made a serf, which is a most vile thing to me, for I must take myself to the walls of the city; and they want me to watch at the gate and to wear a coat of iron on my back. Otherwise I have to go live elsewhere and leave Reims, which gives me little joy.

Another thing that is but small pleasure to me is the Evil Tax,[4] the special levy, and the salt tax, weak currency and the tariff, and the visitation of the pope: we must now pay thirtieths for eight years, and immediately three-tenths for the king. And the devils will finish this! A mine may well be undermined! It would be better for me to be a swineherd elsewhere than to see myself thus skinned alive. And truly the Church is so beaten down that I do not value its prestige a single fish.

Moreover, they say that the King of England is coming to seek out the rest of my substance. I am sick and have little money. Then there are my brothers [fellow canons] by whom I am very annoyed. On top of that I fear that I am forgotten by my true earthly god whom I can never forget; but rather, sighing, I continually lament his absence. But that which most keeps aggravating my unhappiness is that I see well with my one eye that at the court of the king each man is for himself, for there is no man who thinks enough of me that my troubles bother or concern him.

And ever I love the flower of all creation, though I greatly fear that she has no worry about me. Fortune is hard to me, bitter and changeable, who knocks and overturns my cart in this manner. For this reason I am going to leave here and live in the Empire, with an unhappy heart which sighs tenderly, for in this country I am wasted and destroyed. Alas! now I will be in exile in the Empire, for I well see that, priest and lay, we must be treated the same, and all be subject to the commons. But I strongly prefer freedom and few possessions to great riches and servitude.

Now consider, friend, have I plenty of troubles? By the faith you owe Amour, who is my chief, weep with me and complain my sorrow, cover your face and your cheeks with tears, and tell all that thus, without misdeed, I go into exile

– for I have done nothing wrong – and say that never hereafter will I make song or lay. 'Adieu,' I say to you, and I leave all joy.

Despite his personal enmities and straitened finances, there is no indication that Machaut made good on his threat to leave Reims, and he no doubt was there for the siege. The poet's 'earthly god' whose absence he laments must be Jean le Bon in captivity, and 'the flower all creation' a highly placed patroness.

Some years later, Chaucer composed a plea for help that perhaps drew inspiration from Machaut's complaint. He spoke 'To you, my purse' instead of 'To you, Henry,' described his financial condition as 'Shaved as ner as any frere' rather than 'skinned alive,' and threatened to depart 'out of this towne' as Machaut thought of leaving Reims.[5] Chaucer's master-stroke was to make the purse, rather than the patroness and the king, at once his 'lady dere' and 'saveour, as doun in this world here.' In presenting his hardship, he creates a humorous fantasy which a patron would find hard to resist. Machaut's poem offers a contrast in tone to Chaucer's. In enumerating to Henry unhappy personal details of his life, the poet seems much less confident than Chaucer of receiving aid. Yet the work retains a vividness and humour of its own that might well incline his friend to action in Machaut's behalf.

If Chaucer did by any chance attend on Machaut in Reims in 1359, it is possible he also met the boy Eustache Deschamps there, particularly if Deschamps' statement about Machaut, 'Il m'a nourri,' is literally true. One of the fifteenth-century rhetoricians says that Deschamps was the old poet's nephew, and it is a fact that he was born in Reims and that he later recalled events in Reims at the time of the English siege.[6] It is of related interest to this nexus of relationships, as is discussed in the chapter on Deschamps, that he was to write rather similar ballades in praise of Machaut and Chaucer, both of them dependent on Jean de le Mote's ballade addressed to Vitry. The chance that Chaucer and Machaut met in Calais later in 1360 is somewhat greater than the chance of an encounter in Reims, though the sojourns of both writers in the port city were probably brief. A record tells us that Chaucer carried a message for Lionel from Calais to London sometime in October. At that time French and English nobility had massed at the port to carry out the terms of the Treaty of Brétigny. King John was being brought home from captivity in England, while concurrently three of his sons and a mass of others were travelling in the opposite direction as hostages.[7] Chaucer could have been there an extended time, or for a day or two. As for

Machaut, we infer from the *Dit de la fonteinne amoureuse* that he came to Calais in the company of the Duke of Berry and stayed there for four days before seeing him off.

The *Fonteinne amoureuse* was to provide a basic model for Chaucer's *Book of the Duchess*, composed for his own ducal patron. The poem has significant similarities to *Remede de Fortune*, both in its central narrative pattern involving lover's complaint followed by lady's comfort, and in its tableau of lyric set pieces. The story hides under a light veil interesting indications of the human relationship of Machaut with the Duke of Berry, and provides at the same time important insight into the composition and presentation of poetry in the time, especially into the author's adoption of a persona. An anagram near the beginning of the poem identifies Machaut and the duke as the main actors in the poem.[8] At the outset the narrator establishes himself as lover-poet, stating that he writes to honour his lady; at the same time he introduces as central figure a second lover-poet who ostensibly composes two set pieces that he presents in the work: a complaint and a rondeau. The first of these comes at the beginning. The narrator, lying in his chamber, overhears the complaint being recited. The speaker is lamenting that he must go away; he doesn't know how he will survive without his lady. After the lengthy complaint, the narrator leaves his chamber and promptly encounters the young lord who has delivered it; shortly they are friends. The two walk together to a beautiful park where they find a Fountain of Love with a statue of Narcissus, which associates the fountain with the *Roman de la Rose*. Both men, already fully in love with their ladies, refuse to drink the fountain's waters. Falling asleep together, they share a dream in which the lord is solaced by his lady's own poem of comfort. The next day the narrator accompanies him to the port from which he is to sail; on the fourth day, the lord embarks after reciting a rondeau.[9]

In the *Fonteinne amoureuse* the characters are obsessed with poetry; it is a question whether love or composition is more important to them. When the narrator hears the lord complaining, his first impulse is to get pen and paper so that he can copy the complaint; when the lord ends his complaint, though having declared himself desperate, he proudly notes that he has made use of a hundred rhymes, all different; and when they are beside the fountain the lord's primary desire is to preserve the literary moment, so he asks the narrator to write a complaint suitable to the occcasion. Then in the dream the lady answers the original lament with an artful set piece of her own in stanzas that match the complaint. There is, of course, a certain intentional humour in the way poetic impulses compete with amorous urges in this story, a humour that is implicit in the lyric mode itself. When every courtier writes verse, life and passion tend to be replaced by art and poetic pose. But what is lost in feeling is, at least in part, made up in wit and elegance.

Just as the lover in the *Fonteinne amoureuse* is a stand-in for the Duke of Berry, so Chaucer's Black Knight in the *Book of the Duchess* is a surrogate for John of Gaunt. The knight's reason for personal distress (death) is more serious than Machaut's lover's reason (separation), yet he likewise remains conscious of the role of poet which his position as lover and courtier entails. His reaction to his grief is to compose and recite 'a lay, a maner song,' a set piece with its own rhyme scheme (475–86). Later in the story, as he recalls the beginning of his love, he repeats the first lyric he wrote to his lady (1175–80). The narrator too, while deeply moved by the knight's story, is at the same time pleased to have found materials to put 'in ryme.' The concerns of love and those of poetry are hardly divisible, even in this elegy. Within the limits of the conventions, it is suitable if somewhat droll for Machaut's lover to be pleased with his rhyme's effects, and for Chaucer's bereaved narrator to have one eye out for new poetic material. The mode is inherently literary, and its nature is a major factor accounting for the bookishness of the Chaucerian persona in his dream visions.

THE LYRIC NARRATOR: NAÏVE LOVER AND SENSITIVE LADY

The parallel between the *Fonteinne amoureuse* and the *Book of the Duchess* runs deep, and both works are instructive in showing possible relationships of reality to fiction in the contemporary poetic mode. Aided in understanding the representation by subtle but unequivocal clues and our knowledge of events of the time, we see how good poets might fictionalize historical individuals, including the writers themselves. We further see within the narratives lover-poets reciting their lyric poems, presenting idealized pictures of courtiers in action. The works thus provide dramatic contexts for lyrics attributed to the central figures, but no doubt written by the poet himself.

Almost all of the lyrics of the mode, though they typically lack the explicit narrative contexts of the longer poems, are comparably dramatic. There are isolated exceptions like 'A toi, Hanri' when the first-person narrator more or less directly represents the poet, but in general the poet who stood before the court, whether a semi-professional like Machaut or one of the amateur nobility, was an actor assuming a part. The possible roles were mostly standard, and might be readily inferred from the content of the poem. Among the roles were those of the neophyte lover, the deserted or bereft lover, the rebel lover, the lady wise in the ethic of love, the lady deceived and abandoned, the disillusioned courtier, and the wise counsellor. Machaut's lyrics provide examples of all of these, displaying the greatest range of personae found in any Middle French poet's work. He was exceptionally sure and adroit in adopting one and then another character for his first-person lyric speaker. Chaucer's few extant lyrics suggest a comparable mastery and versatility, learned in part from Machaut. It seems clear, furthermore, that both writers found inspiration in their various lyric personas for narrators and characters in their longer works.

The most common speaker in the Middle French lyrics is the young lover who pleads, praises, and complains – the faintly comic neophyte. He employs the same topics the lover used in the earlier Continental lyrics: his desire, her beauty, his fear of separation from her, and his pain at her neglect. But a prime point that distinguishes the lover of the fourteenth-century lyric from the Old French persona is the evident and pervasive artifice of his rhetoric. Lengthy apostrophes, multiple personifications, allegorical situations and actions, literary exempla, complex metaphors and similes, and such comprise the substance of his presentations. Situated as these are in a matrix of the demanding fixed forms, the artifice becomes an overwhelming fact. As in the *Fonteinne amoureuse*, the consequence of the artifice for Machaut's lover-narrator, the nominal poet, is that he appears much more the poet seeking to express himself through the devices of conventional rhetoric than lover drawn by feeling to express himself poetically. Thereby, the audience's natural tendency to identify with the speaker is much attenuated. The artifice does not destroy the poem; instead, it moves the audience's centre of interest away from the force of the lover's sentiments and towards the ingenuity and felicity of his achievement as rhetorician. The lover thereby becomes an instrument of himself as poet, and his love-life becomes a series of occasions to write poetry. One likely effect is comic irony. Over-elaboration of an image or an allegory, for instance, can soon reflect on the character of the speaker and become lightly ironic. The poet envisions and cultivates such an effect for his urbane audience.

The potential of the lover-poet to achieve comic effect is realized in both Machaut's and Chaucer's lyrics. For a relatively simple example we might instance Machaut's virelay, 'Dame, le doulz souvenir,'[10] whose refrain and first stanza were discussed in the first chapter. The opening emphasizes the sweetness of remembering the lady, adumbrating the theme of Chaucer's *Womanly Noblesse*. In the second and third stanzas the lover develops a complex conceit concerning the tears that come to him when the Sweet Thought of the lady deserts him. He will weep so much, he imagines,

> Qu'amoistie soit l'ardour
>   De mon desir
> Et que son aspre vigour
>   Puisse amenrir. (33–6)

... that the burning of my desire will be dampened, so that its sharp force will lessen.

The conventional quenching tears may suggest an authentic lover merely sedulous in following the forms of Amour; but his subsequent completion of the conceit definitively betrays the persona as a poet who will realize rhetorical effects at all costs. Alas, he goes on to say, the tears do not allay the fire; they only act to sharpen and increase the blaze:

> Qu'einsi comme on voit getter
> Yaue en feu pour embraser
>   Et enasprir
> Fait mon desir agrandir
>   Mon triste plour. (46–50)

Just as one sees water thrown on a fire in order to sharpen the flame and make it more harsh, so my sad tears increase my desire.

The provenance of the conceit in the world of domestic fire-tending, and its excessive cleverness, undermine the lover's image of himself as a figure of tragedy. The proper response, which he himself seems to invite, is a smile.

At the same time, the poem is not essentially comic. The persona is an instrument of the actual poet whose aim is not so much to move his audience as to cultivate its ideals of elegance and gaiety. He builds his artful image by means of the elaborate rhetoric, at some cost to the credibility of the lover. But if the lover's behaviour is incongruous, that of most lovers is; the work itself nevertheless is part of an artefact seriously embodying the courtly ideal.

A work of Chaucer's that exemplifies the potential for humour of the lyric persona is *Complaint unto Pity*. Though it too is no comic poem, its narrator still has his humorous aspect. In a well-developed allegory[11] he colourfully intellectualizes his problem and his suffering. The opening lines are pitiful enough to excite sympathy:

Pite, that I have sought so yore agoo,
With herte soore, and ful of besy peyne,
That in this world was never wight so woo ...   (1–3)

One may even be moved by the abstractions Pity and Cruelty when the lover discovers Pity dead:

To Pitee ran I, al bespreynt with teres,
To preyen hir on Cruelte me awreke,
But er I myghte with any word outbreke,
Or tellen any of my peynes smerte,
I fond hir ded, and buried in an herte.   (10–14)

From this point, however, the allegory grows in complexity, increasingly engaging the intellectual interest of the reader but at the same time inhibiting deeper emotional involvement.

Thus, the ensuing development of the funeral imagery and the depiction of the conspiratorial behavior of the abstractions attract us with the ingenuity of the allegory. At the sight of Pity's hearse the lover faints; when he revives, he presses through the crowd in order to approach the body and pray for the soul. Around the hearse he perceives the virtues of the lady, 'Beauty, Lust, Jolyte' (39), and eight more. All of them unmoved by the death of Pity, like cold-blooded Mafia operatives they have conspired with Cruelty to murder the lover:

Confedered alle by bond of Cruelte,
And ben assented when I shal be sleyn.   (52–3)

Now realizing that he will not find a sympathetic audience here for the complaint unto Pity he has brought with him, the lover puts his text aside, but not before sharing its nine full stanzas with the reader.

The poem is not a cold allegory; one can find a suffering lover in it. Early in the allegorical narrative, though, one's interest is diverted from his trials and engaged by the pageant of the funeral and the eleven stony mourners. The whole of the poem has charm, offering good intellectual entertainment, but the audience is hardly expected to grieve with the frustrated lover:

> My peyne is this, that what so I desire
> That have I not, ne nothing lyk therefor;
> And ever setteth Desyr myn hert on fire
> ...
> Me ne lakketh but my deth, and than my bere. (99–105)

We are not quite ready to say with the Franklin, 'Chese he, for me, whether he wol lyve or dye' (F 1086), but our interest lies more in the allegorical scheme than in the lover's fate.

A poem very similiar in interest and effect to Chaucer's *Complaint unto Pity* – and probably providing important inspiration for it – is Machaut's ballade 'Helas! je sui de si male heure nez'[12]; it too shows Pity fatefully absent, allowing the triumph of Cruelty.[13] Superficially, the poem is a desperate lament, but the gallery of abstractions, and the lover's insistent, perverse desire to suffer, undercut the emotional force of the professed desperation:

> Helas! je sui de si male heure nez
> Qu'Amours me het et ma dame m'oublie,
> Tous biens me fuit, tous mauls m'est destinez,
> Nuls ne saroit comparer ma hachie;
> Car Pitez s'est pour ma mort endormie, 5
>   Grace et Eür m'ont guerpy
>   Et Fortune m'est contraire.
>   *Assez de meschiés a ci,*
>   *Eins que joie en puisse attraire.*
>
> Sans nul espoir d'estre reconfortez 10
> Sui et sans cuer; car toudis mercy prie,
> Li las! pour moy, et mes confors est telz
> Que durtez maint où douceur est norrie;
> Cruautez vaint Franchise et Courtoisie,
>   Loyauté est en oubly, 15
>   Mes services ne puet plaire.
>   *Assez de meschiés a ci,*
>   *Eins que joie en puisse attraire.*

Et avec ce si mal sui fortunez
Que, pour faire moy plus languir en vie, 20
Mors ne me vuet pour mes maleürtez.
Mais maugré lui morray, je n'en doubt mie,
Car la durté de ma grief maladie
　A bien la mort desservi,
　Et pis s'on li pooit faire. 25
　Assez de meschiés a ci,
　Eins que joie en puisse attraire.

Alas! I was born in such an unhappy hour that Love hates me and my lady forgets me; all good flees from me, all evils are my lot. None can match my sufferings, for Pity has gone to sleep to bring my death, Grace and Happiness have abandoned me and Fortune is against me. There will be much harm here before Joy can win the day.

I am without hope of being comforted and without my heart; for I ever cry for mercy, alas for me! and my comfort is such that hardness prevails where sweetness was nurtured, Cruelty conquers Openness and Courtesy, Loyalty is forgotten, my service is not pleasing. There will be much harm here before Joy can win the day.

And with all this I am so unlucky that to make me languish longer in life, to increase my unhappiness Death rejects me. But in spite of him I will die; I don't doubt it a bit, for the hardness of my heavy suffering has well earned death, and worse if that is possible. There will be much harm here before Joy can win the day.

Particularly striking here is the extravagant statement of the last stanza, in which the lover stubbornly insists on dying despite Death.

Such perverse resolve recalls comparable contrariness in other lyrics, as in those in which the lover desires to suffer and die because the lady loves to watch his torment.[14] The masochism of this desire has an inherently amusing aspect. In 'Helas! je sui de si male heure nez' the extravagance of the lover's will to die culminates the series of hyperboles that makes up the ballade: *all* good flees, *all* evils come, *none* suffers as I do. Manifestly, the lover enjoys dramatizing his suffering, with the ultimate result that we in the audience are able to respond only to his art, not to his pain. We can admire his cleverness as the nominal poet and the skill of the rhetorician behind him.

The incongruity of the lover's expression certainly acts as a characterizing device. However clever, his words do not reveal a fine sensibility. The charm of the lady, the power of Love, and his own vanity unbalance his poetic ability and make him often amusing, even absurd. Nevertheless, young lovers of limited understanding do not exclusively occupy the world of the Machauvian lyric. Among the several other personae are some who have inborn and spontaneous understanding of the proprieties of love, and of the thoughts, words, and actions proper to it; in the main these are ladies, who typically are the natural agents of Amour and may in the process of time teach the callow lovers. Thus in the numerous lyrics of Machaut in which the speaker is a lady the rhetorical artifice is bolstered by depth of sentiment and appropriateness of thought and expression much more consistently than in the lovers' lyrics. One clear example is the chant royal 'Amis, je t'ay tant amé et cheri,' which is an important original for Chaucer's *Anelida and Arcite*, and a major model for his numerous laments in which women speak.[15] Here, despite her distracted state, the lady maintains credibility and dignity:

> Amis, je t'ay tant amé et cheri
> Qu'en toy amant me cuidoie sauver.
> Lasse! dolente, et je ne puis en ti
> N'en ton dur cuer nulle douceur trouver.
> Pour ce de moy vueil hors joie bouter   5
> Et renoier Amours d'ore en avant,
> Sa loy, son fait et son fauls convenant,
> Quant tu portes sous viaire de fée
> *Cuer de marbre couronné d'aÿmant,*
> *Ourlé de fer, à la pointe asserée.*   10
>
> Quant ta biauté mon cuer en moy ravi,
> Amours me volt si fort enamourer
> De ton gent corps cointe, apert et joli
> Que puis ne pos autre que toy amer.
> Or ne me vues oïr ne resgarder.   15
> Si n'ameray ja mais en mon vivant
> Ne fiance n'aray en nul amant,
> Ne priseray, se bien sui avisée,
> *Cuer de marbre couronné d'aÿmant,*
> *Ourlé de fer, à la pointe asserée.*   20
>
> Si je me plein et di souvent: 'aimi!',
> Qu'en puis je mais? Ne doy je bien plourer?

Car je n'ay pas la peinne desservi
Qu'il me convient souffrir et endurer.
Elle me fait trambler et tressuer,   25
Taindre, palir, fremir en tressaillant,
Quant pour ma mort voy en corps si vaillant
Ouvertement, de fait et de pensée,
Cuer de marbre couronné d'aÿmant,
Ourlé de fer, à la pointe asserée.   30

Honteuse sui, quant je parole einsi,
Et laidure est seulement dou penser,
Qu'il n'apartient que dame à son ami
Doie mercy ne grace demander;
Car dame doit en riant refuser   35
Et amis doit prier en souspirant,
Et je te pri souvent et en plourant.
Mais en toy truis, quant plus sui esplourée,
Cuer de marbre couronné d'aÿmant,
Ourlé de fer, à la pointe asserée.   40

Si ne te quier ja mais faire depri
N'Amours servir, oubeïr ne loer,
Puis que raisons et mesure en oubli
Sont, où tuit bien deüssent habiter.
Et voist ainsi comme il porra aler,   45
Qu'Amours et toy et Joie à Dieu commant.
Et nonpourquant je vueil en ton commant
Estre et fuïr, tant com j'aray durée,
Cuer de marbre couronné d'aÿmant,
Ourlé de fer, à la pointe asserée.   50

L'Envoy

Prince, onques ne vi fors maintenant
Amant à cuer plus dur qu'un dyamant,
Ourlé de fer, à la pointe asserée.

Beloved, I have so much loved and cherished you that I thought my salvation
lay in loving you. Alas! sorrowful, I cannot find in you or in your hard heart
any sweetness; therefore I resolve to shove Joy away from me, and to renounce
Love from now on, his law, his deeds, and his false convenant, since you hide

under your angelic countenance a heart of marble, crowned with adamant, edged with iron, with steel at the point.

When your beauty seized my heart within me, Love wanted to make me so enamoured of your fine noble body, graceful and handsome, that I would then have no other but you. Now you wish neither to see or hear me; so I will never in my life love or have faith in any lover, nor value him, so well have I come to know a heart of marble, etc.

So I lament and often say, 'Aimi!' What can I ever do about it? Should I not well weep? For I have not deserved the pain that I must suffer and endure. It makes me tremble and perspire, to redden and grow pale, to shudder and shake, when I see in such a brave body, clearly intending in thought and deed to kill me, a heart of marble, etc.

I am ashamed when I speak this way; there is ugliness just in the thought, for it is not suitable that a lady ask mercy or grace from her lover, since the lady should refuse smiling, and the lover ought to entreat sighing. But weeping I often beg you, and I find in you when I am most tearful a heart of marble, etc.

But I do not seek for you ever to plead, or to serve, obey, or praise Love, since you, in whom all good ought to reside, have forgotten Reason and Measure. Now may things go as they will, and I commend Love, you, and Joy to God. Despite everything, I still want to be under your protection, while escaping so long as I live the heart of marble, etc.

Envoy

Prince, never did I see before now a lover with a heart harder than a diamond, edged with iron, with steel at the point.

The envoy is characteristic of the chant early and late, but the presence of a refrain indicates that the work is late.[16] Chaucer probably came to know the poem in the late 1360s; it provides one of numerous indications that he kept up to date with Machaut's current writings.

The difference between the character of the lover in Chaucer's *Complaint unto Pity* and Anelida in *Anelida and Arcite*, is similar to the differences between the male and female complainers in the poems of Machaut. On the one hand there is the male lover whose preoccupation with his poetic conceits and uncertain mastery of the ways of Love lead to over-ingenious and strained expression, showing him as clever but somewhat comic; on the other hand there is the lady with fine sensitivities who has an intuitive understanding of Love, even to recognizing the impropriety of her complaining to him. Anelida's delicacy and reserve are closely related to the qualities of the lady in Machaut's poem:

And shal I preye, and weyve womanhede?
Nay! rather deth then do so foul a dede!
And axe merci, gilteles, – what nede?   (299–301)

Even granting that Anelida and such ladies who speak in the lyrics are not entirely free from extravagance, still they typically have an integrity of character that insulates them from the comic overtones associated with many of the male lovers. One hears in the women authentic devotees and philosophers of Love, and is able take their desperation and suffering more seriously than the men's.

DISILLUSIONED LOVER

The young male who hopes and suffers in love represents the most common persona in the Middle French lyrics, and the lovely lady with natural understanding often figures in the works. There are others who appear with some frequency: the moral preacher who praises love and condemns villainy ('Loyal amour est de si grant noblesse, etc.')[17]; the experienced lover who sadly resigns from the life of Amour ('Je pren congié a dames, à Amours')[18]; and occasionally the embittered person who rails at the 'malebouches' ('Langue poignant, aspre, amere et ague'),[19] or at ladies of little faith or excessive rigour. Speakers of the disillusioned type may even in their exasperation become renegades to Love – as in one of Machaut's ballades, which provides an important precedent for similar rebellious and reproachful speakers in two of Chaucer's lyrics:

> Puis qu'Amours faut et Loyauté chancelle
> Et Pité dort et ma dame d'onnour
> Est en tous cas à mon desir rebelle
> N'oncques de moy n'ot pité ne tenrour,
>   Ma dame et Amours renoy   5
> Et leur service et l'amoureuse loy;
> Car miex me vaut de leur dangier partir
> *Qu'en eaulz servant sans joie adès languir.*
>
> Si seray frans, qui est chose si belle
> C'on ne porroit esprisier sa valour,   10
> Et d'autre part n'i a celuy ne celle
> Qui de moy puist oster joie et baudour.
>   Eingsi seray sans annoy

Et drois sires de mon cuer et de moy,
C'on doit .c. fois plus amer et cherir ·   15
Qu'en eaulz servant sans joie adès languir.

Et se ma dame a fait amour nouvelle,
Eüreus yert cilz qui ara s'amour,
Et plus se doit amer qu'autre amans, qu'elle,
Si comme on prent les livres au tabour,   20
   Li portera bonne foy!
A tant m'en tais; mais il vaut miex, ce croy,
Dame et Amour eslongier et fuir
Qu'en eaulz servant sans joie adès languir.[20]

Since Love deserts me and Loyalty wavers, and Pity sleeps, and my honourable lady rebels against my desire, nor does she ever show me pity or tenderness, I renounce my lady and Love, and their service and Love's law; for it is better to escape their power than in serving them ever to languish without joy.

So I will be free, which is such a beautiful thing that one cannot measure its worth; and furthermore there will be neither man nor woman who can rob me of joy and mirth. And I will be without annoyance and true lord of my heart and of myself, which one ought to love and cherish a hundred times more than in serving them ever to languish without joy.

And if my lady has undertaken a new love, he will be happy who will have her love, and should be loved more than another lover, since she – in the same way that one captures hares with a drum – will give him good faith! Now I will be quiet; but it will be better, I think, to depart and flee from one's lady and from Love than in serving them ever to languish without joy.

The excesses and awkwardness of Machaut's young lover-narrators may provoke ironic smiles in the audience, but sarcasm is foreign to them; by contrast, this more experienced disillusioned man brims over with bitter irony, guaranteeing the lady's next lover that she will be faithful just as surely as hares will surrender themselves at the sound of a drum.

Comparably colourful imagery is used to stigmatize the lady throughout Chaucer's *Against Women Unconstant*, especially stanza 2:

Ryght as a mirour nothing may impresse,
But lightly as it cometh, so mot it pace,
So fareth your love, your werkes beren witnesse.
Ther is no feith that may your herte embrace;

But as a wedercok that turneth his face
With every wind ye fare, and that is sene;
In stede of blew, thus may ye were al grene.   (8–14)

The sarcastic tone of the disgusted English lover is quite similar to his French counterpart's, but the third rondeau of Chaucer's *Merciles Beaute* offers a more direct parallel to the Machaut ballade, particularly in the narrator's defiant declaration of independence from Love and his savouring of his freedom:

Love hath my name ystrike out of his sclat,
And he is strike out of my bokes clene
For evermo; there is non other mene.
Sin I fro Love escaped am so fat,
I never thenk to ben in his prison lene;
Sin I am fre, I counte him not a bene.   (27–32)

While the speaker's gloating over his freedom here finds good precedent in the Machaut ballade, the colloquial images of bookkeeping and the 'prison lene,' together with the fatness of the persona, carry the rondeau into a realm of broad comedy that Machaut's lyric does not aspire to.

Chaucer's comedy in this lyric also has a biographical element. From pictures of him and from the host's words in the *Canterbury Tales* we know that Chaucer was broad in the waist, so that there is a certain concurrence in Chaucer the man with his fat persona in *Merciles Beaute*, which of course does not necessarily mean that it concerns a love affair of the poet's. There may be a similar concurrence in Machaut's 'Puisqu'Amours faut et Loyauté chancelle.' It seems that it is a comparatively late work, written when Machaut was in his fifties,[21] and the content bespeaks an older man, thrown over by a lady and reacting with simultaneous ire and resignation. But again the suitability of the poem for the poet's age does not show that it is biographically accurate. It mainly suggests that, as on the stage, in court recitals older characters are played by mature actors.

There is a more patently topical treatment of the contumacious lover in Chaucer's *Envoy to Scogan*, which also lies in the line of descent from Machaut's ballade but is more broadly humorous.[22] The fictional disguise of the real Chaucer and his friend is transparent. Scogan has said, probably in jest, that he is going to give up his lady at Michaelmas.

Chaucer assures him that, despite such 'blaspheme' and 'rebel word' against the 'lawe of love,' he has little to fear from Cupid:

> He wol nat with his arwes been ywroken
> On the, ne me, ne noon of oure figure;
> We shul of him have neyther hurt ne cure.   (26–8)

Chaucer seems more ready than Machaut to exploit the figure of the recalcitrant lover, though the French poem provided a prototype for him.

The references to the poet's fatness and independence of love suggest that *Scogan* and *Merciles Beaute* are late poems. A late date for the latter has interesting biographical implications, suggesting that Chaucer had personal contact with the Duke of Berry subsequent to his stay in London in the 1360s. In a poem that the Duke composed in 1389 he imitates exactly Chaucer's line, 'Sin I fro Love escaped am so fat.'[23] Since records suggest that Chaucer travelled frequently to the Continent on official business into the 1380s, it is not difficult to imagine that he made and maintained a good number of personal friendships in France. It is quite likely that the duke, who was very close to Chaucer's age (and to his shape), befriended Chaucer during the years he spent in England,[24] and that the relationship was renewed from time to time. Since we know that Machaut was close to the duke's family for three generations, that the *Fonteinne amoureuse* was composed for him, and that the duke owned one of the most elaborate of the Machaut manuscripts,[25] a continuing close personal friendship may be assumed between the French poet and the nobleman. Perhaps the most likely place for personal meetings between Chaucer and Machaut would have been one of the duke's residences.

VERSE MADE TO ORDER: KING PIERRE AND THE MARGUERITE POEMS

Another highly placed mutual acquaintance of the two poets – and much more than an acquaintance to Machaut – was Pierre de Lusignan, King of Cyprus, the crusader that 'Alisandre wan by heigh maistrie.' Pierre was a great medieval hero who found his way into Chaucer's poetry as a relatively minor subject; he was a major subject for Machaut, and – what is most significant here – he is the first-person persona for at least two of Machaut's Marguerite poems known to Chaucer. These works illustrate several important aspects of the current poetic mode: how poets might compose on behalf of patrons, the public purposes of such verse, and the development and purveyance of literary materials in the community formed by a few courts. These aspects involve in interesting ways the narrator-persona, which is our present subject, so it will be profitable to look at their background and content.

Modern accounts of Pierre's career suggest that he was a proud tyrant who ruthlessly pillaged and burned the beautiful city of Alexandria, and who was eventually murdered by wronged subjects while in bed with a mistress. If we view Pierre through fourteenth-century eyes, however, we see the premier Crusader of his time, and a great hero of ecclesiastics and poets.[26] Not only did Urban V chararacterize him as true 'athleta Christi,' but his closest counsellors were the eminent and devout churchmen Pierre Thomas and Philippe de Mézières. For Machaut, who celebrated King Pierre's exploits in his last long poem, the *Prise d'Alexandrie*, he embodied the ideal of Christian chivalry and kingship. In this work, and in at least two of his shorter works, Machaut evidences his close relationship with Pierre.

It was while hostages were still in England on behalf of Jean II of France that Pierre appeared in Avignon to undertake a new crusade. On Good Friday 1363 he and King Jean, who was the nominal leader, took up the cross. But it was Pierre who then embarked on a tour of Western Europe in order to enlist help. One of his first stops was England, where he was fêted in a manner appropriate to Edward III's proud court. And while Pierre got only token support from Edward, he evidently made a strong impression on two young writers. Not only did Chaucer subsequently portray him with sympathy in the 'Monk's Tale,' but he also associated his knight with Pierre's greatest successes, 'Alisaundre,' 'Satalye,' and 'Lyeys' ('General Prologue' 51, 58). Jean Froissart was more directly to praise him as valiant king, 'tant creus et honneurés et de raison,' and his patron.[27]

Machaut outdid both poets in his tributes. At the coronation of Charles V in Reims in May 1364, Machaut met Pierre, who was there hoping to enlist the new king in the old king's cause. King Jean's sudden death had deprived Pierre of his main supporter. He failed to get much help from Charles, but he excelled in the jousting and he tremendously impressed Machaut, who thereafter followed his career closely. The two Marguerite poems that he composed on Pierre's behalf inaugurated the fashion of poetry in praise of Marguerite – lady, flower, and gem – which produced a substantial corpus of literature in France and England in the late fourteenth century.[28] The poems Machaut wrote for Pierre are particularly interesting for their handling of the narrator-poet's persona. We have no way of knowing how many lyrics Machaut and his French fellows composed on behalf of others; only an acrostic and some geographical clues tell us about the two Marguerite poems. But we may assume that the writers produced many others for their noble friends. In such works, of course, the narrator would be a more consistently dignified person than in the works in which there is no real-life surrogate. If he is not exactly constrained in his rhetoric, he is at least less excessive in the hyperbole and metaphor he uses to characterize his own state.

The first of the Marguerite poems, Machaut's 'Complainte VI,' has none of the explicit Marguerite imagery that characterizes the genre, though the first stanza identifies the lady as 'flower of flowers' and by name acrostically, and there is an emphasis on praise of the lady characteristic of the type. The initial letters of the lines of the first stanza spell out 'MARGUERITE / PIERRE' (v = u, j = i):

Mon cuer, m'amour, ma dame souvereinne,
Arbres de vie, estoile tresmonteinne,
Rose de may de toute douceur pleinne,
   Gente et jolie,
Vous estes fleur de toute fleur mondeinne   5
Et li conduis qui toute joie ameinne,
Ruissiaus de grace et la droite fonteinne;
   Je n'en doubt mie.
Toute biauté est en vous assevie
Et vo bonté nuit et jour mouteplie;   10
Pour ce plaisence ha dedens moy norrie
   Joie sans peinne,
Et si m'a tout en vostre signourie
Rendu et mis, et par noble maistrie
Ravi mon cuer qui usera sa vie   15
   En vo demeinne.[29]

My heart, my love, my sovereign lady, tree of life, North Star, Rose of May, filled with all sweetness, noble and pretty, you are the flower of all earthly flowers, and the channel which conveys all joy, the well and true fountain of grace; I in no way doubt it. All beauty is perfected in you, and your goodness multiplies night and day; as a result, pleasure has nurtured joy without pain in me, and rendered and placed me in your lordship, and by noble mastery ravished my heart which will lead its life in your service.

The lament that follows this eulogy is motivated by the speaker's impending departure from the country. He hopes to see the lady before he leaves, but if he doesn't he will carry Bon Espoir, Souvenir, and Dous Penser with him (73–5). Far away from her he will be armed and protected by these. Having continued in this vein through the 192-line poem, in concluding he congratulates himself for loving her, and expresses the hope that she will one day call him Ami.

Probabilities borne out by chronological considerations indicate that the poem was written for Pierre while he was still in France with Machaut. The likely historical counterpart for the lady is Marguerite of Flanders, the widow of Philippe de Rouvre, Duke of Burgundy, who from the date of her widowhood at age eleven in 1361 until her remarriage in 1369 to the second Philippe of Burgundy was 'unquestionably the most important heiress of the day.'[30] In having Machaut direct his poem to Marguerite, however, Pierre would have had no ambition to marry the lady. Being already married and occupied with a crusade, he needed high-placed friends, not a wife – especially not one whom his allies in France and England coveted for their scions. Since she was a person of great wealth and influence, Marguerite's support and that of her family would have been invaluable to him.

In the complainte Pierre expresses (or rather Machaut expresses for Pierre's surrogate) determination to see Marguerite if at all possible before he departs (65–8); he was probably with the royal family in France while she was in Ghent. With or without first seeing Marguerite, Pierre travelled through Europe to Venice, whence he set out with his crusaders. In October 1365 he captured Alexandria, but his supporters were unwilling to remain there. So all took their booty and went home, Pierre to Cyprus where he made plans for another crusade. It was probably two years later that Machaut wrote a second poem to a lady named Marguerite on behalf of Pierre, the Dit de la Marguerite.[31] In this work the narrator presents himself as separated from his beloved by the sea, hardly able to conceive his happiness when he sees her once more. Pierre's fortunes, however, never brought him back to France. Frustrated in his attempts to gain support, he was assassinated in January 1369. That same spring, after years of hard diplomacy, Marguerite of Flanders married Philippe le Hardi, Duke of Burgundy.

The Dit de la Marguerite is the first full-fledged Marguerite poem, being the first to celebrate the flower that bears the name – in English, the daisy. The *Dit's* 208 lines are in the same 16-line stanzas as the complainte. The narrator commences by attesting to the great power of the marguerite, for from across the seas it has cured him of his sickness. From the time he first saw it he became its servant, and though he now sees it 'po souvent' (litotes for 'not at all') he remains devoted. Souvenirs and Doulz Pensers constantly recall the flower to him, and when the wind blows from its 'dous pays' he grows healthier. Even from 'd'outre la mer' it seems present to him, and everything he has comes from it. Whether he is in 'Cyprus or Egypt,' he concludes, his heart remains with the marguerite.

The topical references hardly leave in doubt that Machaut wrote this poem also for Pierre, who again appears as an awed young lover addressing a lady who is a nonpareil. In this poem too she probably represents Marguerite of Flanders, whose person even in her youth would have been at some odds with the ideal lady imagined in the poems. Documents indicate that she was not beautiful and that she had a difficult and domineering temperament.[32] The conventions of the poetry nevertheless made the idealizing procedure automatic; we could not expect in the poems realistic characterizations that would accord with the natures of the historical lovers and ladies who lurk in the background.

Though the *Book of the Duchess* provides sure testimony that Chaucer composed occasional poems, we do not know that he wrote lyrics in which the first-person speakers represent historical persons other than himself, as Machaut did in 'Complainte VI' and *Dit de la Marguerite*. Tradition has identified the complainers in *Complaint of Mars* and the *Complaint of Venus* with actual people, though on very unsure grounds. On the whole, it is not unlikely that some narrators in his lyrics, both extant and lost, represent patrons.

Machaut's third Marguerite poem, the *Dit de la fleur de lis et de la Marguerite* (*Lis et Marguerite*),[33] was doubtless written on behalf of a patron who was not Pierre. This is a rather different work in that the 416 lines in octosyllabic couplets are mainly devoted to praising the lady, presenting her as one who combines the virtues of the lily and the marguerite; in addition, there is an allegorical dimension by which the lily, as 'fleur masculine,' represents the lover, and the 'feminine' marguerite stands for the lady (171–2). If we assume that Machaut wrote the poem in 1369 to celebrate the wedding of Philippe of Burgundy and

Marguerite of Flanders, which sealed a great triumph for French diplomacy over the English, the fleur-de-lis represents Philippe, the brother of Charles V and the Duke of Berry.[34]

In contrast to Machaut's first two poems to Marguerite, which focus on the first-person lover's consuming desire to see the lady, *Lis et Marguerite* offers homage and praise to the lady on behalf of Philippe. But the narrator is not a stand-in for Philippe; while he speaks of the lady as '*ma* gracieuse dame,' he focuses on her transcendent nature rather than on her relationship to him. As a poetic character he is comparable to the narrator in the 'Prologue' to the *Legend of Good Women*, Chaucer's own Marguerite poem (for which Machaut's works are prime originals). Instead of representing the patrons, these narrators appear as generic devotees of feminine paragons. The women represented are surrogates within the poems of important historical women whom the poets are celebrating.[35]

MORALIST, AGING LOVER, AND SELF-CONSCIOUS POET

Most of the important personas in Machaut's love lyrics – the naïve young lover, the lady of understanding, the disillusioned mature lover, the patron-surrogate, and the celebrator of the patroness – find counterparts among Chaucer's works. Machaut also wrote a number of short poems on subjects other than love which are built around still other personas. In some the narrator embodies an autobiographical caricature; for example, in 'A toi, Hanri' he takes the part of a cranky and aging poet who seasons his list of gripes with dry humour. In Chaucer's related *Complaint to His Purse*, he accentuates the humour but almost eliminates personal detail from his complaint; he evidently felt more compunction than the Frenchman did about airing his troubles openly. In several other works Machaut is similarly circumstantial, as in two ballades in which he curses the month of March for what it does to his gout and criticizes his fellow canons at Reims Cathedral.[36]

Another persona of Machaut's non-love lyrics that Chaucer took up more willingly is the moralist who decries the world's customs and urges reform. This figure has a background extending from Chaucer's own time back to and past the Romans, but Chaucer drew particular inspiration for the moralist's pose from one ballade of Machaut.[37] Indicating his own fondness for this ballade, the French poet placed it without music in his *Louange des dames*, and also among his ballades with music:

Il m'est avis qu'il n'est dons de Nature,
Com bons qu'il soit, que nulz prise à ce jour,
Se la clarté tenebreuse et obscure
De Fortune ne li donne coulour;
   Ja soit ce que seürté   5
Ne soit en li, amour ne loyauté.
Mais je ne voy homme amé ne chieri,
Se Fortune ne le tient à ami.

Si bien ne sont fors vent et aventure,
Donné a faute et tolu par irour;   10
On la doit croire où elle se parjure,
Car de mentir est sa plus grant honneur.
C'est .i. monstre envolepé
De boneür, plein de maleürté;
Car nuls n'a pris, tant ait de bien en li,   15
Se Fortune ne le tient à ami.

Si me merveil comment Raisons endure
Si longuement à durer ceste errour,
Car les vertus sont à desconfiture
Par les vices qui regnent com signour.   20
   Et qui vuet avoir le gré
De ceuls qui sont et estre en haut degré.
Il pert son temps et puet bien dire: 'Aymi!',
Se Fortune ne le tient á ami.[38]

I think there is no gift of Nature, however fine it may be, that anyone esteems in this time unless the shadowy and dark brightness of Fortune colours it, even though there is no security in her, love nor loyalty. I never see a man loved nor cherished if Fortune does not hold him as her friend.

Her goods are only wind and chance, given by mistake and taken away in wrath. One should believe her where she perjures herself, for lying is her greatest honour. She is a monster covered with happiness, full of misery. No one is valued, however much good he has in himself, if Fortune does not hold him as her friend.

And I marvel how Reason allows this wrong to endure so long, for the virtues are discomfited by the vices who govern as lords. And he who wishes to have the favour of those who are and will be in high station wastes his time and may well say 'Aymi!' if Fortune does not hold him as her friend.

This ballade is permeated with the ideas and images of Boethius, and it is evident that Chaucer used it in constructing his Boethian triple ballade *Fortune*, especially the first ballade. Chaucer achieves more dramatic force by having his narrator address Fortune directly in the refrain, 'For fynally, Fortune, I thee defye,' but his tone and the moral stance are clearly related to Machaut's:

> This wrecched worldes transmutacioun,
> As wele or wo, now povre and now honour,
> Withouten ordre or wys discrecioun
> Governed is by Fortunes errour. (1–4)

Showing the same moral rigour along with more of the personal outrage of Machaut's poem is the indignant speaker in *Lak of Stedfastnesse*, a second work modelled in part on 'Il m'est avis':

> Trouthe is put doun, resoun is holden fable;
> Vertu hath now no dominacioun;
> Pitee exyled, no man is merciable;
> Through coveytyse is blent discrecioun.
> The world hath mad a permutacioun
> Fro right to wrong, fro trouthe to fikelnesse,
> That al is lost for lak of stedfastnesse. (15–21)

In the envoy that follows, Chaucer admonishes King Richard to 'cherish thy folk and hate extorcioun!' His poem, like Machaut's, is political in orientation.

If, as John Shirley says, *Lak of Stedfastnesse* was made in Chaucer's 'laste yeeres,' a final poetic voice of Chaucer was that of the moralist – appropriate to age, one would think. By contrast, 'Il m'est avis' is a composition of Machaut's middle years, and there is little among his later works to match it in tone. Rather, the lyrics that evidently are the latest[39] are love poems expressing conventional ideas and sentiments. Among them is one that deals with the colour symbolism of Amour, which is comparably exploited by Chaucer in several works.[40] The first stanza sets forth the significances of the colours:

> Qui des couleurs saroit à droit jugier
> Et dire la droite signefiance,
> On deveroit le fin asur prisier
> Dessus toutes; je n'en fais pas doubtance.

> Car jaune, c'est fausseté,
> Blanc est joie, vert est nouvelleté,
> Vermeil ardeur, noir deuil; mais ne doubt mie
> *Que fin azur loyauté signefie.*[41]

He who knows how to judge colours correctly and to state their true significance would say that one should prize pure blue above all, I have no doubt of it. For yellow, that is falsity, white is joy, green is fickleness, red is ardour, black is sorrow; but do not doubt that pure blue means loyalty.

In this stanza we perhaps find the last voice that Machaut would choose for himself, that of the experienced arbiter, able 'à droit jugier' in matters within the province of Amour. For Chaucer it was somewhat different; while he did not completely abandon Machaut as a model, in the *Canterbury* period his interest in composing love poetry waned.

Though the first-person persona of any literary work often bears a close relationship to the author, age does not always dictate his subject-matter; while an elderly Chaucer is moralist and ironist, an aged Machaut continues to be essentially a love poet in his lyrics, as in his long *Voir-Dit*. Trying to construct a biography on the basis of the writer's subject-matter, one realizes, is a perilous enterprise. The poems can mislead us even when the poet claims to be narrating only historical fact, as Machaut does in *Voir-Dit*. Of all his works this is the one in which scholars have shown most interest.[42] Many have been sceptical of its claim of truth, and there is ample reason for uncertainty. Nevertheless, there is one matter on which the poem imparts trustworthy – and valuable – information: Machaut's conception of himself as poet. It is not certain that Chaucer knew the *Voir-Dit*,[43] but he could not have failed to perceive the French master's fully developed sense of himself as a literary man.[44] The *Voir-Dit* dramatizes and documents that perception, but his other works and the remarkable manuscripts also testify to it.

The *Voir-Dit* can serve here to extend our concern beyond the lyric persona to a more direct consideration of the poets' images of themselves as authors. The persona of this work is a fascinating blend of convention and autobiography; furthermore, the poem is even more taken up with discussion and illustration of poetic composition than is the *Fonteinne amoureuse*. Written between 1362 and 1365, when Machaut was well into his sixties, it contains about 9,000 verses – including some 60 intercalated lyrics – plus 46 prose letters.

The love story seems quite improbable, involving as it does a pretty lady of eighteen paying court to a gouty, one-eyed old man; however, the poet insists on its truth:

Le Voir-Dit vueil-je qu'on appelle
Ce traictié que je fais pour elle
Pour ce que ja n'i mentiray.   (430–2)

I wish this treatise that I make for her to be called the True Story, for in it I will never lie.

At the outset the poet-narrator, completely surprised, receives a rondeau from the young lady in which she declares that her heart is his; she has not met him, but has been smitten by his poetry. In a lengthy exchange of poems and letters the two carry on a highly literary love affair, both being as concerned with art as with ardour. The exchange culminates in a personal encounter between lady and poet, which has more or less satisfying results (the poem is not explicit, though it teases the reader by presenting the lady in bed dressed only in 'les uevres de Nature'). After the one meeting the lovers do not come together again, though the correspondence continues. The affair and the poem wane away in a series of misunderstandings and unfulfilled promises.

Despite extensive scholarly investigations and discussions, we do not know what if anything of the love story in *Voir-Dit* is true to the poet's life.[45] The loose structure of the narrative stretching out over three years, the January and May love situation, and several bizarre and fanciful events lead me to suspect that it is a fantasy of the poet. Another aspect – the presentation of the narrator's poetic activities – has more certain relevance to his life. Among the numerous passages in *Voir-Dit* which deal with the composition, copying, and transmission of the poet's works, particularly interesting are those which indicate that Machaut maintained a master copy of his poetry from which he had copies of his works made, and which was sometimes unbound so that individual poems might be transcribed.[46] He shows a strong concern that this master copy should be complete and accurate.[47] Throughout the work the narrator presents himself as self-conscious and proud of his identity and stature as poet, and scrupulous in the maintenance and transmission of his oeuvre.

In their comprehensiveness, their consistent and logical ordering, and the beauty and care of their fashioning, the impressive codices that have come down to us bear out the image of the self-aware poet found in *Voir-Dit*. Included among the numerous surviving manuscripts that contain Machaut's poetry and music are several beautifully made collections of his complete works, with generally superior poetic texts, suitable for any nobleman.[48] The four most important manuscripts, representing three stages in his work, were made in Machaut's lifetime, and perhaps under his supervision, probably from a master manuscript such as the one he speaks of in *Voir-Dit*.[49] Various matters allow us to date them within limits.[50] The latest collection made in Machaut's lifetime, the A manuscript, is prefaced by a celebrated table of contents that states categorically, 'Vesci l'ordenance que G de Machaut wet quil ait en son livre' / 'Here is the order that Guillaume de Machaut wishes his book to have.' This statement, the thoughtful arrangement, and the prologue that was specially composed to preface the whole are eloquent testimony to the importance Machaut attached to his calling and to his own work.

The bulk and quality of Machaut's art are most impressive and make understandable his tremendous impact on the literature and music that came after him. The works in the order in which manuscript A places them may be briefly enumerated: 9 long dits amoureux and 4 shorter dits; *La Louange des dames*, a mélange of 282 lyrics of various types not set to music; 8 complaints; *La Prise d'Alexandrie*, a long verse chronicle; and a last long section of 140 musical works with accompanying poetic texts, segregated by type.[51] By contrast with the *Louange*, which presents a judicious mélange of types, the musical pieces are segregated by lyric category: lays, motets, ballades, rondeaux, and virelays, followed by one hoquet and a Messe de Nostre Dame. In total the poetry comprises some 60,000 verses (compare Chaucer's approximately 38,000 verses).

No manuscripts of Chaucer's works from his lifetime exist to testify to a Machaut-like concern for the transmission of his oeuvre, nor is there any indication that he ever collected his works. He obviously allowed the *Canterbury Tales* to circulate in a variety of sequences, and in all likelihood never made a final decision about completing or ordering the work. Of course, in *Adam Scriveyn* and in a stanza in the epilogue to *Troilus* (V 1793–9) he shows anxiety about the accuracy of his text, and he variously evidences a consciousness of his place in the poetic tradition. Nevertheless, Machaut's care for the preservation of his works contrasts strikingly with Chaucer's evident failure to provide for his. One factor mitigating the English poet's apparent neglect is that Machaut's life was about twenty years longer than Chaucer's, and he evidently had more leisure to devote to his poetry in his mature years.

Since both poets rose from the middle classes to enjoy lifelong relationships with the highest nobility, the careers of Machaut and Chaucer have an obvious similarity. The differences between their careers are as substantial. Though he had an active younger life as secretary to Jean of Luxembourg, Machaut's clerical sinecure in Reims allowed him to compose music and poetry in relative isolation from the concerns and cares of public or commercial life. In contrast to Chaucer the public servant, the Frenchman's main point of contact with his royal associates was through his activity as poet and musician, in entertaining, praising, and instructing them, assisting their artistic endeavours, and no doubt playing literary games with them. His fame spread through Europe (in a way that Chaucer's did not), but he always composed for the few, an exclusive coterie of royalty and nobility. At the outset he was an innovator: he followed the Ars Nova in music, and his own version of the poetic mode involved a new synthesis of recent developments. However, the canons of his art changed little in his poetic career. Even when the persona of his later love poetry evokes a writer grown older, he still inhabits the same domain of Amour as the young lover did, a world reflecting the ideals and aspirations of the court, and he expresses himself in the same forms.

Chaucer came into the sphere of the court when Machaut's influence was beginning to be felt strongly in England. He adopted the forms, purposes, and poses pertinent to the mode, and in his earlier court life he perhaps enjoyed some periods of insulation from practical concerns during which his skills in court poetry developed. But his public service as office-holder and diplomat soon began and was to continue throughout his life. His poetic career became and remained subordinate to his life in the world of affairs, and his poetry constantly changed its character. The deaths of Philippa and Blanche and then of the two Edwards, and the preoccupation of Richard II's uncles with governing perhaps gradually deprived the court poet of his royal audience in London. No doubt Chaucer's intellectual interests, combined with his prodigious reading, also led him early to range beyond the limits of the Machaut mode. Even his translation of the *Roman de la Rose* took him into territories that the Machauvians had abandoned, as did the *Book of the Duchess* despite its permeation with Machaut's characters, stories, and verbal expression.

But to come back to the affinities: whenever they might have met before Machaut died in 1377, any discussion of verse between them would have been based on compatible poetic visions, and on the same verbal music. As poems like *Lak of Stedfastnesse* demonstrate, however far Chaucer went beyond the mode of Machaut, he never did abandon it; indeed, its influence was a dominating force on him through the composition of the *Legend of Good Women* in the later 1380s. To show how this claim may be made for the primarily lyric and musical poetry of Machaut, in the face of the Latin and Italian models whose presence is so obvious in Chaucer's work, is now the principal business.

Representations of the Poet, the Persona, and the Audience in Middle French Manuscripts

The following pages present a set of twenty-one manuscript illuminations found in codices belonging to the Bibliothèque Nationale in Paris. All of the miniatures depict some stage in the poetic process – patronage, production, presentation, and audience – of which the Middle French poets were particularly conscious. Except for several sumptuous collections of Machaut's poetry, the manuscripts of fourteenth-century French love poetry were not highly illustrated. It was not until the works of Christine de Pisan (represented in no 8), who wrote most of her poetry in the early years of the fifteenth century, that comparable artistic effort was expended on a French love poet. As a consequence, most of the miniatures shown (thirteen of twenty-one) are from five Machaut collections. The two publications of François Avril listed in the bibliography are valuable for analysis of the style and for the dating of the Machaut illuminations.

The only picture in the two Froissart collections appears here as no 12. The well-known illustration of Froissart in the act of presenting his poetry to Richard II (no 5) is found in a manuscript of the *Chronicles*. The two pictures of Deschamps (nos 6 and 7) are from the small book containing his French verse version of Innocent's *De miseria conditionis humane*; there are no illustrations for his verse elsewhere. All of the illuminations are quite contemporary with the texts, and therefore reflect the painters' – and no doubt the writers' – conceptions. The Machaut and Froissart collections, except for BN français 1587 (no 3), are from the fourteenth century.

These illustrations are reproduced by permission of the Bibliothèque Nationale: BN français 831 f 1v: fig 11; BN français 848 f 1: fig 8; BN français 1584 (Machaut ms A) f D: fig 2, f E: fig 1, f 155v: fig 16, f 367: fig 15, f 414v: fig 13; BN français 1586 (Machaut ms C) f 23: fig 17, f 26: fig 18, f 38v: fig 20, f 51: fig 19; BN français 1587 (Machaut ms D) f 1: fig 3; BN français 2186 f 10v: fig 4; BN français 2646 f 194v: fig 5; BN français 9221 (Machaut ms E) f 16: fig 12; f 107: fig 14; BN français 20029 f 4v: fig 6, f 21v: fig 7; BN français 22545 (Machaut ms F) f 40: fig 10; BN français 24287 f 2: fig 21; BN français 25566 f 10: fig 9.

1 *The poet at work.* Nature presents to Machaut her children, the formative skills necessary for verse composition: Scens, Rhetorique, and Musique.

Comment Amours qui a ouÿ nature
vient a Guillaume de machaut et li
Et luy amours qui nient ester estandi
est bn mener douce z ioieuse vie

Cy comence le liure mestre Guille
De lotis

2 (above left) *The poet at work.* The God of Love presents to Machaut three of his children, the materials needed for poetry: Dous Penser, Plaisance, and Esperance.

3 (left) *The poet at work.* Machaut at his writing desk. In the words above the portrait, the scribe wrongly identifies the poet as 'Guillaume de Lorris.'

4 *Poet and patron.* Thibaut (or the lover) presents his *Romanz de la poire* to his patroness (or the beloved lady).

5 (above) *Poet and patron*. An elderly Froissart presents a book of his poems to an elegant Richard II. This miniature illustrates the passage of the *Chronicles* in which Froissart tells of his trip to England.

6 (above right) *Poet and patron*. Deschamps presents his book to Charles VI. The thick book depicted has the size of the extant manuscript of the poet's oeuvre, compiled after his death, while this manuscript is itself very thin (dated 1383).

7 (below right) *Poet and patron*. Deschamps offers his devotion. Fourteenth-century poets always numbered Mary and Christ among their patrons.

8 *Poet and patron.* Christine de Pisan presents a large book of her poems to Louis d'Orléans. The text is her *Epistle of Othea*.

9 (above right) *Poet and audience.* Two singers, perhaps Adam de la Halle and an assistant, sing the first of Adam's chansons, 'Damerous cuer,' to an audience of men and women.

10 (below right) *Poet and audience.* Guillaume de Machaut reads his *Remede de Fortune* with a didactic finger raised, apt for a poem that contains both an Art of Poetry and an Art of Love.

Ous deues
sauoir que
dedens ce liure
sont contenu
pluisour ditie

11 (above left) *Poet and audience*. At the head of the index in one of Froissart's two verse collections, the poet (?) is seen reading his verse to a man and two women. With the grass at the reader's feet and the elaborate seat, the setting appears to be both outdoors and indoors. Dates of composition shown in text as 1362–94.

12 (below left) *Group singing of lyric*. Six men around a barrel singing a rondeau of Machaut from a rotulus.

13 *Group singing of lyric*. Seven drinkers around barrel singing a Machaut motet from a rotulus.

14 *Group singing of lyric*. Five singers in rather formal posture presenting a lay of Machaut.

15 *The poet-persona*. The lover sings a lay, spontaneously it seems, to his lady. The lay is Machaut's first, 'Loyauté qui point ne delay.'

16 *The poet-persona*. The poet copies the lover's long complaint in Machaut's *Dit de la fonteinne amoureuse*.

18 *The poet-persona.* The lover here is composing the lay 'de son sentement' on a very lengthy scroll. He later reads it to the lady.

17 *The poet-persona.* The lover-poet observes his lady at the beginning of *Remede de Fortune*, presumably gaining inspiration and material for his dit. This miniature and the three that follow are by the distinguished painter of BN français 1586.

19 *The poet-persona.* Coming upon a carole, a round dance, the lover (fourth from right) joins in and sings a virelay. His lady is next to him (facing, with hat).

20 *The poet-persona.* Like Lady Philosophy in the *Consolation of Philosophy*, Lady Esperance sings a song of comfort to the complaining protagonist, who is in a trance, but that doesn't prevent him from including the chant royal in his *Remede.*

21 *Royal reader.* This portrait of Charles V reading appears at the head of a French translation of John of Salisbury's *Policraticus*, but Charles is reading a psalm, 'Beatus Vir.'

CHAPTER FOUR

Machaut's Oeuvre and Chaucer's Early Poems

The several manuscript collections of Machaut's poetry made at different times in his life tell us a great deal about the development of his writing career from the 1340s until his death in 1377; however, they leave us mostly in the dark as to the course he followed in his first forty years. Much of his young adulthood was spent following the peripatetic King Jean of Bohemia, and of his numerous datable works only one was written before 1342.[1] These circumstances indicate that the greater part of his extant poetry and music was composed after he settled down as canon at Reims after 1337, when he was in his late thirties. But further information is sparse. As with Chaucer's career as a young poet, we must rely on inference to reconstruct Machaut's development. His musical expertise and academic background (he had earned the title 'master'), together with the few facts we have, suggest that he began by composing motets, an older, characteristically musical form with liturgical origins; that as he became involved in court life he essayed the secular lyric forms with music and then without; and that after becoming practised in the formes fixes he at length came to write longer dits. This scenario is in line with the simpler one often posited for Chaucer – that he began with lyrics and afterwards started writing longer poems.

The Machaut tradition was quintessentially lyric, and the poets typically began writing verse with the lyric forms. Thus, when Machaut's precursor Nicole de Margival came to compose the *Panthère d'Amours* (c. 1310), he attributed the faults of his dit to his inexperience in composing long pieces: 'It is not at all my custom to versify such a long matter' / 'Ne ce n'est mie mes usages / De si grant chose en rime mettre'

(2609–10). By nature a lyric poet, he felt comfortable mainly with the shorter formes fixes, inserting them throughout the poem. In the final parts of the *Panthère* especially (2190–2665), he succeeds in integrating the lyric passages; no longer mere embellishments of the narrative, they come to dominate. As we saw in the earlier analysis of *Remede de Fortune*, in Machaut's poems lyric discourse likewise reigns; sometimes the pervasive lyric passages are given formes fixes metrics, and sometimes narrative and lyric segments follow one after the other in undifferentiated versification.

In considering Machaut's influence on the development of Chaucer's early work, there is reason to treat the lyric unit as the prime constituent of the verse of both poets. At this point I want to look at Chaucer's longer lyrics and his vision poems as they relate to lyrics of Machaut in particular. We may assume that the young English poet came to know well the greater part of the French poet's large and diverse oeuvre; certainly he was familiar with most aspects of it. In his early poetry he shows knowledge of works from every standard division of the manuscripts: poems with and without musical notation; short lyrics, including numerous ballades, virelays, and rondeaux; long lyrics, including lays, motets, and complaints; and dits of all lengths.[2]

MACHAUT'S LONG LYRICS AND CHAUCER'S EARLY POEMS

Machaut's longer lyric poems are classed in manuscript as 'complaintes' and 'lays.' Not only in versification, but also in rhetorical structure, these forms contrast fundamentally with the ballade. Instead of a logical chain, both involve repetition and accumulation. In effect, in a standard twelve-section lay the poet finds twelve different ways of expressing similar sentiments. The return in the twelfth section of the lay to the versification and music of the first section is emblematic of its circular movement about a single subject. Similarly, in the typical stanzaic complaint the stanzas give the lover an opportunity to make his lament in so many parallel, cumulative verse paragraphs. Both types rely for their primary effects on the natural music of the metrics and phonetics, along with the accretive force of the conventional expression.

No poem of Chaucer is named 'lay,' but the case is different for 'complaint.' Aside from the ABC,[3] all of his lyrics of more than a hundred lines are called 'complaints': *Complaint unto Pity*, *Complaint to His Lady*, and *Complaint of Mars*. *Anelida and Arcite*, which in most ways belongs among the lyrics, is also labelled 'complaint' in two manuscripts; the title is supported by Anelida's lengthy lament.[4] With such titles we might anticipate finding counterparts to these poems of Chaucer in the French works called complaints; however, in no case is the relationship especially close. The Machaut manuscripts include ten poems in a separate 'complainte' section, and several extensive set pieces labelled 'complainte' are intercalated in his longer works. But in contrast to the other lyric classes, Machaut does not assign his complaints a distinctive verse form. Several are in various kinds of couplets,[5] and there are five lengthy pieces that use a stanzaic unit rhyming *aaabaaab*, octosyllabic or decasyllabic except for four-syllable fourth lines.[6] The verse of Chaucer's four long 'complaints' is unrelated to these works. None is in couplets. Thirty-two lines in Anelida's 210-line complaint do have the *aaabaaab* rhyme scheme, but they have line lengths different from Machaut's.[7]

Chaucer knew some of Machaut's complaints. As we discussed previously, he probably was familiar with 'A toi, Hanri' ('Complainte III'), a counterpart in some respects to *Complaint to His Purse*. He may well have known 'Complainte VI,' written for King Pierre of Cyprus. He certainly had read 'Complainte I,' as lines at the beginning of both the *Book of the Duchess* and *Complaint to His Lady* show. 'Complainte I' is notable for its plays on words, particularly involving riche and equivoque rhymes (extended rhymes and homonyms). The first sixteen lines exemplify its character:

Amours, tu m'as tant esté dure,
Et si m'a tant duré et dure
La durté que pour toy endure
   Que d'endurer
Sui si mis à desconfiture
Que de garir est aventure;
Et croy que c'est contre nature
   D'einsi durer.

Car en mon cuer li maulz d'amer
Est si poignant et si amer
Qu'il fait nuit et jour enflamer
   Mon dueil et m'ire,
Ne je ne m'en sçay où clamer,
Puis que ma dame reclamer
Ne me vuet ne ma joie amer
   N'estre mon mire.[8]

Love, you have been so hard on me, and have so much hardened and harden the hardness that I endure for you, that in enduring it I am so discomfited that my recovery is in doubt; and I believe that it is against nature to endure thus.

For in my heart the affliction of loving is so keen and so bitter that it makes my sorrow and anguish flame up night and day, and I don't know where to complain, since my lady doesn't want to accept me, nor to favour my joy, nor to be my physician.

The poem extends to 256 lines; each of the rhyme sounds (after the first) is used eight times. In the virtual absence of personification, allusion, and all but the plainest and most common images, the play of the sounds stands out as the dominant poetic ornament of the work. The poet obviously thought it significant that of the work's thirty-three successive rhyme sounds none is repeated, even though one cannot perceive this subtlety in a simple reading of the work, much less in hearing it.[9]

But Chaucer manifests little interest in the formal features or the word-play. Despite the conspicuous artifice of the work, he is drawn to use it for his dreamer's rather naturalistic lament about sleeplessness in the *Book of the Duchess*:

> And wel ye woot, *agaynes kynde*
> *Hyt were to lyven in thys wyse,*
> For *nature* wolde nat suffyse
> To noon erthly *creature*
> Nat longe tyme to *endure*
> Withoute slep and be in sorwe.   (16–21)

Chaucer uses Machaut's words, but to different effect. Instead of following the rhyme repetitions of the French – seven of 'dure,' reinforced by three of '-ture' – he finds latent realism in the artifice of the French phraseology and evokes an authentic sleepy poet ready for dreamland. The same generalization seems to hold of the relationship of the opening of *Complaint to His Lady* to the same Machaut passage:

> The longe nightes, whan every *creature*
> Shulde have hir rest in somwhat as *by kynde*,
> Or elles ne may hir lif nat *longe endure*. ...

Neither in these lines nor in those that follow is there exploitation of Machaut's obtrusive word-play, or reflection of his verse form.

Chaucer finds neither the form nor the substance of Machaut's complaints of extensive use. His *Complaint to His Purse* is related by imagery and a certain humour to 'A toi, Hanri' ('Complainte III'), and the discussion of sleeplessness in 'Complainte I' is suggestive for opening passages in two other works of his. But the primary models of his complaints certainly lie elsewhere. There is a second long lyric form which we might look to for a model. In contrast to the uniform verse of the complaint, the standard Middle French lay has twelve different two-stanza sections, each with a different stanza form (except that the first and last are the same). The form might suggest, for example, *Complaint to His Lady*, which has four distinct sections with varying versification.[10]

Chaucer shows he knew several of Machaut's lays, among them the *Lay de Confort*, which, like 'Complainte I,' supplied a few lines for the *Book of the Duchess*. A striking image in the *Duchess* was inspired by the first section, which, like all the sections in a lay, consists of two matching stanzas:

S'onques dolereusement
Sceus faire ne tristement
  Lay ou chanson
Ou chant à dolereus son
  Qui sentement
Ait de plour et de tourment,
  Temps et saison
Ay dou faire et occoison
  Presentement.

Qu'en terre n'a element
Ne planette en firmament
  Qui de pleur don
Ne me face et, sans raison,
  Mon cuer dolent;
Et Fortune m'a dou vent
  D'un tourbillon
Tumé jus de sa maison
  En fondement.[11] (1–18)

If ever I could make a lay or chanson sorrowfully or sadly, or a song of sorrowful sound which might convey a sense of tears and of torment, I now have the occasion, time, and season to do it. For there is neither an element in the earth nor a planet in the firmament which does not make me a gift of weeping and, without reason, make my heart unhappy; and Fortune with a whirlwind has thrown me down from her house into the dungeon.

In the course of his complaint in the *Book of the Duchess*, Chaucer's Black Knight exclaims, translating the first lines of stanza 2 above almost word for word,

> For there nys planete in firmament,
> Ne in ayr ne in erthe noon element,
> That they ne yive me a yifte echone
> Of wepyng whan I am allone.   (693–6)

Chaucer's lines capture the sense of Machaut's image fully; notwithstanding, the octosyllables do not simulate the effect of the short lines which are characteristic of the Machauvian lay.

To exemplify a typical variation in verse form between sections of the lay, we might look at another part of *Lay de Confort*, the second half of the eighth section, whose concluding sentiment Chaucer may also have used:

> Et s'Yre ou Despit te lance
>   De sa lance,
>   Recevoir
> Dois en bonne pacience,
>   Ne t'avence
>   De mouvoir,
> Car au goust de souffisance
>   Ta pesence
>   Dois avoir:
> Mieux vaut assez s'acointence
>   Que puissence
>   D'autre avoir.   (155–66)

And if Anger or Despite lance you with their lance, you ought to accept it with good patience, nor react at all, since for a taste of satisfaction you must endure your suffering; just meeting her is worth much more than having another in your power.[12]

The successive sections of a Machaut lay typically have differing but compatible versification. Even though the number of lines, their disposition, and the rhyme schemes differ, the two quoted sections of the lay are obviously related. In both cases lines of seven syllables alternate comparably with shorter lines. By contrast, the parts of Chaucer's *Complaint to His Lady* are not related in verse form, the sharp differences between the size and versification of the four sections making the prosody fundamentally different from the standard lay.

In his 'Retraction', Chaucer admits to 'many a leccherous lay,' and Alceste in the 'Prologue' to the *Legend* attributes to him 'many a lay' (F 430), but there is no real evidence that he ever essayed the form, or for that matter tried a complaint with distinctive versification. It is clear, moreover, that he never standardized his terminology for the various lyric types. The Black Knight's eleven-line poem (BD 475–86) is called successively a *'compleynt'* (464) and 'a *lay*, a maner *song*' (471). And at the conclusion of the *Complaint of Venus*, a triple ballade, Chaucer states, 'Thus wol I ende this *compleynt* or this *lay*' (71). In both cases the terms are used as general designations for lyric laments. Comparably, since the lay form was notoriously difficult for the poet, it seems very doubtful that the poem 'in manere of a *compleynt* or a *lay*' (E 1881) that Chaucer had Damian write out for May in the 'Merchant's Tale' would have qualified as a lay. Froissart states that making a lay is 'a great feat' / 'uns grans fés,' which requires six months of effort.[13] Chaucer's most ambitious feat of versification is Anelida's complaint, which involves a unique medley of French stanzaic patterns rather than a set form. Antigone's song in *Troilus and Criseyde* finds antecedents in several Machaut lays, and in the parallel and cumulative statement of its seven stanzas it resembles the longer French lyric forms. These two pieces are as close as Chaucer's extant poems come to them. Nevertheless, even though he never practised these long lyric forms and did not adopt a standardized terminology for them, his mastery of the ballade and rondeau warrants that he well understood that each of the various formes fixes had a prescribed shape.

Unlike Machaut's lays, the sequence of verse forms in *Complaint to His Lady* has no recognizable rationale, leading some to believe that the parts do not belong together. The length of the sections is very uneven. The first consists of two stanzas of rime royal, in origin a ballade stanza. The second and third sections are famous as the only examples in Chaucer of terza rima, which has led some critics to posit inspiration from the *Commedia*; however, the phraseology in these twenty-five lines is not at all Italianate. It comes directly from the Machaut tradition:

Hir love I best, and shal, whyl I may dure,
   Bet than myself an hundred thousand deel,
   Than al this worldes richesse or creature.
Now hath not Love me bestowed weel
   To love ther I never shal have part?
   Allas, right thus is turned me the wheel,
Thus am I slayn with Loves fyry dart!   (30–6)

Chaucer breaks the interlocking effect of terza rima through stanza divisions, and reduces the Dantean intensity which is potential in the fiery dart of Love with the conventional phraseology characteristic of the French.

Thoroughly French both in spirit and in metrics is the fourth section, which makes up 60 per cent of the *Complaint to His Lady*. It consists of nine uniform ten-line stanzas,[14] rhyming *aabaabcddc*; these are closely related to ordinary ballade stanzas except that Chaucer expands the usual *abab* opening to *aabaab*, as he does in several other poems.[15] The nine-stanza sequence divides readily into three equal sections, thereby suggesting the form of the triple ballades like *Fortune* and *Complaint of Venus*, as well as the ballade sequences of Granson and others. Each three-stanza unit is concerned with a common ballade subject: in the first the lover speaks of his suffering; in the second he vows faithfulness and enduring service; in the third he pleads for pity. Furthermore, the structure of statement of each forms the three-part logical chain characteristic of the ballade. For instance, in the second part (stanzas 4–6, lines 68–97) the lover first admits his poor ability to serve the lady properly (69–70), then declares that his love forces him to ask to serve her (82–3), and finally, with a certain affective logic, concludes that whatever happens she cannot 'drive' him away from serving her 'with alle my wittes fyve' (91–2). Only lacking for the ballade form are the refrain and the continuation of the rhyme sounds between stanzas. Even with Chaucer's long lyrics, it is the ballade form that exercises the primary influence.

MACHAUT'S BALLADES AND CHAUCER'S COMPLAINTS WITH NARRATIVE

The form of the ballade is infinitely more important for Chaucer's poetry than the French lay or complaint. Repeatedly in his stanzaic poetry before the *Canterbury* period, Chaucer employs the three-stanza unit in ballade fashion. In *Complaint to His Lady* and *Complaint unto Pity* there are nine-stanza units that divide naturally into threes. The complaint section of *Complaint to Mars* similarly incorporates five sets of three stanzas each. *Anelida and Arcite* is a complex of three-stanza units and multiples of three: the Introduction has three stanzas, the story has thirty stanzas, the strophe and antistrophe of Anelida's complaint have six stanzas apiece. And as we will discuss below, the *Parliament of Fowls* and especially *Troilus and Criseyde* have numerous ballade-like segments in their unbroken chains of rime royal stanzas. Only when Chaucer comes to employ rime royal in the *Canterbury Tales* do his stanzaic works no longer make important use of the ballade unit.

Daniel Poirion speaks of the 'triangular proportions of the ballade [being] in profound harmony with medieval habits of thought.' He goes on to assert that 'the necessity of distributing the words and the rhymes in three identical series, the images in three symmetrical sections, the ideas in three logical steps made of this lyric genre an efficacious means of expression, an almost universal poetic language.'[16] The ballade was by far the most popular of the lyric forms in the fourteenth century;[17] and Chaucer's lyrics, long and short, reflect that popularity. Though his production of ballades in French and English certainly did not approach the more than one thousand that Deschamps left, Chaucer probably composed many that have been lost; intimate familiarity with the ballade conventions doubtless led him to embed three-step 'logical chains' in his stanzaic compositions. In his longer lyrics, rather than following the lay or complaint development, he favoured combining ballade-like units. There is abundant evidence that Chaucer could have produced verse tours de force like Machaut's longer lyrics had he so desired, but with notable exceptions he favoured sequential development in his poetic statements over the parallelism characteristic of these forms.

There is another respect in which Chaucer's usual procedure in his complaints differs from Machaut's in his long lyrics. Poirion suggestively describes the lay as an 'affective commentary' on an event or adventure, which has its unifying focus exterior to the poem,[18] a description that would hold for most French complaints. Thus, the French poems make unelaborated reference to crucial events outside the works: the lover complains of the lady's treatment of him, or the lady praises the lover's behaviour, but the actions referred to are not narrated. Chaucer's *Complaint to His Lady* is like this; however, the lack of specificity perhaps bothered his concretizing imagination, for in three of his other long lyrics he provides a narrative introduction to which he ties the lover's complaint. The *Complaint unto Pity*, the *Complaint of Mars*, and *Anelida and Arcite* all open with stories that set the stage for formal complaints. Chaucer seems to have developed this organizational pattern independently, though perhaps guided in part by the model of Machaut's *Remede de Fortune* and *Fonteinne amoureuse* in which the formal complaints are part of extended stories. In the *Remede* the lover is so abashed by his experience with his lady that he retreats to the Parc de Hesdin where he unburdens himself in a 576-line 'Complainte,' while the narrator of the *Fonteinne* is awakened one morning by a lover who delivers an 800-line screed, also labelled 'Complainte.' Nevertheless, in these poems the lengthy complaints are subordinate parts of much longer works, while the complaints culminate and dominate Chaucer's three poems.

The first eight stanzas of *Complaint unto Pity* constitute perhaps the first narrative that Chaucer wrote; moreover, as already discussed, it is the only developed personification allegory in his poetry. The opposition of Pity and Cruelty supplies the chief theme. The lover, having gone to Pity's home to deliver a formal complaint about Love, finds Pity 'dead, and buried in an herte' (14). Since the lady's personified characteristics, who surround the hearse, are all 'confedered ... by bond of Cruelte' (52), he realizes that it is useless to present his grievance to them. Instead, he concludes the poem by revealing to the reader the nine-stanza Bill of Complaint, mostly directed against Cruelty.

The whole poem is in rime royal, a ballade stanza. Significant precedents for its allegory are found in the imagery of certain Machaut ballades.[19] And the nine-stanza rime royal complaint which the allegory introduces, as I have mentioned, falls into three equal ballade-like sections, each of which has a separate development and concludes with a couplet rhyming in -*eyne*. In the first set of three stanzas, the lover declares that Pity by right should help him oppose Cruelty. The second set constitutes a direct plea to the lady for mercy. And in the third section the lover resolves that despite the great pain he suffers, he will be faithful. 'Pleyne' and 'peyne' provide the concluding rhymes in the last two sections, and death, pain, and woe become leitmotifs in the last (99–119), recapitulating themes of the whole poem: 'My *peyne* is this' (99), 'encrese my *woo*' (103), 'my *deth* and than my bere' (105), 'parcel of my *peyne*' (106), 'Unto my *deth*' (112), '*peyne* or *woo*' (116), 'for your *deth* I may wel wepe and *pleyne'* (118), 'herte sore and ful of besy *peyne'* (119). The repetitions provide a semantic counterpart to the refrains and continued rhymes in the ballades.

The *Complaint of Mars* has the same story-complaint pattern as *Complaint unto Pity*, but both story and complaint are more elaborate, making it more than twice as long. In total the ingenious combination of lyric and narrative elements that make up *Complaint to Mars* is unique; at the same time most aspects of it have strong precedents in the French. The well-defined organization is formally marked by modern editors. A four-stanza proem prefaces an eighteen-stanza story, both parts in rime royal. The ensuing complaint has a one-stanza introduction preceding five ballade-like units, which Skeat calls 'terns.' Its stanzas are essentially an expanded rime royal, consisting of nine decasyllabic lines rhyming *aabaabbcc*.[20] The narrative point of view in the work is complex. Whereas throughout *Complaint unto Pity* the lover is the first-person speaker, the story prefatory to Mars's first-person complaint is told in the third person by a bird-narrator. The evident point of introducing the bird is to tie the poem to the Valentine tradition, which featured the mating of birds.[21] There are, of course, many talking birds in the Old and Middle French tradition of love poetry, though this bird is especially articulate. He (she?) begins with an aubade warning to birds abed; then his warning mutates into an imprecation to his fellows to prepare for their Valentine's Day selection of mates. While they are preparing, says the bird, he will tell 'the sentence of the compleynt, at the leste, / That woful Mars made atte departyng / Fro fresshe Venus' (24–6). Then he relates not only the complaint but the complex story that gave rise to it.

The story is remarkably clever in blending the planetary conjunction of Venus and Mars with the divine lovers' rendezvous and parting. Wolfgang Clemen speaks of the admirable art 'with which at each stage astronomical conceptions ... woven subtly and aptly in, were used to establish the parallels.' He goes on to admire the effect of determinism Chaucer achieves; the spontaneous feeling of the lovers which appears to control 'is constantly being related to a second plane on which nothing whatever happens by choice and everything is bound by immutable law.'[22] The main problem with the latter part of this compelling formulation is that the sentiments of the lovers, being mechanically subordinated to the highly patterned astronomical action, have little independent vitality and are therefore of little interest. There are admittedly successful parts when all levels are realized both separately and together, as in the wonderful concurrence of the astrological, the mythological, and the romantic when Mars and Venus hie them to bed, a true conjunction of courtly planets:

> This worthi Mars, that is of knyghthod welle,
> The flour of feyrnesse lappeth in his armes,
> And Venus kysseth Mars, the god of armes. (75–7)

They are at one as planets, divine powers, and lovers. Then, in an ingenious complication, Phebus – god, sun, and meddling gossip – approaches the 'mansion' in which they are joined, ready to reveal their misbehaviour to the world. His coming evokes a rich literary context suggesting both the aubade situation of lovers at dawn and the myth of Vulcan and his net.

But mainly the astronomical pattern controls, and the story is adjusted to it. The result is not a sense of determinism, but comedy. Thus, one hardly feels the lovers are victimized when, the pace of Mars the planet having slowed and that of Venus having accelerated, the poet presents us with a knightly lover weighed down by his armour:

> He throweth on his helm of huge wyghte,
> And girt him with his swerd, and in his hond
> His myghty spere, as he was wont to fyghte,
> He shaketh so that almost hit towond.
> Ful hevy was he to walken over lond;
> He may not holde with Venus companye
> But bad her fleen lest Phebus her espye. (99–105)

It is hard to feel sorry for a clumsy or adipose Mars who cannot walk or handle his weaponry.

In the story of *Complaint of Mars* the intellectual problem of coordinating the lover's actions with the astronomical situation clearly has precedence over affective and human implications, so that Chaucer devotes his imagination primarily to a witty working out of the correspondences. A similar 'metaphysical' spirit is an important strain in the Machaut tradition. One might instance such matters as Machaut's repetitions of 'dure' in 'Complainte I', where the word-play rather than the lover's sentiment seems the poet's chief concern, or the lover's pride in the *Fonteinne amoureuse* in the hundred different rhymes of his complaint, which effectively obscures his anguish. In Machaut's work mathematical and phonetic patterns and puzzles often are constitutive. In the music of a rondeau, 'Ma fin est mon commencement / Et mon commencement ma fin,'[23] the poet-composer imitates the text's meaning by having the last half of all three voices of the music mirror the first half. In the *Dit de la Harpe* thirty virtues of the lady correspond to thirty strings on the harp.[24] In other works numerous acrostics and anagrams comparably identify the personages represented.[25] In a ballade, for instance, Machaut spells out the lady's name (Jehane) with numbers: 'Et scez tu, comment on l'apelle? / .xiij., .v. double, .j. avec lie, / Et .viij. et .ix.' / 'And do you know her name? Thirteen, twice five, one happily, and eight and nine.'[26] His followers evinced the same spirit. Deschamps was quite fond of enigmas; Froissart's *L'Orloge amoureus* comprises an elaborate set of correspondences between a love situation and the parts of a clock; and both writers were proud of their virtuouso rhyming feats.

Machaut's vision of the world, states Poirion, is 'dominated by mathematics and astrology.'[27] This appears in various ways in his music, in his word games, and in imagery, like that which connects the lover's weeping with planetary influence. In Chaucer's works the metaphysical urge is manifested in the alphabetical scheme of Chaucer's *ABC*, and perhaps in numerological structuring of numerous works, as in *Anelida and Arcite* discussed below. But he displays the metaphysical spirit of Machaut and his fellows most ostensibly in the story and structure of the *Complaint of Mars*.

In Mars's complaint proper, each of the five terns has a distinct ballade-like development, as Skeat recognizes when he gives each a separate title. He calls the first three stanzas 'Devotion,' the second three 'A Lady in Fear and Woe,' and the third three 'Instability of Happiness.' In these sections Clemen finds a progressive departure from the convention of the complaint, the departure becoming especially marked when Mars comes to question God's treatment of lovers:

> To what fyn made the God, that sit so hye,
> Benethen him love other companye,
> And streyneth folk to love, malgre here hed?
> And then her joy, for oght I can espye,
> Ne lasteth not the twynkelyng of an ye.   (218–22)

Clemen states that 'it would be vain to look for a stanza like this in any comparable French poem';[28] for one thing, he says, 'it is unusual in this type of poem for the poet as it were to challenge God Himself.' This is not quite accurate. The tone and burden of Mars's lament surely is recognizable; it is that of the complaining Boethius, who in the *Consolation of Philosophy* insistently questions divine justice. In lodging his complaint against God, Mars is like many a lover of the tradition who plays the part of the cosmic complainer Boethius, blind to the divine rationale. Perhaps the most notable appearance of the Boethian complainer in Middle French poetry occurs in the discussion of Fortune between Esperance and the lover in *Remede de Fortune* (2403–2812). More directly relevant to *Complaint of Mars*, however, is the lover's questioning of God's ways in the *Jugement du roy de Behaigne*. There the knight, in exculpating the lady for her betrayal, explains, 'Nature et Dieus firent grant ignorance ... / Quant il firent si tres belle semblance / Sans loyauté' / 'Nature and God did a very stupid thing ... when they made such a beautiful face without loyalty' (809–12). Mars expresses virtually the same sentiments in the fourth 'tern' of his complaint when, after comparing his longing for Venus to the desire of men for the priceless brooch of Thebes, he states that the fatal attraction of the brooch was attributable not to it but to its maker; so also it is with the beauty of Venus, which is leading him to his death:

> She was not the cause of myn adversite,
> But he that wroghte her, also mot I the,
> That putte such a beaute in her face. (266–8)

It is both natural and in accord with the French conventions for distracted, despairing lovers to blame the Creator for their woes, and instead of exploring the philosophical implications one should probably see in this a feature of characterization.

Chaucer drew directly from Statius' Latin the image of 'The Brooch of Thebes,' which Skeat adopts as a title for the fourth section of Mars's complaint,[29] but both the image and the sentiments expressed in connection with it accord with the French lyric convention. The pattern of development in the three stanzas, moreover, is typical of the ballade: the first stanza introduces the fatal brooch, the second locates the source of its bane in the maker, and the third applies the lesson to Mars's situation. And the final section of the complaint, which Skeat calls 'An Appeal for Sympathy,' has particularly strong ballade relationships: modelled on conventional appeals for pity, it closely parallels Machaut's ballade 'Plourez, dames,' which was quoted and discussed in the first chapter. The opening stanza of the French, in its request for the sympathy of ladies, is especially like Chaucer's second:

And ye, my ladyes, that ben true and stable,
Be wey of kynde, ye oughten to be able
To have pite of folk that be in peyne.
Now have ye cause to clothe yow in sable,
Sith that youre emperise, the honurable,
Is desolat; wel oghte ye to pleyne.
Now shulde your holy teres falle and reyne.
Alas, your honour and your emperise,
Negh ded for drede ne can her not chevise! (281–9)

The petition to ladies for tears and for them to dress in funereal black, and the warning of the imminent death of the one to be mourned, bolster the more general parallels to 'Plourez, dames.'

Anelida and Arcite is a third poem by Chaucer in which a narrative sets the stage for a lengthy complaint. In this case there are manifest indications that Chaucer planned to continue the incomplete poem well beyond the story-complaint sequence.[30] I have argued that, following the pattern of Machaut's *Fonteinne amoureuse* and other works, the complete poem would have included a 'comfort' addressed to Anelida as a set piece balancing her formal complaint.[31] Of the poem as we have it, the 210 lines that lead up to the complaint are in rime royal, conventionally split by editors into three stanzas of invocation and twenty-seven of story. Another way of dividing the same part is in three 70-line sections: the epic background is presented in 70 lines, and Queen Anelida is introduced precisely at line 71. The next 140 lines tell her troubles; the first 70 relate her devotion to Arcite, the second 70 his treason to her. The ensuing 140-line complaint recited by Anelida also clearly divides into two even parts. The first 350 lines, then, fall into five 70-line groups, and there follows a stanza that looks forward to further events. Were Chaucer to follow out the balanced scheme built on sevens and tens as he had begun, he might well have expanded the work to 700 lines, including 210 more lines of narrative and 140 of 'comfort.' For the numerical scheme, precedents abound in all kinds of medieval poetry,[32] including the Middle French; for the balancing of complaint and comfort, as well as for the story-complaint pattern, Machaut is the most obvious precedent.[33]

The epic opening is based mostly on the *Teseida*, but when Chaucer speaks of Anelida he presents the conventional lyric situation of the lady-love betrayed. A stanza of one of the poems by 'Ch' shows another version of the cast-off lady:

Fauls Apyus, pires que Lichaon,
Sans foy, sans droit, compaignon de Judas,
Cuers d'Erode, voulenté de Noiron,
Je vail Dido parlant a Eneas,
Lasse et deserte; ainsi laissie m'as
Seule, esgaree, ou de tous biens mendie
A cuer dolent et a couleur changie,
Plus que triste, de maulx avironnee.
Ma plaisance est voie desesperee.
En povreté gist la fin de ma vie,
Car cuer de pierre a perverse pensee.
Jone, m'amas, et vieille, m'as guerpie.

False Apius, worse than Lycaon,[34] without faith, without justice, fellow of Judas, heart of Herod, will of Nero – I am like Dido speaking to Aeneas, dejected and deserted. Thus have you left me alone, lost, where I am deprived of all good, with sorrowing heart and changed complexion, more than sad, beset by evils; my pleasure is a path of despair. In poverty lies the end of my life, for a heart of stone has wicked thoughts; young, you loved me, and old, you have cast me off.[35]

Love complaints by ladies in many states, including that of advancing age, are found in numerous Middle French lyrics.[36]

Scholars have associated Anelida's complaint with Machaut's *Lay de plour* and *Lay de la souscie*; in the first the lady weeps over a dead lover, in the second she laments a separation.[37] But more relevant than these is Machaut's chant royal 'Amis, je t'ay tant amé et cheri,' whose text was presented in the last chapter, which provides a precedent for all of Chaucer's betrayed ladies, and particularly for Anelida's formal lament. Her image of the sword of sorrow piercing her heart, mentioned three times, evokes the steel-edged heart in Machaut's refrain:[38]

Cuer de marbre, couronné d'aÿmant,
Ourlé de fer, à la pointe asserée. (9–10, 19–20, etc.)

Anelida's lament has much in common with the chant otherwise. Machaut's lady begins by recalling how she wholly loved her 'amis,' but that where she expected bliss she found only pain, for he now ignores her. Praising his beauty, she confesses her continuing affection and consequent suffering for him; but then she worries that such professions of love are inappropriate for a woman. In the last stanza she renounces both him and love, only to confess at the very end that she would like to have him forever. Anelida makes comparable points at greater length, her complaint being more than twice as long.

One significant parallel to the French chant royal is found in Anelida's desire to behave in a way appropriate to her sex:

> And shal I preye and weyve womanhede? –
> Nay! Rather deth than do so foul a dede! –
> And axe merci, gilteles – what nede?
> And yf I pleyne what lyf that I lede,
> Yow rekketh not; that knowe I out of drede;
> And if that I to yow myne othes bede
> For myn excuse, a skorn shal be my mede.
> Your chere floureth, but it wol not sede;
> Ful longe agoon I oghte have taken hede.   (299–307)

Only the proverb-like image of the visage that blooms but bears no fruit has no parallel in the chant.[39]

The metrics of Anelida's complaint are more complex than in any other verse of Chaucer. There are twelve nine-line stanzas that have but two rhymes each in the scheme *aabaabbab*, plus two sixteen-line stanzas that also use just two rhymes. Adding to the intricacy, two of the stanzas have internal rhyme; in each of their nine-line units there are twenty-seven different words that rhyme. As was discussed earlier, the lines of these stanzas might be cut into short lines such as those found in many lays and virelays. For the complaint as a whole there is no generic counterpart in the French forms; in size it is most comparable to the lay, while the editorial division of the mostly uniform stanzas into six-stanza units of 'strophe' and 'antistrophe' suggests a double chant royal. In the final analysis, in its medley of metrical strategems the versification is unique, but all details have counterparts in the formes fixes, and there is no question about its French affiliations. Nor is there any doubt of its dazzling success as a display of poetic prowess of the kind the Middle French writers most prized. While it is doubtful that any French poet at the time would have thought to produce a work so idiosyncratic in form, there is some justice in W.P. Ker's hyperbolic claim that 'the lyrical complaint of Anelida is the perfection of everything that had been tried in the French school.'[40]

'THE BOOK OF THE DUCHESS' AS A LYRIC STRUCTURE

Three of the extended complaints in Chaucer's verse are attached to explanatory narratives; they tell of the funeral of Pity, the conjunction of Mars and Venus, and the betrayal of Anelida. These stories give point to the lovers' complaints that follow; in contrast to Machaut's separate complaints and lays, where the occasion for complaint lies outside the poem, they bring the focus of the laments into the work. Chaucer did not complete *Anelida and Arcite*, and he evidently gave up composing narrative-complaints after it. Meanwhile, however, he had begun working with a different, more ambitious type of poetic construct; he had composed the *Book of the Duchess*, a work that unites story and complaint, presenting them together in a dream vision in octosyllabic couplets. Despite the traditional association of the couplets with chivalric romance, it is a mistake to see the poem as essentially narrative, for just as with the complaint poems the story is subordinate. It exists primarily to give point and focus to the lyric elements: the dreamer follows the hunt, meets with the Black Knight, and engages him in conversation, giving him the opportunity of celebrating his love and expressing his grief in the body of the poem. It is primarily an elegiac meditation on human loss rather than a story of the narrator's experience.

Chaucer derives much of the substance of his elegy from dits by Machaut. He also finds in those poems models for his complex lyric meditation constructed around a thin narrative. This is well shown by two of the earliest and most successful of them, the *Jugement du roy de Behaigne* and *Remede de Fortune*, which are the works Chaucer used most for specific phraseology in the *Duchess*.

As both the number of extant manuscripts and the many imitations of it show, the *Jugement du roy de Behaigne* was Machaut's most popular dit, and Chaucer evidently had the poem in his mind as well as he did any French literary work.[41] Its narrative element involves a debate on a question of love: who suffers more, the lover whose beloved dies or the one who is deserted? The real point of the discussion is not to determine a 'winner,' but rather to consider why love ends and what the consequences are. Since bereavement or betrayal is theoretically the only way for fin' amors to terminate, the question as posed comprehends the problem. In the background of Machaut's poem are many Old French tençons and jeux partis, which are lyric debates on questions of love; the longer Latin debate-poems that are more immediate models for the work are also highly lyric, featuring lush landscapes and lovely ladies.[42] In all such poems the concern is first to set the scene appropriately and to establish the situation, and then to explore the problem. *Behaigne* accordingly opens in the springtime with a bird which leads the narrator into a locus amoenus; the two main figures, a lady and a knight, each properly described, are then brought on the scene for their debate. The personal histories they narrate are punctuated by extensive descriptions and complaints, which keep the narrative aspect subservient. When their dispute reaches an impasse they proceed to the Castle of Durbui to have the question judged by King Jean of Bohemia. Poetic substance at this stage is provided by praise of the beauty of the castle and of the ideal character of the king, and subsequently by expression of sentiments about Love by such allegorical figures as Youth, Loyalty, and Reason. Such matters are relevant to the central problem as part of its social and ethical background.

Many passages in *Behaigne* are appropriate for individual set pieces. Machaut, however, does not insert any distinct lyric forms in the poem, but instead accommodates and accentuates the lyricism by using a semi-stanzaic verse form throughout, rhyming *aaab-bbbc-cccd*, etc., with short fourth lines regularly interrupting the decasyllables. Several poets followed Machaut's lead in employing this versification in dits amoureux,[43] though Machaut did not use the verse again in his dits, nor did Chaucer use it. In the *Duchess* Chaucer instead employs the versification of Machaut's next long poem, the *Remede de Fortune*, which has octosyllabic couplets interspersed with set pieces in the formes fixes.[44]

I have already discussed *Remede* at some length; it has an important relationship to the *Duchess*, centring on the Boethian discussion between Esperance and the lover. We may take the whole poem as a 'Consolation of Hope,' in which the promises of Esperance fortify the lover against all the torments of his eternally doubtful state. The lyric spirit of the *Remede*, which dominates the narrative, is manifested not only in the separate set pieces but also throughout in extended passages in the couplets that could be made into individual lyrics. One such passage, Amant's report of his first sight of the lady, was quoted previously. Other examples of discrete passages that could stand alone are Esperance's enumeration of the biens of Fortune (2735–72), the lady's exposition of proper conditions for the lover to request mercy (3774–98), and

the lover's praise of Esperance (2294–2326). According to my analysis of
Remede, there are twenty-two developed lyric passages in the poem in
both formes fixes and couplets, amounting to 1,884 of the 4,296 lines.[45]
An additional feature contributing to the lyricism of the work is the
impressive music that Machaut wrote to accompany seven of the set
pieces. In a presentation of the poem, the music would not only add a
lyric dimension to the text but would also greatly extend the time devoted to the set pieces.

As well as providing a model for lyric discontinuity in the *Book of the
Duchess*, Machaut's *Remede* supplies important substance for the Black
Knight's complaints against Fortune. For other aspects of his treatment
of the subject, *Behaigne* is an important precedent. The debate in that
poem systematically investigates how a love affair ends through a comparison of two exemplary cases. The process of analysis has a somewhat
academic air as the two despondent lovers become deeply engaged in
the problem of exactly who is suffering more. In the *Duchess* Chaucer
is more naturalistic, but he too explores with some thoroughness main
aspects of his subject, the loss of the loved one. To begin with he presents
three parallel instances of grief and loss – the narrator's unspecified grief
that he has suffered for eight years, the death of Seys (narrated in an
Ovidian exemplum), and the loss of the hart in the hunt of Octavian –
which provide reflectors that reveal different facets of human loss. In
the Black Knight's story which ensues, his particular bereavement is
explored in conventional terms that have the effect of universalizing it.

The *Duchess* is a succession of more or less lyric passages, beginning
with the dreamer's complaint about his sleeplessness, but the Black
Knight's presentation is most obviously made up of them. Like the lover
in *Remede de Fortune*, he recites poems of his own composition, one a
statement about death (475–86), another a sample of the verse he sent
the lady (1175–80). Both are in octosyllabic lines, varying in rhyme just a
bit from the couplets. Though the rhyme sequences are not strange –
aabbaccdccd (475–86) and *aabbaa* (1175–80) – in total the pieces are anomalous and undeveloped, in contrast to the elaborate pieces of *Remede*;
perhaps they should be seen as metonymic representations of larger
poems. In the continuing couplets, though, the Black Knight's complaints, his description of the lady, and his account of his early devotion
to Love and the lady comprise very well developed lyric passages. The
149-line complaint in which he describes his anguish in a series of oxy-
morons and then launches a volley of invective against Fortune (561–709)
might be converted into a stanzaic piece like a Machaut complaint; and

the 225-line passage characterizing the lady, combining external and moral description (notatio and effictio) (817–1041), could readily be adapted to a lay in praise of the lady. Chaucer chose instead to disrupt the couplets as little as possible.

In the Black Knight's complaint and his description of the lady, Chaucer was working largely with comparable passages in *Behaigne* and *Remede*. He also draws phrases and images from Machaut's lyrics. Some of these minor correspondences have an interesting relevance to the *Duchess*, while others seem simply dug from the mine that Chaucer found in Machaut's oeuvre. The *Lay de Confort*, which is the origin of the Black Knight's planet-induced tears, has indirect historical relevance to the death of the duchess. The image of the tears was perhaps meant to sound a major chord in John of Gaunt's memory, for it is probable that Machaut had sent the lay to the Duke of Berry when he was a prisoner in London in the early 1360s. The poem treats of the longing of the duke's wife for him. John of Gaunt and Chaucer, who were about the same age as the duke, may well have been among those in the company when this poem of separation was first read, in which case the striking image could have had a particular poignancy for John.[46]

The three motets of Machaut that Chaucer echoes in the course of his complaint against Fortune do not have similar historical relevance, but Chaucer's familiarity with the motets is itself significant since the motet is not a form that an unmusical poet would have composed. It is unfailingly musical, with three voices – triplum, motetus, and tenor – that are assigned poetic texts of different verse-forms to be sung at the same time. With the sense of the words suppressed by this simultaneous singing, Chaucer hardly could have learned the motet texts from performance. Nor would their complex melodies have drawn his special interest. His use of them, then, strengthens the image of his reading through the Machaut manuscripts methodically, not just surveying them for particular works or picking up odd passages aurally.

We perhaps may speculate that the motets made a stylistic as well as a verbal contribution to the knight's presentation. They provide models for his differing rhetorical stances, which help to articulate his long monologues. For instance, his direct address to Death in his 'maner song' is based in part on a comparable apostrophe in Machaut's third motet:

> He! Mors, com tu es haïe
> De moy, quant tu as ravie
> Ma joie, ma druerie,

> Mon solas,
> Par qui je sui einsi mas
> Et mis de si haut si bas,
> Et ne me pouiés pas
>   Assaillir. (1–8)

Ah! Death, how I hate you since you have snatched away my joy, my love, my comfort, which has so stunned me and thrown me down from so high to so low, and yet you couldn't strike me (dead).

These lines come from the 'triplum' of *Motet III*; the motetus, which would have been presented simultaneously, involves a commentary on Love ('Love, which just wounded my heart, did me a great wrong,' etc.), and the tenor text, also sung at the same time, is a rhetorical question ('Wherefore am I not dead?'). The Black Knight's song reflects the question of the tenor as well as the direct address of the triplum:

> Allas, deth, what ayleth the
> That thou noldest have taken me,
> Whan thou toke my lady swete,
> That was so fair, so fresh, so fre,
> So good, that men may wel se
> Of al goodnesse she had no mete? (481–6)

In *Motet VIII*, which the Black Knight echoes in his invective against Fortune, Machaut again uses varying stances in the different voices. The triplum is a comment about Fortune composed of vivid images, as in the following lines (cf *BD*, 626–9):

> C'est fiens couvers de riche couverture,
> Qui dehors luist et dedens est ordure.
> Une ydole est de fausse pourtraiture,
> Où nuls ne doit croire ne mettre cure. (7–10)

She is excrement hidden under a rich covering, which shines without and stinks within. She is an idol of false portraiture in whom one ought to have no belief or interest.

In contrast to this third-person comment, the motetus involves direct address to Fortune ('Ha! Fortune!'), and the tenor a meditative lament

('And there is no one to help me'). The knight comparably mixes colourful vituperation (See BD 620–41) with repeated oxymora that characterize his depressed condition ('My song ys turned to pleynynge,' etc., 599–615), rhetorical questions ('How myghte I fare werre?' 616), and exclamations ('Allas!' 598, 619, 661). In other words, he uses the various voices of the complaining lover that are characteristic of the lyrics, the polyphonic variety of the voices in the motets being particularly suggestive for his long complaint.

Finally, Chaucer accentuates the lyricism of his poem by using striking images from the short works, drawing them readily from non-pertinent contexts: for invective against Fortune, he applies a scorpion image (BD, 636–41) from the triplum of Motet IX (45–8), which is a Latin text wholly addressed to Satan; and he draws liar and monster images (628, 630–1) from 'Il m'est avis' (12–14), a moral ballade. In these cases we must think that isolated images simply arose from Chaucer's retentive memory, with contexts not especially pertinent to the Duchess, to enrich the description of Fortune.

In the total of their word-for-word borrowing, Machaut's lyrics make a minor contribution to the Duchess; none the less, they help demonstrate a major point, for it is telling that the rhetorical stances of the speakers and the materials of their statements adapt readily to Chaucer's poem. As with the dits amoureux of Machaut and his French followers, the components of the Duchess are largely compatible with the lyrics of the mode. Its narrative is an attractive aspect, but it is slender, serving mainly to provide an explicit dramatic setting for the essentially lyric passages. Accordingly, the Black Knight is little different from the generic complainer, though like the poetic representatives of Machaut's patrons he tends to be less awkward than some. Moreover, as is appropriate for lyric, the situation and the development of the poem are relatively static, with the content highly figurative and emotive.[47]

THE 'HOUSE OF FAME' AND 'PARLIAMENT OF FOWLS'

If one recognizes that the Middle French dits amoureux are primarily chains of lyric passages, it is not much of a leap to see the Book of the Duchess as similarly constituted since it draws so much of its substance from poems of Machaut. With the House of Fame and the Parliament of Fowls it is a different matter, for their dependence on contemporary dits is less apparent. Nevertheless, there are basic features that derive from the French. Chaucer again designs the structures of these works to serve the themes rather than the narratives, and he again uses versification typical of the French verse. And though the poems do not participate in the Machaut mode to the degree that the *Duchess* does, French elements are important.

The pattern of action in the *House of Fame* has no clear parallels in Machaut, but it has been associated with two French works of closely related writers, the *Temple d'Onnour* of his disciple Froissart[48] and Nicole de Margival's *Panthère d'Amours*,[49] a poem that Machaut had learned from. Like Chaucer's poem, these are works in which a dreamer visits a Wonderland, and learns from what he sees and hears. The *Panthère* has much the more interesting relationship to the *House of Fame*.[50] In it and Chaucer's work the dreamers are instructed initially by what they are shown, then by lectures, and in the end by visiting edifices belonging to traditional personifications (Fortune in Nicole, Fame in Chaucer). A major difference between the narrators is that Nicole's lover-narrator is more personally involved in the happenings than Chaucer's dreamer, who is a witness seeking 'tidings' of Love.

There is another vision poem, a five-stanza serventois, 'En avisant les eschés Atalus,'[51] which provides particularly intriguing parallels to the *House of Fame*. They are intriguing both because of the strangeness of the poem and because they pose the possibility that Chaucer's work has some non-courtly origins in the puy. The poem is from the 1360s or before. It is found in University of Pennsylvania manuscript French 15, whose contents have considerable relevance to the literary environment of mid-fourteenth-century England and may have been particularly known to Chaucer.[52] This serventois does not have the coherent subject-matter of the *House of Fame*, all of whose episodes develop the theme of fame; but it does present a narrator who has a series of strange adventures very similar to those of Chaucer's dreamer, and like his are material for comic fantasy. The two poems also allude to a wide range of literary figures.[53]

The first action of the narrator in the serventois is to enter the beak of a giant eagle – a golden eagle which Theseus in another story had entered; he views within the marvellous statue Pygmalion made.[54] In the second stanza, with the eagle in flight, he looks out from the beak and sees various signs of the zodiac. Parallels to these unusual actions are found in Chaucer's much longer poem, in the first part 'Geffrey' views carved representations in a temple of Venus, and subsequently an eagle with golden plumes takes him through the air where he catches sight of the 'ayerrish bestes' – the zodiac again. Still another unusual correspondence is found in the later visits of both narrators to the House of Daedalus. It seems unlikely that parallels in such bizarre events could be the result of coincidence, but a simple imitation by Chaucer also seems improbable.

One gathers from the opening lines of the serventois that the vision that ensues results from the narrator's dazed contemplation of the problems of chess:

> En avisant les eschés Atalus
> et tous les trais qu'il fist soubtillement,
> je me boutay en l'aigle Theseus
> pour aviser un ymage excellent.
> Et si sachiez, par le mien serement,
> que c'estoit celle que fist Pymalion,
> car elle avoit les cheveux d'Absalon,
> les yeulx jaspar, corps, port, et vis d'Elaine.
> Et si chantoit trop miex une chançon
> *que onques ne fist Orpheus ne Seraine.*
>
> Mais elle fist comme Herodés ou plus,
> et si avoit vestu le vestement
> de Dalida et Taÿs, que vestus
> furent d'orgueil en fait et en jouvent.
> Parmi le bec de l'aiglete patent
> choisi Leo qui le tint par le gron.
> Avec Cancer si repris compaignon,
> Capricornus qui marcheant fu de graine,
> que m'ayda mieulx en ma conclusion
> *que onques ne fist Orpheus ne Seraine.* (1–20)

While pondering Atalus' game of chess and all the moves he subtly made, I pushed myself inside the eagle of Theseus in order to study a fine statue. On my word, I wish you to understand that this was the image that Pygmalion made, for it had the hair of Absolon, eyes of jasper, and the body, bearing, and face of Helen. And it sang a song much better than ever did Orpheus or the Siren.

But she acted as badly [as] or worse than Herodias, and she had donned the clothing of Dalila and Thaïs, who were clothed with the pride of deed and youth. Out through the open beak of the eagle I perceived Leo who held him [?] by the cloak. With Cancer I saw a companion Capricorn, who is a merchant of grain [the first sign of winter, when grain must be purchased], who helped me solve my problem better than ever did Orpheus or the Siren.

The subsequent stanzas present experiences that are no more coherent. The narrator alights from the eagle, sends a pigeon with a message from Solomon to Sheba, and at the sound of a trumpet sees Cupid jump on Jason's horse. The parallel to *House of Fame* is completed in the fifth and final stanza when the narrator goes into the House of Daedalus with its baffling means of exit:

La Mort happe Cupido et Venus,
et dansay tant qu'encore m'en repent,
car entrez sui en l'ostel Dedalus;
ne je ne sceu de quel part issir ent.
Ou lit Gauvain m'endormi longuement,
et la songay que veoye Sanson
rere tout jus, deffacier sa façon;
si tressaili, mais je veil qu'on me traine
se je ne fu mieux trompez a claron
qu'onques ne fist Orpheus ne Seraine. (40–50)

Death seized Cupid and Venus, and I danced so much that I still repent it, for I entered the house of Daedalus; and I did not know which way to leave. I slept long on the bed of Gawain, and I dreamt that I saw Samson lying there with his appearance marred [with his hair cut]; then I shuddered, and I wish to be drawn by horses if I wasn't more betrayed by the sound of a horn than ever was Orpheus or the Siren.

The horn awakens the narrator. In the Envoy he speaks of Amour's having put him in a hideous prison wherein he lost breath and sense.

When the reader finishes the work he may feel as outdone as the narrator, but there is a certain charm in the wild collocation of incidents and references. Its tone is hardly like Machaut; the fanciful use of allusion perhaps evokes Jean de le Mote's free use of names, and the form – five stanzas of ten decasyllables plus envoy – is thoroughly Middle French. The work was probably not written for the court, however; in the fourteenth century all of the five-stanza forms were especially practised in the puy, the serventois foremost.[55] For this reason, it is of signal interest that this bizarre if intriguing vision poem is a legitimate analogue to the *House of Fame.* It tempts one to add to the surfeit of theories the possibility that this vision poem of Chaucer is itself a product of the puy, and that the mysterious 'man of gret auctorite' who appears just before the poem breaks off is the 'Prince' of the puy.[56]

At the same time the strange serventois is no typical lyric; its most lyrical features are the versification and the tuneful refrain. Its substance is mainly a series of incidents and sights briefly described; there seems to be no theme that provides occasion for lyric development. The *House of Fame*, of course, has such a theme in the exploration of the nature of fame. Before broaching the main subject, however, it introduces the vision with a meditation on dreams. The opening can profitably be compared with that of Machaut's *Lis et Marguerite*, a lyric dit probably composed for Marguerite of Flanders. Both poems begin with long sentences in which intellectual inquiry is discussed – inquiry into the nature of dreams in Chaucer's poem, into the colours of flowers in the French work. There is a striking similarity in expression, first of all in expressions of puzzlement over *why* one thing and *why* another:

> And why th'effect folweth of somme,
> And of somme hit shal never come;
> Why this is an avision
> And why this a revelacion,
> Why this a drem, why that a sweven,
> And noght to every man lyche even;
> Why this a fantome, why these oracles,
> I not ...   (5–12)

> Pour quoy les unes sont blanchettes,
> L'autre est jaune, l'autre est percette,
> L'autre ynde, l'autre vermillette,
> N'i a celle qui n'ait verdour
> En esté et diverse odour,
> Ou qui n'ait ou greine ou semence,
> Ce seroit moult belle science.   (4–10)

Why some are white, another yellow, another blue-grey, another dark blue, another vermilion, nor is there one which lacks foliage and distinctive perfume in summer, or which does not have seed or pollen – this would be wonderful knowledge

In the *House of Fame* the narrator goes on to say that he will not busy his brains about the miracles of dreams, using terms quite like those that Machaut used in representing scientists who painfully inquire into the secrets of nature:

> But whoso of these miracles
> The causes knoweth bet then I,
> Devyne he, for I certeinly
> Ne kan hem noght, ne never thinke
> To besily my wyt to swinke,
> To know of hir signifiaunce
> The gendres, neyther the distaunce
> Of tymes of hem, ne the causes,
> Or why this more then that cause is. (12–20)

> Mais je ne congnois creature
> Qui tant des secrez de Nature
> Sache, qui me sceust aprendre
> Pour quoy c'est ne la cause rendre,
> Comment que c'est chose certeinne
> Que pluseurs s'en sont mis en peinne
> Et fait tout leur pooir sans feindre,
> Mais onques ne poient ateindre
> Ad ce que la chose sceue
> Fust clerement et congneue. (11–20)

But I don't know anyone who knows so many of Nature's secrets that he can teach me why or tell me the cause, even though it is sure that many have taken pains and used all of their powers without stinting, but they never could achieve a clear knowledge and understanding of the thing.

In addition to the parallels in content, stylistic similarities include the loose, involved syntax, an unusual amount of enjambment, and numerous polysyllabic rhymes.

The opening of the *House of Fame* keynotes the style of the work; the same curious and diffident narrator speaks throughout. Despite the three-book structure and the invocations and the plentiful correspondences with the *Comedy*, Dante contributes minimally to the poetic effect, while the qualities of the dit amoureux show up in the versification, verbal style, and structural pattern. At the same time, though the eagle promises Geffrey tidings of love, after the first part of the poem the substance is hardly amorous and is not especially lyric. The connections with Middle French love poetry that we can impute to *House of Fame* are thus limited. Despite its French matrix one may feel that in it Chaucer is moving away from the lyricism of his French contemporaries. However, that movement is not carried through in three long poems that followed: the *Parliament of Fowls, Troilus and Criseyde*, and the *Legend of Good Women*. Indeed, the relationships become increasingly strong.

As with the two preceding dream poems, the narrative line in the *Parliament* is slender, its purpose being to facilitate thematic development; once more, the presentation of various aspects of the subject is made to cohere about the experience of the dreamer. In this case, the theme concerns the nature of love. The main types of love dealt with are love of the common profit, as celebrated in the Dream of Scipio; sexual love without procreative end, as seen in the Temple of Venus; and procreative love in various social guises represented by the different kinds of birds. The manner of development is similar to the earlier dream visions, but Chaucer changes one basic feature, the versification. For the first time he chooses to use the rime royal stanza throughout a long poem, except for the rondeau near the end.

In adopting a uniform stanza for his poem, Chaucer probably was influenced by Boccaccio's example in his stanzaic works, the *Filostrato* and *Teseida*. Evidence for his growing familiarity with Boccaccio is supplied by his adaptation of a passage of the *Teseida* for the garden and temple description in the *Parliament* (183–294). Nevertheless, Chaucer's stanza itself does not come from the Italian. However close ottava rima (*abababcc*) is superficially to rime royal (take out line 5 and you have rime royal), before he came to Boccaccio, Chaucer had used the seven-line stanza in both ballades and long complaint poems where its manifest source is the ballade. The difference in effect between ottava rima and rime royal is substantial, for the former has had all of its impressive successes, from Boccaccio to Byron, as a narrative stanza,[57] while the rime royal unit rose to popular use in the lyrical ballade. The consequent increased lyricality of Chaucer's verse over Boccaccio's is more strongly evidenced in *Troilus and Criseyde* than in the *Parliament*, as we will discuss in the next chapter. Nevertheless, the *Parliament* has much of the dit amoureux about it, including developed passages that with little alteration could be made into independent lyrics.

Beyond the essentially non-narrative structure of the poem, and the versification, the most obviously French aspects are associated with the bird debate. The discussion involving different types of birds has ana-

logues in dits that precede the Machaut tradition and in a poem of
Granson in which he imitated the *Parliament*.[58] The relationship to the
Middle French is most evident in the rivalry of three noble lovers (tercel
eagles) for a lady of great attraction (a formel eagle). The use of falcon-
class birds to represent nobility was well established in the current poetic
practice, the most relevant antecedent for the *Parliament* being Machaut's
Dit de l'alerion.[59] In that poem the narrator's lady-loves are figured successively by a sparrow hawk ('esprivier'), an alerion, an eagle, and a
gyrfalcon. Chaucer's poem features a variety of birds, but when the
falcons come on the scene the quality of the diction changes noticeably.
In contrast to the colourful colloquialism of the debate between the
different species of birds ('Al this is not worth a flye!'), the three tercel
eagles compete for the lovely formel in the refined language of court
poetry. Each of the three presents his case in a short set piece very like
myriad ballade requests for mercy. The royal tercel with bowed head
sues for the formel's love:

> Unto my soverayn lady, and not my fere,
> I chese, and chese with wil and hert and thought,
> The formel on youre hond, so wel iwrought,
> Whos I am al, and evere wol hire serve,
> Do what hire lest, to do me lyve or sterve;
>
> Besekynge hire of merci and of grace,
> As she that is my lady sovereyne;
> Or let me deye present in this place.
> For certes, longe I may nat lyve in payne,
> For in myn herte is korven every veyne.
> Havynge reward only to my trouthe,
> My deere herte, have of my wo sum routhe. (416–27)

He goes on professing his devotion and loyalty for two more stanzas.
The second tercel elaborates for two stanzas his greater devotion and
longer service (449–62), and the third in precise ballade length (463–83)
asserts that his love is the deepest and truest. Their diction and the form
of their statements have their origins in Middle French poems. The
following lines from a Machaut ballade represent a typical lover's declaration:

> Douce dame, tant vous aim et desir
> De cuer, de fait et d'amour fine et pure,

Que mi penser sont et tuit mi desir
En vous que j'aim seur toute creature.
  Et puis qu'Amours ad ce mis
M'a que je sui vos fins loiaus amis,
Dame, vueilliez en grace recevoir
Moy qui tous sui vostres sans decevoir.

Et je vous jur qu'honnourer, oubeir,
Amer, garder, sans penser mespresure,
Vous vueil de cuer et faire vo plaisir
Com vos amis qui d'autre amour n'ay cure.[60]   (1–12)

Sweet lady, I so love and desire you in my heart, in my deed, and in my love fine and pure, that my thoughts and all my desires are in you whom I love above every creature. And since Love has caused me to be your true loyal lover, lady, deign to receive me graciously, who am yours without deceit.

And I swear to you that from my heart I want to honour, obey, love, and protect you without thought of wrongdoing, and to do your pleasure as your lover who cares for none other.

Unless the lady loves him, the lover continues, he will never be cured. Similarly, each of the three tercels, having sworn his faith and service, attests that his life is in the formel's power. The story of the *Parliament* provides appropriate speakers and dramatic situations for the conventional ballade-like lovers' petitions.

The various other developed lyric passages of the *Parliament* have diverse origins, including the *Roman de la Rose* and the *De planctu naturae*; the Middle French stanza affects the basic character of all of them. And of course the contemporary French mode rules in the concluding rondeau with its standard thirteen-line form.[61] A French rubric designates its 'note,' which, the narrator believes, 'imaked was in Fraunce' (677).[62] The invocation of Saint Valentine in the rondeau again associates the *Parliament* with poems of Oton de Granson, whose work is considered below.

I have attempted to bring out the degree to which all of Chaucer's early compositions are essentially lyric in conception and, in much of their substance, largely inspired by the Machaut tradition. The Middle French mode inspired the verse-form and structure of the complaints and the dream poems, and it likewise accounts for a large part of their subject-matter, even of the eclectic *House of Fame* and *Parliament of Fowls*.

For virtually all of Chaucer's long verse before *Troilus and Criseyde* the basic inspiration plainly was French. That the influences are less clearcut in *Troilus* one can hardly dispute, since an Italian work was its main narrative model. After composing that work Chaucer drew on diverse native and Continental narrative types for the famous stories of the *Canterbury Tales*. The seemingly sudden development may suggest that a great transition takes place with the appearance of *Troilus* around 1386: a modern narrative Chaucer suddenly emerges triumphantly from medieval lyric Chaucer, the Italians acting as his literary mother and then as midwives to his English self, Machaut all forgotten. The 'Prologue' to the *Legend*, in the light of its manifest dependence on the French, is the most obvious obstruction to such a view; nevertheless, the 'Prologue' does not supply the most powerful argument against it. That is provided by *Troilus* itself.

CHAPTER FIVE

Machaut and His Tradition:
Troilus, the *Legend*,
and the *Tales*

Though Chaucer is particularly renowned today for his narrative powers, he began writing poetry in the style of the consummately lyrical Middle French court literature. First coming under the influence of writers like Jean de le Mote in Edward III's London, and then leading or joining the crowd who adopted Guillaume de Machaut as mentor and model, he was essentially a lyric poet right up to his composition of *Troilus and Criseyde*. The complaint poems and the dream poems indeed have stories, but they are stories that dramatize and give focus to the lyric-matter rather than dominating as in a fabliau or a saint's legend. It is much more true to the *Book of the Duchess* to read it as a series of lyric pieces characterized by discontinuity than to focus primarily on the progress of the Black Knight towards consolation. Of course some progress may be discerned, but it resembles that of an orchestrated sequence of lyric poems that shows a forward narrative movement. Such a narrative is always secondary to the thematic, characteristically lyric development.

THE BALLADE AND 'TROILUS AND CRISEYDE'

Troilus and Criseyde is the first work that Chaucer modelled on a strong narrative, *Il Filostrato*. In some ways he fortifies Boccaccio's story. He adds passages that foreground the Troy legend, as John A. Burrow has emphasized,[1] and also 'eches in' Pandarus' elaborate strategems, thereby introducing fabliau-like complexity to the plot, as well as a good amount of circumstantial detail which concretizes the action.[2] Yet it is an exaggeration to say with Burrow, 'For Chaucer as for other Ricardians, the story is the thing. *Troilus and Criseyde* is, above all, an incomparably vivid and authentic *narrative poem*.'[3] There is as much truth in the contrasting statement of Rossell Hope Robbins, who finds in *Troilus* 'an intricate and closely worked *dit amoureux*' – a series of lyric passages.[4] The fact is that *Troilus* is both a vivid narrative and an effective lyric sequence. Critics have long assumed and adequately recognized the first, but the second has not been apparent to them. None the less, I believe it to be demonstrable that *Troilus*, besides being Chaucer's most important manifestation of Italian narrative inspiration, represents the high point in his work in the French lyric mode. The most obvious witness to its lyric nature is the series of lyric set pieces it embodies. These are not decorations, but are essential to its nature, as is symptomatized by the pervasive debt of the poem to the French court mode for diction, imagery, sentiment, and characterization.

A cursory reading of *Troilus* turns up a number of lyric pieces: the two 'Cantici' of Troilus (books I and V), the song of Antigone, the prayers of petition and praise to Love and the planets (book III), the lovers' exchange of aubades, the 'Literae' of the two lovers (book V), the portraits of the characters (book IV), and the sequence of envoy and invocation in the epilogue. Closer analysis reveals many more 'developed lyric passages,' that is, essentially non-narrative sequences of verse which with moderate alteration could be made into separate short poems. In the whole work, counting conservatively, I have identified fifty-six which take up about a fifth of the total lines.[5] They are distributed quite evenly throughout, and each of the major characters – Troilus, Criseyde, and Pandarus as well as the narrator – delivers a substantial number of them (Pandarus, with ten, presents the fewest; Troilus presents twenty-six). The range of subjects in the set-pieces is comparable to that in Machaut's collection, the *Louange des dames*. While love predominates, there is some variety. Other topics of the *Troilus* pieces include instructions for composing a letter, a commentary on the value of dreams, and a discourse on fate and free will.

The regular recurrence of lyric passages throughout, and the fact that all the major speakers take advantage of the narrative situations to comment expressively or sententiously, so that each is in effect a lyric poet, imparts lyricality to Chaucer's entire work. A comparison with *Il Filostrato* helps make the point. In Boccaccio's poem there is no scarcity of set pieces; in it too almost 20 per cent of the work is occupied by developed lyric passages. But they are fewer (twenty-six as compared with fifty-six), they are much longer, and Troilo is the speaker in three-fourths of them. The effect of his lonely poetic gift is to set him off from the other characters as an idealist fallen among realists and cynics. He is not even closely connected with the narrator, who nominally identifies himself with Troilo. In seven of nine books Boccaccio's narrator goes right to the story with no prefatory comment, whereas at the beginning of all five books of *Troilus* Chaucer's narrator involves himself emotionally in the action, invoking, predicting, and otherwise commenting poetically. Along the way he constantly inserts sympathetic and instructive remarks ('Forthi ensample taketh of this man, / Ye wise, proude, and worthi folkes alle,' etc I 232 ff). It is paradoxical that Chaucer's narrator is much more effectively implicated in the story he tells than is Boccaccio's, for whom Troilo is professedly a surrogate.

The contrast between go-betweens is even more telling. Boccaccio's Pandaro is thoroughly prosaic in his practicality; none of his statements resembles a lyric poem. Chaucer's Pandarus is quite a composer of rime royal set pieces replete with the phraseology of Middle French lyric. In book II alone he recites one to advise Criseyde to make the most of time, another to report Troilus' full confession to Love, another to assure Troilus that when the oak or Criseyde finally falls there will be no getting up, and a fourth to tell Troilus in Ovidian and Horatian terms how to write a letter. Except for the first of these, suggested by two lines of *Il Filostrato*, there are no counterparts in Boccaccio. The Italian Criseida is only a little more poetic than Pandaro, delivering three set pieces in total, while the English Criseyde presents eleven. In book II she responds to Pandarus' advice to seize the day with a three-stanza complaint ('Allas for wo, why nere I ded?' II 409 ff), while her Italian counterpart briefly agrees with Pandarus' statement. When Pandarus departs from her shortly after this, there ensues a three-hundred-line representation of her progress towards love, culminating in her dream in a symbolic exchange of hearts (II 659–931); it is all a lyric flight, interrupted only by several stanzas indebted to Boccaccio in which practical considerations obtrude. At the same time, in contrast to the dissonance between lyric and narrative in *Il Filostrato*, mostly attributable to the coarseness of Criseida and Pandaro, the frequent emotive and reflective statements of each of Chaucer's characters tend to be consonant with those of the others and of a piece with the apparent spirit of the story.

Even granting the basic role of these lyric pieces in Chaucer's story, though, what evidence is there that contemporary French poetry was the major influence on the lyricism of *Troilus*? Boccaccio is the more important source for the passages themselves, offering a substantial precedent for twice as many as Machaut does (twelve to five). The crucial fact in the matter of influence is that the structures and content of almost all the passages – including those inspired by Boccaccio, Dante, and Petrarch – are marked by the conventional forms and materials of contemporary French poetry.

It is of first importance, of course, that Chaucer's rime royal stanza finds its origin in contemporary French lyric poetry, being Machaut's and le Mote's favourite for the ballade, while Boccaccio's ottava rima is primarily a narrative stanza. Furthermore, when we consider the structures of the full passages, it is striking how many in *Troilus* conform to the length and rhetorical pattern typical of the ballade. In rhetorical structure, as already discussed, the Middle French ballade characteristically consists of the three-part logical chain that Poirion describes, each stanza making one link.[6] The poem usually develops a single theme around a central image or set of images, a literary exemplum, a personification allegory, or an uncomplicated combination of these. To illustrate the form and the way in which Chaucer makes use of it in *Troilus*, we might consider four ballade-length specimens: two separate rime royal ballades, one by Machaut and one by Chaucer, and two developed lyric passages from *Troilus*. All four of these are on a theme particularly germane to Chaucer's story, that of loyalty in love.

Like 'Plourez, dames,' discussed earlier, Machaut's 'Se pour ce muir' was obviously one of the poet's favourites since he found three places for it in his manuscript and wrote music for it.[7] It is still another poem in which the colour symbolism of love is featured:

Se pour ce muir, qu'Amours ay bien servi,
Sy fait mauvais servir si fait signour,
Ne je n'ay pas, ce croy, mort desservi
Pour bien amer de tres loyal amour.
Mais je voy bien que finé sont mi jour,
Quant je congnois et voy tout en appert
Qu'en lieu de bleu, dame, vous vestés vert.

Helas! dame, je vous ay tant chieri,
En desirant de merci la douçour,
Que je n'ay mais sens ne pooir en mi:
Tant m'ont mué mi souspir et mi plour.

Et m'esperence est morte sens retour,
Qu'en souvenirs me monstre à descouvert
Qu'en lieu de bleu, dame, vous vestés vert.

Pour ce maudi les yex dont je vous vi,
L'eure, le jour et le tres cointe atour,
Et la biauté qui ont mon cuer ravi,
Et le plaisir enyvré de folour,
Le doulz regart qui me mist en errour,
Et loyauté qui sueffre et a souffert
Qu'en lieu de bleu, dame, vous vestés vert.[8]

If I die because I have served Love well, then it is an evil thing to serve such a lord, for I am sure I have not deserved death for loving well with a very loyal love. And I see well that my days are ended when I recognize and perceive openly that instead of blue, lady, you are wearing green.

Alas! lady, I have cherished you so while desiring the sweetness of your mercy that I no longer have sense nor strength in me, so much have my sighs and tears changed me; and my Hope is irrevocably dead since in my mind I see clearly that instead of blue, lady, you are wearing green.

Therefore I curse the eyes with which I see you, the hour, the day, and the very lovely attire, and the beauty which have ravished my heart, and the pleasure intoxicated with folly, the Sweet Look which led me astray, and Loyalty which suffers and has suffered, since instead of blue, lady, you are wearing green.

This ballade may well be described as a chain with a logical progression. Each stanza is completed and closed by the refrain, but at the same time the three are effectively linked by thematic continuity, and by a well-orchestrated heightening of emotional intensity. The lover begins with a general declaration that he is dying because of his lady's disloyalty; then in the next stanza he directly addresses her, declaring his past devotion and present despair; finally his heightening emotion leads him to curse all those things that led him to love her. A discreet use of conventional personification throughout works with the vivid colour symbolism to create a metaphorical level of action and to support the unity of the poetic statement.

Chaucer's rime royal ballade *Against Women Unconstant*[9] no doubt derives its refrain from 'Se pour ce muir,' though the substance and rhetorical structure of the two poems are different enough to provide an instructive contrast in the possibilities of the form:[10]

Madame, for your newefangelnesse,
Many a servaunt have ye put out of grace.
I take my leve of your unstedfastnesse,
For wel I wot, whyl ye have lyves space,
Ye can not love ful half yeer in a place,
To newe thing your lust is ay so kene;
In stede of blew, thus may ye were al grene.

Right as a mirour nothing may impresse,
But, lightly as it cometh, so mot it pace,
So fareth your love, your werkes beren witnesse.
Ther is no feith that may your herte enbrace;
But, as a wedercok, that turneth his face
With every wind, ye fare, and that is sene;
In stede of blew, thus may ye were al grene.

Ye might be shryned, for your brotelnesse,
Bet than Dalyda, Creseyde or Candace;
For ever in chaunging stant your sikernesse;
That tache may no wight fro your herte arace.
If ye lese oon, ye can wel tweyn purchace;
Al light for somer, ye woot wel what I mene,
In stede of blew, thus may ye were al grene.

Here all three stanzas are directly addressed to the lady. In the first the lover announces his intention of departing from her because of her fickleness. Then he describes the behaviour that has led to his resolution in the remaining two stanzas, both of which make much the same point – that she is incurably inconstant. However, the two are not reversible; their differing rhetorical approaches serve to intensify the emotion as the poem proceeds. In stanza 2 there is sarcasm in the developed similes of the mirror and the weathercock but hardly the bitterness of the last stanza. That begins with the unfavourable comparison of the lady to three notorious women, including Criseyde; then it moves to the paradox that 'ever in chaunging stant your sikernesse,' a description that directly associates her with Dame Fortune; and it concludes with invective. The significance of 'al light for somer' may not be crystal clear, but the disapproval is unmistakable.

These two poems offer effective examples of Machaut's ballade style; each develops the theme of disloyalty in love in an orderly progression. Reiterated colour symbolism and continued and consistent imagery support the thematic unity. We may compare the two poems with two developed lyric passages from *Troilus and Criseyde* which also deal with the question of loyalty in love. In the first example Pandarus tries to cheer up Troilus by proving that a commitment to love a certain lady need not bind one for ever. For this purpose he invokes the scholastic notion that love is not a matter of substance, but an accident that may be found in various substances. The lines that immediately precede and follow point up the relative self-containment of the three-stanza unit:

Forthi be glad, myn owen deere brother!
If she be lost, we shal recovere an other.

What! God forbede alwey that ech plesaunce
In o thyng were, and in non other wight!
If oon kan synge, an other kan wel daunce;
If this be goodly, she is glad and light
And this is fair, and that kan good aright.
Ech for his vertu holden is for deere,
Both heroner and faucoun for ryvere.

And ek, as writ Zanzis, that was ful wys,
'The newe love out chaceth ofte the olde';
And upon newe cas lith new avys.
Thenk ek, thi lif to saven artow holde.
Swich fir, by proces, shal of kynde colde;
For syn it is but casuel pleasaunce,
Som cas shal putte it out of remembraunce.

For also seur as day comth after nyght,
The newe love, labour, or oother wo,
Or elles selde seynge of a wight,
Don olde affecciouns alle over-go.
And, for thi part, thow shalt have oon of tho
T'abregge with thi bittre peynes smerte;
Absence of hire shal dryve hire out of herte.

Thise wordes seyde he for the nones alle ...   (IV 405–28)

The three stanzas again have a neat logical structure that leads directly to the conclusion drawn in the last three lines.

The unit begins with Pandarus' statement that love can be produced in various circumstances by different virtues inhering in different ladies:

beauty, musical talent, personality (love is then an accident rather than a substance). From this generalization he deduces in the second stanza that since love depends on 'cas', some new circumstance inevitably will provide a new 'plesaunce' to supersede old love. In the last stanza he summarizes and specifies. With Criseyde absent, new occasions – women, work, problems – will drive her out of Troilus' heart. The logical argument is supported by vivid imagery of new things: new ladies with varying talents, new loves born in fresh events, new concerns of quotidian existence. These will enter into Troilus' life to stoke the fire cooled by Criseyde's absence. Repetition of rhymes and rhyme-words ('*wight*,' '*pleasaunce*') between stanzas supports the logical and imaginative unity.[11] Once more, a small adjustment could make an independent ballade of the passage.

Pandarus' set piece is built up from mere hints in *Il Filostrato*. Criseyde's oath of constancy, a second passage from *Troilus* on the theme of fidelity, finds an origins in a lay of Machaut.[12] Criseyde speaks here in one of the final conversations of the recumbent lovers just before their separation. Troilus has expressed misgivings about her ability to remain true in new circumstances; she responds by protesting her unshakeable constancy. Again I provide the framing lines to the set piece:

And helpe me God so at my mooste nede,
As causeles ye suffren al this drede!

For thilke day that I for cherisynge
Or drede of fader, or for other wight,
Or for estat, delit, or for weddynge,
Be fals to yow, my Troilus, my knyght,
Saturnes doughter, Juno, thorugh hire myght,
As wood as Athamante do me dwelle
Eternalich in Stix, the put of helle!

And this on every god celestial
I swere it yow, and ek on ech goddesse,
On every nymphe and deite infernal,
On satiry and fawny more and lesse,
That halve goddes ben of wildernesse;
And Attropos my thred of lif tobreste,
If I be fals! now trowe me if yow leste!

And thow, Symois, that as an arwe clere
Thorugh Troie rennest downward to the se,

Ber witnesse of this word that seyd is here,
That thilke day that ich untrewe be
To Troilus, myn owene herte fre,
That thow retourne bakward to thi welle,
And I with body and soule synke in helle!

But that ye speke, awey thus for to go ...   (IV 1532–5)

Criseyde expresses her vow in quasi-legal form. She specifies the possible nature and motivation of the imputed fault: falsity because of love, father, property, pleasure, or marriage. Then she swears by all the gods and demigods her determination to be true. The punishment she specifies for recreance is the damnation of her body and soul, while the witnessing river Simois will manifest the unnaturalness of her act by reversing its course. Unity is reinforced by the repeated evocation of the pagan supernatural through references to the gods, the underworld and its inhabitants, and divinely decreed event. Coherence is also achieved through repetition. The last lines of stanzas 1 and 3 give the effect of a refrain. And Criseyde's repeated vow is incantatory: 'thilke day that I ... Be fals to yow,' 'If I be fals,' 'thilke day that ich untrewe be.'

This set of four lyric pieces, two independent, two from the long poem, demonstrates how a common topic of love poetry, such as loyalty, submitted to similar development in different literary contexts. In book IV of Chaucer's work the imminent separation of the lovers provides occasion for lyric development by asking how they will abide by the laws of Amour. Will they remain loyal to death as the ideal presumably requires, or will they find practical solutions? Practical Pandarus rationalizes a change for the ever-loyal Troilus, while faithless Criseyde vows eternal faith, both expressing themselves in near-ballade form. In book V Troilus will produce further lyric sequences on the topic with his strictures on Criseyde's behaviour (V 1254–74, and the 'Litera Troili,' especially V 1345–58). The question of loyalty is an obvious subject for the set pieces of the story. Chaucer takes advantage of many other lyric situations offered by the double sorrow of Troilus: from the narrator's exegesis of the power of Love after Troilus is struck, to Troilus' complaint against Fortune when he is awaiting solace, to Antigone's praise of the life of Amour as Criseyde is pondering her situation, and eventually to the testaments of the lovers when they are to part.

MACHAUT'S LOVERS AND 'TROILUS AND CRISEYDE'

For the versification and structure of the lyric passages of *Troilus*, Chaucer mostly found his inspiration in the French ballades rather than in the *Filostrato*. And in his attention to individual development of the lyric occasions that the whole of the narrative provides – not only those pertinent to the hero, as in Boccaccio's poem – he was following the tradition of the dit amoureux. The immediate models for such practice in *Troilus*, as in the *Book of the Duchess*, are two of Machaut's dits, the *Jugement du roy de Behaigne* and *Remede de Fortune*. Like others of the type, both poems have thin narratives with continual lyric elaborations and excursuses.

The debate topic of Machaut's *Behaingne*, involving the question of who suffers more, the betrayed or the bereaved, brings to the fore the same problem the story of *Troilus* poses: when if ever is it permissible to stop loving the mate whom Love has assigned? In *Behaigne* there are at least ten relatively separable lyric statements about the problem of faithfulness in love. For instance, in explaining why he cannot hope to have his lady's love again, the knight asserts in a tight five-quatrain passage (1069–87) that something which is not a unified whole cannot be stable; the lady's heart, therefore, split as it is, can never rest in one place. In a second excursus of five quatrains (1092–1107) he states that just as one cannot divide a wolf from its pelt without killing it, so the lady is inseparable from her changeable nature. Again, he complains for three quatrains of the notoriety the lady will endure because of her betrayal (1148–59). These are of course commonplace topics of the poetry; for instance, Criseyde in the Greek camp states the last worry, about future notoriety (V 1054–71), and the other concerns find comparable expression in *Against Women Unconstant*.

The king's counsellors in *Behaigne*, personified figures who embody different aspects of the king's character, present further extended commentary on the fickle lady's behaviour. Lady Reason, making use of a brief personification allegory, states (1724–75) that she herself would allow the knight to leave the lady, but Amour, Beauty, and Youth forbid it. Loyalty in turn uses colourful images in advising the knight – perhaps surprisingly – to feed the lady the kind of bread she has fed him, to dance as she dances (1822–47). But Amour and Youth each enter eloquent, well-developed protests to this opinion (1790–1811; 1859–91); they are adamant in demanding that the knight remain faithful to the lady and maintain faith in Love's power yet to reward him. As with the other passages in *Behaigne* dealing with the problem of loyalty, each of these four statements of the counsellors could exist as separate poems or be readily adapted to another story in which the topic figures, such as *Troilus and Criseyde*.

The *Remede de Fortune*, a work dominated by nine lyric set pieces with their music, provides a more general and important model for *Troilus*. In line with the difference in their narratives, the lyric topics in the *Remede* diverge from those of *Behaigne*. Whereas in the latter poem the main emphasis is on the end of the love affair, on death and betrayal, the *Remede* treats the progress of the lover from despair to hope to the obtaining of mercy, providing a narrative analogue to the first books of *Troilus* and topics for discursive development. The work further had a major influence on Chaucer's conception of the characters and their expressions of sentiment. Some important differences between *Troilus and Criseyde* and *Il Filostrato*, and some parallel passages in *Troilus* and Machaut's works, especially the *Remede*, will help to clarify the influence. The importance of the parallels in language lies not in the similarities of phraseology as such, but rather in the more profound relationships in which the similarities are grounded and to which they point.

In the story the characterizations and actions of Troilus, Pandarus, and Criseyde successively evidence Machaut's influence. In the first place the presentation of Troilus in his 'first sorwe,' which involves a marked modification and elaboration of Boccaccio's treatment of Troilo's enamourment, has clear filiations with the French poet's dits. Troilus is altogether more naïve, impressionable, and idealistic than his Italian counterpart. He lives, as it were, under a different code. When the Italian Troilo sees Criseida in the temple the effect is not earth-shaking; at first he doesn't realize that Love has shot him, and the whole process of his falling in love is briefly, even perfunctorily, described. Chaucer's Troilus, by contrast, is so stunned by Criseyde's look that he can hardly stagger to his room; the ensuing effects on him of her appearance are given lengthy treatment. In the *Filostrato* as soon as Troilo becomes conscious of Love's wound an unstated assumption is made that he wants sexual satisfaction; his first discussion with Pandaro explicitly confirms this. And when Troilo eventually meets Criseida, he without difficulty carries on a conversation with her that soon leads to the satisfaction of his desires. Troilus on the other hand, until he finds himself in bed with Criseyde, affirms that just a kind look from her will satisfy him. In their first meeting he speaks to her with the greatest difficulty, and in their later tryst only by virtue of his swooning and Pandarus' timely action is the consummation achieved. Machaut's influence in such matters is manifest. Troilus' reactions and his manner are directly related to those of the knight in *Behaigne* and of Amant in the *Remede*, and ultimately are founded on the typical lover of the French lyric.

A comparison of certain passages is telling. Both Chaucer and Boccaccio describe the circumstances of the lover's seeing the lady and the effect of her first look. The Italian poet, however, is not interested in the lover's psychological reactions nearly to the degree that Chaucer is. It is in Machaut, who almost completely neglects concrete detail in concentrating on mental event, that Chaucer finds his methods of presenting these reactions. Thus the knight in *Behaigne* reports that with the first look of his lady,

> Dedens mon cuer la douce impression
>> De sa figure
> Fu telement emprainte qu'elle y dure. (411–13)

Within my heart the sweet image of her person was so imprinted that it remains there still.

Troilus, upon seeing Criseyde, likewise feels such desire

> That in his hertes botme gan to stiken
> Of hir his fixe and depe impressioun.[13]

The effect of the look, Machaut's knight goes on to say, was pleasurable but dizzying:

> Si me ploit tant cilz dangiers a sentir,
> Quant ses regars se daignoit assentir
> A descendre sur moy, que, sanz mentir,
>> Je ne savoie
> Qu'il m'avenoit ne quelle part j'estoie;
> Car senz, vigour, et maniere perdoie. (437–42)

It so pleased me to feel her dominion when she deigned to let her glance fall on me that, to tell the truth, I didn't know what was happening to me or where I was, for I lost sense, strength, and presence of mind.

Of Troilus Chaucer states that after Criseyde has 'let falle / Hire look' (I 290–1) he feels such desire and affection that 'unnethes wiste he how to loke or wynke' (I 301). In a comparable passage in *Remede de Fortune* Amant tells how under the influence of the lady's look he is dazzled, struck dumb, and left without strength (1264–7); indeed, he continues,

Nature en moy s'en esbahist
Et mes sens s'en esvanuist,
Dont li cuers me tramble et fremist.   (1269–71)

Nature was astounded within me by it, and my senses deserted me, which made my heart tremble and shake.

When Troilus' eye 'smot' (I 273) on Criseyde, he 'wax therwith astoned' (I 274), and his heart 'gan to sprede and rise' (I 278).

Following the initial sight of their ladies, the fire of love burns comparably Machaut's Amant, Boccaccio's Troilo, and Chaucer's Troilus. The lovers in the French and English poems, however, endure states of emotional distraction rather more extreme than Troilo's. At the end of his first complaint the Italian weeps and sighs (I 57), but Chaucer's Troilus at this point is nearly 'in salte teres dreynte' (I 543), even as Amant in *Remede de Fortune*, finishing his complaint against Amour, has his sighs drowned in tears ('souspirs en larmes noiez' I 489). And Troilus and Machaut's lovers are especially unlike Troilo in desiring only the refreshment of the lady's look. Amant states that he could be cured 'if only she deigned to nourish my desire with her look' (1319–20), even as Troilus wants but a look from Criseyde: 'with som frendly lok gladeth me' (I 538; cf III 129–30).

In the subsequent meetings between the lovers, most aspects of Troilus' behaviour have their counterparts in Machaut's dits. When in the second meeting Troilus is confronted by Criseyde's tears and the possibility that he may get more than a look from her, he faints. Chaucer's presentation at this point is inspired by Amant's description in *Remede de Fortune* of his fainting:

Aussi fui je tous desvoiez
De sens, de memoire, et de force
Et de toute autre vigour. Pour ce
Estoie je cheüs en transe.   (1490–3)

Thus I had wandered far from the way of sense, memory, and strength, and every other power. As a result I fell into a swoon.

Troilus' faculties and powers are comparably stunned and shut up deep within him:

And every spirit his vigour in knette,
So they astoned or oppressed were.
The felyng of his sorwe, or of his fere,
Or of aught elles, fled was out of towne;
And down he fel al sodeynly a-swowne. (III 1088–92)

In following Machaut's description of the lover's disoriented sensibility, Chaucer nicely transforms 'desvoiez,' meaning in origin something like 'strayed from the road,' into 'fled ... out of towne.'

The personality of Machaut's lovers shows up throughout Chaucer's story in Troilus' hyperemotionalism, which leads him to complaints that despite their Boethian content amount more to inner churning than to constructive philosophic statement. It has been rightly said that Troilus' long speech about predestination is not dialectical, but is an emotional outburst.[14] In *Behaigne* the knight indulges in the same kind of emotive speculation (715–860). He cannot decide whom to chide for his lady's infidelity. He cannot blame the lady because Amour led her to take another; he cannot blame Fortune because changeability is Fortune's essence. Therefore, God and Nature must be culpable in providing the lady with every virtue except Loyalty. But he cannot blame them either, for they are above reproach. As Troilus, after his agonizing inward debate, ends where he started, so also the knight concludes with no solution.

Amant's lengthy formal complaint in *Remede de Fortune* (905–1480) likewise exudes fruitless mental turmoil. At its end he describes it as a fight with himself ('et quant a par moy debatus ... et combatus' 1481–2). At this point Esperance appears to assist him. So too Troilus' long monologue, similarly described ('And whil he was in al this hevynesse / Disputyng with hymself' IV 1083–4), is immediately followed by Pandarus' appearance. A Boethian situation involving complainer and instructor-comforter is present at this point in both works. As a matter of fact, the whole of *Remede de Fortune* turns on this allegorized inner debate constructed on the model of *Consolation of Philosophy*. Just as Lady Philosophy, representing the faculty of reason, appears to Boethius to answer his complaint, so Amant's hope takes on the body of Lady Esperance and comes to him to provide comfort, drawing her arguments mainly from the *Consolation*.[15]

If Troilus' emotionalism and sensitivity find their origins in Machaut's lovers, so also the characterization of Pandarus has roots in the French works. As go-between he is hardly a product of the formes fixes, but as lover and philosopher of love he belongs to the fourteenth-century court. He is certainly something of a false Lady Philosophy – a bogus Reason unequal to genuine difficulties – but he is also in part a true representative of Esperance, a bearer of hope. Like Esperance with Amant, Pandarus encourages Troilus, sometimes using her very words. Thus, early in her conversation with Amant, Esperance reminds him of his unworthiness, which makes it very easy for his lady to give him an adequate reward:

> Tu ne dois pas las clamer,
> Se tu l'aimes bien, n'esmaiier
> Qu'elle ne te doie paiier
> Plus mil fois que ne desers
> En ce que tu l'aimes et sers.   (1636–40)

You should not cry alas, if you love her well, nor be dismayed that she doesn't pay you a thousand times more than you deserve for loving and serving her.

The lady's least reward ('guerredon') is worth much more than you can merit, Esperance asserts. Using identical terms, Pandarus reminds Troilus that merely serving his lady is a great reward for a lover:

> What? sholde he therfore fallen in dispayr,
> Or be recreant for his owne tene,
> Or slen hymself, al be his lady fair?
> Nay, nay, but evere in oon be fressh and grene
> To serve and love his deere hertes queene,
> And thynk it is a guerdon hire to serve,
> A thousand fold moore than he kan deserve.   (I 813–19)

As usual the verbal parallels signal deeper affinities in situation and in thought.

To encourage Troilus Pandarus answers his early complaint about Fortune in words patterned on Esperance's lessons to Amant. Fortune is bound to change, says Esperance, for 'if she were always the same / ... she would not be Fortune, but since she won't stay still [sejourne] ...' (2531, 2534–5). Amant has described Fortune earlier as one

> Qui n'atent mie qu'il adjourne
> Pour tourner; qu'elle ne sejourne ...   (913–14)

Who does not intend in any way that [the wheel] stop turning; and she does not stay still ...

The two passages issue in Pandarus' wise comments:

> For if hire whiel stynte any thyng to torne,
> Than cessed she Fortune anon to be.
> Now, sith hire whiel by no way may sojourne ...   (I 848–50)

Machaut acts as intermediary in providing much of the Boethian commentary about Fortune in *Troilus*. The well-known opening passage in book IV, in which Fortune makes a face at Troilus, then twists her countenance away from him, has a rather full parallel in *Behaigne* (684–93).

In his encouragement of Troilus, Pandarus draws one of his strongest arguments directly from Esperance. The lady is so good, the reasoning goes, that she must possess Pity. Says Esperance: 'You ought also to think, in order to drive away worry, that since she perfectly possesses all the excellences that one may well imagine, express, or conceive, which increase in her unceasingly, and since she is adorned with virtues and is without vices, then it follows of necessity that Franchise and Pity are in her' (1671–82). Pandarus summarizes this thinking in making the same point to his patient:

> And also thynk, and therwith glade the,
> That sith thy lady vertuous is al,
> So foloweth it that there is som pitee
> Amonges al thise other in general.   (I 897–900)

Such philosophizing has little precedent in *Il Filostrato*. His French heritage makes Pandarus a more complex and interesting figure than Pandaro.

After intense suffering, Troilus, the knight in *Behaigne*, and Amant in *Remede de Fortune* do find 'pity' – 'mercy' – in their ladies. Though Machaut's lovers never specify what has constituted or might constitute the desired mercy,[16] they are convinced, as Troilus is by his more explicit reward, that it has taken providential powers to achieve it. To make this point, Machaut echoes a Christian commonplace about mercy. Happily for you, says Amant's Esperance to him, 'Pitez est dessus droiture' (*Remede* 1686). Troilus in bed likewise rejoices that 'mercy passeth right' (III 1282) and that Love's 'grace passed oure desertes' (III 1267). For Troilus and the knight in *Behaigne*, however, it turns out that Fortune, not Providence, is at work. Having sat atop the wheel for a time, they both are cast down; for both of them it turns out that the ladies lack not Pity, but another vital virtue, Loyalty.

In much of Chaucer's story Criseyde has close affinities to the ladies of the French dits. She is like them in that she is 'dangerous' – hard to get, much harder than Boccaccio's Criseida. It takes greater and more extended proof of devotion on Troilus' part, and much more wheedling and trickery by Pandarus, before Criseyde is conquered. Her intriguing display of 'danger' is very much that of the women of Machaut, who have (in contrast to the men) complex and interesting psyches. As a matter of fact, the lovers recognize the ladies' superiority and look to them for salutary precept and example. Thus Amant in *Remede de Fortune* tells at length (167–247) how his lady's words and behaviour taught him gentle and polite ways. So also Troilus looks to Criseyde for instruction:

> So techeth me how that I may disserve
> Youre thonk, so that I thorugh myn ignoraunce,
> Ne do no thing that yow be displeasaunce. (III 1293–5)

His phraseology here comes from the knight in *Behaigne*, who tells the lady when she has accepted him into her service that if he does anything contrary to her pleasure ('contre vostre plaisance' 665) it will be from ignorance ('par ignorance' 667).

In order to satisfy Troilus' concept of Criseyde as his worthy mentor, Chaucer endows her with a sententious bent foreign to the Italian Criseida. In the process he transfers to Criseyde and heightens a speech that Boccaccio assigns to Troilo concerning the virtues of the beloved. It was not Troilus' rank or bravery that attracted her to him, Criseyde tells him,

> But moral vertu, grounded upon trouthe –
> That was the cause I first hadde on yow routhe! (IV 1672–3)

Without minimizing the influence of Troilo's words, we may compare Criseyde's earnest speech here with the first lines of a Machaut ballade, spoken by a lady with a penchant for lofty pronouncement:

> Ce qui contreint mon cuer à toy amer,
> Amis, ce fait ta bonne renommée,
> Pleinne d'onneur, c'on ne peut trop loer.[17]

What constrains my heart to love you, Ami, is your good name, full of honour, that one cannot praise excessively.

This lady's tendency to high-minded generalization in matters of Amour, shown throughout the lyric, is like that of Criseyde and most of Machaut's female narrators.

Assigned to the lover by Amour, the lady is Love's representative, presumably embodying the god's wisdom and virtue. It is from this lofty position that Criseyde makes her two lengthy promises of loyalty to Troilus: the oath just before their parting, which we looked at earlier in this chapter, and her promise of eternal love after their first night together. For her to desert Troilus, she states solemnly, would be contrary to nature:

The game, ywys, so forforth now is gon,
That first shall Phebus fallen fro his speere,
And everich egle ben the dowves feere,
And everi roche out of his place sterte,
Er Troilus out of Criseydes herte.   (III 1494–8)

This speech finds a relevant counterpart in Machaut's Lay des dames (Lay X); the lady who speaks testifies again as one who has a natural understanding and virtue in Love's affairs. 'Do not doubt, Ami,' she says to her absent lover, 'that you will see the trees walk, the mountains collapse, the beasts speak, the fish fly, before I leave you; time stop, laws maintained, envy dead, the Seine flow backward, and the sea dry up, when I do not love you above all' (141–52). This lady's statement is not presented in a dramatic context; we do not see her loyalty put to the test as Criseyde's is, fatefully. Chaucer's narrative provides a dimension of irony that the lay lacks. There is a good deal of implicit humour in the presentation of the callow lover in the French lyrics, but little in the image of the dignified lady.

The reader feels the irony of Criseyde's vow, but one would not say that the Criseyde whom we have come to know in book II is by nature a faithless female. From the beginning of Il Filostrato we may feel that Boccaccio's heroine is not trustworthy, that she is too conscious of practicality and too compliant to stay committed if events encourage infidelity. But Chaucer's Criseyde is primarily a romantic who requires Antigone's praise of love to make her 'somwhat able to converte' (II 903). The song of Antigone indeed is a high point of the poem; it is central to the presentation of Criseyde and to the construction of the paradise of Love which the lovers find – or think to find – in book III.

The song is built on several lyrics of Machaut, the most important being two lays. It is itself like a lay in that its seven stanzas provide parallel and cumulative statements in praise of the lover and the life of love. As we have seen, the typical lay similarly consists of a twelve-part series of statements which centre on one subject, providing variations on a theme rather than forming the logical chain characteristic of a ballade. It seems that Machaut always designed his lays for singing, so that Chaucer's emphasis on the musical nature of Antigone's presentation also suggests the lay. As the ladies walk in a 'blosmy bower grene,' Antigone

> Gan on a Troian song to singen cleere,
> That it an heven was hire vois to here.   (II 825–6)

The reader is reminded three times after she finishes that she has sung a 'song' (III 875, 877, 883). And when Criseyde shortly goes to bed, a nightingale provides a fitting sequel; the bird

> Ful loude song ayein the moone shene,
> Peraunter in his briddes wise, a *lay*
> Of love ...   (II 920–2)

In its substance Antigone's song is perhaps as near to a lay as anything in Chaucer's poetry.

The two Machaut lays that he particularly draws on for the song have female first-person speakers; they are called in manuscript the *Paradis d'Amour* and the *Mirouer amoureux*.[18] Either title might serve for Antigone's piece, which emphasizes the 'blisse of love' (II 849, 885, 891) and the perfection of the lover:

> As he that is the welle of worthynesse,
> Of trouthe grownd, mirour of goodlihed,
> Of wit Apollo, stoon of sikernesse,
> Of vertu roote, of lust fynder and hed,
> Thorugh which is alle sorwe fro me ded.   (II 841–5)

In the *Mirouer amoureux*, the lady who speaks says her lover is known as

Mireoir qui les bons parfait
Et de ce monde l'excellence.
  C'est la flour,
  C'est l'onnour
De ce monde et la valour,
C'est uns drois flueves de joie.   (15–20)

A mirror who perfects the good, and the excellence of this world. He is the flower, the honour, and the prize of this world, a true source of joy.

In her continuing praise she says he is one 'who will put an end to my sorrows by his virtue' (85–7).

True to the lays and several other Machaut poems, Antigone constructs an image of the life of love as an ideal that can be realized on earth. Thus Criseyde's wondering question gets an unequivocal answer:

  'Lord, is ther swych blisse among
  Thise loveres, as they konne faire endite?'
  'Ye, wis,' quod fresshe Antigone the white,
  'For alle the folk that han or ben on lyve
  Ne konne wel the blisse of love discryve.'   (II 885–9)

This is the message that the romantic Criseyde carries to her bed and to a dream of an eagle who exchanges heart for heart.

The song draws on Machaut's poems for its testimony that love between man and woman has the power to make a heaven on earth. Such elevated love in the French works involves nothing overtly carnal; its implicit setting is courtly: the garden or the parlour. In book III Troilus and Criseyde, in a different setting, believe that their bed of delight is fixed in a paradise of love, and all of their experience in the book encourages them to believe the paradise is authentic. On the brink of his change in fortune, Troilus talks to Pandarus of the 'hevene' (III 1599) that he has found. But of course the ensuing events show the paradise to be not only ephemeral but deceptive.

In Boccaccio's story only Troilo is thoroughly taken in by the romantic illusion; Pandaro and Criseida give it lip service, but they mostly attend to practical matters. Troilo's dream is his alone. In Chaucer's poem, by contrast, the lovers, Pandarus, and the narrator all join in constructing and lending credence to an idealized world of love built on Machaut's model. However, the narrative increasingly undermines the illusion. In the world of this story, in contrast to Machaut's world, the lovers are seen going to bed, and their procedure in getting there necessitates compromise with ideal behaviour: calculation, deception, and awkwardness. And after Criseyde is exchanged for Antenor, the train of external event so dictates the behaviour of the characters as finally to render meaningless the commonplaces of romance they continue to utter.

The lyric structures characteristic of the dit amoureux continue until the end of *Troilus and Criseyde*, but it is not in the romance idealisms of the French works that Chaucer's poem finds its final meaning. However important the idealisms are in the development and working out of the story, they prove much too fragile when carried into a world of endless contingency. This culmination of Chaucer's work in the French mode also constitutes his most definitive undercutting of its values. In his subsequent *Legend of Good Women*, he is much gentler with these values.

FRENCH LYRICISM ONCE MORE: THE 'LEGEND OF GOOD WOMEN'

The God of Love's strictures against *Troilus and Criseyde* in the 'Prologue' to the *Legend* (F 332–3; G 264–6) suggest that the characterization of Criseyde was not well received by some of the noble ladies in Chaucer's audience. The problem was similar to that which Machaut had with the *Jugement du roy de Behaigne*. In presenting a perfidious lady, and in stating that the knight suffered more from this lady's perfidy than did the lady whose gentle lover had died, Machaut evidently stimulated a protest from at least one great lady, perhaps Bonne of Luxembourg.[19] He made amends by composing the *Jugement dou roy de Navarre*, in which Bonneurté and her ladies catechize and chide the poet – identified specifically as Guillaume, as he had not been in *Behaigne* – and the King of Navarre condemns and reverses the decision of the earlier work. In stating their case the ladies tell several well-developed stories demonstrating that the death of the loved one is the greatest tragedy in love and that the lady rather than the man is the greater sufferer in love. For the poet's misrepresentations, the king assigns him as penance the task of writing a lay, a chanson, and a ballade.

In composing *Troilus* Chaucer had anticipated that ladies in his audience might similarly be offended by the characterization of Criseyde. Late in the poem he specifically asks

... every lady bright of hewe,
And every gentil womman, what she be,
That al be that Criseyde was untrewe,
That for that gilt she be nat wroth with me. (V 1772–5)

He hopes to exculpate himself, yet he well understands that his depiction gave the ladies good reason to be upset. The Machaut tradition had accustomed them to better treatment, for it presents women who are superior to their lovers morally and intellectually. To make matters worse, Chaucer's characterization initially identifies Criseyde with the superior ladies of that tradition. She is a convert and a subscriber to the ideals of romance, and she speaks the conventional wisdom and sentiments that women as adjutants of Amour are particularly qualified to enunciate. But then her high-minded statements and deeply sworn vows prove to be a deceptive veneer. Stepping right out of the flattering picture of society that the court poetry paints, she proceeds to betray Troilus. One may well find the implication in the story that when the lady of the lyric tradition is placed in an actual situation, she will prove to be just like Eve, Dalila, and all the others. Thus, while Chaucer doesn't invent the story of Criseyde's falseness, he does give her the character of the Middle French lyric lady with whom the ladies of the court had been encouraged to identify themselves, and then her behaviour makes the characterization deeply ironic. By implication it calls into question the ideals of the court literary tradition.

Chaucer offers the *Legend of Good Women* as a palinode to *Troilus*. Appropriately, the important 'Prologue' is a genuine return to the French, as its antecedents witness. To review briefly points covered previously, the *Jugement dou roy de Navarre* inspired the governing idea of the palinode by which the poet is confronted by powerful individuals who order him to make amends with specified poetic compositions. *Navarre* also suggested the theme of Chaucer's penitential legends, which were to show the natural virtue of women in matters of love. And Machaut's poem presents counterparts to the legends themselves: in arguing the virtuous suffering of women, Bonneurté's counsellors relate several developed classical exempla, including the stories of Dido, Ariadne, Medea, Thisbe, and Hero. The histories of the first four are found among Chaucer's legends, and the fifth is part of his plan. In addition, the basic structure of the *Legend,* a series of stories on a single theme preceded by an introduction, has a significant analogue in le Mote's *Regret Guillaume,* with its introductory narrative followed by thirty complaints about the death of the count. Each of the last twenty-eight complaints features a narrative, a number of them drawn from classical sources.

The probability that le Mote's *Regret* suggested to Chaucer his pattern of introduction plus exempla is increased by the likelihood that Machaut drew on the same work for his *Navarre;*[20] Chaucer time and again shows an understanding of the genealogy of his originals by having recourse to their antecedents.[21] In any event, the main point is that his structure is dictated by the theme rather than a narrative. Le Mote's thirty complaints with their substantial exempla provide complementary and sometimes overlapping statements of the theme of grief, constituting a rhetorical exploration of the subject; similarly, Chaucer's series of legends develops the idea of virtuous suffering in love that characterizes women. Thus, though the narrative element dominates in the individual legends, it is subordinated to the lyric subject of the whole work. The principle by which the stories are assembled in the *Canterbury Tales* is entirely different from that of the *Legend.* The 'General Prologue' introduces no unifying theme, and there is no explicit thematic program for the tales.

In its subject of feminine virtue and its rhetorical structure the *Legend* accords well with contemporary French practice; it is in versification that the poem most differs from that practice. In none of the literatures that Chaucer knew were there long poems in decasyllabic couplets. The only real precedents among works he was familiar with are weak ones; they include the couplets of four short complaints of Machaut and a 142-line set piece in the *Panthère d'Amours.*[22] These are all lyric pieces, while the couplets became for Chaucer primarily a narrative vehicle, though not exclusively.

The 'Knight's Tale' evidently represents Chaucer's first extensive use of the long couplets. The tale has numerous developed set pieces, especially those formed by the complaints and prayers of the lovers, and by the various descriptions of persons, structures, and ceremonies, but these and the narrative of the love affair are not deeply affected by the French lyric tradition. In contrast to the earnest narrator of *Troilus* the Knight is detached, almost perfunctory, in describing the reactions of the lovers, as if he does not take them seriously. The character of the ingenue Emily, moreover, is far from that of the wise deputy of Love whom the French poets create. In sum, lyric sensibility largely is missing from the story. Confirming the clear difference of the 'Knight's Tale' from the dit amoureux is Chaucer's failure to draw on the French poets' work except for a few passages in which the expression is markedly French. Thus, when he sees Emily, Arcite exclaims briefly but to good lyric effect:

> The fresshe beautee sleeth me sodeynly
> Of hire that rometh in the yonder place;
> And but I have hir mercy and hir grace,
> That I may seen hire atte leeste weye,
> I nam but deed; ther nis namoore to seye. (1118–22)

And his 'roundel' (1529), of which we are given the charming three-line refrain, is thoroughly in the French manner:

> May, with alle thy floures and thy grene,
> Welcome be thou, faire fresshe May,
> In hope that I som grene gete may. (1510–12)

The graceful conventional phraseology in the first passage and the neat repetitions and alliterations in the second give them a recognizable French character, but on the whole the 'Knight's Tale,' in sharp contrast to *Troilus*, has little of the dit amoureux about it.

From the witness of the 'Knight's Tale' one might speculate that the decasyllabic couplets did not adapt well to the lyric mode – that the versification inherently tends to the effects of epigram and wit, as ultimately realized in the neoclassical heroic couplet. This may be true in part, but one need only look to the 'Prologue' of the *Legend* to see that Chaucer could write an extended lyric piece quite effectively in the couplets. The 'Prologue' is discontinuous, descriptive, and discursive, thoroughly in the spirit of the natural music of the dit amoureux, and the materials that Chaucer builds it from are almost all French.

Chaucer draws from *Navarre* the idea of writing a palinode to a work that affronts women, the idea of a penance that involves writing verse, and models for the general situation of a poet's being indicted for his work and for the peerless lady who confronts the poet.[23] In Machaut's dit the poet is out hunting in the fields when he is confronted by Bonneurté and brought to the king for judgment. The parallel between this pair and Alceste and the God of Love in Chaucer's poem is reinforced by Raison's encomiastic explanation to Machaut of the name and virtues of Bonneurté (3833–3968), quite like the God of Love's revelation to the poet of Alceste's name and peerless nature (F 497–515). Much of the overall plan of the poem, then, is owed to *Navarre*; likewise, a great deal of the substance comes from lyrics of the Marguerite tradition written by Machaut and Froissart.

John L. Lowes's study of the literary background of the 'Prologue' to the *Legend* has long been standard;[24] it provides a wealth of valuable information about the Marguerite poetry, but two important weaknesses vitiate it. In the first place, Lowes thought Deschamps provided a model for Chaucer's praise of the daisy (the marguerite), which is doubtful.[25] In addition, Lowes wrote in ignorance of Machaut's *Dit de la fleur de lis et de la Marguerite*, a late work found in only one manuscript that was not edited when his essay was published. *Lis et Marguerite*, together with Machaut's *Dit de la Marguerite* and Froissart's *Dittié de la flour de la Marguerite*, are the main models for the phraseology and imagery of Chaucer's 'Prologue.'[26]

Each of these French works is a continuous lyric statement without a connected story, while as in the longer dits amoureux, the 'Prologue' has a narrative connecting its lyric passages. *Lis et Marguerite* originated a great part of the Marguerite imagery which later became conventional. In it and in the 'Prologue' the professions of devotion to the flower are often strikingly similar, and in particular Alceste's clothing has its only real antecedents in the description of the two flowers of Machaut's poem. As her robe and crown give her the appearance of a daisy, so in *Lis et Marguerite* the lily is said to be clothed ('revestus' 150) in white petals and to have a crown of yellow pollen, signifying its manifold virtues (137–54). And the petals of the marguerite are said to form a white girdle of joy around it (213–16), with its centre providing a red crown of honour (217–24). With more concern about matching the human figure Chaucer accommodates the features of the daisy to Queen's Alceste's figure. He depicts Alceste's gown as possessing the green of the flower's foliage, while her crown is a counterpart to the whole bloom. The white 'flowrouns' (F 217) are carved from a single pearl, and correlatives for the yellow centre and the red tips are supplied by a 'fret of gold above' (F 225) and inset rubies (F 534).[27]

The metrics of the two other poems that chiefly inspired Chaucer's verse of the daisy, Machaut's *Dit de la Marguerite* and Froissart's *Dittié*, are stanzaic; while this distinguishes their versification clearly from

Chaucer's couplets, their series of decasyllabic lines provide some stylistic parallel.[28] The effect may be gathered from the opening of Machaut's *Dit*:

> J'aim une fleur qui s'uevre et qui s'encline
> Vers le soleil, de jours quant il chemine;
> Et quant il est couchiez sous sa courtine
>   Par nuit obscure,
> Elle se clot einsois que li jours fine.

I love a flower which opens and bends towards the sun as it goes on its way in the daytime; and then the flower goes to bed under its cover of dark night when it closes as the day ends.

The long, frequently enjambed lines assist the representation of the quasi-personal interaction between the narrator, the flower, and the sun. Comparably, Chaucer's narrator tells of his getting up in the morning,

> With dredful hert and glad devocioun,
> For to ben at the resureccioun
> Of this flour, whan that yt shulde unclose
> Agayn the sonne, that roos as red as rose.   (F 109–12)

Extended rhymes and alliteration strengthen the affinities to the French verse.

But probably closer to Chaucer's style in the 'Prologue' are the octosyllabic couplets of *Lis et Marguerite*, which are not divided into stanzaic units. Earlier I compared the opening of the *House of Fame* with that of *Lis et Marguerite*. Both works begin by discussing metaphysical problems; Chaucer's narrator is concerned with the mysterious nature of dreams, and Machaut's puzzles over the colours of flowers and their causes, which no one understands. The 'Prologue' presents another version of this opening in which an enigma is propounded and probed; the process begins here with the narrator's observation that no one knows for sure what hell and heaven are like, since no one now alive has been there. We need the help of books, he goes on, to know about things we don't witness,

> And as for me, though that I konne but lyte,
> On bokes for to rede I me delyte.   (F 29–30)

He continues in this informal way to say that the only thing that can take him from his books are the attractions of May and his devotion to the daisy. Machaut's narrator is equally informal and associative in eventually confessing that 'although the understanding that Nature has given me is worth little' (23–4), he wants to describe as best he can the fleur de lis, and also the little flower that is called the marguerite (25–30). In all three works we are led by way of musing on the inscrutable to the main subjects, which are dealt with subsequently in verse paragraphs.

The 'Prologue' serves as preface to a sequence of legends, so that a substantial section of its later part is devoted to supplying a motive for telling them. This entails a review of Chaucer's poetic deeds, bad and good, leading up to assignment of a penalty for the bad. Otherwise, the 'Prologue' mostly is made up of a series of set pieces which present the daisy as a nonpareil and Alceste as its embodiment. The focus on praise of the flower accords with the French Marguerite poems, all of which were no doubt written for actual court ladies. Chaucer in this must be writing in response to and in honour of an important lady, probably Queen Anne. The developed set pieces in the first part of the F 'Prologue' include two passages in praise of the marguerite (40–65, 84–96), a long reverdie (125–77), a description of Alceste and the God of Love (212–46), and the lovely intercalated ballade in rime royal, 'Hyd, Absolon, thy gilte tresses clere' (249–69), which is thoroughly French, inspired mainly by Froissart, it seems.[29]

Chaucer speaks openly to his French contemporaries in complaining of their monopoly on poetic stores: 'Ye lovers that kan make of sentement ... han her-biforn / Of makyng ropen, and lad awey the corn' (F 69, 73–4). He professes to be reduced to following after them,

> glenyng here and there,
> And am full glad yf I may fynde an ere
> Of any goodly word that ye han left.   (F 75–7)

It may be that the 'Prologue' genuinely tired him of gleaning after the French, for this was the last of his long works that show heavy Middle French inspiration, except perhaps the 'Squire's Tale.' The legends of the women themselves, to be sure, are integrated into the thematic scheme that the 'Prologue' sets up, but their substance is mostly narrative and their models classical and Italian. The characters of the women, along with that of Alceste, one may note, do restore the standard Middle French image of the lady as the true heroine and savant of Love, fulfilling the ostensible purpose of counteracting the effect of Criseyde's characterization.

SURVIVAL OF THE MIDDLE FRENCH MODE IN THE 'CANTERBURY TALES'

In his compositions after the 'Prologue' to the *Legend* Chaucer was much less close to his French contemporaries in spirit. One might anticipate finding strong French characteristics in the four rime royal stories of the *Canterbury Tales*, at least one of which, the 'Second Nun's Tale,' was composed before the 'Prologue' to the *Legend*. But, as with the poems in decasyllabic couplets, versification is not a controlling matter. In the *Tales* Chaucer uses rime royal to an effect quite different from that of *Troilus* and the *Parliament*. The stanzas function more exclusively as narrative units, and where they act to define rhetorical excursuses they tend to be less extractable, as with the frequent one- and two-stanza apostrophes in the 'Man of Law's Tale,' which function importantly as narrative dividers but usually would not make effective independent pieces.

Only in the stanzaic prologues to the rime royal tales do we find typical lyric set pieces, though unlike most formes fixes verse the prologues are moral and religious in content. It is perhaps with conscious purpose that Chaucer uses rime royal for the Second Nun's attack on Idleness, the keeper of the garden in the *Roman de la Rose*. The first three stanzas of her prologue form virtually an anti-ballade, in which 'ydelnesse' (used five times), 'slouthe,' and 'slogardye' are like refrain words bouncing off their contraries: 'bisynesse,' 'werche,' and 'swynke':

> The ministre and norice unto vices,
> Which that men clepe in Englissh Ydelnesse,
> That porter of the gate is of delices,
> To eschue, and by hire contrarie hire oppresse –
> That is to seyn, by leveful bisynesse –
> Wel oghten we to doon al oure entente,
> Lest that the feend thurgh ydelnesse us hente. (G 1–7)

The Nun follows up her introduction on idleness with an impressive eight-stanza prayer to the Virgin. It forms a companion piece to the Prioress's three-stanza rime royal apostrophe in her prologue, 'O mooder mayde, O mayde mooder free!'[30] Still another three-stanza rime royal piece, a disquisition on poverty, is found in the prologue to the 'Man of Law's Tale' (B 99–119). All of these passages from the prologues fall clearly into the category of sequences that could be made readily into separate lyrics.

The tales themselves, however, with limited exceptions, use rime royal for narrative purposes. 'The Monk's Tale' likewise, though also in a common ballade stanza, shows no tendency to develop separable lyric passages. Of the other stanzaic verse in the *Tales*, then, only 'Lenvoy de Chaucer' appended to the 'Clerk's Tale' remains especially associated with Middle French lyric. It is a metrical tour de force, with six stanzas using the same rhymes, *ababcb*, the rhymes extended and markedly French (*-ence*, *-aille*) except for the *c* lines. Aside from the brevity of its stanzas and its lack of a refrain, it is quite like a double ballade; the Clerk's repeated reference to it as a song (E 1174, 1176) properly suggests its lively musicality.[31]

With a number of the tales, like those of the Canon's Yeoman and the Pardoner, or the prose treatises, the relationship to the Machaut tradition is non-existent. With those that feature love relationships, though, there is generally some poetic use of the conventional language of the formes fixes. It is probably most apparent in the sequence of the Merchant's, Squire's, and Franklin's tales. In the 'Merchant's Tale,' as with the stories of the Miller and the Nun's Priest, the standard cant is used to humorous effect, as when the Merchant frames a complaint for Damian as he lies in bed, aching for May:

> I seye, 'O sely Damyan, allas,
> Andswere to my demaunde, as in this cas.
> How shaltow to thy lady, fresshe May,
> Telle thy wo? She wole alwey seye nay,
> Eke if thou speke, she wol thy wo biwreye.
> God be thyn help! I kan no bettre seye.' (E 1869–74)

Of course Damian immediately begins to find a remedy by writing a letter 'In manere of a compleynt or a lay' (1881). The conventional phraseology is also applied to January, a comic amant. When he is struck blind, the Merchant echoes a Machaut ballade and rondeau in complaining against Fortune for the old man:[32]

> O sodeyn hap! O thou Fortune unstable!
> Lyk to the scorpion so deceyvable,

That flaterest with thyn hed whan thou wolt stynge;
Thy tayl is deeth, thurgh thyn envenymynge, etc. (E 2057–64)

In such a matter as January's praising his squire to May ('He is as wys, discreet, and as secree / As any man I woot of his degree' E 1909–10), the language is also put to effects of wry humour.

The fact that Chaucer used the French mode for the purposes of humour in this mature tale, however, does not indicate that he became at some point contemptuous of the poetry so that he found only comedy in it. As we have seen, a certain degree of humour was implicit in the mode, and it accommodated a range of humorous commentary. Moreover, the 'Squire's Tale' and the 'Franklin's Tale,' both also probably late compositions, use the conventional expression more straightforwardly. The falcon episode in the 'Squire's Tale,' indeed, is a clear reversion to the earlier mode. In her avian representation of a courtly lady, the falcon recalls the *Parliament of Fowls* and Machaut's *Dit de l'alerion*. In character the falcon is particularly like Machaut's lady of the chanson royale who complains against her false lover and his steel-edged heart, and she also evokes Anelida. Her story is a reprise of the betrayed lover's tale, told several times in much the same terms by Machaut and the younger Chaucer. She tells of the long service of 'this god of loves ypocrite' (514), which in due course led to her entrusting her heart to him; but then he showed his true colours, as the falcon briefly explains in familiar terms:

Though he were gentil born, and fressh and gay,
And goodlich for to seen, and humble and free,
He saugh upon a tyme a kyte flee,
And sodeynly he loved this kyte so
That al his love is clene fro me ago;
And hath his trouthe falsed in this wyse.
Thus hath the kyte my love in hire servyse,
And I am lorn withouten remedie! (F 622–9)

Throughout this section (F 409–650), the language is comparably characteristic of the Middle French love poetry. The Squire's bird narrative does not form a full-fledged dit amoureux, however, since it largely lacks the extended lyric passages of most such works. It is as if Anelida had told her story without delivering her complaint. Nevertheless, this part of the 'Squire's Tale' comes closer to the contemporary French tradition than does any narrative in the *Canterbury Tales*.

The 'Franklin's Tale' at points also comes near the spirit of the mode's poetry. The Franklin's comment on the accord between Dorigen and Arveragus, whereby neither assumes mastery, is a matter of French love philosophy, finding a notable counterpart in the *Remede de Fortune* where the lady lectures Amant on mastery. Lovers ought to treat each other as equals, she says,

> Sans pensée avoir de maistrie,
> De haussage, et de signourie,
> Qu'adès ha tençon et rumour
> Entre seignourie et amour.   (4049–52)

With no thought of having mastery, supremacy, or lordship. For there is ever discord and discontent between lordship and Love.

The Franklin delivers a neat, separable thirty-line discourse on mastery, developing the same sentiments:

> Love wol nat been constreyned by maistrye.
> Whan maistrie comth, the God of Love anon
> Beteth his wynges, and farewel, he is gon!
> Love is a thyng as any spirit free.   (E 764–7)

The effect of their liberating agreement, concludes the Franklin, is ultimately to place Arveragus 'in lordshipe above' (E 795).

A good deal of the language connected with the squire Aurelius and his love for Dorigen is drawn from contemporary French poetic usage. Like many a Middle French lover, Damian is

> Oon of the beste farynge man on lyve;
> Yong, strong, right vertuous, and riche, and wys,
> And wel biloved, and holden in greet prys.   (E 932–4)

The series of adjectives is quite characteristic of Machaut's personal descriptions; we might compare the beloved knight of the lady in *Behaigne*, who had

> Gent corps faitis, cointe, apert et joli,

Joine, gentil, de maniere garni,
Plein de tout ce qu'il faut a vray ami.   (141–3)

A fine well-made body, attractive, lithe, and handsome; he was young, noble, of gentle bearing, possessed of all that a true lover needs.

Aurelius' affair follows the predictable course. Afraid to speak to the lady, despairing, he can express his woe only in a 'general compleynyng'; that is, in writing poems to no specified lady:

He seyde he lovede, and was biloved no thyng.
Of swich matere made he manye layes,
Songes, compleintes, roundels, virelayes,
How that he dorste nat his sorwe telle,
But langwissheth as a furye dooth in helle;
And dye he moste, he seyde, as did Ekko
For Narcisus, that dorste nat telle hir wo.   (E 946–52)

The matter, manner, and types of Aurelius' love poems, and the brief reference to the Ovidian story, strictly accord with the Middle French lyric tradition. His behaviour is described in consonant terms.

At times the Franklin shows impatience with Aurelius' carrying on; when he takes to his bed, the Franklin comments sardonically, 'Chese he, for me, wheither he wol lyve or dye' (E 1086). He is expressing the impatience of the uninitiated with court ways and expressing for his society a disapproval of Aurelius' morals. But there is no implicit criticism of contemporary French love poetry per se, which bears within itself a detached amusement at the lovers' excesses, and whose lyric expressions are never specific enough to depict or condone adultery. The 'Franklin's Tale' is probably one of Chaucer's last significant reflections of French court poetry, though it is a condensed reflection used to present a passion that eventually is discredited and disavowed by Aurelius. Rather than manifesting a disdain for the poetry by associating it with Aurelius' designs, however, Chaucer once more is showing a recognition of it as the suitable medium for depicting lovers of the gentle class.

In his long poems Chaucer never rejected the Machaut tradition, and yet even at the beginning he did not, as Froissart did, simply accept and imitate Machaut's forms. The dramatized complaints and the dream poems represent original approaches to the building of long dits within the bounds of the highly lyric tradition. Surprisingly, however, it was when Chaucer first used a strong narrative in *Troilus* and *Criseyde* that he made his most creative use of the mode. After *Troilus*, only in the 'Prologue' to the *Legend* and Chaucer's lyrics does the Middle French poetry remain a dominant force in his work. Estates analysis, the inclusive moral treatise, and especially the narrative forms of fabliau, saint's life, and chivalric romance henceforward supplied his materials and structures, while the French model of natural music was reduced to a subsidiary position, to be called upon conveniently to serve auxiliary functions in the love stories. Because of Chaucer's willingness to experiment and his radical evolution from lyric to narrative writer, it is especially surprising that the French poets of his mature days, his coevals and associates, showed little tendency to venture outside the matrix that Machaut in large part constructed. Their failure to follow him into a wider literary world, however, did not prevent Chaucer from having close relationships, personal and literary, with these poets. It is to his important relationships with Froissart, Deschamps, and Granson that most of the rest of this book will be devoted.

CHAPTER SIX

Chaucer and
Jean Froissart

Despite Machaut's potentially repressive dominance in young Chaucer's literary world, all evidence suggests that the English poet willingly accepted him as poetic father, and never came to reject his influence; his later adoption of other models did not involve rebellion. The character of faithless Criseyde constitutes no critique of Machaut's poetry, which on occasion also presents faithless women; in the apology for her that is implicit in the *Legend*, Chaucer with good humour simply presents the standard, more edifying, type of woman from the mode. The *Canterbury Tales* too embodies no reaction against the court verse. The 'General Prologue' begins with a reverdie that places the work in a conventional context, but then in a few lines the poet gracefully turns first to the spiritual purposes of pilgrimage and then to the social participants; in a sentence Chaucer takes his audience into a new and much broader, but not incompatible, literary milieu.

And just as there is no strain evident in his relationship with Machaut as literary parent, despite the power of his authority, so also Chaucer seems to have reacted with unfailing serenity to the genius of Jean Froissart, the literary older brother who most nearly matched his powers as court writer in London. For several years he and Froissart both lived in London, learning side by side the lessons of Machaut's work, and both were affected by the legacy of Jean de le Mote, who was from Froissart's home town; at the same time, in their experiences and observations of life they were laying the groundwork for their later diverging presentations of contemporary life. As far as one can determine, for a decade or so they went along similar paths as poets in the same city without envious eyes, though not without mutual effects, and afterwards they followed different ways. Their personal and literary relationships, and the impact of these on one another, are quite significant for both, and well worthy of study.

FROISSART AND CHAUCER IN LONDON

In the early 1360s London saw itself as a great political centre, home and host to powerful kings and magnates. The city had cultural pretensions also, and its citizenry would not have been stunned to learn that two men destined to rank among the greatest writers of the epoch were young servitors in the courts. Nevertheless, Jean Froissart and Geoffrey Chaucer had as yet to distinguish themselves, and there are few records of their activities in those years. Beyond the indirect evidence of their literary borrowings from each other, there is no document which tells us even that they were acquainted. But without such documentary evidence we can still make certain assumptions confidently. Given the small population of London by modern standards (some fifty thousand inhabitants), the confined and overlapping nature of the court society to which both men were attached, their common bonds of age and interests, the gregarious natures and the passion for knowledge which the writings of both betray, together with the fact that Chaucer married a woman who, like Froissart, was from Hainault and closely connected with Queen Philippa, how could they not have been well acquainted? The question seems to be not whether they knew each other, but what the nature of their relationship was.

Their silence about each other in their writings is not much evidence, though it is something. It says that they probably were not intimate friends, as Chaucer must have been with Gower and Strode, whom he names in *Troilus*. In the *Chronicles*, which are filled with names of Englishmen, Froissart mentions Chaucer but once, citing him and Sir Richard Stury as diplomats on a mission in France in 1377.[1] It may be indicative that when Froissart returned to England in 1395 after decades of absence, he reports his eagerness to see Stury, but not Chaucer. The 'Sir' that marked Stury's name but not Chaucer's may have had something to do with it, since Froissart always cultivated those in high positions. Nevertheless, Froissart does not come through finally as a snob, as has been suggested,[2] nor as a subservient courtier like Placebo in Chaucer's 'Merchant's Tale,' who thinks his lord is always right. While he loved to hobnob with royalty and nobility, even declared that his fondness for

nobility was inborn,[3] his delight in such association and in name-drop-
ping seems remarkably without conceit and guile. When in the *Joli buisson de jonece*, for instance, Froissart enumerates thirty of his great patrons,[4]
the list serves an immediate autobiographical function, and also has the
ingenuous charm of a lottery winner's counting his gains. His favouring
the aristocracy in his writings results largely from his being an author
in their service. At the same time it is true that his English confrère did
not as obviously dote on his court connections, which were just as strong
as Froissart's. Chaucer evidently frequented the circles of the highest
nobility throughout his life, but in his later poetry, instead of numbering
the kings he had met, he writes to Philip de la Vache and Henry Scogan,
whose positions at court were clearly of secondary interest to him.

The reactions of the two poets to the court environment in the early
1360s differed appreciably. Chaucer was a Londoner at home in a milieu
in which his father had moved easily. He was a citizen of family and
talent, unselfconscious among the nobility, while Froissart was a Hainuyer outsider fascinated by the newness and glory of the foreign court,
a commoner delighted by each new nobleman he added to his string of
friends. The reactions of each are in themselves legitimate, but they
would not have made the two soul-mates. In addition, the men became
de facto rivals as poets, with the rivalry having much more potential
effect on Froissart than on Chaucer.

Though his poetry is little known today, it is usually accepted that
Froissart thought of himself as a poet first and a historian second.[5] When
he came to England in about 1361 he brought to Queen Philippa what
must have been a chronicle of his own composition, in verse rather than
prose,[6] and he later emphasizes the 'beaux dittiés and traittiés' with
which he provided her during his service.[7] His chronicling activity evidently took second place until well after he left England. Indeed, one
reason Froissart had been summoned to England was probably to write
poetry, for it seems that his countryman Jean de le Mote, who had been
composing verse in England perhaps into the latter 1350s, by then had
faded from the scene. Le Mote's departure could have left a noticeable
void, since the patronage of poets was a practice that Queen Philippa
had learned from her father, Count Guillaume of Hainault, and King
Edward would have learned the custom from both of his parents. To
fill the void left by le Mote, Philippa perhaps thought to find another
poet from her home, Valenciennes, which had both a strong tradition
of court writers and a well-established puy. Froissart's advent could have
been the result.

In England Froissart had a semi-official status as court poet. His report in *La Prison amoureuse* shows that he was looked to for verse composition when in 1368 he travelled to Milan in the nuptial entourage of Lionel of Clarence, which included 455 people and 1,280 horses. Froissart recalls the three days' layover at Chambéry with Amadée, Count of Savoy, and the lavish feasts and endless music for which he wrote the lyrics:

> Trois jours dura la feste. Mes
> Il y eut danses et carolles,
> Pour quoi j'ai empris les parolles.
> Car bien .vixx. jones et belles,
> Toutes dames et damoiselles ...[8]

The celebration lasted three days; there were dances and carols continually, for which I composed the words. For there were some 120 young and beautiful women, all ladies and damsels.

When in the evenings the minstrels stopped playing their instruments, the ladies continued with virelay after virelay, customarily sung without accompaniment, for which Froissart presumably also contributed some of the lyrics.[9]

Another rising young poet, Oton de Granson of Savoy, probably joined the wedding party at Chambéry and stayed with the company in their travels to Italy. He may also have accompanied them on their return to England. As a nobleman of appropriately limited literary aspirations, Granson was no rival to Froissart's position as poet at the English court; by contrast, Chaucer may unwittingly or at least unpurposefully have posed a substantial threat to that position. Ostensibly merely an amateur poet, for his duties were those of an all-purpose courtier and fighting man, Chaucer was younger than Froissart and without his background in the French literary milieux. Yet by the late 1360s it must have become apparent that Chaucer could do more wonderful things with the current poetry than had been done, and that he could do it in the increasingly prestigious vernacular, English. Some seven years earlier, when Froissart had arrived in England, he found disciples and apostles of the Machaut tradition in the hostages of the Battle of Poitiers and their retinues, also newly arrived. The forms and conventions of the poetry they brought with them blended well with what he already knew, allowing him to assimilate the mode quickly and become one of its prime disseminators. At that time, the situation for him was ideal: he was a protegé of the queen, the court was prosperous, his audience was receptive, and he had no real rivals.

By 1369, however, when Philippa died, the audience was diminished, the political situation in England was deteriorating, and there was a courtier-poet composing in English who could upstage any career writer. Chaucer's presence may well have been a factor, conscious or unconscious, in Froissart's decision to remain with Wenceslas of Brabant in Brussels rather than to return to London, where he doubtless still had many friends. But the greatest were gone.[10] In Brussels, Wenceslas, son of Jean of Luxembourg and himself a poet, was delighted to receive an established writer like Froissart, and there was no question about the ascendancy of French in literature there.

Froissart's position in Brabant was about what it had been in London: unofficial court poet. In the next four years he wrote his most ambitious dits amoureux, but it is doubtful that Chaucer knew these. Of his long dits, we can be sure only that he knew the one Froissart had written in England, the *Paradis d'Amour*.[11] We can be sure of that because Chaucer translates the opening passage of the *Paradis* at the beginning of the *Book of the Duchess*. It is clear, moreover, that the relationship goes beyond this passage. The *Paradis*, we might say, supplies a compositional model for the *Book of the Duchess* based on dits of Machaut. Froissart's poem has a dream frame inspired in part by Machaut's *Fonteinne amoureuse*, with the substance of the work modelled on *Remede de Fortune*. In turn Chaucer's elegy has a dream frame inspired first by Froissart's *Paradis* and second by the *Fonteinne amoureuse* (Froissart's source), with the substance modelled mainly on *Remede de Fortune* (also Froissart's source) and the *Jugement du roy de Behaigne*. Thus, in making his opening passage of the *Duchess* a near-verbatim translation of Froissart's first lines, Chaucer ostentatiously announces that he is following the compositional procedure of Froissart in the *Paradis*. He does not show knowledge of the dits that Froisssart subsequently wrote in Brussels, however. There is a striking similarity between the *Duchess* and another poem by Froissart, the *Dit dou Bleu Chevalier*, composed in Brussels, but that work shows Froissart imitating the English poem,[12] thus revealing another facet of the relationship between the two poets.

We may ask how Froissart got to know the *Duchess*, which was written after he left London. One possibility is that Richard Stury brought a copy when he visited Froissart in Brussels in 1371.[13] The *Duchess* would have been an appropriate gift to Froissart, since both poets were admirers of Chaucer's subject, the Duchess Blanche,[14] and Chaucer's imitation of

Froissart's *Paradis* in the elegy certainly entailed a poetic compliment. When Froissart composed the *Bleu Chevalier* in 1372, then, by imitating the *Duchess* he would have been returning the compliment. Literary borrowing was the way of their world, but with these men it could have had particular significance in marking their mutual respect and good will.

It is interesting that just as Chaucer commemorated Blanche in the *Duchess*, so Froissart in his *Lay VII* elegized Queen Philippa, who died a year after Blanche.[15] Uncharacteristically for a lyric lay, the 219-line poem offers unmediated factual commemoration. Froissant dwells on such matters as the number of Philippa's children and her provision of a tomb for herself: 'Elle eut son vivant / Sept fils et cinq filles, / Preu et hardi' (162–4) / 'In her life she had seven sons and five daughters, valiant and brave'; 'Son vivant fist dediier / A Wesmoutier / Sa sepulture et taillier / Ricement et par excellense' (64–7) / 'While living, she had her tomb richly and excellently carved, and consecrated at Westminster.' This factual matter seems too prosaic for the verse medium, especially for the short lines and complex rhymes of the lay. None the less, Froissart's lyrics are for the most part light and graceful, and compare favourably with the best work in the mode.

The well-known ballade on the marguerite in the *Paradis*, for instance, has an ease and beauty that evokes Chaucer's delightful tribute to the daisy in the 'Prologue' to the *Legend*, as the first stanza exemplifies:

Sur toutes flours tient on la rose a belle,
Et en apriés, je croi, la violette;
La flour de lis est bielle, et la perselle;
La flour de glai est plaisans et parfette.
Et li pluiseur ainment moult l'anquelie,
Le pyone, le mughet, la soussie.
Chascune flour a par lui son merite,
Mais je vous di, tant que pour ma partie,
Sur toutes fleurs j'aimme le margerite. (1627–35)

Some hold the rose to be beautiful above all flowers, and after it, I think, the violet; the fleur de lys is lovely, and the corn-flower; the gladiolus is pleasant and perfect; and many love the columbine, the peony, the lily of the valley, the marigold. Every flower has its particular virtue; but I tell you, for my part, above all flowers I love the daisy.

The remaining two stanzas are of comparable simplicity and liveliness, making the poem a fine example of Froissart's lyric skill. Among Machaut's many fourteenth-century French disciples Froissart is undoubtedly the most successful poet. Chaucer was impressed, for the *Duchess* testifies that Froissart's use of Machaut as literary model led the English poet to a comparable imitation.

It is probable that Froissart met Machaut on more than one occasion, but, as with Chaucer, a meeting with the older master cannot be documented. Nevertheless, there is an interesting textual correspondence between Machaut's *Fonteinne amoureuse* and Froissart's *Espinette amoureuse* that suggests one possible scene for an encounter. Under cover of a fiction involving a young lover and an older poet, the *Fonteinne amoureuse* represents Machaut as keeping the Duke of Berry company just before the duke's trip to England to become a hostage for his father, King Jean. At the end of the poem the companions come to a port, presumably Calais, whence the lover-duke is to set sail. At the port, the poem reports, there were many 'avolés' (2812)[16] – foreigners or refugees. In Froissart's semi-autobiographical *Espinette amoureuse*, which makes substantial use of the *Fonteinne*, he employs the same unusual word (2474) – consciously imitating Machaut, it seems – in describing the great crowd he found at the port from which he sailed on his way to serve a lady overseas, no doubt Philippa in England. The suggestion one may draw from the *Espinette* is that Froissart was going to England in the same momentous time that the Duke of Berry and other French hostages were travelling to England under the terms of the Treaty of Brétigny. The actual year and date of Froissart's trip is a matter of dispute, but the latter part of 1360 is a reasonable possibility.[17] There is, then, just a chance that the two French poets were at Calais at the same time, and that the enterprising Froissart saw the aging Machaut there. I have already mentioned the possibility that Chaucer encountered Machaut in Calais on this occasion; thus, as in Reims in 1359 where Chaucer, Machaut, and Deschamps could have gotten together, there is again the imaginable chance that three major poets of the age were together at once.[18]

Once in England, Froissart states, he lived 'in the Court and Household of the noble king Edward ... and of the noble queen ... and amongst their children and barons of England.'[19] He also states that he belonged to the household of King Jean of France, which perhaps refers to a situation that existed when Jean was in England.[20] In any event, we can gather from his many references to some of the French hostages as friends and patrons that he enjoyed a close relationship with them. As mentioned before, they probably were the occasion of his first extensive acquaintanceship with Machaut's works; the main prior influences on the young poet from Valenciennes would have been the Picard dialect writers rather than those of Champagne.

MACHAUT TO CHAUCER BY WAY OF FROISSART

It is typical of the writers of the time that Froissart never names Machaut. The closest he comes is in the *Joli buisson de jonece*, when the narrator and a group of friendly personifications walk along singing a motet that had been sent from Reims (5076); though no further specification is made, the reference surely is to a work of the canon of Reims, Machaut. This slight tribute is hardly indicative of the relationship, for Machaut is Froissart's most powerful model. In turn, it was partly from Froissart that Chaucer learned the possibilities for creative imitation of Machaut. The relationship of the *Duchess* (c 1368) to the *Paradis* (c 1365) provides the clearest instance of Froissart's instructing Chaucer in the use of Machaut.[21] Also evidencing his mediating influence is the 'Prologue' to the *Legend of Good Women*, in both the ballade and the daisy passages, though it was composed long after Froissart had left England.[22]

For Chaucer's ballade in the prologue, 'Hyd, Absolon, thy gilte tresses clere,' the chain of influence is complex, involving three authors and three attractive ballades, each with the refrain 'Je voy assez, puis que je voy ma dame.' The first two form a double ballade, presented among the balades notées and in *Voir-Dit* in the Machaut manuscripts, and the third is Froissart's imitation of the two. The first part of the double ballade, which engendered the series, is actually by Thomas Paien, as Machaut reveals only in *Voir-Dit*.[23] I quote the the first stanza and a half:

Ne quier veoir la biauté d'Absalon,
Ne d'Ulixès le sens et la faconde,
Ne esprouver la force de Sanson,
Ne regarder que Dalila le tonde,
   Ne cure n'ay par nul tour
Des yeux Argus ne de joie gringnour,
Car pour plaisance et sanz aÿde d'ame
Je voy assez, puis que je voy ma dame.

De l'ymage que fist Pymalion

Elle n'avoit pareille ne seconde;
Mais la belle qui m'a en sa prison
Cent mille fois est plus bele et plus monde ...

I don't seek to see the beauty of Absalon, nor the wit and ready tongue of Ulysses, nor to test the strength of Samson, nor to watch Dalila cut his hair, nor do I have in any way longing for the eyes of Argus or of greater joy, for to my pleasure, without the aid of anyone, I see enough since I see my lady.

As for the statue that Pygmalion made, it had no equal nor imitation, but the lovely one who has put me in her prison is a hundred thousand times more pure and beautiful ...

Machaut's ballade, the second part of the double ballade, imitates the stanza form and refrain of this work, but syntactically and rhetorically the style is quite different, as can be seen from his first stanza:

Quant Theseus, Herculès et Jason
Chercherent tout, et terre et mer parfonde,
Pour acroistre leur pris et leur renom
Et pour veoir bien tout l'estat dou monde,
    Moult furent dignes d'onnour.
Mais quant je voy de biaute l'umble flour,
Assevis sui de tout, si que, par m'ame,
Je voy assez, puis que je voy ma dame.

When Theseus, Hercules, and Jason went everywhere, both on the land and the deep sea, to augment their glory and renown, and to inspect well all the condition of the world, they were very worthy of honour. But when I see the humble flower of beauty, I am satisfied in all ways, so that, by my soul, I see enough since I see my lady.

Dispensing with the first ballade's anaphora ('Ne quier ...' 'Ne trop ...,' etc.) and parataxis, Machaut builds his stanza of two heavily subordinated sentences, a syntactic form that accords well with his usual practice.

Froissart's poem, in addition to using the same refrain, combines phraseology, allusions, and rhyme words from the two earlier ballades. However, he uses rime royal rather than their eight-line stanza. I quote the ballade in full as an excellent example of Froissart's creative imitation:

Ne quier veoir Medee ne Jason,
Ne trop avant lire ens ou mapemonde,
Ne le musique Orpheüs ne le son,
Ne Hercules, qui cerqua tout le monde,
Ne Lucresse, qui tant fu bonne et monde,
Ne Penelope ossi, car, par Saint Jame,
Je voi assés, puisque je voi ma dame.

Ne quier veoir Vregile ne Platon,
Ne par quel art eurent si grant faconde,
Ne Leander, qui tout sans naviron
Nooit en mer, qui rade est et parfonde,
Tout pour l'amour de sa dame la blonde,
Ne nul rubis, saphir, perle ne jame:
Je voi assés, puisque je voi ma dame.

Ne quier veoir le cheval Pegason,
Qui plus tost ceurt en l'air ne vole aronde,
Ne l'ymage que fist Pymalion,
Qui n'eut parel premiere ne seconde,
Ne Oleüs, qui en mer boute l'onde;
S'on voelt savoir pour quoi? Pour ce, par m'ame:
Je voi assés, puisque je voi ma dame.[24]

I don't seek to see Medea or Jason, nor to study deeply the map of the world, nor do I seek the music or the tone of Orpheus, nor Hercules who travelled the whole world, nor Lucrece who was most good and pure, nor Penelope either, for, by Saint James, I see enough when I see my lady.

I don't seek to see Virgil or Plato, nor to find out by what learning they possessed such great skill, nor to see Leander who without any oar drowned in the sea, which is rough and deep, all for the love of his fair lady, nor to see any ruby, sapphire, pearl, or precious jewel: I see enough when I see my lady.

I don't seek to see the horse Pegasus who races through the air faster than a swallow, nor the image that Pygmalion made which had no equal, first or second, nor Eolus who stirs up the sea. Do you wish to know why? For this, by my soul: I see enough when I see my lady.

Despite his indebtedness to the language of both poems, the syntax and rhetorical structure of this lyric is comparable to the first ballade. In following that poem, Froissart may have thought he was imitating a work of Machaut; instead, it seems that he was employing the stylistic trait that most frequently distinguishes his lyrics from the master's: a heavy use of lists, anaphora, and parataxis.

Like a number of his contemporaries, Froissart was much more given to catalogues and series in his short poems than was Machaut; for instance, in all of Machaut's lyrics there is nothing similar to Froissart's catalogue of flowers in the ballade to the Marguerite quoted above.[25] This feature perhaps enables us to see Froissart's particular influence on the ballade in the 'Prologue' to the *Legend*. The likeness is telling, though it involves few verbal echoes,[26] as the first two stanzas illustrate:

> Hyd, Absolon, thy gilte tresses clere;
> Ester, ley thou thy meknesse al adown;
> Hyd, Jonathas, al thy frendly manere;
> Penalopee and Marcia Catoun,
> Make of youre wifhod no comparysoun;
> Hyde ye youre beautes, Ysoude and Eleyne:
> My lady cometh, that al this may disteyne.
>
> Thy faire body, lat yt nat appere,
> Lavyne; and thou, Lucresse of Rome toun,
> And Polixene, that boghten love so dere,
> And Cleopatre, with al thy passyoun,
> Hyde ye your trouthe of love and your renoun;
> And thou, Tisbe, that hast for love swich peyne;
> My lady cometh, that al this may disteyne. (F 249–62)

There is a manifest similarity between Chaucer's refrain and that of the French ballades; a simple assertion of the lady's presence ('my lady cometh,' 'je voi assés') is followed by the implication in a brief subordinate clause that she surpasses all that has before seemed worthy. Other likenesses of Chaucer's ballade to the poem are indicative. These include Chaucer's and Froissart's use of rime royal, and their mutual citations of Penelope, Lucrece, and Jason. Chaucer also importantly echoes the first ballade in the opening reference to Absalom as a paragon of beauty. Chaucer's use of parataxis and anaphora ('Hyd' and 'And' begin nine lines) also is like Froissart's and the first ballade's.

Froissart's fondness for lists and series evidently goes back to his very beginnings as a poet. His first ballade has the following opening stanza:

> Jone, joians, jolie et amoureuse,
> Bonne, belle, bien faite et bien parlans,

Sage, soués, courtoise et gratieuse,
Lie, loyaus, legiere et avenans,
France, frice, faitice et trés plaisans,
Dame d'onneur, de bien enluminee,
Dame digne d'estre en tous lieus amee:
Tel est li corps feminins ou mis ai
Corps, coer, avis, sens, entente et pensee
Et au ssourplus quanque faire porai.[27]

Young, joyful, pretty, and loving, good, beautiful, well-formed, and well-spoken, smart, gentle, courteous, and gracious, happy, loyal, easy, and agreeable, noble, animated, shapely, and very pleasant, a lady of honour, shining with goodness, a lady worthy to be loved everywhere: such is the womanly one in whom I have placed body, heart, mind, sense, purpose, and thought, and what is more, whatever I may do.

The barrage of alliterating adjectives may well suggest that this is the effort of a quite young poet, but it is not uncharacteristic of later Froissart. Machaut, by contrast, in his search for the smooth and understated in his lyrics, generally stops far short of such enumerations and effects. His status as musician-poet no doubt contributed to his avoiding interruptions in the melodic flow of the words. In this respect too, Chaucer generally follows Machaut. Aside from his ballade in the 'Prologue,' in his lyrics he keeps the lists short,[28] and in his stanzaic works generally he favours the long subordinated sentences characteristic of Machaut's work.

Froissart was not to reside near Chaucer after 1368. After leaving England in 1368, he did not return to the country for twenty-seven years. Since it seems that his poetry did not circulate widely,[29] any of his works that Chaucer knew either were composed before 1368 or were brought to him, probably by personal acquaintances, such as Stury, who were in contact with both poets. Whether Froissart wrote the ballade 'Ne quier veoir' before leaving England is uncertain, but another poem that leaves its mark on the 'Prologue' to the *Legend* was doubtless composed later. This is Froissart's *Dittié de la flour de la Marguerite*,[30] his most important celebration of the marguerite flower, and the only one he wrote which Chaucer's praise of the daisy specifically recalls.[31] Here again is the same chain of influence, with Chaucer using a work of Froissart plus Froissart's models. In his description of the daisy Chaucer echoes both of Machaut's short dits on the marguerite, the *Dit de la Marguerite* and *Dit de la fleur de lis et de la Marguerite*.[32]

A brief analysis will illustrate once more how Froissart guided Chaucer's handling of poetic topics. Machaut's *Dit de la Marguerite* opens:

> J'aim une fleur qui s'uevre et qui s'encline
> Vers le soleil de jours quant il chemine. (*Dit* 1–2)

I love a flower which opens and bends towards the sun every day as it makes its way.

These lines are transformed by Froissart to

> Car tout ensi que le solaus cemine
> De son lever jusqu'à tant qu'il decline,
> La margherite encontre lui s'encline ... (*Dittié* 53–5)

For even as the sun makes its way from its rising till its setting, so the marguerite follows, inclining toward it ...

Later in the *Dittié*, when he is focusing more on the narrator's assiduous attentions to the flower, Froissart is inspired by Machaut's second poem, *Lis et Marguerite*, as in the following passage:

> Einsi par nuit elle se cuevre,
> Et au matinet se descuevre.
> Lors la voy volentiers de l'ueil. (*Lis* 249–51)

Thus [the marguerite] conceals herself in the night, and uncovers herself in the morning. Then I happily see her with my eyes.

Froissart transforms the willing inspections made by Machaut's narrator into an obsessive habit:

> Car n'ai aultre desir
> Que del avoir pour veoir a loisir
> Au vespre clore et au matin ouvrir ... (*Dittié* 162–4)

For I have no other wish than to be free to observe her close in the evening and open in the morning.

Chaucer, conscious of all of the four passages quoted above, expands the drama further by having his narrator walk in the meadow night and day to observe the flower:

> ... in my bed ther daweth me no day
> That I nam up and walkyng in the mede
> To seen this flour ayein the sonne sprede,
> Whan it upryseth erly by the morwe.   (F 46–9)

> And whan that hit ys eve, I renne blyve,
> As sone as evere the sonne gynneth weste,
> To seen this flour, how it wol go to reste,
> For fere of nyght, so hateth she derknesse.
> Hire chere is pleynly sprad in the brightnesse
> Of the sonne, for ther yt wol unclose.   (F 60–5)

As with the *Book of the Duchess* and the ballade of the 'Prologue,' so with the love affair with the daisy: Froissart both acts as an intermediary, guiding Chaucer's use of previous writers, and makes a separate integral contribution to his poem.

It is logical and natural that Froissart in his first years in England should have instructed Chaucer in the art of poetry by both precept and example. Born in 1337,[33] he was old enough for young Geoffrey to look up to him, and he had a professional's experience in the current poetic modes that Londoners could not match.[34] The two men probably also had similar backgrounds in the merchant class. Froissart's father might well have had a connection with the Hainuyer court similar to that which Chaucer's father had with Edward III's, which provided his son an entrée. But no doubt the two poets had rather different personalities, as their reactions to the nobility indicate. And they differed in their feelings about involving themselves in commerce. At some early point in his life, Froissart tells us in the *Joli buisson de jonece*, he had tried his hand at 'marchandise'; however, he had soon rejected that calling, disdainfully deciding that 'learning is worth more than money.'[35] By contrast, Chaucer evidently found such commercial activities as keeping a customs inspector's accounts neither uncongenial nor anti-intellectual.

These two wise and gregarious authors, whose backgrounds and circumstances gave them a great deal in common, nevertheless headed ultimately in different directions – the one to be the celebrator of the nobility and court ideals in both his poetry and his chronicles of the

Hundred Years' War, and the other the prober and analyst of human nature and society in the *Troilus* and the *Canterbury Tales*. To an extent, Froissart sacrificed his own welfare for the fame of his betters, expending his own substance to follow and associate with them and to write about their feats. They rewarded him but did not make him rich. For Chaucer, the court probably seemed a qualitatively undifferentiated part of his widening social scene. At the same time his practical aims and administrative talents helped to raise his family to an elevated social and financial position.

While there were close parallels in the early circumstances and experiences of the two poets, their later careers increasingly diverged. Froissart's later history is nevertheless relevant to Chaucer's, if only because it shows a road that the English poet did not take – and it shows more than that. When in 1368 Froissart chose Brussels over London, he found himself part of one of the liveliest courts in Europe, associated with a most congenial leader in the person of Duke Wenceslas of Brabant. Son of blind King Jean of Luxembourg, and brother of Bonne, great patrons of Machaut, Wenceslas likewise was a man of culture and attainment who presided over a gay court alive with poetry and music.[36] Nevertheless, however agreeable the surroundings for the sociable poet, the status of a professional man of letters in that time was highly insecure, and Froissart evidently tended to be a spendthrift. In 1372 he seems to have been in financial trouble and to have borrowed from the Lombards. With the help of his patrons he found the logical way out, and by 1373 he had become a priest and accepted the living of Lestinnes in Hainault. His change in situation led to changes in his writing activities. Until this time his main compositions had been poetry in the lyric mode of the court. Thenceforward, though he wrote some lyrics and shorter dits, his main works were the thirty-thousand-line Arthurian romance *Meliador*,[37] in which Wenceslas' own lyrics are intercalated, and the *Chronicles*, the project that gained him his later fame. About 1382 Gui of Blois helped him to a canonacy at Chimay, which enabled him to travel and write, much to the profit of his historical writings. He died sometime after 1404.

Froissart's *Chronicles* are preserved in a large number of manuscripts involving several redactions, and were printed frequently from the beginning of printing through every century. Translated into English by Lord Berners in the sixteenth century and by others later, they are seen as the authentic record of some of England's most glorious moments. They continue to be popular in England as well as in France.

The fortunes of his poetry have been much different. Were it not for two manuscript collections of his lyrics and dits, not one poem of his would be extant today; the only records of his verse would be his own scanty remarks about them in the *Chronicles*, and the appearance of his name in a list of poets made by a fifteenth-century rhetorician.[38] It is especially notable that not one of his lyrics is to be found in any extant manuscript anthology. We no doubt owe the two manuscripts that we have, dating from 1393 and 1394, to Froissart's own initiative. We know that in those same years he had one copy made for Richard II, for which he was handsomely rewarded. Despite the general neglect of the poems, Richard's munificence was not misplaced, for Froissart was probably the best French poet of the century next to Machaut.

The two Froissart manuscripts evidently were compiled and produced on the model of the Machaut collections, though they are not so sumptuous as some of those.[39] The order and contents vary significantly between the two Froissart collections, but each begins with several of the longer poems, then presents the lyrics segregated by category, and concludes with two or three long dits. As in the Machaut manuscripts, the order in which the works are presented, both the dits and the lyrics within their categories, tends to be chronological, but there are a number of obvious exceptions.[40]

Froissart's four longest dits amoureux show him at his most Machauvian. While there are original features, structually and in content they are modelled mainly on the dits of Machaut which have programs of intercalated lyrics: *Remede de Fortune, Dit de la fonteinne amoureuse*, and *Voir-Dit*. As mentioned, Froissart wrote the first of the long dits, the *Paradis d'Amour* (c 1365), while he was in England. In its plot and its set of five lyric types, it follows the *Remede*, and in some details the *Fonteinne amoureuse*. Chaucer knew it, but he probably did not know Froissart's other three long poems. The next, *Espinette amoureuse* (c 1370), imitates Machaut's *Fonteinne amoureuse* in particular, and contains fourteen intercalated lyrics that take up a third of its length. In the *Espinette* there is much pseudo- or crypto-autobiography, including the veiled presentation of his trip to England at the instance of a great lady (Queen Philippa). In the poem a motive for the trip is the narrator's disappointment in his love for a lady named Marguerite, but there is no way of knowing if the love represented had an actual counterpart in the poet's personal experiences, or is a pure poetic imagining.

The third major dit, the *Prison amoureuse*, has a close affinity to Machaut's *Voir*-dit, shown most obviously in its incorporating eleven prose

letters and seventeen lyrics ostensibly written by the two protagonists
– Rose, who represents Duke Wenceslas, and Flos, who stands for Froissart. In its purpose of comforting Wenceslas in his ten-month captivity
in 1372–3, it is also like Machaut's *Confort d'ami*.[41] The *Joli buisson de
jonece* is the fourth and longest of these major dits.[42] Though the poem
commemorates a vision of November 1373, when Froissart was but thirty-
six, it is a summing up of his career, a retrospective autobiographical
mate to *Espinette amoureuse*, with the poet reviewing his experiences of
Amour and his career as poet, and concluding with a lay to the Virgin,
which implicitly points the way towards his new life as priest.[43] One
finds in the work, which incorporates twenty-eight lyric pieces that occupy over a fifth of its length, strong influence of all three of the Machaut
dits: the *Remede*, the *Fonteinne*, and the *Voir-Dit*.

In the thin narrative lines, the numerous inserted lyrics, and the rhetorical embellishment, these poems share the basically lyric nature of
Machaut's dits. A lyric feature that is often central in these works is the
classical exemplum.[44] With these, however, Froissart frequently goes
well beyond his mentor's practice. Instead of simply retelling stories of
Ovid, he invents lengthy pseudo-classical exempla. This characteristic
of his dits has attracted more scholarly attention than any other, and it
is of particular interest here because of the significant convergences and
contrasts between Chaucer's and Froissart's employment of classical references and narratives.

FROISSART'S CLASSICAL INVENTIONS

Froissart makes frequent brief allusions to figures from classical legend
and sometimes retells the stories at length. The *Paradis d'Amour*, his first
long dit and the only one that Chaucer surely knew, contains numerous
brief allusions. In the poem he refers to Morpheus, Iris, and Juno, Achilles
and Polyxena, Leander and Hero, and many such. He associates with
these figures names that have an authentic ring but are found in no
classical dictionary: Leucothea, an alleged inamorata of Neptune; Me-
lampus, a wailing dog attributed to Acteon; and Enclimpostair, messenger of the God of Sleep, whose marvellous name Chaucer later could
not resist (*Duchess* 167). In his evident invention of such names Froissart's
main predecessor was Jean de le Mote.[45] One may recall from the earlier
discussion that le Mote excited the contempt of Philippe de Vitry and
Jean Campion for his use of inauthentic classical names. Froissart undoubtedly was familiar with le Mote's practice and with the exchanges

of ballades between le Mote and his antagonists,[46] and in his verse he was of le Mote's party, who after all was also a Hainuyer and Queen Philippa's man. But in the dits that came after the *Paradis* Froissart's inventions went beyond le Mote's coining of names and brief narratives to the creation of lengthy Ovidian stories.

The only one of his extensive Ovidian inventions found in a poem that Chaucer clearly knew occurs in the *Dittié de la flour de la Marguerite*,[47] in a passage explaining the flower's origin. As Froissart recognized, this was a subject typical of classical myth-makers:

> S'ai bien cuesi
> Quant j'ai en coer tel flourette enceri
> Qui sans semence et sans semeur ossi
> Premierement hors de terre appari.
> Une pucelle ama tant son ami –
> Ce fu Heros, qui tamaint mal souffri
> Pour bien amer loyaument Cepheï –
> Que des larmes que la belle espandi
> Sus la vredure
> Ou son ami on ot enseveli.
> Tant y ploura, dolousa et gemi
> Que la terre les larmes requelli;
> Pité en ot, encontre elles s'ouvri
> Et Jupiter qui ceste amour senti
> Par le pouoir de Phebus les nouri;
> En belles flours toutes les converti
> D'otel nature
> Comme celle est que j'aim d'entente pure
> Et amerai tous jours quoi que j'endure.   (64–82)

Thus I have well chosen when I have cherished in my heart such a flower [the daisy], which first appeared from the earth without seed and without being sown. A maiden loved her lover so much – this was Hero, who suffered great distress for loving Cepheï well and faithfully – that the beautiful girl spread tears over the grass where her lover lay buried. She so wept, mourned, and sighed that the earth received the tears; it had pity on her and opened itself to them. And Jupiter who felt this love nourished them with the power of Phebus. He changed them all into the beautiful flowers that have the same nature as she whom I love with pure intention, and will love so long as I live.

In the stanzas that follow the poet goes on to describe how Mercury discovered the flowers that grew from the tears. He was inspired to make a chaplet of them for his reluctant mistress, who was so moved by the daisies that she granted him her love.

In the *Dittié* we don't find out how Cepheï had died. But Froissart fills in the beginning of the story in the *Joli buisson de jonece* (3216–41). It seems that one day Hero failed to keep a rendezvous, and in his distraction Cepheï lost his hold on the tall tree from which he watched for her, falling to his death. As is typical of his practice, Froissart concocts the tale mainly from features inspired by the *Metamorphoses*. He delights in strange Latin- and Greek-sounding names, as in his more notable inventions: Papirus and Ydorée, Pynoteus and Neptisphelé, Ydrophus and Neptiphoras, Architelés and Orphane.[48]

It has been remarked that Froissart's fondness for putting together pieces of classical stories in new configurations, readily attributing the product to Ovid, and piling up lists of names in which he mixes the obscure with the well-known is not in the spirit of Humanism, which already was flourishing in Italy.[49] It is also not in the spirit of Machaut's practice. In mid-career Machaut came to employ Ovidian narratives, like the well-developed exempla in the *Jugement dou roy de Navarre*, and in his long dits – though not in his lyrics – he lists exemplary figures from Ovid and other sources. In these, however, he generally adheres to his authorities and is not fanciful.[50] We may perhaps associate Machaut's conservatism in this regard with the attitude of his fellow Champenois, Philippe de Vitry, who was a friend and correspondent of the ur-Humanist Petrarch, just as Froissart's medievalist freedom of invention may originate with his countryman le Mote.

As discussed previously in reference to le Mote's use of names, Chaucer seems to alternate between rather careful adherence to classical authority and freedom of invention. The *Legend of Good Women* illustrates both approaches. In the 'Prologue' Chaucer follows much the procedure of Froissart or le Mote in creating his Alceste on the model of a famous faithful wife, Alcestis, and fabricating for her an Ovidian metamorphosis into a daisy (511–12); he further invents her stellification, a detail he imputes to an obscure authority, Agathon (525–6). But then in the legends themselves Chaucer adheres quite faithfully to his sources, mainly classical, though he 'medievalizes' details. In the story of Seys and Alcyone in the *Book of the Duchess*, likewise, Chaucer draws a good deal from Ovid, but he bolsters his exemplum with materials both classical and medieval that were not proper to Ovid's narrative, including Froissart's

Eclimpostair. Also in the *Duchess* we find a hunter, Octavian (368), not readily identifiable either with the ancient or the medieval emperor, a Cesiphus (589) lying in hell in a position appropriate to Tityus, and the names Antilegyus (1069) and Tubal (1162) when Archilochus and Jubal are appropriate. In the *House of Fame*, with its heavy use of classical reference, the 'carelessness' is more pronounced: Julus and Ascanius, the same person in Virgil, are treated as two (177–8); Jupiter instead of Neptune quiets the storm that scatters Aeneas' fleet (198–225); a mysterious Elcanor is listed among famous dreamers (516); Helicon is a well instead of a mountain (522); Orion appears for Arion (1205); the strange names of Atiteris and Pseustis are found among the musicians (1227–8); Marcia (a female?) appears instead of Marsyas (1229); Limote evidently signifies Elymas (1274); the temple of Isis at Athens is substituted for that of Diana at Ephesus (1844–5). We might also see Chaucer's whole conception of Fame and her house, and the activities therein, built as it is with free improvisation on the precedents of Virgil, Ovid, and Boethius, as in some ways comparable to what Froissart does in building the story of Hero and Cepheï by combining features from the tales of Pyramus and Thisbe and of Venus and Adonis with his own additions.

In *Troilus* Chaucer improvises similarly in presenting a new instance of Cassandra's futile prophecy (v 1450–1533). There are numerous 'anomalies' in this passage, but such matters as Chaucer's calling Cassandra 'Sibille,' as if that were another name for her, and her misidentification of Tydeus as a descendant of Meleager probably does not reflect simple ignorance on Chaucer's part. Of course, the free treatment of classical materials has long been recognized as a trait of medieval authors, but in the case of le Mote and Froissart there is a conscious extension of the practice, while with Vitry, and probably Machaut, there is a conscious reaction against it, which might be called Humanistic. Chaucer may be placed on either side; his habits of classical allusion were probably learned from both le Mote and Machaut, with Froissart exerting subsequent influence.

FROISSART AND CHAUCERIAN REALISM:
CHRONICLE, PASTOURELLE, AND DIT

Geographical separation was not the primary reason for the divergence of Chaucer's and Froissart's authorial careers. Even after they were separated they made use of each other's verse in their love poetry, but as they became less involved with composing in the manner of Machaut neither showed a tendency to follow the other. Froissart became the historian par excellence of the Hundred Years' War, while Chaucer presented his great mirror of society in the *Canterbury Tales*. One might speculate that a similar desire to depict their world as they found it stimulated the two writers, since both the *Canterbury Tales* and Froissart's *Chronicles* present a wide spectrum of contemporary society. Nevertheless, at bottom, the works are far apart. It is not simply that neither writer was influenced directly to any extent by the other's later work,[51] nor is it mainly the difference between prose and poetry or between fiction and non-fiction. In their later writings the authors reveal basically different sensibilities.

It is significant that much of the fictional *Canterbury Tales* is more realistic in presentation than the factual *Chronicles*; the former has passed as a reasonably objective presentation of contemporary society, while the latter is imbued with the aristocratic bias and tendency to idealization characteristic of chivalric romance. Indeed, it is Froissart's romantic vision that accounts for much of the appeal of his narratives. The reader is enthralled with his presentation of Edward III, the Black Prince, and Bertrand du Guesclin as successors to Arthur and Roland, of Philippa as the the 'best queen since Guenevere,' and the battles of the war as the greatest 'puis le temps du bon roi Charlemagne.'[52] His statement of purpose for his *Chronicles* does not exhibit a particular concern to find out and report the facts, but rather a passion to present the 'honourable enterprises' and 'noble adventures' of the war as examples to future generations, the same motive that inspired Malory and his publisher Caxton to present the *Morte Darthur*.[53] Froissart's thirty-thousand-line (unfinished) Arthurian poem *Meliador*, composed mainly in the 1370s, is very much a literary companion of the *Chronicles*.

It is true that Froissart does not glorify without qualification the historical practice of chivalry or the behaviour of particular people. He not only presents the Black Prince as heroically modest in the honour he showed to the captured King John by serving him at table, but also as unacceptably cruel in slaughtering the innocent citizens of Limoges. At the same time, in contrast to Chaucer's often wry report of the deeds of Troilus and Theseus, there is no hint of irony in Froissart's narration of the deeds of great men. In Froissart, brave deeds, even when linked to unspeakable callousness, purposeless destruction, and social chaos, earn praise for the military leader.

Since chronicling was very fashionable in Chaucer's time, we might have expected such writings to have an important effect on his work.

Besides the impressive activity of Froissart and his Hainuyer country-men, Machaut himself had written a long verse chronicle, the *Prise d'Alexandrie*. Numerous others in England and France joined in. But the contemporary instances in the 'Monk's Tale' are as close as Chaucer comes to chronicle. He did not find congenial the subjects or the cus-tomary romancing style that Froissart employs so effectively. For Chau-cer, looking back from the 1380s to his beginning as a soldier in the abortive campaign of 1359, and at the downhill progress of the English military fortunes in the years since, the sad paths of war evidently were not inviting. Thus, one must turn to writings other than the *Chronicles* to find a parallel in Froissart's work to the realism in Chaucer's pres-entation of the Canterbury pilgrimage. More cogent material is provided by the verse of Froissart that recent critics have most generally admired: twenty pastourelles, the prologue to a long dit, and two humorous au-tobiographical pieces. Much as traditions of painting were developing in Flanders and northern France that manifest acute observation of con-temporary life, so Froissart's work variously evidences a poetic tradition of realism that developed in the same area. In this aspect the parallels to Chaucer are general ones of technique and effect.

Froissart's pastourelles are not in fact highly realistic, but when taken together with some related French poems of the same type they provide interesting evidence of a poetic tradition of realism. We have already seen that Froissart's use of classical allusion may be associated with the practice of le Mote's Hainault rather than Machaut's Champagne. An-other evidence of his origins is the influence of the puys, which throve in the northwest especially; in his manuscripts a total of five chansons and serventois are identified as 'crowned' poems – that is, poems hon-oured at meetings of the mainly bourgeois societies of poets.[54] Puy verse was not only less aristocratic in tenor than the poetry of the courts, but in addition each puy had its own customs and rules of composition. In form also some of Froissart's lyrics evidence influences other than Ma-chaut; in particular, we might think of the longer stanzas and the shorter lines characteristic of his ballades.[55]

The most obvious differences from Machaut and affinities to local tradition show up in Froissart's twenty pastourelles, five-stanza forms commonly practised in the puys.[56] Machaut the court man wrote no pastourelles. In reviewing Froissart's poetry, B.J. Whiting notes with evident jubilation, 'Here [in the pastourelles] at least Froissart is not endebted to Machaut.'[57] Notwithstanding, in one respect Machaut had a crucial, if indirect, influence on the development of Froissart's pastourelles, the picture being more complex than Whiting was in a position to know. An inspection of the pastourelles in conjunction with some related poems composed in Froissart's region shortly before 1360, only recently edited,[58] suggests strongly that Froissart was domesticating the non-court form to the tradition of the court – that is, conforming it to the Machaut tradition.

It has been commonly thought that Froissart revived the thirteenth-century pastourelle while effecting important changes in the type, but the newly edited poems from the Pennsylvania manuscript suggest that he began with a local tradition that had already made the changes, and that he modified the type as he came under other influences. Thus, Froissart's first two pastourelles offer an interesting contrast. The first, probably written before his English sojourn,[59] involves a discussion between several shepherds about the houppelande, a long cloak that was just coming into fashion. Some of the shepherds express wonder and curiosity about it while others show that they are up to the minute on fashion, and in the course of the five stanzas provide an interesting and thorough description of the garment. The subject is one generally appropriate to the conversation of shepherds, and the reader's attention is focused on their interests throughout the poem. The work is not unlike the first of the Pennsylvania pastourelles, which also has to do with styles of clothing.[60] Old Herman instructs his young son to be conservative and modest in his dress; in particular, he is not to wear tight-fitting garments that display his lower parts.[61] The son responds properly, showing appropriate respect for his aged father. Froissart's lyric on the houppelande, which pays more attention to description, has neither the dramatic interest of this poem or its moral implications, but in both cases the shepherds treat matters of dress in a way natural to them.

Froissart's second work in the genre, however, written after he had been in England for a while, uses the shepherds as a device to focus on a court occasion, the return to London in 1364 of King John of France. It is a lively discussion by figures from an idealized simple life. Here, and in most of Froissart's remaining pastourelles, the subject-matter and treatment do not evoke the life of actual shepherds; they belong to the long tradition of artificial Arcadianism, contrasting in this regard with the Pennsylvania pastourelles. Two of these poems in particular, which centre on events of natural interest to shepherds, suggest that a tradition of effective realistic poetry existed in the Picard dialect, a tradition that Chaucer and his fellows would have known, though it has now been largely lost.

In the light of the rather large body of French work that has survived from the fourteenth century, such a lost tradition may seem unlikely. If it had existed, statistics seem to dictate that substantial evidence of it would remain. But selective disappearance of distinctive literary types, even of excellent works, is quite possible when they go out of fashion. That which conforms to the current modes, both the good and the marginal, will be retained and assiduously preserved, while very good work that does not appeal to the taste of the time may well be ignored and as a consequence, in medieval conditions, quickly lost. Circumstances were ripe for this to happen in the later fourteenth century because of the dominance of the Machaut tradition. Machaut's work in the various types of lyric and longer dits effectively crystallized major developments of the early century and overshadowed all else until the end of the next century. It was the conventional court poetry that was admired, and which therefore was likely to be collected and survive. Conversely, poetry that deviated was liable to perish. One may then reasonably postulate a body of high-quality realistic poetry that has been forgotten simply because the work was not prized. The two fine pastourelles I have mentioned are compelling witnesses to the possibility. Because they are virtually unique among extant fourteenth-century French lyrics and are peculiarly successful, and because they represent a style that could have influenced Chaucer's later work significantly, they are worth discussing here in some detail.

Centring on the everyday behaviour and repartee of country people, the genre scenes created in the two poems are thoroughly engaging and true to life. Certain factors conduce to their realism: their evident puy origins, which allowed non-court subjects; the requirement that as pastourelles they deal with the lower classes; and their concern with current historical events. But these factors do not assure effective realism. To produce lively and authentic representations of life the poet required fine powers of observation and the good models for verse techniques which a developed tradition provides. The lyrics speak well for themselves. In accord with contemporary pastourelle practice, each of the two poems has five stanzas, a refrain at the end of each stanza, and an envoy.[62] The stanzas are exceptionally long, consisting of fifteen lines of octosyllables in one case and sixteen in the other; and the rhymes carry over from stanza to stanza. Both works involve complaints by shepherds that concern current political events.

The refrain of the first poem laments that a wolf has been set to guarding the sheep, which in context probably refers to the peace treaties that were being negotiated between England and France in 1359 and 1360.[63] It would have been natural to feel that by the proposed political agreements the people of several Continental areas, as well as the hostages, were being given into the power of their natural enemies – sheep in the power of wolves, as the refrain has it. As is the case with most fourteenth-century pastourelles, the narrator's role contrasts with earlier convention. The Old French type generally opens with a narrator of the upper class telling how he came upon a shepherdess or some shepherds and became involved with them. In the Middle French development the narrator usually is present only as a reporter. In the poem at hand his presence is indicated only by the verb 'trouvay' – 'I found' or 'came upon' – and the whole of the lyric is devoted to telling what he observed. The first stanza introduces three old shepherds resting at noonday:

> Trois bergiers d'ancien aez,
> pour le chault dessoubz un buisson,
> manjans lait, burre, et pois pelez,
> aulx nouveaulx, et maint gros maton,
> trouvay qui tenoient sermon
> de faire manches a cousteaux.
> Atant vint a eulz Maroteaux,
> une pucelle de Helli
> son quien amenant devant li,
> en disant, 'Oez de nouvel:
> je oy hier dire au Carduel,
> l'aisné filz Brunel le Sauvage,
> que ne sçay quel gent de parage
> ont esleu (de quoy j'ay merveilles)
> *un leu pour garder les oeilles.* (1–15)

I came upon three old shepherds, sitting beneath a bush because of the heat, eating milk, butter, and peeled peas, new garlic, and a number of large cheeses. They were talking about carving knife-handles. Then Maroteaux, a girl from Heilly, came up to them with her dog in front of her, saying, 'Hear the news that I heard yesterday from Carduel, the eldest son of Brunel the Sauvage, that some very strange kind of nobility has chosen – for which I marvel – a wolf to guard the sheep.'

Maroteaux's revelation, never explicitly glossed, produces a predictable reaction from each of the old shepherds. Hinauls of the Meadows responds first (16–30), announcing that he is going to sell his leatherworking tools and materials, his punch and his ointment (since there won't be any sheep left to supply hides). He recalls some of the exceptional events he has lived through: King Louis' seige of Tunis in 1270 (when Louis died), the great battles of Mons-en-Pévèle and Cassel, and the recent burning of Rethel that prevented the Black Prince from crossing the Aisne River. 'But never,' he concludes indignantly, 'have I heard of putting a wolf to guard the sheep.'

Hinauls the Hairy ('li herupez') chimes in with another speech (31–60) in character for an old shepherd reacting to such news. 'Good times for shepherds have passed,' he says. 'Though I am the oldest of you I have never seen such a thing. Wolves love lambs only to eat; such shepherds are unworthy of their trade. David and Asahel [in the Bible] were shepherds, and shepherds have often received divine revelation [as at the Nativity]. Though I am a hundred years old I have never seen such an outrage as putting a wolf to guard the sheep.' He has been to Rome twice, he goes on to say, and he names some important battles of the Hundred Years' War that he has witnessed: the seiges of Sheudt, Tun-l'Evêque, and Tournai, and the battle of Vannes when the English mounted the walls. 'And I swear by Saint Rémi that I saw the King of England do homage to Philippe. But afterward he led the fleet [against France] at the battle of Cadzant.' Turning to the third shepherd, he asks, 'Hubaut, did any of your ancestors ever see – tell me! – a wolf put to guard the sheep?'

'Never,' responds Hubaut (61–75), 'though I have seen many things. I have seen the plague and afterwards the flagellants who cruelly whipped themselves until the blood ran in streams, causing the sheep and goats to flee in terror. By the blood of God, at that time a master was I don't know what [that is, not much good]. Don't I speak the truth, Ansel?' The fourth shepherd, Ansel, who evidently has just joined the group, responds with his 'bel langage,' an ironic commentary. 'Yes, but Reason corrected their custom, and you won't see such things any more, only a wolf to guard the sheep.' This speech leads directly into the envoy, addressed to the prince of the puy:

Franc prince, qui ces mos ymage,
on en puet s'aquier hault ouvrage
mais qu'on ait veu les imparielles,
un leu pour garder les oeilles. (76–9)

Generous prince who hears these words, one may learn an edifying lesson if he has seen such inequities – a wolf put to guarding the sheep.

In the force and authenticity of its realism, this work is unsurpassed in fourteenth-century French verse. Its language is lively and colloquial, it presents shepherds engaged in everyday pursuits reacting in character, and it makes reference to important and interesting historical events in a convincing dramatic context, all of this embedded in a difficult but effective verse form. If it imputes to the shepherds a more sophisticated understanding of event than seems likely – as the 'Miller's Tale' imputes to the Miller a cleverness far beyond the ability of such a figure – it nevertheless remains centred on their proper interests. The second pastourelle, no doubt the work of the same poet, makes a worthy companion to it, and it differs sufficiently in its cast of characters and subject-matter to suggest the potential range of the kind. It has the same metrical form, except that the stanzas are sixteen lines long with a consequent modification of the rhyme scheme.

The subject of this poem clearly is one of the disgraceful exploits of the routiers, the out-of-work mercenaries who pillaged northern France in the time of truce after the battle of Poitiers in 1356. Specifically, the poem probably grows out of events of 1357 or 1358. The battle cry of the routiers, 'Saint George,' repeated in the refrains, obviously had become a general slogan not confined to the English. The setting of the work is near Amiens; the two characters who speak are an old shepherd, Madoulz, and his son. At the poem's outset they are weeping bitterly because the son has just been robbed of all their sheep, lambs, ewes, and yearlings. Madoulz, who had not been present, asks somewhat incoherently, 'Were they Navarrese? Why didn't you defend yourself?' 'I would have been hanged,' responds the son, 'I knew that I was completely lost as soon as they cried "Saint George"' (1–16). In his helplessness, Madoulz is angry with both his son and the ruffians:

'L'ouïs tu crier, quoquevieulz?'
'Mon Dieu, pere,' dist l'enfes, 'oye.
Et me tollirent mes ostieuls,
ma boete, et alesne aguisie
qui avoit le manche entaillie.
Noyez soient il en le Canche!
Que font leurs chevaux de nuisanche!
Je leur ay tresbien avisé.'
'Et leur as tu point demandé
se ce sont Flamens ou François?'
'Si ay. Ilz sont de Boulenois

et ont trestout ouan consu
canchiers et en grange batu.
Mais je ne sçay laou c'est qu'on forge
les armes quë ilz ont vestu
aussi tost c'om crie "Saint George." '   (17–32)

'You heard them hollering, idiot?' 'My God, father, yes, and they took my tools, my box, and sharp awl with the carved handle. May they drown in the Canche! What havoc their horses caused! I saw them well.' 'And did you ask if they were Flemish or French?' 'Indeed I did. They are from around Boulogne, and have been out all year raiding along the rivers and destroying granges. And I don't know where they got the arms they put on as soon as someone cried "Saint George." '

The son then says that while they are now well armed, it wasn't long before that such men didn't have bread to eat. Madoulz comments bitterly on the circumstance that the pillagers are near neighbours: 'If three wolves had attacked the flock they would have carried off [only] three of the sheep; isn't it a great outrage when our countrymen are worse than wolves? Never before did it happen that people raised on barley bread become feared as noblemen as soon as they cry "Saint George" ' (33–48).

In the remainder of the poem proper (49–80), the brigands are further characterized. The son asks if they are brave men. 'Not in the least,' responds Madoulz. 'They are good only for robbery. Do you think such a gang of good-for-nothings would dare to joust on the battlefield, even two against one armed man? Never! But these cowards will pillage a defenceless citizen; in that they are marvellously brave. All such people stink of hanging. Certainly, I'd rather be way over in Montagu as soon as they cry "Saint George." ' With sad humour the son picks up the refrain and wonders if Saint George would steal old sheep worth less than wolves or foxes. 'Don't be silly!' rejoins Madoulz. 'These are not gentlefolk but cowards; and if peace were made all such scoundrels would be hanged right away; as many of the rascals would be tortured and gibbeted as those who have died in battle.' 'That would be well done,' comments the son. 'May such a fly bite them that they can no longer do a thing when they cry out "Saint George!" '

Once more the envoy is a direct commentary by the narrator, reinforcing the dramatic message of the poem:

Franc prince! Houlier et cabit,
coquart, coquin, et malostru
le crient; mais ce est qui l'acorge.
Je lo quë on les gette ou fu
aussi tost qu'on crie 'Saint George!'   (81–5)

Generous prince! Mercenaries, thugs, fools, rascals, and boors cry it, yet there are some who support them. I beg that they be thrown into the fire as soon as they cry 'Saint George!'

These two poems, and to a lesser extent some others of the Pennsylvania pastourelles, provide good evidence for a vigorous tradition of realism which probably developed in the puys of northern France in the early fourteenth century and flourished until the 1360s. What happened to the tradition? Why is there no further evidence of it when it was producing effective works like these? As suggested above, it is likely that the Machaut tradition simply smothered its competition, and that the puy poets were seduced into following the triumphant court style perfected by the two great musician-poets, Philippe de Vitry and Machaut. Froissart's pastourelles show how a talented court poet with puy experience could help to redirect the form. His first pastourelle, probably written before he came under the direct influence of the Machaut style, partakes of the Pennsylvania type. His second pastourelle, composed in England, adapts the type to court uses.

Whiting asserted as an accepted fact that of all of Froissart's poems his twenty pastourelles 'show the greatest literary merit, interest, and originality.'[64] His evaluation reflects the desire of many modern readers to find something different from the Machaut model in fourteenth-century lyrics, and it is true that in its dramatic presentation the medieval pastourelle differs from the usual court lyric; it is the only lyric type that requires dialogue. As Whiting also notices, Froissart's pastourelles are written from an aristocratic point of view and 'are not very realistic.' He sees all such traits as natural to the Old French genre.[65] However, if we set Froissart's poems alongside their counterparts in the Pennsylvania manuscript we see that instead of reviving something old, his pastourelles embody an attempt to domesticate the fourteenth-century genre to the court mode, and in the process much of the vigour and immediacy is lost. Thus, in his 'Pastourelle IX' the shepherds talk of current events as they do in the two Pennsylvania poems, but in a far different manner.

The purpose is to celebrate Gaston de Foix, the shepherds providing a convenient vehicle to that end:

En un biau pré vert et plaisant,
Par dessus Gave la Riviere,
Entre Pau et Ortais seant,
Vi l'autrier ensi qu'a prangiere
Maint bregier et mainte bregiere
Qui devisoient des estas,
Des haus, des moiiens et des bas,
Sans parler de leur bregerie,
Mais d'armes et d'armoierie
Leur oÿ biau cop deviser
France et Engleterre nommer,
Portugal, Castille aus castiaus,
Navare, Arragon et Bourdiaus,
Osterice, Bretagne et Blois,
Et pas n'oublioent entre iauls
Les armes de Berne et de Fois.[66]

The other day around noon, in a lovely meadow, green and pleasant, situated on the Gave River between Pau and Orthez, I saw many shepherds and shepherdesses who were talking about the world, about the high, the low, and the middle classes, not discussing shepherding, but rather I heard them speaking extensively of arms and heraldry, naming France and England, Portugal, Castille with its castles, Navarre, Aragon, and Bordeaux, Austria, Britain and Blois, and they did not forget among these the arms of Béarn and Foix.

The concern of these shepherds with describing coats of arms seems about as unlikely an occupation as any ascribed to them in the classical tradition of pastoral.

When we know the Pennsylvania pastourelles, we see that everything that has appeared new in Froissart's work in the genre – the metrical form, the historical references, and the reduced role of the narrator – has precedents that he undoubtedly knew. In the matter of metrics there is the striking fact that of all five-stanza poems in Middle French that have been published, only the two Pennsylvania pastourelles and thirteen of Froissart's pastourelles have stanzas of fourteen or more octosyllabic lines.[67] And while Hoepffner credited Froissart with the creation of the 'pastourelle historique,'[68] several of the Pennsylvania pastourelles, composed earlier, are based on historical event. Likewise, the narrator's role as passive witness, which has seemed original with Froissart, finds a direct counterpart in the Pennsylvania poems. If, as is quite possible, the materials for the Pennsylvania manuscript were assembled in England, Froissart could have been the one who brought the pastourelles texts there.

Froissart knew the tradition and very likely these particular poems. Indeed, it seems that he took up the form just after the two Pennsylvania poems that we have looked at were composed. They were written very close to 1360; Froissart's second marked an event of 1364, and his first was probably composed in 1360 or 1361. Before composing the second, he evidently came under the powerful influence of Machauvian court poetry. Assisted by his subsequent use of the form, uncourtly realism went out of style even in the puy genres that previously had been hospitable to it. The dramatic presentation, so vivid in the poems we have looked at, became primarily a mechanism in Froissart's pastourelles; in general his shepherds and shepherdesses, rather than interacting dramatically with their fellows, simply take turns in speaking and elaborating on the subject at hand. And whereas the shepherds in the Pennsylvania poems remain stubbornly concerned with their own affairs, making the historical material relate to their personal interests, in most of Froissart's pastourelles the shepherds exist to celebrate court events or subjects of court poetry, or engage in idealized activities.[69] As a result Froissart's pastourelles comprise another form that integrates into the Machaut tradition; with their court subjects, dramatic presentation, and their own proper forme fixe they provide a pleasant variation, but little more than a variation, on the standard ballades, rondeaux, virelays, and chants royaux. While they clearly grew from the puy practice that we see in the Pennsylvania poems, they altered it drastically and signal the end of the pastourelle as a substantially different type. Thus, Deschamps later writes several five-stanza works that use the pastourelle framework and historical reference, but the drama is static and the focus is on the public subject presented from an aristocratic perspective.

If Chaucer knew the tradition of realism found in the complex lyric forms of the Pennsylvania pastourelles, therefore, though his knowledge of it would not have come mainly through Froissart's poems, it might have come from verse and compositional practice that Froissart brought with him to England. The very fact of the tradition is surely significant for Chaucer's work, for in these pastourelles there is contemporary precedent for his effective presentation of men of common occupations in action, in works like the 'General Prologue,' the 'Miller's Tale' and the 'Reeve's Tale,' and the 'Canon's Yeoman's Tale.' In them also is precedent for the well-realized dramatic dialogue found throughout Chaucer's poetry, and especially for the stanzaic dialogues of the *Parliament of Fowls* and *Troilus and Criseyde*. Instead of offering congruencies in detail to Chaucer's works, the texts provide evidence that there existed a rich contemporary tradition of verse realism – not closely related to the moralization of estates literature or the sermon – pertinent to Chaucer's own developing techniques.

Froissart directed the pastourelle genre away from, rather than towards, realism. Like his shepherds, he is aristocratic in his sympathies. Permanently fascinated by nobility and royalty, most of his poetry and his chronicles manifest a great interest in the courtly occupations of love and war. One should not, of course, deplore this aspect of his character, for without it his matchless *Chronicles* would not be what they are, nor would his lyrics and dits amoureux, which also are of very high quality. Yet had he turned his attention more often towards subjects of popular application and concern he might have produced a substantial body of lively poetry that could be related to Chaucer's usually humorous realism. In the *Chronicles* Froissart shows a consistent ability to capture details of narrative interest, and occasionally in both prose and poetry he deals compellingly with domestic and uncourtly situations and events.

One passage of notable popular interest in his love dits is his description in the *Espinette amoureuse* (1–296) of himself as a schoolboy. In an ingratiating enumeration he describes more than thirty of his childhood games. It was not chess or backgammon that caught his fancy, he says, but building little mills on brooks, making mud pies, tying strings to butterflies, riding stick-horses named Grisel, and such. And he goes on to tell of taking gifts to the little girls at school, and how he would get beaten for his lessons, beaten by his fellows, and beaten again for his torn clothes, none of which daunted him for long. Another verse piece that appeals to modern readers is the *Débat dou Cheval et dou Levrier*,[70] a ninety-two-line poem in octosyllabic couplets which Froissart wrote after his trip to Scotland in 1365. Froissart's horse and dog, as they travel, in turn complain about the rigours of travelling and the treatment they receive. Each thinks the other has all the advantages: the dog asserts that the horse is lucky to be strong and well shod, well suited for travel, while the horse thinks the dog very fortunate in having no burden and never being whipped. The horse has a stall, is curried at night, and is often covered with a cloak; the dog is favoured with food from the table and gets in on the fun everywhere. So it goes until they see their destination ahead.

Froissart's most ambitious poem of the autobiographical sort is the *Dit dou florin*,[71] a work that makes a trio with Machaut's 'A toi, Hanri' and Chaucer's *Complaint to His Purse*, though it is considerably longer (492 lines) than either of those poems. The *Dit* resembles Chaucer's poem in the narrator's preoccupation with his empty purse, and in its use of personification to dramatize his plight: Chaucer makes his purse his 'lady dere' to whom he complains, while Froissart, finding in his purse one clipped and battered florin that has not disappeared with its fellows, addresses it as a culprit that he's caught. At the same time, in its wry presentation of the poet's autobiography under the pressure of a difficult situation, the *Dit* is reminiscent of Machaut's address to 'Hanri.' What especially associates the three works is the consistent irony with which each of the poets presents himself and his plight.

The setting for Froissart's poem is Avignon, where he is in pursuit of a new benefice. He has just spent three months with Gaston Phebus, Count of Foix, reading to him every night from his endless romance *Meliador*. On his departure the count gave him a hundred gold francs, but in Avignon a thief relieved Froissart of these while he was at Sunday Mass. The poem begins with a hundred-line exposition of his own ability to spend money, and of the life of ease and influence which money leads. He slides easily into treating money as a person:

> Argens est de pluisours lignies,
> Car, lors qu'il est issus de terre,
> Dire poet: 'Je m'en vois conquerre
> Pays, chasteaus, terre et offisces.'
> Argent fait avoir benefisces,
> Et fait des drois venir les tors
> Et des tors les drois au retors.
> Il n'est chose qu'argens ne face
> Et ne desface et ne reface.
> Argent est un droit enchanteur,
> Un lierres et un bareteur:
> Tout met apoint et tout toueille. (52–63)

Money belongs to many races, and as soon as it comes from the ground it can say, 'I am going to conquer countries, castles, lands, and offices.' Money confers benefices, and makes wrong of right and in return right of wrong. There is nothing that money does not make, destroy, and remake. Money is a true magician, a thief, and a grafter: it settles everything and messes everything up.

The poet then considers that in the past twenty-five years he has had more than two thousand francs in addition to the benefice of Lestinnes, and he wonders what he has done with them. Coming upon the lone florin in the purse, he decides to make it tell him what has happened to the money he has had.

Like a good jailer, he first submits the florin to cruel torture ('jehine' 110) and then questions it abusively. In the first line of the following quotation, 'vallet' has a nice ambiguity, signifying both a serving-man and a coin:

'Diex, dou vallet!'
Di je lors. 'Es tu ci quatis?
Par ma foi, tu es uns quetis,
Quant tous seulz tu es en prison
Demorés, et ti compagnon
S'en sont alés san congié prendre!
Or ça, il t'en fault compte rendre.'
Adonques le pris a mes dens
Et le mors dehors et dedens
A la fin qu'il fust plus bleciés.
Et quant je me fui bien sanciés,
Sus une piere l'estendi
Et dou poing au batre entendi.
Et puis si tirai mon coutiel
Et jurai: 'Par ce hateriel,
Je t'esboulerai, crapaudeaus!
Bien voi que tu es uns hardeaus
Tailliés, rongniés et recopés.
Pour ce n'es tu point eschapés!
Les aultres t'ont laissié derriere!
Se tu fuisses de leur maniere,
De bon pois et de bon afaire,
Tu eusses bien o eulz a faire.'   (112–34)

'By God, you fellow,' I said then, 'are you skulking here? By my faith, you are a caitiff since you have remained in prison when your companions have fled without any leave-taking. Come here! You must account for yourself.' Then I took him in my mouth and bit him inside and out, so that he was even more cut up. And when I was satisfied, I stretched him out on a stone and began beating him with my fist. And then I took out my knife and swore: 'By this head, I will disembowel you, scoundrel! I see clearly that you are a knave – cut, trimmed, clipped. This is why you didn't escape! The others left you behind! Had you been their sort, of proper weight and good condition, you could have gone with them.'

Froissart handles the metaphor and the colloquial diction very skilfully, maintaining at the same time the florin's dual character as coin and mistreated prisoner, as well as his own dual character as destitute poet and cruel inquisitor. He goes on to threaten the florin with being cut in pieces and burned at the foundry unless it tells where the two thousand florins he has earned have gone.

The florin responds with proper respect: 'Pour dieu merci, Sire!' and says that it has been in Froissart's purse a long time, so that it has learned French, English, and Flemish,[72] and also knows where its more fortunate fellows have gone. It says that seven hundred have gone for books that Froissart has had made, and five hundred to the tavern at Lestinnes, and he must have paid a thousand for his travels from city to city, 'en arroi de souffisant homme' / 'outfitted like a prosperous man' (224). The conversation continues, and both the poet and the florin recall past experiences, particularly Froissart's visit with Gaston de Foix and the theft of his gift. The florin asserts that there is no use crying about the lost money, which there is no hope of recovering, and reassures Froissart that his patrons will take care of him. Froissart agrees that the florin is right; in any event, he concludes, as Antoine de Beaujeu and Gérard d'Obies have often said laughing,

'Autant vaudront au Jugement
Estront de chien que marq d'argent.'

'At the Judgment a dog-turd will be worth as much as a mark of silver.'

Froissart successfully relieves the crudity of the proverb by putting it in the mouth of jesting noblemen, much as Chaucer evades responsibility for coarseness by having appropriate pilgrims present the fabliaux in the *Canterbury Tales*.

If the *Dit dou florin* is a begging poem, as it seems to be, it is very skilfully presented. Instead of exposing his troubles to his patrons directly in an aggrieved recitation, Froissart puts his plight in a humorous context, showing that he does not view himself with excessive gravity. The poem also demonstrates that he had a fine talent for dealing humorously and circumstantially with everyday events in verse. Taken together with the Pennsylvania pastourelles – and we also might include Machaut's 'A toi, Hanri' – the *Dit* is a good indication that Chaucer's style of realism was not alien to fourteenth-century French poets. In the final analysis, it seems, they simply found the court mode of love lyric more compelling.

Of the several French poets with whom Chaucer had a significant relationship, Froissart was the one with whom he had most in common. Their family backgrounds, their ages, their situations in the London court, and their virtuoso literary talents all serve to associate them. The natural gregariousness, the tolerance, and the sense of humour that each manifests in his writings also must be counted among their major affinities. Though the identifiable direct borrowings of Chaucer from Froissart are confined to the frame of the *Book of the Duchess* and various passages and features of the 'Prologue' to the *Legend of Good Women*, still the influence must be counted as much broader than this. In an important way Froissart showed Chaucer what Machaut had to offer, and he may also have contributed to Chaucer's development of a realistic style. In return Froissart did not disdain to learn from the younger Chaucer, as his imitation of the *Duchess* in the *Dit dou Bleu Chevalier* shows. In the process he perhaps learned some of his own limitations as poet. If the two writers probably did not become close friends, they still were men who must have liked and appreciated each other. Coming together in London in a remarkable time in history, they converted that time into remarkable literature.

CHAPTER SEVEN

Chaucer and
Oton de Granson

For the royal government in London and for citizens of England, the wedding trip of Lionel of Clarence to Milan in the spring of 1368 marked a change in the political and social climate that was far from happy. As the party made its grand progress across France to Italy, no one could realize how far down on her wheel Fortune shortly would carry the English and Edward III. The bridegroom was to die in Italy in October; back in England Blanche of Lancaster would die in September, Queen Philippa the next August; thereby Edward's second son and the two leading women of his court were quickly taken away. Meanwhile in Spain the first son, the Black Prince, was sick and bogged down in a fruitless military operation, and John Chandos, one of the greatest English warriors, had recently died there. As the English glory dwindled, in France the stars of Bertrand du Guesclin and the court under Charles V were rising. No longer was London the cynosure Froissart had found in 1362, and when on his return from Italy he went to Brussels rather than England he took from it the bit of Continental gaiety that he had brought with him.

'FLOUR OF HEM THAT MAKE IN FRANCE'

Nevertheless, a replacement for the absent Froissart did appear – not a professional French man of letters but a skilled amateur poet. Oton de Granson, probably a participant in Lionel's wedding in 1369, was to serve in England and on its behalf, with long periods off in Savoy, for the next twenty-eight years until his death in a duel in 1397. His lord in

Savoy, the Green Count Amadée VI, obviously was a lover of French court poetry. It was he who had entertained the wedding party in Chambéry for three days, providing Froissart occasion for presenting his virelays, and on 5 May 1368 Amadée paid Machaut handsomely for a manuscript collection of his poetry.[1] Encouraged to try his hand at verse in the favourable climate that the Counts of Savoy provided, Granson no doubt had become experienced in the formes fixes by the time he arrived in London. Comparable interest in verse and similarity in age evidently led Granson to a long friendship with Chaucer, who was to celebrate him in the envoy of the *Complaint of Venus* as 'flour of hem that make in Fraunce.'

The words show Chaucer's respect and affection for Granson. Yet by the words he is hardly giving his poetic powers 'pre-eminence above Froissart, Deschamps, and Machaut,' as has been claimed.[2] For Chaucer's phraseology is not applicable so much to Granson's 'making' as to his accomplishments as a knight. An inspection of medieval usage shows that the term 'flower' or 'fleur,' when signifying the élite or the choicest in a class, was originally and most commonly applied to the nobility and to men of arms. From the *Song of Roland*, where Charlemagne laments the fall of the Douze Pers, 'De France m'ont tolude la flor' / 'They have taken from me the flower of France', to the *Morte Darthur*, where Malory identifies Lancelot as 'the floure of knyghtes,' the term evokes the special qualities of the warrior or the prince. It is a favourite of Froissart in the *Chronicles*, as when he calls the Black Prince 'la fleur de toute la chevalerie dou monde,' or speaks of a French garrison as consisting of the 'fleur de gens des armes.'[3] 'Flower' connotes the characteristic virtues of the nobility. Chaucer's words signify that Granson is a great knight-poet, even the best of the knight-poets then active, but they are hardly an affidavit that he is the best of French poets. Froissart and Deschamps, not to mention Machaut, were more skilled. Granson never presented himself as more than an amateur in the world of such professionals.

Granson was the first of a new group of noble poets which would include in the late century Jean de Garencières, the authors of the *Cent ballades* and its responses, the members of the Cour amoureuse,[4] and ultimately Charles d'Orléans and René d'Anjou. In general, these writers did not as intently study and exercise the art of poetry, nor as systematically preserve their oeuvre, as did contemporaries of lesser birth like Machaut and Froissart. This is not to say that Granson did not approach verse composition in a serious manner. He wrote in all the lyric genres, and a substantial number of his works are preserved in several collections of formes fixes poetry.[5] As we will discuss, he was probably responsible for having manuscripts made that included his work. Still, the total of his extant verse is but a fraction of what remains of the other prominent French poets whom we associate with Chaucer, and it is uneven in quality.

Almost all the numerous references to Granson by those who knew him and came after him show that he was an impressive courtier and knight, a person whose life invited the creation of legend. Froissart, who no doubt knew Granson personally, speaks of him in the *Chronicles* as 'banerés et riche homme durement' / 'a banneret and a most worthy fighter,'[6] but he makes no reference to his poetry. Christine de Pisan, Granson's most ardent encomiast, praises his chivalric virtues in two poems. In one instance, she says he was 'courtois, gentil, preux, bel et gracieux,' possessing all virtues. In the second, she speaks of his prowess like that of Telamonian Ajax, and of his devotion to the ladies whom he wished 'to serve, esteem, love,' but she too says nothing directly of his poetry.[7] Though Granson was a composer of poetry in praise of the ladies, there is no indication that he was a lover on the order of Lancelot. Whoever 'Isabel' was, whom he addresses and names in several poems, his aims in writing verse to her in all probability were diplomatic and social. He was very active in warfare most of his adult life,[8] and he was generally a man of affairs; in the early 1390s, for instance, he took part in peace negotiations between France and England, and in Philippe de Méziéres' influential Order of the Passion of Jesus Christ he was one of the 'four evangelists' charged with preaching a new crusade.[9] Not inconsistently, Granson's death manifests the warrior's willingness to involve himself in violence. In 1397, when he was over fifty, he died defending his honour in a judicial duel. His manner of dying did nothing to discourage the legend of the man.

As Granson in a fashion filled a vacancy in the English court left by Froissart, so also he fills a gap in our history, succeeding to le Mote and Froissart as French poets with whom Chaucer might well have had regular contacts in London. Granson, as a landed knight, was higher on the social scale than Chaucer and his previous associates. But he made more extensive use of Chaucer's poetry than did any other French poet, which indicates that he had a writer's capacity to appreciate Chaucer's genius, and he probably had a personal warmth that nurtured their friendship. His position as a warrior-knight in the service of John of Gaunt no doubt was socially convenient for him, facilitating association with court men at all levels.

The *Complaint of Venus* provides our best clues to Chaucer and Granson's relationship. Implicitly, it is a tribute by Chaucer to his noble friend, being a triple ballade that translates three of the five poems in Granson's five-ballade sequence, called in one manuscript *Les Cinq balades ensievans*.[10] Chaucer's ten-line envoy provides rare historical information and literary commentary; it is the envoy that speaks of Granson as 'flour' and also of the difficulty of translating his verse's 'curiosite'– a word with a nicely ambiguous quality. Chaucer's envoy nevertheless is a somewhat anomalous appendage to the triple ballade, having no counterpart in the Granson ballades that he is translating. The 'princes' (princess?) to whom it is addressed is just one of its problems:

Princes, receyveth this compleynt in gre,
Unto your excelent benignite
Direct [dedicated] after my litel suffisaunce.
For elde, that in my spirit dulleth me,
Hath of endyting al the subtilte
Wel nygh bereft out of my remembraunce,
And eke to me it ys a gret penaunce,
Syth rym in Englissh hath such skarsete,
To folowe word by word the curiosite
Of Graunson, flour of hem that make in Fraunce.   (73–82)

Chaucer's preceding three ballades conform perfectly to common French verse practice, as this envoy does not. Its versification does not relate it to the preceding poem as envoys commonly did,[11] it is much longer than the French poets ever made their envoys, and indeed it is not even like any current ballade stanza.[12] If it were not for Chaucer's complaining about the scarcity of rhyme in English, which suggests that he has just emerged from wrestling with the translation, one would feel that the envoy is an ad hoc performance, hurriedly composed to adapt the translation – made long before – as a presentation piece. We cannot rule out that possibility. The complaint about rhyme being scarce also constitutes a crowning anomaly. Perhaps it is just an aging poet's quiet joke: using but two rhyme sounds in ten lines, Chaucer employs a rhyme scheme for the envoy that is much more demanding than that which either poet uses in the ballades proper.

The envoy seems a thing apart. The originals for the ballades of *Complaint of Venus*, found in Granson's *Cinq balades ensievans*, were probably composed during his imprisonment in Spain in 1372–4.[13] In all likelihood

Chaucer knew the poems by 1374, when Granson entered into the service of John of Gaunt. Both the French and the English sets of ballades might have been written for Isabel of York, wife of Edmund; if so, the *Complaint of Venus* could date any time from 1374 to 1392, when she died.[14] Chaucer's statement that 'elde' is dulling his spirit suggests the later date, at least for the envoy. But whenever he composed the work, an inspection of Chaucer's handling of Granson's text in his three ballades provides a unique opportunity to study the relationship of his poetry to formes fixes lyric in general and Granson's work in particular.

CHAUCER TRANSLATES GRANSON: 'THE COMPLAINT OF VENUS'

Two of Chaucer's lyrics, *An ABC* and the *Complaint of Venus*, are commonly identified as translations, but neither is a close reproduction of its original. Each does draw on a single work for its main materials and adheres to the appropriate literary mode, yet both make substantial changes in the wording and form of their originals. *An ABC*, a prayer to the Virgin, is based on a verse prayer intercalated in Guillaume de Deguilleville's *Pèlèrinage de la vie humaine*; it consists of twenty-five twelve-line stanzas using a tail-rhyme scheme. Chaucer's changes add to the traditional Marian expression and also contribute courtly features to the poem. The 'Monk's Tale' stanza that Chaucer uses (*ababbcbC*) originates in the courtly ballades, and phrases that Chaucer adds, like 'of alle floures flour,' were current in the love lyrics. Nevertheless, Chaucer's changes are quite in the spirit of Deguilleville's original; that is, they conform to its type, the Marian prayer, in which courtly usages are common.

In their conformity to the conventions of the types, the affinities between Granson's *Cinq balades* and Chaucer's *Complaint of Venus* are comparable to those between *An ABC* and Deguilleville's prayer, but they are more complex. Both series of ballades are spoken by a courtly figure about the beloved, both make use of standard ballade forms, and the English poem bases its rhetorical plan and a high percentage of its phraseology on the French. At the same time there are major differences between the love poems: Chaucer's *Complaint* is a triple ballade with an envoy, while Granson's has five ballades with no envoy; and Chaucer's narrator is a woman (called Venus in the traditional title), while Granson's is a man.

Chaucer provides versions of three of Granson's ballades. Adapting Skeat's labels for Chaucer's ballades, one might entitle Granson's five poems (1) 'The lady's worthiness,' (2) 'Her worthiness and danger,' (3) 'The lover's devotion and resolution,' (4) 'His disquietude and suffering,' (5) 'His satisfaction in constancy.' Chaucer omits the second and third ballades, thereby abbreviating but not reorienting the content. By his reduction Chaucer also suggests a forme fixe type related to the motet, the triple ballade, originally designed for polyphonic performance.[15] The last ballades of the two series provide perhaps the most interesting comparison of the English to the French, which is not entirely to Chaucer's advantage. Granson is at his best in the *Cinq balades*, especially the last one, and Chaucer may genuinely be baffled by the difficulties of translation.

I present the corresponding stanzas together, and italicize the matching phraseology:[16]

His Satisfaction in Constancy
But certes, Love, *I sey not in such wise*
That for t'escape out of your las I mente,   50
For I so longe have ben in your servise
That for to lete of wil I never assente;
No fors thogh Jelosye me turmente.
Sufficeth me to sen hym *when I may,*
And therfore certes, to myn endyng day   55
To love hym best ne shal I never repente.

Amours, sachiez *que pas ne le veulz dire*
Pour moy getter hors des amoureux las,
Car a porté si long temps mon martire
Qu'a mon vivant ne le guerpiray pas.
Il me souffit d'avoir tant de soulas   5
Que vëoir puisse la belle gracieuse;
Combien qu'elle est envers moy dangereuse
De li servir ne seray jamais las.

And *certis, Love, when I me wel avise*
On any estat that man may represente,
Then have ye made me thurgh your fraunchise
Chese the best that ever on erthe wente.   60
Now love wel, herte, and lok thou never stente,
And let the jelous putte it in assay
That for no peyne wol I not sey nay;
To love him best ne shal I never repente.

Certes, Amours, quant bien a droit remire
Les hauls estas, les moiens, et les bas,　　　　　　10
Vous m'avez fait de tous les liex eslire,
A mon advis, le meilleur en tous cas.
Or ayme, Cuer, si fort com tu porras,
Car ja n'avras paine si douloureuse
Pour ma dame qui ne me soit joieuse　　　　　　15
De li servir ne seray jamais las.

Herte, to the hit oughte ynogh *suffise*　　　　　　65
That Love so high a grace to the sente
To chese the worthieste in alle wise
And most agreable unto myn entente.
Seche no ferther, neythir wey ne wente,
Sith I have suffisaunce unto my pay.　　　　　　70
Thus wol I ende this compleynt or this lay;
To love hym best ne shal I never repente.

Cuer, il te doit assez plus que *souffire*
D'avoir choisi si bien que choisi as.
Ne querir plus royaume n'empire,
Car si bonne jamais ne trouveras,　　　　　　20
Ne si belle par mes yeulx ne verras.
C'est jeunesse sachant et savoureuse;
Ja soit elle de m'amour desdaigneuse
De li servir ne seray jamais las.

In this ballade about 60 per cent of Chaucer's phraseology closely parallels Granson's.

The syntax in both poems is like Machaut's, highly subordinated, with liberal enjambment, with the smaller grammatical units largely conforming to the line divisions. Thus both poems begin with four-line sentences that have four subordinate clauses each. In more conspicuous matters of the 'natural music,' Granson's poem seems to have the advantage. In the first place, his rhymes are considerably more homogeneous. His -ire, -as, -euse involve in all cases a single consonant; two of them are sibilants, and all three continuants. Chaucer's -ise, -ente, -ay, by contrast, present a thoroughly disparate consonant set: sibilant, nasal plus stop, and diphthong (no consonant). Moreover, Granson's rhymes have a better alternation of masculine and feminine endings, as French practice and the poetic treatises favoured.[17] The French refrain 'De li servir ne seray jamais las' has a phonetic subtlety that Chaucer's does not match. Every vowel sound is echoed as liquids and sibilants flow through the line: *de, ne; li, -ir; ser-, ser-; -ay, -ai; ja-, las.* The echoing achieves an inconspicuous but telling euphony which is not responded to in Chaucer's phonetically patternless 'To love hym best ne shal I never repente.' Similarly, one might cite the effectiveness of Granson's rhymes in lines 6 and 7 of each stanza: 'gracieuse' / 'dangereuse', 'douloureuse' / 'joieuse, savoureuse' / 'desdaigneuse.' Chaucer's monosyllables in the same position – 'may,' 'day,' 'nay,' etc. – are quite colourless.

Granson's concluding stanza seems especially effective in comparison with Chaucer's. Notably, he takes advantage of the rhyming couplet in lines 4 and 5, avoiding the usual grammatical stop dividing the stanza's middle lines[18] in order to make parallel assertions about the goodness and beauty of the beloved, culminating in line 6 with an enthusiastic comment on the attractions of her youth. The parallelisms and the sibilants in these three lines are particularly important in the effect:

Car si bonne jamais ne trouveras,
Ne si belle par mes yeulx ne verras.
C'est jeunesse sachant et savoureuse.

In gracefully concluding the poem in the lines following, Granson combines a concessive clause with the refrain, producing 'Even though she disdains my love, I will never tire of serving her.' Chaucer's last lines, by contrast, are for him unusually maladroit. The lady advises her heart, in rather discordant colloquial terms, to seek no further 'wey ne wente' (matching Granson's elevated 'realm nor empire'), since she has 'suffisaunce.' Then in the penultimate line the poet can do no better than the filler 'Thus wol I ende this compleynt or this lay' (71), which stands alone and adds virtually nothing. Even the lyric types named in the line are uninformative.

In no respect, of course, does Granson finally compare with Chaucer as poet, but he appears to advantage in this pair. It may be that the lament about rhyme in the envoy was occasioned by difficulty Chaucer experienced with the third ballade. His first two ballades seem more successful. In particular, he handles well the various changes required to switch the narrator's sex from male to female, which are far from perfunctory. Though experienced scholars have assumed that because of the conventional nature of the lyrics little reorientation of the poem's language was necessary beyond the gender of the pronouns,[19] this is hardly the case. Convention in these poems does not entail lack of discrimination. Thus, whereas in the first ballade Granson's speaker says that his lady has 'bonté, beauté, et grace,' Chaucer's lady avoids ascribing to her lover 'beauty' and 'grace' and speaks instead of his 'wysdom' and 'governaunce.' Rather than presenting a beautiful, graceful young man, who might seem effeminate, she singles out his intellect and his exemplary behaviour.

Chaucer makes numerous other important adjustments for his female speaker in his *Complaint*. For instance, Danger, a feminine reaction, would be thought incongruous in a lover, so in the first stanza of the third ballade he avoids Granson's adjective 'dangereuse' (6). Likewise, since it would be inappropriate for a lady to serve her lover untiringly, as Granson's speaker claims to do in the refrain of the French poem, in Chaucer's refrain the lady expresses a proper feminine constancy by declaring that she will never repent her loving. In the first balade the French lover's worship of the lady's 'doulz fais feminins' / 'sweet feminine traits' (5) becomes the English lady's praise of the 'manhod' of her lover (4).

Not all such changes are limited to a few words. Chaucer completely alters the third stanza of the same poem because of the sex-bound nature of the French presentation. Granson's stanza celebrates the joyfulness that the lady imparts to all:

> Ou qu'elle soit bien fait et mal efface;
> Moult bien li siet le rire et le jouer;
> Son cuer esbat et les autres solace
> Si liement qu'on ne le doit blasmer;
> De li veoir ne se puet nulz lasser;
> Son regart vault tous les biens d'un royaume;
> Il samble bien qu'elle est tresnoble femme ...   (17–24)

Wherever she is she performs good and does away with evil; laughing and playing suit her well; her heart so joyfully cheers up and solaces others that one must not blame it; no one can tire of seeing her; her look is worth the wealth of a kingdom; it is apparent that she is a most noble woman ...

By the conventions of the lyric mode the lady is the purveyor of joy, providing the major vitalizing force in the fictional society; her beauty and her glance are an inspiration to all. The lover at the same time is the beneficiary rather than a source of such inspiration. In the corresponding stanza, therefore, Chaucer's lady abandons Granson's wording. Attributing appropriate male virtues to her beloved, the lady celebrates his humility in serving her 'in word, in werk, in contenance' (17–24). Similar considerations of sexual congruence may even have caused Chaucer not to translate Granson's second and third ballades, which are more sex-bound than the others; the second focuses especially on the lady's beauty, and the other is largely a plea for mercy, inappropriate in the mouth of a lady.

While many of Chaucer's alterations of Granson's phraseology are made in response to the switch in the sex of the speaker, one prominent change that is not so motivated involves the subject of jealousy. Granson's lover mentions 'jealousy' but once in the five ballades; he opens the second stanza of his fourth poem with the colourful exclamation, 'Jalousie, c'est la mere du diable!' and then drops the subject. Chaucer's lady alters the image, not treating Jealousy's association with the devil. Instead she exclaims with equal vividness in the second ballade, 'Jelousie be hanged by a cable!' We may attribute this change to the exigencies of rhyme, but her further interest in the subject of jealousy, to which she returns three times in the next three stanzas, must have a deeper motivation.[20] One would guess that in a poem where the additions and fundamental changes are limited, the new emphasis was governed by the occasion that produced Chaucer's poem. The occasion would also govern the sex of the speaker. It is entirely probable that both works were written for and about particular people and events, and it is intriguing to speculate who in the courts might have been jealous of whom.[21]

Whatever the personal and occasional reference of *Complaint of Venus*, one strong motivation for Chaucer's translating the French poem was to compliment his Savoyard friend. The adaptations usually went the other way, from Chaucer to Granson, for the very good reason that Chaucer was much the better and more practised poet. Granson had an extensive opportunity to familiarize himself with the English works, and his poetry shows that he read and absorbed a good number of them. Clearly he had begun with Machaut, but in his poetry he also followed Chaucer back to the master.

MACHAUT TO GRANSON BY WAY OF CHAUCER

The *Complaint of Venus* probably marks the only time that Chaucer based any of his verse on Granson's. There are numerous other concordances between works of the two poets, but in these cases the line of influence runs from the English to the French. It is obvious that from the 1360s Chaucer's accomplishment as poet far outstripped Granson's, and that his contemporaries, including Granson, were not long in recognizing the English poet's genius. In so far as the two were men of the court and the battlefield, Chaucer would certainly have granted Granson precedence; but with regard to their writing, the latter naturally would have deferred. Moreover, the internal evidence provided by the poems makes clear the direction of influence. In general those features and passages in Granson's work that are like Chaucer's provide unelaborated and abbreviated parallels. His uses of Chaucer remind one of other writers' uses of the *Roman de la Rose*. Just as poets writing after the *Rose* employed motifs of that work, such as the dream or the garden, through abbreviated evocation of the original passages, so Granson employs features of Chaucer's narratives – the man in black, the overheard lover's complaint, the offer of help, the parliament of birds – through references and descriptions that are less developed than Chaucer's.[22]

Granson's extant work as presented by Piaget includes ninety ballades, nineteen rondeaux, a virelay,[23] six lyrics of moderate length called 'complainte,' a 'pastourelle' of nineteen stanzas, three lays, and two poems with a narrative thread that are long enough to call dits amoureux. Throughout this poetry one finds uses of Machaut's forms and echoes of his wording, but the range of reference to other literature, either Latin or vernacular, is very limited.[24] It is indicative of Granson's particular relationship to Chaucer, then, that his more substantial works have important models in poems of Chaucer. Works like the *Complainte de Saint Valentin* and the *Complainte de l'an nouvel* have narrative frames derived from the *Book of the Duchess*, though they still show primary dependence on Machaut. More completely Chaucerian – no doubt the most thoroughly Chaucerian of all poems of the Machaut tradition – is the dit called the *Songe Saint Valentin*. In it verbal and substantive parallels show Granson's familiarity with the *Book of the Duchess*, the *Parliament of Fowls*, *Troilus and Criseyde*, and probably the *House of Fame*. Parallels of poetic strategy that are notably Chaucerian appear in features such as the buildup to the dream, the narrator's self-presentation, and the tendency in the work to echo overtly other poems.[25] A work that evidences significant but more limited influence from several of the same Chaucer pieces is Granson's second dit, the *Livre Messire Ode*, which is the longest of his extant works. Both the *Songe* and the *Livre*, in the light of evident dependence on *Troilus*, must have been composed after 1385, late in Granson's career. Granson's father died in 1386, and in the years that followed Oton evidently spent much of his time in Savoy and France taking care of his inheritance and becoming enmeshed in various political problems. But in 1392 he was back in England, where King Richard awarded him an annual income of a hundred marks, and shortly after that he went campaigning with the Earl of Derby, the future Henry IV.[26] It seems likely that the *Songe* and the *Livre* were composed in the years between 1386 and 1392,[27] when Granson was bogged down in the political mires of France and Savoy; he could while away his idle hours composing poetry for the queen.

Like most experimental poems, the *Songe Saint Valentin* has its successes and its failures; but it is all interesting because it shows what a contemporary French poet who had read much of Chaucer through to *Troilus* found to imitate. As the title tells us, the *Songe* is a vision poem. In his dream the narrator goes to a garden looking for a diamond and a ruby that he has lost, but when he finds a Valentine's Day gathering of birds there, he devotes all his attention to that. A multitude of various kinds of fowl is busy selecting mates for the coming year (36–68). Presiding over them is an eagle, who has with him his chosen companion (69–73). The narrator notices a peerless peregrine falcon, 'almost a tercelet' – that is, very nearly grown – holding itself apart; the eagle addresses it and reproaches it for not having taken a mate (104–29). The falcon responds with the unhappy story of his having loved and lost the best of all falcons, to whom he has resolved to be ever true (130–301). With the eagle's approval he flies off alone, and the other birds depart with their mates (302–14). The narrator wakes up when they leave, feeling rather unhappy (315–19). Up to this point Granson has kept a storyline going, but for the last 130 lines of the poem (320–449) the narrator muses on the joys and sorrows of lovers, the difference between men and birds, and his own inaptitude for loving, and he prays to the God of Love to increase the honours of both men and women who love. Here at the end, then, we find the essentially lyric impulse of Granson and the mode overcoming even the thin narratives of his models.

One patently Chaucerian feature of the *Songe* is found in the commentary after the dream, when the narrator adopts the pose of being himself inapt for love. The opening lines of *Troilus* are the most immediate model for the statement that begins with the narrator's professing sympathy for those who suffer in love, even though he has no firsthand experience with loving:

Ja soit ce que je ne suy mye
Nesun de ceulx qui ont amie,

Et si ne suy n'amé n'amis,
Ne oncquez ne m'en entremis,
Ne pas ne me vueil acointier
A moy mesler d'autruy mestier.
Car trop me tenroit on pour nice,
Se je prenoie tel office
Ou je ne sçay chanter ne lire,
Fors ainsy que par ouy dire.
Mais, non obstant ma grant simplece,
Tant est navré qui amours blesse,
Que j'ay pitié de tous amans,
Soyent englois ou alemens,
De France né ou de Savoye
Et prie a Dieu qu'il lez avoie
Et conforter a leurs besoings.   (390–406)

... even though I am not at all one of those who has an amie, nor am I loved or or a lover, nor did I ever undertake it, nor do I wish to busy myself in the occupation of others. For people would consider me very stupid should I take up such an office in which I do not know how either to sing or read, except by hearsay. But notwithstanding my great ignorance, he whom Love strikes is so severely wounded that I have pity for every lover, be he English or German, or born in France or Savoy, and I pray to God that he receive them and comfort them in their need.

Earlier we discussed the opening of *Troilus* as it related to Machaut's ballade 'Plourez, dames.' There the attempt to enlist sympathy for the lovers of the poem associates the French poem with the English passage. Other topics, however, relate these lines of Granson's poem to the opening of *Troilus*. Here it is the narrator's profession of ignorance about love, coupled with his strong sympathy for those who suffer, that issues in his plea to God to help them. We recall that while the *Troilus* narrator does not 'dar to love' because of his 'unliklynesse,' nevertheless he prays to God for lovers' success even if he should die, 'so fer am I from his help in derknesse' (I 15–18). Of course, there are other passages in works of Chaucer in which the narrator similarly belittles his own aptness for love, as in the second book of *Troilus*, where he apologizes for speaking of love 'unfelyngly,' because 'a blynd man kan nat juggen wel in hewis' (II 19–21), and in the *Parliament of Fowls*, where Africanus tells the narrator plainly that the writing on the gates of the garden pertains to lovers, not to him (155–66). But the association of the narrator's incapacity for loving with his concern for lovers links the French passage most closely with the opening of *Troilus*.[28]

Granson's evocation of the inept Chaucerian narrator here is rather surprising. Typically, he strikes the conventional pose of the lover who may be desperate, ever-yearning, and unfulfilled, but not one who is incapable. Indeed, the image of Granson that popular history has handed down is of the archetypal knight and lover – Christine's 'gentil, preux, bel et gracieux' man of the court. So his imitation of the *Troilus* narrator is unexpected, and in it his poetic judgment may be somewhat misguided on two counts. In the first place, the pose could not serve the social function for him that it probably served for Chaucer. We admire Chaucer's narrator as a strategy employed to make the poet and his poetry more acceptable to the highly placed people he addresses. We imagine that when an untitled poet such as he assumes the persona of an inept or comic figure, the nobility in his audience feels more comfortable with his poetry than it would if his narrator posed as an equal. However, this rationale would not transfer to knights of prominence and substance like Granson, who would have no need to hide behind ineptitude. Second, and more fundamentally, Granson's introduction of this narrator after the dream seems poorly timed. In *Troilus* Chaucer establishes his self-deprecating narrator in the very first stanzas; the entire story is filtered through the personality of this servant of Love's servants. But Granson's narrative is complete before one finds out that the narrator of his love vision professes himself unsuited for love. It can exert no retrospective power on the reader's understanding of the dream.

Notwithstanding, the passage possesses a certain lyric value simply as the emotive statement of a self-effacing poet anxious to help lovers; this redeeming quality emerges particularly as the prayer for 'tous amans' continues:

Et si requier au dieu d'Amours
Qu'il vueille savoir leurs clamours
Et ouir les pleurs et les plains
Et les regars dont ilz sont plains.
Et face lez cuers souvenens
A cez damez de leurz amans,
Et leur envoit bonnez nouvellez
A ellez d'eux et a eulx d'ellez,
Et les face brief retourner

Et tous leurs fais a bien tourner.
Et quant ilz seront revenus
Pour si loiaulx soient tenus
Que envieux ne mesdisans
Ne leur puissent estre nuisans,
Mais leur soit mis en habandon
D'amour le gracieux guardon ... (410–25)

And I also ask the God of Love that he deign to attend to their cries and to understand the weeping and the complaints and the plentiful glances. And may he make the hearts of these ladies mindful of their lovers, and send them glad tidings, she from him and he from her, and make them return soon to their loves and turn all their experiences to good. And when they have returned may they be found so faithful that neither the envious nor the slanderer can harm them; but rather may the gracious reward of love without limit be theirs.

The prayer continues for some twenty lines to the end of the poem;[29] though it doesn't contribute to the narrative, it does have lyric relevance in the work. Such passages serve to confirm that in the Middle French dits – and here of course *Troilus* differs – the story-lines existed mainly to provide occasion for lyric development.

More integrally fitted into the narrative is another part that is notably Chaucerian – the first twenty-eight lines of the poem that preface the dream. In the first six lines there is an acrostic such as Machaut might have used;[30] at the same time the motif of the 'panser,' the process of thought, that the lines introduce suggests the *Book of the Duchess* and Froissart's *Paradys d'Amour*. The poem begins:

*I*l est grant aise de panser,
*S*e ce n'estoit que pour passer
*A*ucune fois l'eure d'un jour.
*B*ien met le corps en grant sejour,
*E*n grant repoux et en grant aise,
*L*e panser qui le cuer apaise. (1–6)

Thought is a great comfort, if only at times to pass an hour in a day. The thought which puts the heart at ease also provides the body great relaxation, great repose, and great comfort.

Froissart and Chaucer also open the *Duchess* and *Paradys* with talk about 'thoughts,' though in contrast to Granson's easeful meditation theirs are the restless thoughts that accompany insomnia.[31] They need supernatural help from Juno and Morpheus to overcome their disquiet, whereas Granson finds that thoughts naturally lead to sleep. He states that a man is able to meditate any time, having either good or bad thoughts,

Et si fait au cuer grant soulas,
Quant ung homs est pesans ou las
Et il veult prandre son repoux,
Il puit panser sur tel propoux
Qu'en son propoux s'endormira. (13–17)

And therefore it is great solace to a heart, when a man is depressed or weary and wishes to get his rest, that he can meditate on such a matter that in considering this matter he will go to sleep.

The progress to the dream at this point becomes aligned with the process presented in the *Parliament of Fowls*, which is to be Granson's main model for the vision proper. In the *Parliament* the narrator reads the dream of Scipio, which supplies inspiration and subject-matter for his own dream. Just as a hunter dreams of hunting or a drinker dreams of the bottle, he suggests, so he dreamt of Africanus. Similarly, the narrator of the *Songe* has a love vision on an appropriate day of love, 'Le jour de la Saint Valentin' (22), presumably as a result of thinking of his lady.

Granson abbreviates and creatively varies his models, and a little narrative inconsistency does not bother him. At this point in the introduction to the dream, he seems to realize that the matter will not be as agreeable as the restful thoughts of the first lines might promise, so the narrator experiences the troubled sleep-inhibiting thoughts of the *Duchess* and the *Paradis*:

Celle nuit avoie voillié,
Car mon cuer m'avoit travaillé
Pour plusieurs diverses pansees
Qui ne sont pas toutez passees. (23–6)

That night [of the dream] I had lain awake, because my heart had laboured over several troubling thoughts, which are still not all past.

As with the eight-year sickness of Chaucer's narrator, the reader is led to imagine an adamant mistress who brings persistent sad thoughts. (Granson evidently was not concerned about the inconsistency of the dreamer's implying a lady-love here and later professing an incapacity for love.)

The dream that now begins draws in quick succession on the *Duchess*, the *Roman de la Rose*, and then apparently the Middle English *Pearl*, before taking for its primary model the *Parliament*, with Machaut's *Dit de l'alerion* in the background. The narrator falls asleep on his bed, and it seems to him in his sleep that it is morning; he has gone to seek out a ruby or a diamond that he had lost in a garden ('vergier' 27–33). But instead of finding his jewels, he sees numerous birds of all sorts,

> Blans et noirs, privés et sauvages,
> Sors, muez, nyais et ramaiges,
> De bois, de champs et de rivieres,
> De maisons et de colommieres.
> Petiz et grans, tous y estoient.   (37–41)

White and black, tame and wild, yearlings, moulted, unfledged and fledgling, from wood, field and river, from houses and dovecotes, large and small, all were there.

For Chaucer's inclusive classification of waterfowl, seedfowl, wormfowl, and birds of prey (323–9) and the lengthy list of species (330–64) in the *Parliament*, Granson substitutes this set of less precise binary classes. But his birds are like Chaucer's in that they have all come together on Valentine's Day to choose appropriate mates (44–6). When the dreamer arrives at the vergier, the selection process has evidently taken place already. The fowl are embracing wing in wing and preening in the sun (48–52); the nightingale and lark are singing and the doves kissing, each acting according to his nature (53–60).

In Chaucer's poem Nature herself presides over the parliament, holding in her hand an exemplary female eagle. The one who presides over Granson's assembly ('qui tenoit sa justice' 70) is an eagle with his chosen mate at his side. The narrator is so pleased to discover that he can understand the discussion the birds are having that he forgets about the jewels he was seeking and listens as the handsome peregrine falcon, which has been sitting apart from the proceedings, tells its sad tale.[32] In speaking about the falcon it fell in love with, the peregrine celebrates its great ability and nobility as a hunter (166–225). It could fly faster and dive farther than any other hawk; none could hope to outfly it. Thus, whereas Chaucer characterizes his lover-birds and the love relationships anthropomorphically, Granson follows Machaut's *Dit de l'alerion* in bringing out avian attributes. The peregrine ends its story conventionally, nevertheless, with a sad lament over his separation from the beloved. Invoking the lady, 'A Dieu vous commens, je m'en voys' (303), he flies away alone. The others depart with their mates, and the narrator awakens on his bed.

NEW DIRECTIONS: THE 'LIVRE MESSIRE ODE'

Literary echoes, sounded in a very Chaucerian manner and largely involving works of Chaucer, occur throughout the *Songe Saint Valentin* and indicate Granson's familiarity with Chaucer's works and his respect for them. That its narrative is as connected and well structured as it is in itself suggests the English poet's influence. With its 449 lines it is Granson's second-longest poem. By far the longest is the *Livre Messire Ode*, a compendious work modelled roughly on Machaut's *Voir-Dit*; its 2,495 lines represent about 40 per cent of Granson's extant verse. It possesses the highly episodic structure of most dream vision poems; its discontinuity is accentuated by numerous inserted lyrics of the formes fixes and letters in prose and verse. It is especially like the *Voir-Dit* in that much of the *Livre* deals with the process of the poem's composition and compilation. In addition, the work reflects Granson's familiarity with several other dits of Machaut, including the *Remede de Fortune*, the *Fonteinne amoureuse*, and the *Dit de l'alerion*, and also once more with the *Songe vert* and Froissart's *Paradis d'Amour*. Granson again shows his familiarity with Chaucer's *Troilus* and, especially, the *Book of the Duchess*.

The narrator makes a great deal of his dressing himself in black (417, 480, 570, 865, etc.), a motif that originates with the *Duchess*, though in the *Livre* it symbolizes unhappiness rather than bereavement. In addition, there is one particularly Chaucerian episode in the main dream. In the vergier in which the dream experience takes place, several figures appear at different points: a happy lover, a handsome young squire and pretty lady, a messenger, and a sad lover. In the final instance (1134–1515) there is a clear evocation of the situation in the *Duchess* involving Chaucer's dreamer and the Black Knight.[33] Granson's dreamer looks up from his love meditation and sees the unhappy man who has hidden himself in the bushes. The man comments on the dreamer's unhappiness and offers to help him if he will describe his troubles:

Mais s'il vous plaisoit a moy dire
L'achoison de vostre douleur,
Se faire vous pouoie doulceur,
De tresbon cuer je le feroye.   (1153–6)

And if you would tell me the nature of your sorrow, if I could comfort you, I would willingly do it.

The narrator replies that he is beyond help, but he himself would still like to comfort the man and amend his troubles (1163–72). Both offers of help – the man's and the narrator's – echo the dreamer's offer of comfort to the Black Knight in the *Duchess* (547–57).[34] The model for the man's response that immediately follows, however, is a situation in book I of Chaucer's *Troilus*: Pandarus' offer to help Troilus in pursuing his love for Criseyde. There Troilus objects that since Pandarus can't help himself in love, he surely cannot help others:

Thow koudest nevere in love thiselven wisse:
How devel maistow brynge me to blisse?   (I 622–3)

Pandarus responds at length with proverbs and examples to the effect that he may be able to advise Troilus to his profit even though he cannot help himself. He concludes:

And yet, paraunter, kan I reden the,
And nat myself; repreve me na more.   (I 668–9)

Comparably the stranger asks 'par mocquerie' (1173) how the narrator might aid him when he doesn't know which way to turn. He persists:

Comment me pourroit conseiller
Ung qui aydier ne se sauroit,
Combien que faire le vouldroit?   (1177–9)

How could a person advise me, even though he is eager to help, who can't help himself?

The narrator responds:

'Doulx frere,' adonc je luy disoie,
'Peult estre que mieulx vous saroye
Conseiller que je ne faiz moy.'   (1180–2)

'Sweet brother,' I then said to him, 'it may be that I can better advise you than I can myself.'

Now the model shifts back to the *Duchess* as the stranger consents to tell his story and instructs the narrator: 'Escoutés!' / 'Listen!'
   The stranger relates a narrative of a falcon that recalls Granson's own *Songe Saint Valentin*, as well as Machaut's and Chaucer's bird narratives. He tells how he loved, won, and lost a beautiful falcon, and laments bitterly. In response the narrator reveals once again his affinity to the narrator of the *Duchess* in declaring

Il me semble que c'est folour
Pour ung oysel mener tel fin.   (1364–5)

It seems to me folly to carry on in such a manner for a bird.

Chaucer's obtuse narrator chides the Black Knight: no one alive 'wolde for a fers make this woo!' (740). Both narrators are slow to catch on to poetic metaphor, and their companions have to explain their meaning. Just as the Black Knight reveals that his 'fers' or chess queen is actually his lady, so the stranger explains that the falcon he has spoken of is 'une damoiselle / Gente de corps, durement belle' (1488–9). He has spoken poetically, he explains:

J'ay debatu par poetrie
Et ainsi que par rimerie
La douleur que mon cueur sentoit.   (1478–80)

I have discussed poetically, in the tradition of rhyming, the sorrow that my heart felt.

Granson thus again has used a feature of Chaucer's comic narrator, his obtuseness, and again at some cost to the characterization of his persona, who this time is *the* lover of the poem. Of course, the slowness of the narrator to understand the significance of the bird allegory does give the poet a chance to warn the more literal-minded in his audience against misunderstanding his metaphors.

The artistry of the *Livre Messire Ode* is quite interesting. Like the *Songe Saint Valentin*, in addition to the specific correspondences, it owes a more general debt to Chaucer. Both works illustrate the technique Chaucer uses in his dream poems of adapting and combining narrative motifs, language, and characters from other works and refashioning them in genuinely new creations. At the same time, while we may find the *Songe* in its architectonics rather like Chaucer's dream poems, the structural principles of the *Livre* are quite original. Only some eleven hundred of its lines, 40 per cent, are in the narrative couplets; the remaining verse is in the lyric forms of ballade, rondeau, lay, and complaint. Moreover, the couplets are often used in places where we might expect a stanzaic piece, as with his letter to the lady (448–514), while the lyric forms are employed for narrative. There are many precedents for lyric sequences in couplets where a stanzaic piece would be appropriate, but the use of the lyric forms for narrative sections of the long dits is quite unusual. For instance, while Chaucer's Black Knight, like his predecessors in Machaut, narrates his first meeting with the lady in couplets, Granson's sad lover tells in a graceful ballade the story of finding his 'esprivier':

A l'entree de ma jeunesse,
A mon premier commancement,
J'estoie destraint de leesse
Et de trouver esbatement.
J'avoye hostel bel et plaisant,
Pres de bois et plain de jardins,
Ou je m'aloie deduisant.
De mon deduit tresmal m'est prins!

Ung jour que j'estoie sans presse
En ung jardin tout privement,
Je regarday a la tournesse
Et vy voler si gentement
Ung esprevier, en menassant
Trestous les oyseualx du pourpris,
Car j'y prins grant soulassement.
De mon deduit tresmal m'est prins!

Au plus tost me mis en l'adresse
De regarder voye comment

Prendre le pourroye, maiz tristesse
M'est venue novellement
Que je l'ay prins, maiz malement
L'ay gardé, comme m'est advis.
Dont je pleurë et diz souvant:
De mon deduit tresmal m'est prins! (1190–1213)

In the doorway of my youth, in my first beginning, I was embraced tightly by joy and the search of pleasure. I had lovely, pleasant lodgings close by a wood and with many gardens where I took my delight. By my delight I was most evilly taken.

One day when I was quite alone and at ease in a garden, I looked at the turret and saw flying very nobly a sparrow-hawk, threatening all the birds in the enclosure, and indeed I took great solace from that. By my delight I was most evilly taken!

Immediately I set to studying how I might capture it, but sadness came upon me anew after I had taken it, for I poorly kept it, I think. For which I weep and say often: By my delight I was most evilly taken!

After this the man finishes his story in couplets, and the narrator responds to it with a ballade. In making the lyrics serve narrative purposes we might feel that Granson is simply mixing his categories and showing again his limitations as a poet, but the fact is that as he uses them the lyrics make generally effective mediums for the narrative.

The fragmentation of the *Livre* into numerous set pieces, with the couplets often merely providing links, and the indiscriminate assignment at the same time of narrative to couplets and stanzaic pieces, actually represents a logical development of the long love poem in the Middle French mode. The essential nature of the works, long and short, is lyric, and it is appropriate that the lyric forms should expand to encompass even the narrative elements just as the couplets were made to include extensive lyric interludes. The next logical step was the long poem's becoming a series of lyrics, which actually happened in the *Cent ballades*, a collaborative ballade collection of the 1390s. Granson's *Cinq balades ensievans* and *Six balades ensievans* also look forward to the developed ballade sequence.

The dream which takes up the main part of the *Livre* (188–1716) culminates in the interview with the unhappy stranger. All of the incidents relate to the narrator's own unfulfilled love for his wonderful lady, whom he identifies several times as the best in all France ('nonpareille de

France,' etc 1586, 1931, 2065, 2271). As Piaget argues,[35] this seems to refer to Isabel of Bavaria, Queen of France, who had in her personal library a 'livre des ballades de messire Ote de Grantson.' What makes the identification of the lady more certain is the acrostic 'ISABEL' in the *Songe Saint Valentin*, which is closely related to the *Livre Messire Ode*.[36] Moreover, in the poem even the stranger agrees that the narrator's beloved is the best of all ladies, an unusual concession for a medieval lover unless a sovereign queen is in question.

As with all dits in the mode, the story in the *Livre* is not complex. After the stranger leaves, a debate between the narrator's body and heart is staged in several spates of lyrics and couplets (1526–1711), and then he awakens. Once more about a third of the poem is left after the dream, though the narrative is virtually complete. What remains is eight hundred lines of complaint by the lover and his commentary on the love affair and loving in general. The poem is mostly framed in lyric set pieces: complaints, ballades, and rondeaux. In this part, too, certain interesting references to specific people are found. The references to the lady as the nonpareil of France are mainly found here; the narrator names his 'compaignons gracieux / Prigent, Regnault et Jamect' (1951–2), requesting that they be faithful in serving their ladies; and he refers to 'Guion' (2140), evidently a messenger. None of these figures can be identified with any confidence. An identifiable person is named much earlier when the narrator, depressed by the progress of his love, writes a letter to John of Cornwall – a well-known military figure in the service of Edward III – challenging him to combat (1081–1117). He doesn't issue the challenge 'pour orgueil,' he says, but rather as a quick way to death and resolution of his unhappy love. Surely Granson is here exploiting the humour implicit in the poetic mode; the lover picks a fight with the world champion in order to end his life the shortest way.

This use of specific names in a poem that is written in the rather abstract generic terms of the dits amoureux seems out of tune, but it does provide clues to an implicit historical context for the composition. Such naming is not entirely new to the type. The narrator is given a proper name in a few related works – 'Guillaume' in Machaut's *Jugement dou roy de Navarre* and 'Geffrey' in the *House of Fame* – and at one point Jean de Meun identifies 'Guillaume de Lorris' as the lover in the *Roman de la Rose*. But *Voir-Dit* is again Granson's main model. In that poem there are some very clear personal references, including several to Charles v. Despite such references, neither the *Livre* nor the *Voir-Dit* represents a strong movement towards realism. The basic manner of expression continues metaphoric, abstract, and exemplary. Oton's *Livre* is no closer to the realism of the *Canterbury Tales* than the *Songe*.

The various correspondences between Chaucer's and Granson's works suggest certain things about the relationship between the two poets, which we might summarize at this point. Granson's use of the narrative motifs of the *Book of the Duchess* in poems that he probably composed in the early 1370s[37] indicates that he read or heard Chaucer's elegy shortly after it was written and that the two had come to know each other near the time of Lionel's wedding. Around the same time Granson was also writing the *Cinq balades ensievans*, which provided the model for Chaucer's *Complaint of Venus*. Though Chaucer did not to finish the *Complaint* until later, it seems reasonable to think that he acquired copies of the ballades around 1374; he may even have experimented with translating them into English about that time.

The sketchy historical records suggest that the late 1370s and the early 1380s were busy times for Granson: we find him variously back in Savoy in 1376, serving with the English garrison at Cherbourg in 1379, and on a mission to Portugal for the King of England in 1382. No positive evidence shows literary interchange between him and Chaucer in this period, but they probably continued to have friendly dealings when they were both in London. By the time Granson went to Savoy after his father's death in 1386 he must have come to know the *Parliament of Fowls* and at least the first book of *Troilus and Criseyde*, in addition to the *Book of the Duchess*. Before this time his poetic practice had not been adventurous; though composing poetry was a grace appropriate to a knight, he was first a military man and had been content in his writing to follow closely his predecessors, principally Machaut, while devoting his primary efforts to military campaigning. But when in the years 1386–92 he was forced by obligations attendant on his inheritance to stay close to home in Savoy and France, he evidently used the spare time to experiment with longer works, the *Songe* and the *Livre*, for which Chaucer's works provided an important model, suggesting perhaps that he carried manuscripts of the English poems with him.

Back in service in England in 1392, Granson probably showed Chaucer his own recent literary efforts, and the English poet, recognizing the tribute implicit in the imitations (however they ignored the literary and philosopical complexities), responded by composing or completing his translation or adaptation of *Cinq balades*, the *Complaint of Venus*, and adding a commendatory envoy. Granson went back to Savoy in 1396, whence he did not return; he died in judicial combat in August 1397.

His adversary's motivation for challenging him was mainly political, it seems, and the death must have saddened Granson's friends, including Chaucer, though his writings give us no direct clue. The fact that he died in combat, having had a distinguished military career extending past his fiftieth year, perhaps extenuated any sense of frustration or outrage that his friends felt at his fate.

GRANSON'S VALENTINE POETRY AND CHAUCER

In Granson's relatively small extant oeuvre is the impressive number of seven works whose rubrics identify them as Valentine poems; in addition, the dream in the *Livre Messire Ode* takes place on Valentine's Day. Granson shared his literary interest in Saint Valentine with Chaucer, who features Valentine's Day in several poems; most notably, his *Parliament of Fowls* is 'the book of Seint Valentynes day.' As two important recent studies by Henry A. Kelly and Jack B. Oruch have demonstrated,[38] the connection of Valentine's Day with the pairing of lovers was unknown before Granson and Chaucer; they virtually originated the occasion as we know it. Both scholars give Chaucer credit as the 'original mythmaker.' I essentially agree with their conclusions, but I would suggest a possible modification. The evidence we have for dating the relevant works suggests to me that the myth-making was a cooperative enterprise of the two poets. It indicates that Granson was the first to write love poems for Valentine's Day, while Chaucer pioneered the crucial involvement of birds in the observance. Tending to confirm such a division of labour is the fact that the first English Valentine poems after Chaucer's, those of John Gower and Sir Thomas Clanvowe, speak of Valentine's Day as the day when birds choose their mates, whereas birds do not figure in the next French Valentine verse, that of Christine de Pisan and Jean de Garencières.[39]

The very existence of the works, composed by the two poets over the same span of years, is symptomatic of a lasting close relationship between them. The works may be read as manifestations of a continuing literary game played by friends over a period of many years. Granson's Valentine poems are scattered among the manuscripts that contain his works. Four are found in the Paris collection, in which his poems have a generally chronological arrangement; they occur third, eighth, ninth, and twenty-second in order, and five of them are similarly spread out in the Neuchâtel group.[40] The *Balade de Saint Valentin double* may be the first Valentine poem, being found in the Barcelona collection, which, as has been said, probably presents works of Granson's from before 1374.[41] Another early one, which makes use of the *Book of the Duchess*, is the first of two poems called *Complainte de Saint Valentin*. Reasoning from the wide distribution of the verse within and among the manuscripts, and extrapolating from our understanding that a good part of his work doubtless is lost, one might conjecture that from early in his career he habitually composed poems for Valentine's Day, perhaps one each year when he was not campaigning.

The extensive research of scholars has revealed comparatively little in the legend of the saint to connect him with lovers. Yet it may be significant for the association that the *Balade de Saint Valentin double*, which could be the earliest of the poems, makes the most extensive reference in any of them to the saint and his feast. The speaker begins the poem by noting that he chose his lady seven and a half years ago, and declares that on this day he once again chooses her; he invokes the day and the saint in the fourth stanza, which he addresses to Valentine:

> Saint Valentin, humblement vous suppli
> Qu'a vostre jour me soyez en aÿe,
> Et me faites avoir le doulz ottri
> Ou il n'a riens que bien et courtoisie
> Et bonne foy, c'est jeu sanz villanie.
> Bien y pouez un miracle monstrer,
> Car de plusieurs vous ferez aourer
> Et requerir de maint loyal amant,
> Se en ce cas vous m'estes bien aidant.
> Or me aidiez, tresdoulz saint debonnaire.
> Et se riens diz qui vous soit desplaisant,
> *Pardonnez moy, besoing le me fait faire.* (37–48)

Saint Valentine, I humbly beseech you to help me on your day, and cause me to have the sweet consent in which there is nothing but good and courtesy and good faith; it is a game without villainy. You can well manifest a miracle, for you will make yourself praised by many and prayed to by numerous lovers if you are good help to me in this cause. Please help me, most kind and noble saint, and if I say anything which displeases you, pardon me, for need constrains me to do it.

Throughout the poem the notion that a person chooses a mate on Valentine's Day is strong; the mating of birds is not in question.

In succeeding poems the notion of lovers pairing up and choosing one another becomes more explicit. The first *Complainte de Saint Valentin* opens with the narrator's lamenting that he sees every lover intending to 'apparier' / 'pair' with his beloved on this day, but his own lady is gone forever. Saint Valentine appears to him, along with the God of Love, but the saint has nothing to say while the god is quite voluble. The work ends with the lover's consenting to accept the new lady whom Love has assigned him. This all occurs on 'le jour de la Saint Valentin,' as the last line (272) informs us. The *Souhait de Saint Valentin*, whose first six lines show an acrostic on 'Isabel,' mentions the saint's day in the final lines when the narrator wishes that his lady would choose him for her servant, 'ce samedi matin / Pour ce qu'il est jour de saint Valentin' (63–4). The specification of Saturday, along with the acrostic, leaves no doubt that the poem was composed for the feast on a particular year and for a particular person.[42] Also overtly written for a specific occasion is the second *Complainte de Saint Valentin*, in which the narrator laments his impending separation from the lady because 'I must leave the country' (25); however, nothing beyond the rubric connects this work with Valentine's Day. Saint Valentine's name also is not found in the text of the *Balade de Saint Valentin* which follows the *Complainte* in the Paris manuscript, though a strong indirect association with the day is found in the notion of the lover's choosing his lady; twenty of the twenty-four lines begin 'Je vous choisy.'[43] In the *Complainte amoureuse de Sainct Valentin*, by contrast, the stated occasion of the poem seems only perversely appropriate to the day; for 150 lines the speaker laments his lady's lack of fidelity, even wondering 'Qui doist jamés avoir fiance / En femme?' / 'Who should ever have faith in woman?' (67–8). He concludes that of necessity he will meet a sorrowful end 'Ce jour de la Saint Valentin' (160). The sentiments are so out of harmony with Granson's other works that one suspects the authenticity of the ascription to him.[44]

In the six Valentine poems discussed so far, then, Saint Valentine is presented as an appropriate object of a lover's prayer, and his day implicitly is the time for choosing a mate. The saint even makes an appearance to the lover. But nothing is mentioned about birds finding mates; indeed, in these poems no bird appears. Only when he composed the *Songe Saint Valentin* did Granson associate birds with the day. Since the poem is inspired in large part by Chaucer's *Parliament of Fowls*, we gather that Granson's Valentine birds originate with that poem. Chaucer states that his assembly of birds occurred 'on Seynt Valentynes day, / Whan every foul cometh there to chese his make' (309–10), and he makes clear that Nature summons them each year on that day for the purpose (322, 386). At the conclusion his birds also address the saint in Heaven, 'Saynt Valentyn, that art ful hy on-lofte' (683), professing to sing for his sake. In the *Songe Saint Valentin* the dream occurs on Valentine's Day, and the gathering of birds which the dreamer forthwith sees is taking place for each to choose 'son per' (45).

Chaucer never mentions Valentine's Day without introducing the motif of the birds choosing mates. Thus, in the frame-story of the *Complaint of Mars*, a bird summons other fowls to awaken on Valentine's Day, reiterating like Granson that this is the time to *choose*:

And ye that han not *chosen* in humble wyse,
Without repentynge *cheseth* yow your make,
And ye that han ful *chosen* as I devise,
Yet at the leste renoveleth your servyse.   (16–19)

In the Chaucerian *Complaynt d'Amours* too, the complaint is made on Valentine's Day, 'whan every foughel chesen shal his make' (86), and we find virtually the same words in the *Livre Messire Ode*, where Valentine's Day is said to be the time 'que tous oyseaulx prennent leur per' / 'When every bird takes its mate' (1242).[45] After Chaucer has introduced the bird motif, it becomes integral in Granson's dits.

To summarize, taking such evidence as the Valentine poems of Chaucer and Granson supply, we might imagine that Granson developed early in his career the custom of writing a love poem on Valentine's Day. He presented the saint as a suitable patron for lovers to pray to, and the day as one appropriate for human lovers to choose their companions. Then about 1380, perhaps at Granson's instance or in his absence, Chaucer wrote a Valentine poem introducing an assembly of birds. That Granson was pleased, and probably flattered, by Chaucer's elaboration of the myth is shown by his later *Songe*, which imitates the *Parliament*. Afterwards Chaucer composed a second Valentine poem, the *Complaint of Mars*, and Granson continued to show his attachment to the occasion by his references in the *Livre Messire Ode*.[46] The subsequent mode of Valentine poetry, then, is testimony to the combined activity of the two poets.

From the various aspects of the friendship that we can reconstruct from Chaucer's translation in the *Complaint of Venus*, Granson's various adaptations of Chaucer, and the vogue of Valentine poetry, our evaluation of Chaucer and Granson's relationship must be a positive one.

Chaucer in youth had been a soldier, he was a public servant all his adult life, and he was a poetic genius. Simply having a friend in London who was also a soldier, a diplomat, and a versifier – one who could in some fashion appreciate his genius and who offered him the sincere flattery of imitation – surely was of tremendous importance to him. Granson was a man of literature who might draw Chaucer aside at court to discuss current French verse, if not the poetry of Rome and Florence. He was a man who would want to know what Chaucer was composing at the moment, rather than simply what was going on at the custom-house.

In his poetry Granson shows knowledge of a variety of French poets in addition to Machaut: Froissart, Deschamps, the *Songe vert*, and the *Roman de la Rose*. He was a gifted and informed amateur who travelled extensively, and he was in an ideal position to mediate in the international circle of Middle French poets, to transport copies and news of his own and his friends' verse from one writer and court to another. It may indeed have been he who assembled the most substantial anthology of fourteenth-century French lyrics that has come down to us. I refer to the 310 poems in University of Pennsylvania manuscript French 15, which includes 27 works of Granson and 15 poems headed 'Ch,' which could well be Chaucer's. Appropriately, the anthology is built around a core of 109 works of Machaut. There is a good possibility that the manuscript is the very 'livre des Balades Messire Othes de Grantson' that belonged to Isabel of Bavaria.[47] His assembling the anthology would serve as a substitute for the complete collections that others made of their oeuvres, and Oton would thereby manifest both an innate modesty about his accomplishment[48] and the good taste of an avid amateur collector.

We may postulate, then, that throughout his career – in Savoy, England, France, and elsewhere – he picked up texts of poems of friends and acquaintances and also had transcribed the works he came across. When he was in France in the late 1380s, newly acquainted with the lively and intelligent young Queen Isabel, he could have arranged and had copied a substantial collection of the poems for her, designed in part to cultivate her interest in what was to her a new literature. The book would have been an appropriate gift for her ceremonious reception into Paris in 1389. If Granson had it made, it would of course reflect his literary judgment; in general it is tastefully selected and arranged. A variety of poets, known and unknown, is represented. Even more pleasing than the balanced representation of the poets is the good distribution of the verse by type, speaker, and mood.

Such reconstruction of the possible origin of the manuscript is speculative, but any understanding of Granson to be gained is significant for the Chaucerian. Of all the French poets – and I do not include Gower in this classification[49] – he probably knew Chaucer best and over the longest period. For this reason, further study of his works in the context of their manuscripts, analysis of the texts that lie behind them, and study of the available documents could prove very revealing. Among the most intriguing pieces of the historical puzzle is a ballade by Eustache Deschamps about an event at Calais involving Granson and himself. It tells a great deal about the character of the two French poets and their relationship.

The ballade evidently was written in 1384, when the English and French were treating for a permanent peace. The two poets were serving different sides. Deschamps haplessly enters the English territory to visit Granson, having forgotten to bring his pass. His friend decides to play a joke on him, which Deschamps reports colourfully, with comic representation of the English words. The refrain refers to the French legend that the English had tails like animals:

Je fu l'autrier trop mal venuz
Quant j'alay pour veir Calays;
J'entray dedenz comme cornuz,
San congié; lors vint .II. Anglois,
Granson devant et moy après,
Qui me prindrent parmi la bride:
L'un me dist: 'dogue,' l'autre: 'ride';
Lors me devint la coulour bleue:
'Goday,' fait l'un, l'autre 'commidre.'
Lors dis: 'Oil, je voy vo queue.'

Pour mal content s'en est tenuz
L'un d'eulx, qui estoit le plus lays,
Et dist: 'Vous seres retenuz
Prinsonnier, vous estes forfais.'
Mais Granson s'en aloit adés
Qui en riant faisoit la vuide:
A eulx m'avoit trahi, ce cuide;
En anglois dist: 'Pas ne l'adveue.'
Passer me font de Dieu l'espite;
Lors dis: 'Oil, je voy vo queue.'

Puis ay mes talons estenduz
De mon roucin, le serray près,
Lors sault, si furent espanduz;
Delez Granson fut mes retrais.
La ne me vault treves ne pais,
De paour la face me ride,
De tel amour ma mort me cuide;
Au derrain leur dist: 'Je l'adveue.'
'Chien,' faisoit l'un, 'vez vous vo guide?'
Lors dis: 'Oil, je vois vo queue.'[50]

The other day I was poorly welcomed when I went to see Calais; I entered without leave, like a fool; so two Englishmen came up to me – I was behind and Granson was in front – who took me by the bridle. One said to me, 'Dog,' the other, 'Ride!' Then I became pale: the one said 'Good day,' the other, 'Come here!' Then I said, 'Yes, I see your tail.'

The uglier of them acted quite peeved and said, 'You will be held prisoner, you are forfeit.' But Granson kept going, and laughing left me: he had betrayed me to them, I think. In English he said, 'I disclaim him.' They made me endure God's own humiliation. Then I said, 'Yes, I see your tail.'

At that point I stretched my spurs over my horse and clasped it tight. It jumped and they scattered. I retreated over by Granson. There I found neither truce nor peace; my face creased with terror. With that kind of friendship I thought I'd die. At last he said to them, 'I vouch for him.' 'Dog,' said the one, 'Do you see your guide?' Then I said, 'Yes, I see your tail.'

The joke seems a little rough and dangerous, but Deschamps had a reputation for practical joking, so Granson was not tricking a helpless innocent, and the poem shows that Deschamps savoured the incident.

In any event, this gives us a view of Granson different from that of Piaget, who, reading Granson's conventional love poetry as autobiography, speaks of him as 'a timid man, overly sensitive, faithful to death, having at heart only a single passion, serving his lady.'[51] In contrast to this lugubrious portrait, the poem shows the man as a lively, full-blooded individual, interacting with an impish friend in an interesting and human way. Granson and Chaucer too would have had their times of merriment together, talking over such incidents as the poem recounts. We get a sense from the poem too of the closely knit nature of French-speaking court society. Despite the problems attached to foreign travel, we perceive that this was a small world in which men of affairs moved as a matter of course between national territories and centres of government. The mobile Granson, in touch with royalty and poets in various capitals and camps, clearly would have been an important link for Chaucer to the international circle of French poets.

CHAPTER EIGHT

Chaucer and Eustache Deschamps

The inclusive bibliography of Chaucer's sources lists thirty-nine different works of Eustache Deschamps that scholars have presented as offering significant parallels to Chaucer's poetry.[1] With such professional testimony to the relationship of the two poets' works, it is somewhat surprising to find that no one of the parallels that has been cited is so close that we can say that *in this case* Chaucer was surely following Deschamps, or vice versa. In all cases the similarities that are alleged, whether in conception, plan, or wording, are inconclusive, and attractive alternatives of filiation exist. This is not to say that Chaucer did not know the poetry of Deschamps; it would be surprising if he did not. And we have Deschamps' own word that he read Chaucer: his ballade to Chaucer bears explicit witness to his knowledge of Chaucer's writing. It is to say that the common bracketing of Deschamps with Machaut and Froissart as a French contemporary whose work had a major and direct influence on Chaucer is based on tenuous evidence.

It is fairly clear why Chaucerians have given Deschamps so much attention. His ballade to the English poet explicitly establishes the connection and the rest of his extensive and diverse oeuvre opens many possibilities. The corpus is very large, composed of some 80,000 lines of poetry plus 3 pieces in prose. There are 1,017 ballades, 171 rondeaux, 84 virelays, 139 chansons royales, 14 lays, and 59 other pieces, including 12 poems in Latin.[2] Since Deschamps' subjects are many and varied, and often topical, and the manner often comic or satiric, the work has appealed to critics of our age as the conventional love poetry has not. Furthermore, the fact that his writing is extant mainly in a single manuscript facilitated the early editing of his work, little collating being required. His poetry became generally accessible well before Machaut's, while Chaucer source scholarship was still in its first bloom. The eleven volumes have been an inviting treasury for scholars to plunder since they began appearing in 1878.[3]

Deschamps enjoyed a close personal association with Machaut, and he knew most of the prominent formes fixes poets of his time. But his talents do not ally him closely with these writers. Despite his apt characterization of poetry in the mode as 'natural music,' Deschamps' ability to produce such music was limited. A number of his lays particularly dramatize the problem. The lay form as perfected by Machaut, with its short lines, intricate rhymes, and varying strophes, is highly lyric; it assorts poorly with the 'professorial attitude' Deschamps often assumes in these poems. As Poirion states broadly of Deschamps' work, 'The lyrical movement hardly gives force to the doctrinal teaching. That practical morality which Machaut and Froissart reserved for their *dits*, Deschamps makes the very substance of the greater part of his lyric poems. Conversely, when he relaxes, it is to descend into a familiar and anticourtly wit. The poet only submits superficially to the tradition inherited from Machaut. The service of ladies as it is reflected in his ballades, rondeaux, and virelays of love has only a tinge of *courtoisie*. Furthermore, the poet readily abandons the praise of ladies for which Machaut had given him the example.' Poirion finds that Deschamps is in his element only in the critical vein, in sermon or satire; he concludes that it is only then that Deschamps' poetry is effective, and even shows 'a certain talent.'[4] This denial of Deschamps' lyric ability is perhaps a little harsh. In particular, some of Deschamps' thousand ballades seem to me effective embodiments of the natural music proper to the mode; still, even the best are uneven.

Deschamps was born near Reims in a town called Vertus in Champagne in about 1346; he was probably two years younger than Chaucer.[5] He states that as a youth he long studied grammar and logic; afterwards he apparently spent a number of years reading law, probably at Orléans, but without receiving a degree.[6] About 1367 he entered the service of the king. For most of his life subsequently he was attached in various capacities to Charles v and his sons, Charles vi and Louis of Orléans. Of the poets we have considered, he was the most closely associated with the courts throughout his life, and though all the poets were travellers, his excursions on the king's business carried him the farthest.

Whether he spent time in England is uncertain. It would have been natural for him to travel to England for much the same reasons that led Chaucer to travel to France, and his poem about the misadventure with Granson in Calais shows that he knew some English words well enough to find rhymes for them;[7] nevertheless, there is no solid evidence.[8] His attitude towards the English was equivocal. At times his poetry manifests rather modern-sounding partisanship for France and dislike of the English. This dislike was fuelled by events of the war, especially the burning by the English of his natal home at Vertus in 1380. At the same time, no antipathy is apparent in his personal friendship with Lewis Clifford or in his admiration for the valour of Guischard d'Angle or his praise of Chaucer's poetry, discussed below. He no doubt shared with such men a liking for the literature of the day. He knew and had dealings with a large number of poets and aficionados of poetry; even his son-in-law was a versifier.[9] If anyone was at the centre of literary life in France, it was Deschamps. We have already looked at some evidence of his friendship with Granson.[10] His familiarity with literary personages began much earlier, however, with his relationship with Guillaume de Machaut, which we can view mainly through several ballades. These ballades are important because they show the strong ties between the two poets and because they provide a context for the ballade to Chaucer, a text of unique significance for Chaucer studies.

DESCHAMPS AND MACHAUT

Deschamps often writes poems about events and places that were important in his personal life. One such ballade celebrates his home province of Champagne; among other matters he praises its great authors, including Chrétien de Troyes, and also

> Vittry, Machault de hault emprise,
> Poetes que Musique ot chier.[11]

Vitry and Machaut of great enterprise, poets whom Music held dear.

It was almost two centuries too late for Deschamps to have known Chrétien, and Vitry died in 1361, virtually assuring that Deschamps would have had no more than a passing acquaintance with him. However, numerous references suggest that his relations with Machaut, who lived until 1377, were very close. A fifteenth-century treatise claims that Machaut was Deschamps' uncle.[12] Nothing we know makes the kinship improbable, except that it is attested nowhere else. More immediate evidence that they were close, however, is provided by Deschamps himself. In a poem written shortly after Machaut's death, he says that the older poet 'm'a nourri et fait maintes douçours' / 'educated me and did me many kindnesses.'[13] Just how far Machaut's teaching or nurturing extended is surely uncertain, but the wording does evoke the image of long visits by young Eustache to the canon at Reims. Thus, when Deschamps says in the midst of an account of the siege of Reims of 1359, 'bien m'en remembre' / 'I well remember it,'[14] we seem invited to imagine the thirteen-year-old boy sitting out the threat with his aging benefactor.[15]

Several of Deschamps' works show that the close personal relationship between the poets continued after the younger poet matured. In the dream vision of his *Lay amoureux*, which he probably wrote in his early adulthood,[16] some lovers in attendance on the God of Love point out the dreamer, who has concealed himself behind a bush (like the narrator in Machaut's *Jugement du roy de Behaigne*). They exclaim,

> Vez la Eustace
> Qui doit bien estre en vostre grace.
> Guillaume et lui noz faiz escriprent;
> Venus et Juno les nourrirent.[17]

See Eustache there, who well deserves to enjoy your grace; Guillaume and he have written our [lovers'] deeds; Venus and Juno nurtured them.

The poet with some presumption brackets himself with the master, almost suggesting collaborative effort. At another time, perhaps in 1369,[18] Deschamps in a ballade reports to Machaut that he has delivered a copy of his *Voir-Dit* to Louis de Mâle of Flanders. This ballade is revelatory of the way verse circulated and was presented, and of the relationship between the two poets. It is the first of four lyrics by Deschamps that celebrate and praise the older poet's work:

> Treschiers sires, vueillez remercier
> L'art de musique et le gay sentement
> Que Orpheus fist en vous commencier,
> Dont vous estes honouriez haultement:
> Car tous voz faiz moult honourablement
> Chascuns reçoit en maint pais estrange,

Et si n'y a nul, a mon jugement,
Qui en die fors qu'a vostre louenge.[19]

Most dear lord, please thank the art of music and the glad sentiment which Orpheus stirred in you, for which you are highly honoured: everyone receives your works very honourably in many foreign countries, and I believe there is no one who speaks of them anything but in your praise.

In the subsequent stanzas he reports delivering 'Vostre Voir Dit' to the Duke of Flanders, and reading to the assembled company a passage from it on the cruel behaviour of Fortune.[20]

Deschamps' devotion to Machaut and his admiration for his work are confirmed in the double ballade that he wrote on Machaut's death, probably designed to be set to music Andrieu provided.[21] The first ballade particularly recalls Machaut's 'Plourez, dames,' which we considered in the first chapter. The opening calls on

Armes, Amours, Dames, Chevalerie,
Clers, musicans et fayseurs en françoys,
Tous soffistes et toute poetrie,
Tous cheus qui ont melodieuses vois ...   (1–4)

War, Love, Ladies, Chivalry, clerks, musicians, and French poets, all learned men and every Muse, all those who have melodious voices ...

The summons is to lament ('Demenés duel, plourés' 7) the death of Machaut. Deschamps continues, 'He never spoke idly about love, but he was courteous [*courtois*] in all his writings' (9–10); he proceeds to call on three mythological figures to join the complaint:

Hé, Horpheüs! assés lamenter te dois
Et regreter d'un regret autentique,
Artheüs aussy, Alpheüs tous trois,[22]
La mort Machaut le noble rethouryque.   (13–16)

Come, Orpheus! You must greatly lament and regret with genuine sorrow, Arethusa also, and Alpheus a third, the death of Machaut, the noble rhetorician.

The poem makes special note of how Machaut's 'chanterie' (11) and 'bonne pratique' (22) pleased counts and kings; and it ends, echoing 'Plourez, dames,' with a call to all Champenois to don black ('Vestez vous de noir' 23) and lament Machaut's death.

The second part of the double ballade begins with an elaborate encomiastic apostrophe to the dead poet:

> O flour des flours de toute melodie,
> Tres doulz maistres qui tant fuestes adrois,
> Guillaume, mondain diex d'armonie,
> Aprés vos fais, qui obtendra le choys
> Sur tous fayseurs? (1–5)

O flower of flowers of all melody, very dear master who was so skilful, Guillaume, worldly god of harmony, after your achievements, who will be preeminent above every poet?

The term 'master' denotes both the poet's academic rank and Deschamps' personal subordination to him. Again, each stanza concludes with the call to weep for 'La mort Machaut le noble rethouryque.' Mythological imagery is once more prominent; in the second stanza Machaut is called

> Le fons chierie et la fontayne Helie
> Dont vous estes le ruissel et le dois ... (9–10)

The precious well and fountain of Helicon, of which you are the stream and current ...

And among the series of musical instruments summoned for the lamentation in stanza 3, 'rebebe, viele et ciphonie,' etc., a place is found for the 'nymphes de bois.'

A virtual sequel to the double ballade is a poem in which Deschamps' asks Peronne, the young beloved of Machaut celebrated in the *Voir-Dit*, to accept him as her 'ami' now that Machaut is dead.[23] The appeal is not so bizarre if we think of Peronne as a product of the old poet's imagination rather than an actual person. Deschamps' poem, then, would be simply another instalment in the elaborate fiction of the 'True Story.' In any event, most of the first two stanzas of this ballade are devoted to discussion and praise of Machaut,

Noble poëte et faiseur renommé,
Plus qu'Ovide vray remede d'amours,
Qui m'a nourry et fait maintes douçours ...   (3–5)

Noble poet and renowned maker, above Ovid a true consolation in love, who nurtured me and did me many kindnesses ...

The poem goes on to report how 'Music played his obsequy ... and Orpheus buried his body' (9–10). Now, with Machaut's 'tresdoulx chans' silenced, Orpheus is deaf and mute (11–12). By a certain logic, Peronne now becomes a recourse for Deschamps (16), who seems to suggest an amorous sharing of grief. This surely is not to be taken seriously. In any event, another ballade indicates that the plea was unsuccessful; he addresses 'tresdoulce Gauteronne,' begging her in the refrain, 'Recevez moy: j'ay failli a Perronne' / 'Take me, I failed with Peronne,'[24] and assuring her he loves her more than Paris loved Helen (9). Gauteronne might be excused for harbouring some scepticism.

The absurd aspect of the Peronne sequel to the poetic observance of Machaut's death accords with the pose as clown and butt which Deschamps adopts in a substantial number of poems, as in the adventure with Granson.[25] But it does not negate the serious content of his words about Machaut, testifying to the importance the relationship had for him, his high admiration for Machaut's musical and poetic talent, and the genuine distress he felt on Machaut's death. The poems to and about the older poet, taken together with some other texts, also provide some useful parameters for analysing his praise of Chaucer.

'GRANT TRANSLATEUR, NOBLE GEOFFROY CHAUCIER'

There is no solid evidence on which to base a dating of Deschamps' poem to Chaucer. He specifically mentions Chaucer's translation of the *Roman de la Rose*, but that was one of Chaucer's first works, so that the remark is little help in fixing a date. Some have thought to find in the ballade specific reference to other poems which might give a useful *terminus post quem*.[26] However, as we will discuss, the references are highly questionable. Lewis Clifford is named in the poem, but that provides only a vague clue. A date in the late 1380s seems to me most likely.[27] Fortunately, the dating does not appreciably affect the poem's significance for Chaucer studies. The text that follows is standard,[28] but the translation presented offers a few changes, notably a new understanding of 'pandras' (9):[29]

O Socratés plains de philosophie,
Seneque en meurs, et Auglus en pratique,
Ovides grans en ta poëterie,
Briés en parler, saiges en rethorique,
Aigles treshaulz, qui par ta theorique
Enlumines le regne d'Eneas,
L'Isle aux Geans – ceuls de Bruth – et qu'i as
Semé les fleurs et planté le rosier,
Aux ignorans de la langue pandras,
Grant translateur, noble Geoffrey Chaucier.

Tu es d'Amours mondains Dieux en Albie,
Et de la *Rose*, en la terre Angelique
Qui, d'Angela Saxonne, est puis flourie
Angleterre – d'elle ce nom s'applique
Le derrenier en l'ethimologique –
En bon anglès le livre translatas;
Et un vergier, où du plant demandas
De ceuls qui font pour eulx auctorisier,
A ja long temps que tu edifias,
Grand translateur, noble Geffroy Chaucier.

A toy pour ce de la fontaine Helye
Requier avoir un buvraige autentique,
Dont la doys est du tout en ta baillie,
Pour rafrener d'elle ma soif ethique,
Qui en Gaule seray paralitique
Jusques a ce que tu m'abuveras.
Eustaces sui, qui de mon plant aras;
Mais pran en gré les euvres d'escolier
Que par Clifford de moy avoir pourras,
Grand translateur, noble Gieffroy Chaucier.

Envoy

Poëte hault, loënge d'escuirie,
En ton jardin ne seroie qu'ortie,
Consideré ce que j'ay dit premier,
Ton noble plant, ta douce melodie;
Mais, pour sçavoir, de rescripre te prie,
Grant translateur, noble Geffroy Chaucier.

O Socrates versed in philosophy, Seneca in morals, Aulus in practical affairs, great Ovid in your poetry, brief in speech, wise in poetic composition, soaring eagle who by your theoretical understanding illuminate the kingdom of Aeneas, the Island of Giants – those whom Brut destroyed – and who have sown there the flowers [of poetry] and planted the rose-tree, you will spread light to those who do not know French, great translator, noble Geoffrey Chaucer.

You are the worldly God of Love in Albion, and you translated the book of the *Rose* into good English in the Angelic land which, beginning with Angela the Saxon, then flourished as England – the name comes from her, the last in the etymologic series. For a long time you have been making a garden for which you have asked plants from those who write poetry for posterity, great translator, noble Geoffrey Chaucer.

For this purpose I ask from you a genuine draught of the spring of Helicon, whose stream is wholly in your charge, in order to gain relief from it for my burning thirst, for in France I will be paralysed until you give me a drink. I am Eustache, and you will have some plants of mine. So accept kindly the school exercises which I will send you by Clifford, great translator, noble Geoffrey Chaucer.

Esteemed poet, eminent among squires, I would only be a nettle in your garden, if you consider what I have described before, your noble plants, your sweet melody. Still, I would like to know your opinion; please respond, great translator, noble Geoffrey Chaucer.

There are a number of puzzling words and passages in the poem, which different translators have variously resolved, but the general sense is not in question.[30]

With its three stanzas of ten decasyllabic lines and the six-line envoy, it is a particularly full ballade, and it is one of Deschamps' more effective pieces. The image of the garden full of flower poems does multiple duty, helping to unify the work. England is a garden in which Chaucer has sown his works, and he has made the island the garden of the *Rose*. To add to his own garden Chaucer has asked for new flowers, which Eustache will supply. However (making a rapid switch) Deschamps sees himself as a nettle alongside Chaucer's flowers. The image of the fountain of Helicon, from which Deschamps requests a drink, fits well into the poetic landscape as a place of beauty within the garden and a source of nourishment for the flowers. At the same time, some of the figures and diction have a pedantic tone that does not accord readily with the floral imagery. These are introduced mainly in connection with rhymes in -*ique*: 'theorique,' 'ethimologique,' 'autentique,' and are found in words like 'auctorisier,' and in the digression etymologizing 'England' (12–15).

Scholars have seen in 'pandras' a reference to Pandarus of *Troilus and Criseyde*.[31] As attractive as that meaning might be for imagining a Continental circulation of Chaucer's great poem, I believe the word is not a proper noun but instead the future of a verb; I propose 'pandre,' signifying 'to disseminate or illuminate.'[32] If one discounts this single word as referring to *Troilus*, there is no reminiscence of the poem in all of Deschamps' work; in addition, suggested evocations of Chaucer's other poems – for instance, that the epithet 'soaring eagle'(5) derives from the *House of Fame* – come to seem quite remote. At the same time, the absence of such reference does not mean that Deschamps knew only Chaucer's *Rose* or only his translations. Indeed, the vision of Chaucer's garden as strewn with flowers suggests that Deschamps was familiar with a good number of his English works. Furthermore, one would surely expect the high praise in the poem to be based on a corpus of original works in English. Ranking Chaucer with the great classical writers and ceding him sole possession of the Muses' pool is no small praise, particularly from a functiondary of the French king.

But to gauge more exactly how literally one should understand Deschamps' eulogy of Chaucer and his expression of modesty, we must put it in the context of the several similar poems he wrote. It is apparent, of course, that phraseology in this work overlaps with that of the poems to Machaut. Chaucer is 'great Ovid,' while Machaut is 'above Ovid'; Chaucer possesses Helicon, Machaut is its 'stream and current'; Chaucer is 'worldly God of love,' Machaut 'worldly God of harmony.' Chaucer is 'wise in rhetoric,' Machaut 'the noble rhetorician.' The comparison is certainly not unfavourable to Chaucer. We would expect Deschamps' estimate of Machaut not only to be high because of his genuine accomplishment, but also to be partial because of the close relationship between the poets. Nevertheless, the praise of Chaucer is phrased in terms just as strong and more extended and specific.

Deschamps writes an encomiastic ballade to another poet, Christine de Pisan, which is also instructive in gauging the praise of Chaucer and interesting for understanding contemporary literary relationships in France.[33] Deschamps is responding to her laudatory letter, dated February 1403.[34] His language is fulsome. In opening he addresses her as 'eloquent Muse among the nine ... Nonpareil ... in understanding and learning' (1–3), and he speaks of her books as showing 'great philosophy,' averring that God has given her the sign of Solomon (11). He asserts that she is unique in her writings (refrain), and worthy of great honour among both men and women (21–2). In the final stanza and the envoy the poet confesses his own inferiority: he wants to learn from Christine (22), in every respect he makes obeisance to her (28), and he beseeches her to allow him

> Comme ton serf, d'estre en ta compaignie
> Pour bien avoir d'estude congnoissance. (32–3)

To be among your attendants as your servant so as to well gain knowledge from studying with you.

Judging by such praise and modesty, we understand that Deschamps was not averse to polite flattery and self-abasement. At the same time, he had good justification for being ingratiating. Christine was a recognized and talented author with good connections, so the old poet was prudently, as well as gallantly, responding to her own lavish compliments of him.

Not surprisingly, Deschamps was not always so modest about his own talents. In the *Lay amoureux*, as we saw, he bracketed himself with Machaut as love poet. And in a ballade lamenting the loss of a manuscript he presents himself as working in the garden of poetry alongside some of the great names of antiquity.[35] His missing works, he tells us, formed 'such a sweet-smelling, precious and beautiful garland that its perfume could heal all sickness' (6–8). He extends the description in the second stanza:

> Continuelz fut vint ans mes labours
> Aux fleurs semer ou Ovides planta
> De Socrates et Seneque les mours,
> Et Virgiles mains beaus mos y dicta
> Et Orpheus ses doulz chans y nota.
> Poeterie fut au tour du sercel,
> Rethorique le fist ront comme annel.
> Lettres y mist et les noms des plus haulx
> Si plaisamment que maleureus m'appel:
> *S'ainsi le pers; c'est trespovres consaulx.* (11–20)

I laboured twenty years continuously to sow flowers where Ovid planted the virtues of Socrates and Seneca, and Virgil spoke many lovely words, and Orpheus recorded his sweet songs. Poesy surrounded the flower bed, and Rhetoric made it round like a ring. It placed literature and most eminent names there so pleasingly that I call myself miserable if I lose it thus; it is a very sad matter.

If Deschamps does not here claim equality with the sages, he certainly sees himself working in the same flower-bed.

An interesting original for several of Deschamps' ballades celebrating poets, particularly the one to Chaucer, is the ballade that le Mote wrote to Vitry, probably in the late 1350s, discussed and quoted in chapter 2. The form and substance of the first lines in particular are echoed. Compare the following lines of the poems to Vitry and Chaucer:

le Mote:	*O Victriens, mondains dieu d'armonie* (line 1)
Deschamps:	*O Socratès* plains de philosophie (1)
	Tu es d'Amours *mondains dieux en Albie* (9)
le Mote:	*Supernasor de la fontaine Helye* (3)
Deschamps:	*Ovides grans* en ta poeterie (3)
	A toy pour ce *de la fontaine Helye* (21)
le Mote:	Doctores vrays, *en ce pratique Anglus* (4)
Deschamps:	Seneque en meurs, *Auglius en pratique* (2)

The parallels show a clear filiation between these works. As I have remarked elsewhere, the ballade exchange between le Mote and Vitry no doubt was well known to Deschamps, writing twenty-five years later; and he would have expected his audience, certainly Chaucer, to hear echoes of the earlier less friendly interchange of poetry across the Channel.[36]

Deschamps lauds Christine for her 'sens,' 'dotrine,' and 'philosophie,' and says little about her skill in versifying. He praises Machaut both for his music and his 'rethorique' (versifying), but he says nothing about his thought or moral sense. No doubt his silences were not underlining failings; rather, he was being selective in pointing out the particular strengths of the two. And what he chooses to compliment in both writers shows discrimination; he is emphasizing real strengths. It is significant, then, that in his poem on Chaucer his litany of merit encompasses all facets of the poet's métier: thought ('philosophie,' 'theorique'), morals ('meurs,' 'pratique'), and verse ('poeterie,' 'rethorique'). He even praises him for his music, obviously 'natural' music ('douce melodie,' a phrase that we will return to in chapter 9). From such evidence we might attribute to Deschamps a real understanding of Chaucer's genius, founded on an appreciative reading of a substantial number of his works. What might give us pause is our knowledge of the difficulty that the language barrier would have presented to a French poet if he had not spent time in England, and the fact that there is no solid evidence of borrowing by either poet from the other such as we find in the parallels between Chaucer's works and the poems of Machaut, Froissart, and Granson.[37]

As previous chapters have shown, Froissart's works reveal a knowledge of the *Book of the Duchess* and Granson's a knowledge of several of Chaucer's poems, including *Troilus and Criseyde*. But there is no indication that either French poet was familiar with the *Canterbury Tales*. Among the Middle French poets, it is Deschamps who would have found the *Tales* most consonant with his literary practice. He writes poems on subjects suggestive of various *Tales*, and a number of the parallels that scholars have pointed out between Deschamps' and Chaucer's works involve one or another of them. In the ballade to Chaucer, moreover, his description of the English poet as the well-rounded poet of philosophy and morals as well as love could well refer implicitly to the late work. Nevertheless, evidence that he knew the *Tales* is far from conclusive.

Deschamps' ballade has provided scholars a basis for assuming that the two poets were broadly familiar with each other's work, but the extent of their knowledge is very much an open question. In the remainder of the chapter, in the course of treating the various aspects of their relationship, we will consider the more notable correspondences that scholars have previously asserted. This will permit an assessment of the total literary debt such as has been attempted only in Brusendorff's summary survey.[38]

DESCHAMPS' GIFT TO CHAUCER: 'LES EUVRES D'ESCOLIER'

In his ballade to Chaucer, Deschamps says that since Chaucer has asked for verse from other poets, he is sending him some of his own schoolboy efforts by way of Lewis Clifford. Clifford had probably reported Chaucer's interest in receiving poetry from the Continent. Deschamps doubtless did not think as poorly of the works he sent as his pejorative description of them would indicate; as with the poem to Christine, his modesty is somewhat overdone. What Deschamps actually sent Chaucer has been the subject of speculation, and scholars have loaded Clifford down with a substantial part of the oeuvre. It seems likely that Deschamps had copies made of a variety of the shorter works that he most savoured and that he thought would impress Chaucer. Making copies of longer works, or of many poems, would have been expensive and time-consuming. As a way of talking about the relationship between Chaucer's literary activity and Deschamps' myriad lyrics, we might postulate some of the texts he sent, without meaning to imply that this is the only way Chaucer could have seen his work.

Since Deschamps' verse had a strong moralistic streak, he might have thought first of sending some of his edifying verse. One likely possibility would be his double ballade on Fortune, one ballade a statement of defiance addressed to Fortune and the other Fortune's answer.[39] These are thought to be originals for Chaucer's *Fortune*, and that likelihood is strengthened by their place in the great Deschamps manuscript immediately following the ballade to Chaucer.[40] The opening of the first ballade frames it as a challenge to Fortune:[41]

> Encontre toy, Fortune fortunée,
> Bonne et male, fait Franche Volunté
> Sçavoir a touz qu'elle est en homme née
> Pour empeschier toute ta pouesté;
> Ne nulz ne puet estre par toy tempté
> Qu'il ne demeure en son propre pouoir,
> S'en lui ne tient, tant l'aies tempesté.
> *Franc Cuer ne puet de son siege mouvoir*!

Against you, capricious Fortune, good and bad, Free Will makes known to all that it is born in man to thwart all your power; nor is there any who can be tempted by you if he trusts in his own strength, and keeps control of himself, however you might shake him. A Free Heart cannot be moved from its stronghold!

The succeeding stanzas elaborate on the power of Free Will, which operates from the 'high secret place of its thought, seeking eternal good' (17–18). The companion ballade uses the same form and rhymes; it is entitled 'Response de Fortune.' Rather than taunting the defiant speaker, Fortune agrees with him:

> Lasse! je voy pluseurs a la volée
> Qui cause sont de leur grant maleurté,

Eux soubmettans, comme gent aveuglée,
Aux chetis biens de temporalité;
Et la ont tant mis leur affinité
Qu'ilz n'en puelent leur penser remouvoir;
C'est ce qui fait, et par grant lascheté,
Lasche et moul cuer de son siege mouvoir.

Alas! I see many who at a stroke are cause of their great wretchedness, submitting themselves like blind people to the contemptible goods of the temporal world; and they have so devoted their hearts to them that they cannot remove their thoughts from them. That is what causes the cowardly and weak heart, in its great cowardice, to be moved from its stronghold.

Such a person, continues Fortune, devotes himself to acquiring goods, which are then taken away 'par cas soudain' (14), while the Free Heart scorns them in favour of 'le bien parfait' (22).

It is clear that Deschamps' double ballade could have suggested to Chaucer the general outline of his triple ballade, *Fortune*, which involves a dialogue between the 'Pleintif contre Fortune' and Fortune.[42] As Brusendorff says, 'In these poems we meet with the same spirit of defiance against Fate, which is the key-note of Chaucer's [*Fortune*] and especially of his first two *balades*, spoken as in Deschamps by Man and Fate respectively.'[43] This is compelling, but the relationship is not as neat as Brusendorff would have it. The narrator's dramatic challenge to Fortune does not extend past Deschamps' opening lines, while it is in force throughout Chaucer's work. In the second poem Fortune agrees with Deschamps' first speaker, while she and the speaker have an acerbic debate in Chaucer's poem. Also, the topics of the discussion are rather different; Chaucer is mostly concerned with friendship and mutability, Deschamps with free will. Finally, none of Chaucer's language has that neat congruency with Deschamps' wording which marks his borrowings from other poets.[44] The fact that the stanza forms are identical is not a powerful argument for the close relationship of the poems, since the *ababbcbC* rhyme scheme is the favourite of Deschamps, Granson, and Christine de Pisan, and second only to rime royal in Chaucer.[45] All in all, we may say that the similarities are significant but not conclusive, and the direction of influence is uncertain. If we decide that Chaucer knew these French poems on Fortune, then we probably also will decide that he was not taken by Deschamps' wording.

Another moral ballade that Deschamps might have included in his gift of poesy to Chaucer is one that bears the manuscript rubric 'Comment tout change sa condicion,' which Brusendorff saw as the primary model for Chaucer's *Lak of Stedfastnesse*.[46] The poem begins with a general lament that everything is changing its state and all are abandoning the rule that has governed them. The servant commands, lordship no longer characterizes lords, and so on. In a lively second stanza Deschamps gets carried away with oxymoronic descriptions of the unnatural behaviour of animals:

> Es bestes, voy debonnaire lyon,
> Aignel crueus, entreprenant lyeppart,
> Le loup piteus, le poucin champion,
> Et pour le gros voy voler le busart,
> L'aigle et l'austour voy devenir fetart,
> Et le coulon veult faire vassellage,
> Et le cenglier veult estre papelart:
> *Dont peut venir au jour d'ui tel usaige?*

Among the animals, I see the lion mild, the lamb cruel, the leopard timid, the wolf compassionate, the chicken defiant, the buzzard sent on the long flights,[47] the eagle and the goshawk become lazy, and the dove aspires to great prowess, while the boar turns hypocrite: where could such behaviour today come from?

In the last stanza Deschamps continues with examples of those who are not content to live according to their natures, concluding that 'for everyone his proper skill ought to suffice' (21). The whole poem amounts to little more than an amusing list of beings behaving contrary to their nature or calling, punctuated by a refrain that asks how the world got in such a state. Deschamps returns in several lyrics to the theme that one cannot depend on anything any more,[48] and expresses his outrage rather effectively at times. However, as with the poem quoted, the statements he makes are simplistic in comparison with Chaucer's sophisticated presentation in *Lak of Stedfastnesse* of the 'up-so-doun' condition of the world, which culminates with a request to King Richard to 'wed thy folk agein to stedfastnesse.' With similarities in phraseology lacking, the best one might say is that if Deschamps sent such a work to Chaucer, it might have stimulated him to consider writing a poem on the theme.[49]

In his ballade praising Chaucer, Deschamps does not refer to his sense of humour, but he would not have needed to read much of Chaucer's work to know about it. He would surely think to send some verse demonstrating his own comic and satiric bent. One frequent target of his satiric humour was marriage. Scholars have related his ballades and chants on this subject particularly to *Lenvoy de Chaucer a Bukton.*[50] Two of Deschamps' favourite themes are found in Chaucer's poem: it is inexcusable for a man to marry twice, and marriage is servitude. These are both expressed in the ballade that Brusendorff thinks a source for the specific wording of Chaucer's *Bukton.*[51] The manuscript contains only two stanzas of the ballade, quoted here as representative of the set of poems:

> Homs hors du senz, plains de forçonnerie,
> Tristes, dolens, chetifs et malostrus
> Est li meschans qui deux foiz se marie;
> Puisqu'il s'i est une foiz embatus,
> Du premier cop il doit estre tenus
> Pour ygnorant, mès s'il y entre arriere,
> *Des maleureux doit porter la banniere.*
>
> Car en exil met son corps et sa vie
> Et devient serfs, laches et espandus,
> Et d'un errour fait seconde folie
> Quant deux foiz est par femme confondus.
> Adonc vouldroit estre ars, mors ou pendus,
> Quant priz se voit, et par telle maniere
> *Des maleureux doit porter la banniere.*

A man out of his mind, filled with folly, sad, suffering, miserable, and uncouth is the unhappy one who marries two times; when he gets mixed up one time in marriage, in that first case he ought to be excused as ignorant, but if he gets into it again, he must carry the banner of the wretched.

For he consigns his body and his life to destruction and becomes a slave, cowardly and ruined, and from one error he falls into a second madness when he is confounded by woman two times. Then he wishes himself burnt, dead, or hanged, when he finds himself thus taken, and in such plight he must carry the banner of the wretched.

Chaucer's poem to Bukton does not seem so mordant as this or Deschamps' other poems on the subject; perhaps it is the light tone he establishes from the beginning that relieves the harshness of passages like the following:

> But thilke doted fool that eft hath levere
> Ycheyned be than out of prison crepe,
> God lete him never fro his wo dissevere,
> Ne no man him bewayle, though he wepe.   (13–16)

Neither poet shows much pity for the poor fools. But again the affinity between the works is quite general in both content and phraseology.[52]

An important formal consideration, the ballade envoy, provides further potential evidence of the Chaucer-Deschamps relationship. *Fortune*, *Lak of Stedfastnesse*, and *Lenvoy de Chaucer a Bukton* all have envoys. Deschamps is the chief poet who established the practice of composing envoys for ballades. Before his time envoys were peculiar to the five-stanza forms; Machaut's ballades never had envoys. We might assume, then, that Deschamps is influencing Chaucer's practice when he appends envoys to his ballades. However, the forms of Chaucer's envoys have little in common with those of Deschamps. Poirion, noting what Deschamps says about envoys in the *Art de dictier* and his practice in his poems, finds that the French poet aimed to give his envoys as many verses as there are strophes in the work, adding a line for the refrain: six lines total for the chant royal and four for the ballade. At times he mixed these up, giving some ballades six-line envoys and some chants four-line envoys, but his variations ended there. Deschamps also had a set practice for the rhyme scheme; in his envoys the rhymes reproduce the rhyme sequence of some part of the main stanzas.[53]

In contrast to Deschamps, Chaucer uses no established system in his ballade envoys.[54] The seven-line length of the envoy of *Fortune* has no particular rationale, and its rhyme scheme bears no relation to the 'Monk's Tale' stanza of the poem. Furthermore, its mere possession of an envoy sets *Fortune* apart from other multiple ballades, for none of the French examples, such as Deschamps' double ballade, have envoys. Chaucer's envoy to King Richard which concludes *Lak of Stedfastnesse* is also aberrant; it is simply a fourth rime royal stanza using the same rhymes. Comparably, the envoy of *Bukton* is a 'Monk's Tale' stanza that matches the three stanzas of the poem proper, though none of its rhymes repeat those of the stanzas. None of Chaucer's envoys, in sum, seem modelled on the practice of Deschamps.

To return to the possible contents of Deschamps' packet for Chaucer:

after choosing some moral and satirical lyrics to send, he probably would think to include poems in other forms and on the subject of love. A virelay that has been adduced as a source for *Merciles Beaute*[55] would satisfy the two desiderata. The main similarity between the works is in the common image of the eyes as dangerous weapons:

> *Comment pourra mon corps durer*
> *Ne les Doulx Regars endurer*
>   *De voz biaux yeux?*
> *Se Bon Espoir ne me fait mieulx*
> *Que je n'ay, il me faut finer.*
>
> En traiant m'ont voulu navrer
> Jusqu'au cuer, par leur regarder
>   Tresperilleux;
> Dont du trait ne puis respasser,
> Mais m'en convendra trespasser.
>   Ayde moy, Dieux!
>
> Fay que Pitié vueille garder
> Et Bon Espoir reconforter
>   Mon plaint piteux;
> Car se Dangier le despiteux
> Me nuist, je doy bien demander
>   *Comment pourra*, etc.

How can my body survive or endure the sweet look of your beautiful eyes? If Good Hope does not do better for me than I have done, my end is bound to come. In lancing their very dangerous look, they wished to wound me to the heart. Now from the shot I cannot recover, but I must die. Help me, God! Cause Pity to stand guard, and Good Hope to comfort my piteous lament; for if dispiteous Danger wounds me, I must then ask, How can, etc.

This foreshortened virelay is undistinguished but reasonably representative of Deschamps' rondeaux and virelays. Since its relationship to *Merciles Beaute* is very general, as with the other lyrics that Lowes adduces as sources for the poem, there is little reason to believe that it was more than vaguely suggestive to Chaucer.[56]

Another class of poem from which Deschamps might have chosen an example to send to Chaucer is that of topical works dealing with the activities and diversions of the court. One group of four such poems that is related to Chaucer's 'Prologue' to the *Legend of Good Women* concerns the debate over the comparative virtues of the flower and the leaf. The subject evidently amused courtiers on the two sides of the Channel.[57] The first three of Deschamps' poems – a ballade, a chant royal, and a rondeau – argue for the virtues of the flower, while the fourth, a chant, takes the side of the leaf.[58] In the 'Prologue' (F 72, 188–93) Chaucer professes absolute neutrality, even indifference, to the question, but he clearly implies that the debate is a lively one in England. We might speculate that Deschamps composed the second of the works especially to send to England with Clifford, since it names Philippa of Lancaster, daughter of John of Gaunt, as a distinguished partisan of the flower. The first stanza of this chant royal indicates the tenor of the debate as it was carried on by the various poets. The mention of France in the first line suggests that Deschamps had in mind an international audience:

> Pour ce que j'ay oy parler en France
> De deux ordres en l'amoureuse loy,
> Que dames ont chascune en defferance,
> L'une fueille et l'autre fleur, j'octroy
> Mon corps, mon cuer a la fleur; et pourquoy?
> Pour ce qu'en tout a pris, loange et grace
> Plus que fueille qui en pourre trespasse
> Et n'a au mieux fors que verde couleur,
> Et la fleur a beauté qui trestout passe.
> *A droit jugier je me tien a la flour.*[59] (1–10)

Since I have heard discussed in France two orders under Love's law, which every lady holds to differently, one to the leaf, the other the flower, I grant my body and heart to the flower; and why? Because in every respect it has worth, praise and grace more than the leaf, which decays in dust and has nothing superior except green colour, while the flower has beauty that surpasses all. I rightly take the part of the flower.

The three following stanzas elaborate on his reasons for choosing the flower; and he asks Guillaume La Trémouille, who was a chamberlain of Charles VI, to permit him to wear the symbol of the order. In the fifth stanza he recommends as the 'fleur de valeur' Philippa, a lady to be found in Lancaster. The envoy is addressed to the 'Royne d'amour,' Philippa as the flower, who surpasses all in understanding and honour.[60] Both the subject and circumstances of the poem suggest a possible connection with Chaucer, though again there is nothing to establish it with any certainty.

A substantial number of other short poems by Deschamps have been associated with Chaucer's work: ballades to the marguerite connected with Chaucer's praise of the daisy,[61] a begging poem to Charles v which is seen as a source of the *Complaint to His Purse*,[62] and other lyrics found to be relevant to passages in the longer works. Clifford might have carried these too back to England. And even if, as I have suggested, the 'euvres d'escolier' dispatched with Deschamps' ballade were limited to the short poems, any of his works could have circulated in other ways in both France and England, and thereby been available to Chaucer. Clifford's special delivery is not needed to account for Chaucer's indebtedness to some of Deschamps' lengthier poems, notably the *Lay de franchise*, *Lay de la fragilité humaine*, the *Fiction du lyon*, and especially the *Miroir de mariage*. But an inspection of the evidence scholars have presented of a direct relationship once more reveals nothing conclusive.

CHAUCER AND DESCHAMPS' LONGER WORKS

In addition to a prodigious number of works in the shorter formes fixes, some fifty of Deschamps' longer verse pieces survive. They are of various kinds: fourteen lays, a number of stories and letters of moderate length in octosyllabic couplets, and two long unfinished poems, the *Fiction du lyon* (2,954 lines) and the *Miroir de mariage* (12,103 lines).[63] They include love visions, political satires, moral treatises in verse, poetic charters for humorous societies, and adaptations of older Latin works; Deschamps draws from more sources than any other Middle French poet. Nevertheless, he does not show a mastery of literature comparable to Chaucer's. Despite the fact that he spent many years in school and composed poems in Latin, his knowledge of the classics seems very thin. Most of his references to Ovid and Virgil, for instance, seem derived from sources other than the originals.[64] Deschamps' knowledge of medieval literature, especially of Boethius, the *Roman de la Rose*, and Machaut, is more impressive. But in comparison with Chaucer his use and understanding of older literature consistently seems superficial.

While Deschamps' longer works tend to be derivative, they usually have original touches in form and content. Similarly, the versification and organization generally adhere to common practice, but there are surprising deviations and discontinuities. His fourteen lays as a group show such characteristics.[65] Clearly, their main inspiration is Machaut's practice. But Deschamps varies the standard lay form much oftener than Machaut does, and unlike Machaut he uses the lay for a wide variety of purposes – narrative, moral didacticism, political and social statements, and love poetry.[66] Two of his more Chaucerian poems are the *Lay amoureux* and the *Lay de franchise*, which are contiguous in the manuscript. In both of these the narrator goes out maying and hides himself behind a bush to view springtime activities. The *Lay amoureux*, quoted previously, is a dream vision in which the dreamer views from behind a bush a court held by the God of Love.[67]

We may label the *Lay de franchise*, which lacks the dream device, a 'dit d'aventure.'[68] Lowes saw the poem as a major source for the 'Prologue' to the *Legend of Good Women*, but Marian Lossing found his evidence defective.[69] Aside from other considerations the question is important because the time of composition of Deschamps' poem is indicated in the work, and it can provide a terminus for the composition of the 'Prologue'; it has been one of the anchors of traditional Chaucer chronology. Without going over the detail of the relationship, already described by Lowes and Lossing, it may be worthwhile to consider more general features of the lay, especially as they relate to Chaucer's poem. It is notable that Deschamps' work does not fit completely his own prescription for the lay, since instead of having twelve pairs of stanzas with different metrics, all twenty-four stanzas are the same, each having thirteen decasyllabic lines. The long uniform lines facilitate narration in the poem, which would be difficult to handle in the uneven lines and stanzas customary for the lay. They also make it more like Chaucer's 'Prologue,' which is likewise made up of decasyllabic lines.

Though it is not a dream poem, the lay's first ten stanzas evoke a number of passages in Chaucer's dreams. True to Chaucer's custom of beginning with a general meditation, the work opens with the narrator's speaking of the custom of 'going to gather in the May' (13). He discusses his own habit of rising early on May Day and going into the countryside where many an Amant goes to seek love. His thoughts are of a flower, obviously the marguerite, though he never names it in the poem:

De mon hostel me pars au point du jour.
Prins et sousprins d'amoureuse dolour,
M'acheminay pensant par une plaine
A la beauté de la tresdouce flour
Qui en bonté, en douçour, en honour
Et en tous biens, est la flour souveraine. (27–32)

I leave my home at dawn. Surprised and seized by love's sorrow, I went across a meadow thinking of the very sweet flower which in goodness, sweetness, honour, and every good is the supreme flower.

The next two stanzas describe the flower's nature and appearance in the familiar terms of Marguerite poetry. There are a number of similarities in wording to Chaucer's characterization of the daisy in the 'Prologue',[70] but nothing which is not matched – generally more closely – in Machaut and Froissart.

The narrator then tells of arriving at a grand park and seeing a great castle which had many statues on its pillars (82). Catching sight of a company of noblemen dressed in green, he hides himself behind a bush to watch them and observe the animal life. He enumerates the birds – goldfinches, linnets, etc. (105–14) – and describes the suitable disport of the celebrants of May (118–30). They are singing new songs, cutting flowers, fashioning girdles and wreaths of the branches, making flutes from the stems, and reciting poems of love together, 'speaking of honour and of loyal loves, by which all true hearts ought to be ravished' (129–30).

We now discover that the sixteen-year-old Charles VI and his brother Louis are present. The king speaks, adjuring all to be diligent in observing May, and he summons them to dine at the Castle of Beauté. The impressive person of the king and character of the company is described. Their topics of discussion are edifying and courtly:

La fut Honours; la fut Joie et Soulas;
La fut monstré de Vaillance le cas;
La fut parlé des grans faiz anciens;
La sont aucuns pour armes avocas;
La pour Amours murent pluseurs debas
Et questions ...   (183–8)

There was Honour, there was Joy and Solace; there the character of Valour was demonstrated; there the great deeds of old were discussed; there some defended arms; there several people posed debates and questions about Love ...

The lady whom the flower objectifies, the subject of the poet's prior meditation, concludes the discussion at this point. 'With her beautiful words she wisely stated that prowess is not possible without love' (210–11), and she invokes as witness the stories of Troy, of the *Brut*, and of classical heroes like Jason and Hercules (212–19).

The group goes off 'dansant' to Beauté (235). The narrator depicts the castle and its impressive furnishings, and then describes the festive dinner with its many courses, each announced by horns. He somehow has been able to observe all this from his hiding-place. At length he comes out and starts back home. But the poem does not end here as a standard kind of compliment to the king and his way of life. Deschamps the moralist now strangely replaces Deschamps the extoller of the court. On his return journey he overhears the rustic Robin speaking to his Marion, praising the simple life. Though he has just finished describing in admiring terms the king's luxurious life and lavish feast, Deschamps now has Robin speak of great meals as indecent ('deshonneste') and warn that those who partake are in danger of dying from them (274–6). Musing on Robin's words, the narrator finds 'haulte prudence' (304) in them. Then, returning to the 'douce fleur' once more, he closes the poem with the hope that she will willingly receive his lay.

Lowes thinks the poem was written to honour Marguerite of Burgundy after her marriage in April 1385, but Marian Lossing questions his assumption.[71] Nevertheless, it is not necessary to pin down the particular lady in order to fix the date of the events celebrated in the poem as 1 May 1385, since they take place on May Day, and the king – born 3 December 1368 – is said to be sixteen years old. If Chaucer used the *Lay de franchise*, then he must have written the 'Prologue' after the middle of 1385. But his use is not at all sure. Lossing disposed effectively of most of Lowes's evidence, showing that the individual verbal parallels asserted were 'far too general to offer valid evidence,' and that the parallels in structure also 'fail to stand the test of examination.'[72] In general, Lossing's critique of Lowes seems valid; nevertheless, there remains a congruity between the opening sequences of the lay and the 'Prologue' which is not duplicated in any of the other related works. None of the others has the opening sequence in which the narrator goes out at dawn at the beginning of May thinking of the daisy-flower's virtues.[73] and subsequently has an experience involving the woman who embodies those virtues. Furthermore, while the *Lay de franchise* is no dream poem, the dream vision of the narrator in the closely related *Lay amoureux* presents some interesting parallels to the 'Prologue,' including the appearance in fiery brightness of the God of Love, who presides over a group of legendary lovers, and the discovery of the eavesdropping narrator who is identified as a composer of love poems.[74]

This sequence of parallels between Chaucer's 'Prologue' and the two lays, which is unduplicated in the tradition, does not prove a relationship between the poems, certainly not with the conclusiveness that Lowes asserted. At the same time, it does seem to me that it makes a filiation between the works probable. Which way the imitation might have gone, however, from Deschamps to Chaucer or vice versa, there seems no way of determining on the basis of internal evidence.[75] On the broad question of the relationship between the poets, the similarities in these works add another modest indication of their first-hand knowledge of each other's verse.

The same cannot be said for the relationship of another of Deschamps' lays to Chaucer's work. Any direct connection between the two writers' versions of Innocent III's *De miseria conditionis humane*[76] is quite doubtful. Chaucer says he translated this treatise,[77] though the text is not extant, but we do have verse translations of limited passages in the 'Man of Law's Tale' and the 'Pardoner's Tale.' A few years previous to these translations by Chaucer, Deschamps composed a verse version of certain parts of Innocent's work under the title *Double lay de la fragilité humaine*, and he presented a handsome manuscript copy of the work, together with the relevant parts of the Latin text, to Charles VI in 1383.[78] It is tempting to assume that Chaucer was inspired by Deschamps' model; however, there is virtually nothing in the available evidence to suggest a relationship. In the first place, since Innocent's treatise was very popular, it would be quite understandable if the poets had chosen independently to produce versions of it.[79] In the second place, the fragmentary translations of Innocent's work scattered in Chaucer's verse have very little in common with what Deschamps produced.

As was the case with the form of *Lay de franchise*, the versification of Deschamps' 'double lay' is not quite what one would expect. Instead of twenty-four sets of two stanzas, the size of two standard lays, it has thirty-three; the stanza forms do not differ as prescribed, but all the lines are heptasyllabic, gathered in stanzas of seven to ten lines. The work actually covers but a fraction of Innocent's work, and there is very little overlap between the parts used in Chaucer's extant verse and what Deschamps produced.[80] The one notable instance in which both poets translate from the same part, which provides an opportunity to compare the poets' handling, is in book I, chapter 14, 'Of the Misery of the Poor and the Rich,'[81] where the plight of the poor man is dealt with. The first twenty-three lines of the prologue to the 'Man of Law's Tale' translates this part of *De miseria* into rime royal, often word for word. The Latin original and the passage from the tale begin:

Pauperes enim premuntur inedia, cruciantur erumpna, fame,
siti, frigore, nuditate ... O miserabilis condicio merdicantis!
Et si petit, pudore confunditur ...[82]

O hateful harm, condicion of poverte!
With thurst, with coold, with hunger so counfoundid!
To asken help thee shameth in thy herte ...   (I 99–101)

After following the Latin for over three stanzas, the Man of Law goes
off in a direction opposite to Innocent's. Whereas *De miseria* continues
with a balancing lament for the plight of the rich man, the Man of Law
celebrates the happy state of 'riche marchauntz' (122).

Deschamps' treatment is different: he is faithful to Innocent's general
scheme, but he summarizes rather than translating fully. In a matched
pair of stanzas he contrasts the sorrows of the rich and the poor. His
short stanza on poverty is a third as long as Chaucer's version.

Mais povres homs est digiteus,
Vilz tenus et si maleureus
Que tousjours languist en doubtance;
Il est de tous biens langoreus,
Tristes, chetis et fameilleus;
Chascuns le het et desavance;
Mieulx lui vault mort que mendience,
Car de truander est honteus;
Povres homs est d'amis trop seuls,
Chascuns le met en oubliance.   (279–88)

The poor man is subject to continuous want, considered contemptible, and ever
languishes in fear; lacking every good, he is sad, miserable, and starved; all
detest and reject him; death is better for him than begging, for to ask alms is
shameful; the poor man is without friends, everyone forgets him.

This is as close as Chaucer's and Deschamps' verse versions of *De miseria*
get to each other. Doubtless Chaucer's prose would not have been closer
to the French. The fact that the two poets translated the treatise into the
vernacular testifies to the similarity of their cultural backgrounds, but
there is no evidence that either knew or was affected by the other's
version.

Another lost writing of Chaucer which has been related to a poem of Deschamps, the 'Book of the Leoun,' is one of the 'enditynges of worldly vanitees' that Chaucer retracts at the end of the *Canterbury Tales* (I 1084, 1087). The more common speculation is that the lost work is a version or adaptation of Guillaume de Machaut's *Dit dou lyon*, a dit amoureux in which the lion represents the faithful lover; the centrepiece of the poem is a lecture on love by a worthy old knight.[83] Brusendorff, however, on rather weak evidence, assumes that the poem must have been written very late in Chaucer's career, at a time when he had 'outgrown long ago' his taste for Machaut's love poetry.[84] Instead of Machaut's work, then, Brusendorff suggests as a model Deschamps' *Fiction du lyon*.[85] Since the latter is a 'satire directed against the political situation in France' in the early 1380s, says Brusendorff, Chaucer 'may have adapted it to suit the disorderly state of affairs in England' in the late 1390s. There are a number of arguments against such a suggestion, among them the uninspired content of the *Fiction du lyon* itself.

As already noted, the *Fiction* represents one of Deschamps' two attempts to write an extensive work in verse; he left both unfinished. The mere fact that they were not formally completed would not have prevented a medieval author from circulating the works, of course, but both poems have informative explicits, presumably attributable to the compiler of the manuscript, which call attention to the fragmentary states of the works. After the *Fiction* we read, 'Cy mourut l'acteur, et pour ce demoura la fiction cy dessus imparfaicte' / 'At this point the author died, and therefore the above fiction remains incomplete.' This is probably misleading. Since at its beginning the work treats of the early years of the reign of Charles VI, it is unlikely that Deschamps had worked on the *Fiction* at any time near his death. The explicit is probably otherwise indicative of the compiler's lack of information. If he was a literary friend of Deschamps, as is likely,[86] then the statement may be his rationalization of the poem's inchoate state. The very confusion of the compiler suggests that the work had not circulated and become known.

The content of the poem is diverse, chiefly related to two monuments of medieval literature: the *Roman de Renart* and the *Roman de la Rose*.[87] Its narrative is a political allegory featuring Noble the Lion, representing Charles V, together with the young lion, Charles VI; also important are Renard the Fox, a surrogate for Charles le Mauvais of Navarre, and the leopard, Richard II of England. In the midst of the fable the poet inserts a great council of the pagan gods in which they decide to destroy the world in a progressive process, and a monologue of Nature, who speaks of her divine mission and pleads vainly that the gods spare man and the animals. The poem breaks off with Renard visiting the leopard and determining to foment discord.

Badel's statement that the poem 'adds nothing to the credit of Deschamps'[88] is probably just. Its execution is uninspired and one understands Deschamps' having abandoned it. The beast fable nevertheless appealed to him as a subject-matter. There are a half-dozen short poems in which he uses the Renard material for political allegory, and numerous others that contain references to figures in the fables.[89] Although Deschamps makes diverse uses of the materials, Chaucer's one great beast fable, the 'Nun's Priest's Tale,' has almost nothing in common with them. If we add to this the facts that the *Fiction du lyon* may have never circulated, that it is a mediocre poem which has little to attract imitation, and that there are no correspondences between the *Fiction* and Chaucer's other works, the chance that it provided a model for the 'Book of the Leoun' seems very small. On the other hand, Machaut's *Dit dou lyon*, extant in numerous manuscripts, obviously had a broad circulation. It is written in a mode thoroughly compatible with that of Chaucer's dream poems, and in fact Chaucer made use of it in the *Book of the Duchess*.[90] If Chaucer's lost work is based on one of the French poems, by all odds it is Machaut's.

We come finally to the work that is Deschamps' longest, that has the best claim to being his master-work, and that has been importantly associated with poems of Chaucer. This is the *Miroir de mariage*. The poet left it incomplete after 12,103 lines; if he had closed it 1,000 lines earlier at the end of the debate about marriage, with which it had been occupied to that point, it probably would be judged a reasonably well-constructed and successful work. It opens with a discussion of friendship, which leads to the main subject – the question whether a young man, called Franc Vouloir (Free Will), should marry. His false friends Desir, Folie, Servitute, and Faintise advise it, and engage in extensive praise of the benefits of marriage; but before acting Franc Vouloir seeks the advice of Repertoire de Science (Wisdom), the true friend. After consulting the authorities, Repertoire de Science in a detailed response enumerates the dangers and ills of carnal marriage, and contrasts the superiority of spiritual marriage. At length, having considered both sides of the question, Franc Vouloir chooses to live unmarried. The most important texts from which Repertoire de Science draws his advice are Saint Jerome's *Adversus Jovianianum*, the Bible, Matheolus' *Lamentations*, and Ovid's *Ars amatoria*. His presentation also no doubt draws on Deschamps' firsthand observation or experience, as with the discussion of costly weddings, and the picture of the prodigal son at the university.[91] Though the work has some slow places, much of the debate is lively and it contains numerous interesting exemplary narratives.

The thousand lines that follow Franc Vouloir's decision, however, distract and detract. When Folie blames Franc Vouloir for refusing to marry, the latter attacks Folie, enumerating the historical disasters that she has caused: the imprisonment of Boethius, the death of Roland, the fall of Troy. Eventually, his historical survey comes to the Hundred Years' War; in telling of Crécy, Poitiers, the seige of Reims, and the Treaty of Brétigny (1360), he follows closely the account of the *Grandes Chroniques de France*. After some hostages are named, the work breaks off. As with the *Fiction du lyon*, the explicit attributes the unfinished state of the work to the death of the author. 'De la matiere de ce livre ne traicta l'acteur plus avant pour maladie qui lui survint, de laquelle il mourut. Dieu lui pardoint a l'ame! Amen!' / 'The author wrote no more on the subject of this book before sickness came upon him, from which he died. God forgive his soul! Amen!' Again the manuscript's compiler seems to look on the poem as work in progress, and evidently assumed that it had not circulated.

Nevertheless, in 1911 Lowes asserted that Chaucer had made extensive use of the *Miroir de mariage*. In two articles he detailed evidence of its influence on the marriage discussion in the *Canterbury Tales*, especially on the 'Wife of Bath's Prologue' and the 'Merchant's Tale.'[92] Though not all scholars were thoroughly convinced, this influence was generally accepted until an article by Zacharias Thundy appeared in 1979. The article calls into doubt any direct use of the *Miroir* by Chaucer.[93] Where Lowes found influence of Deschamps, says Thundy, either the *Lamentations* of Matheolus or its translation by Jehan Le Fèvre offer closer parallels.[94] Thundy's case appears sound. Even without attempting to judge the case for Matheolus' influence, one sees that the particular echoes of Deschamps that Lowes alleges are not impressive. The close word-for-word parallels between Jerome or the *Roman de la Rose* and the 'Wife of Bath's Prologue' are simply not present between the *Miroir* and Chaucer's text.

At the same time there is a broad similarity between the *Miroir* and the *Canterbury Tales* in the treatment of the marital discussions. Numerous points that Repertoire de Science makes in arguing against marriage are made dramatically in the Wife's presentation, which is in part a response to the Pardoner's request that she teach 'us yonge men of youre praktike' (D 187), an ironic parallel to Franc Vouloir's request to his mentor. Moreover, arguments for marriage made by the false friends of Franc Vouloir are presented ironically by Chaucer's Merchant at the beginning of his tale. Similarly, the advice for and against of Placebo and Justinus in the 'Merchant's Tale' has an analogue in the advice of Franc Vouloir's false and true friends. Once more the evidence is inconclusive. While we cannot say with any assurance that Chaucer knew the *Miroir*, there are parallels that show Chaucer's marriage discussions could have been inspired in part by it.[95]

All told, the significant evidence for Chaucer's use of Deschamps, or vice versa, is disappointingly small. The framework of Deschamps' double ballade on Fortune is quite like that of Chaucer's triple ballade *Fortune*. Some of Deschamps' warnings against marriage are suggestive of the tone and ironic message of the *Envoy to Bukton*. The *Lay de franchise* and the *Lay amoureux* present narrative and situational parallels to the 'Prologue' to the *Legend of Good Women*. Deschamps' flower-and-leaf poems could figure in the reference of the 'Prologue' to the *Legend*. And some aspects of the debate in the *Miroir de mariage* are like the discussions of marriage in the *Canterbury Tales*. This is the sum of it. It is particularly significant that there are no extensive unduplicated verbal parallels in any of the works. The promise of the ballade to Chaucer, which creates an image of an active cross-Channel exchange of poetry between the writers, is simply not fulfilled in the evidence of the extant works. We will perhaps be better satisfied if we put aside the question of the direct relationship and deal with the two as poets who worked on different sides of the Channel in the same years with similar materials and with understanding and wit.

In one article on Deschamps and Chaucer Lowes does exactly this. The article offers a series of notes, gathered not 'to suggest new sources' but to 'add fresh vividness here and there to the background of contemporary manners and customs against which some of Chaucer's lines demand projection.'[96] The first note illustrates the cultural setting for the gamesters' oaths in the 'Pardoner's Tale,' by which they 'to-tere' Christ's body: 'By goddes precious herte, and by his nayles, etc.' (C 474, 651). Lowes finds a 'vivid, even lurid, commentary' on the Pardoner's statements here in two of Deschamps' poems that describe dice games. One of them presents the Dukes of Berry and Burgundy and other nobles at play; their behaviour, says the editor, suggests 'drinkers sitting in a cabaret' instead of great lords in a chateau.[97] The picture is indeed un-edifying, with one cursing his luck, another coughing in the fireplace, and another accused of hiding money in his sleeves.

> Il dit que non fet,
> Et s'on ne se taist, qu'il laira
> Le gieu, et que plus ne jourra.
> Lors veissez Dieu despecer
> Du sang, et sa mort parjurer ...

He said that he didn't do it, and if he [the accuser] was not quiet, he would leave the game and play no longer. Then see him tearing God apart, with His blood, and swearing by His death ...

These are only a few of the oaths associated with the game Deschamps describes. The whole depiction certainly provides a colourful commentary on the Pardoner's lines, as well as a fresh view of the life of medieval magnates.

It would be easy to see a great part of Deschamps' work as a vast commentary on Chaucer's. Obviously, the backgrounds and many of the experiences of the poets were comparable. Both served in royal and ducal courts from a young age. Both may have studied law. Both travelled far on the king's business. Both were married men with children whose wives predeceased them by many years; neither remarried. Both composed a large body of poetry in a variety of modes on a great variety of subjects. So also might they be compared in personality. As young men they obviously practised the graces of a courtier and participated in military actions. As they aged they both took an increasingly ironic view of the world about them and a comic view of themselves. But neither became cynical. In some of his work Deschamps played the part of the buffoon; Chaucer, by contrast, took the role of the humorous elf. They both died in late middle age, no longer especially productive.

If they met, Chaucer would have played no tricks on Deschamps such as his court friends and Granson did. Deschamps in turn would have been respectful of Chaucer for his poetic prowess. With their common interests, common history, and comparable curiosity, each would have been content to spend hours drawing the other out. Chaucer would not have found in Deschamps as good a friend as Granson or as impressive a man of letters as Froissart, but he would have felt him a kindred spirit in his broad experience, his usual self-effacement, and the irony with which he viewed the world.

CHAPTER NINE

Natural Music
in 1400

It suits the Procrustean tradition of literary historians, who like to divide materials into time segments of one century, that the deaths of Chaucer and Richard II neatly close off the great age of Ricardian poetry in 1400. Langland and the Gawain Poet had disappeared by the end of the century, and if Gower lived on into the fifteenth century (until 1408) it was only for a few less productive years, which can be safely ignored. So also in France the major disciples of Machaut – Froissart (died c 1404), Granson (1397), and Deschamps (c 1406) – faded from view near the turn of the century. Moreover, the founding of the French Cour amoureuse, a significant sign of the times,[1] took place in 1400. This is all to say that facts as well as the appeal of round numbers justify our focusing on the year 1400 in this concluding chapter.

In the course of the fourteenth century the poetry of the formes fixes evolved perceptibly. After Machaut the most prominent writers no longer provided music for their texts, but many poet-musicians remained active.[2] More of the nobility, and perhaps more of the townspeople, took part in verse composition. The forms themselves changed; only in relative terms were they 'fixed.' Ballades became much longer with stanzas of eight or ten decasyllabic lines, and often with substantial envoys; the rondeau form, increasingly popular, became diversified and generally longer; and by 1400 the lay and the virelay were moribund. Such are some obvious features in the evolution. However, my purpose is not to review and forecast the broad development of Middle French poetry, most of which became tangential to Chaucer's work in the last decade of his life. Instead, I will concentrate on two limited questions about developments that particularly concern Chaucer at the end of his career. One question is retrospective, having to do with the relationship of the puys and the courts as far as we can follow that shadowy history from the late thirteenth century to 1400. The other looks forward, and probes the essence of Chaucer's 'natural music'; it asks how successful Chaucer was in overcoming the great barrier of his Germanic stress language in translating the French natural music into English, and to what degree he then was able to pass along his version of that music to subsequent English poets.

THE COURT AND THE PUY

Since the available information about the medieval civic literary societies, the puys,[3] is fragmentary, and since no comprehensive study has been made, the common understanding of them is based more on impression than on fact. Because they are said to have been middle-class, the membership is readily imagined to be Philistine; because the intentions were outspokenly religious and moral, the verse is assumed to be unpoetic; and because certain aspects of the practices imitate the court – a prince presides, a lyric is 'crowned,' its author becomes 'king' – the writers are thought to be epigones of the court poets. All of these assumptions were no doubt true some times in some places; like most medieval social phenomena, the puys were quite varied from one group to another. Nevertheless, in the fourteenth century eminent and highly cultivated men took part in the concours, the poetry that we know to have emanated from the puys is not notably inferior to the common run of the 'courtly,' and the puy writers were often the same as the court writers. Indeed, instead of battening on the court tradition, the puys through the fourteenth century seem to have been a source of nourishment and strength for court poetry, and the century ended with the court groups openly imitating the 'bourgeois' literary societies. The formes fixes mode in part shared Chaucer's middle-class origins in the city, and it retained its ties there.

We may connect the very beginnings of the formes fixes with the puys. The oldest body of extant lyrics that clearly belongs to the mode was composed by the original and versatile genius Adam de la Halle. His *Jeu de la feuillée*, itself perhaps written for a concours, strongly suggests that he wrote such lyrics for the puy at Arras. Thanks in part to Adam, we know more about the organization in Arras than any other of its kind. An important aspect of the puy there – and of puys elsewhere, it seems – is that it brought together a diverse group of devotees on a relatively equal footing. Scholars have seen this social inclusiveness as serving importantly to elevate the status of the minstrels.[4]

One evidence of the democratic nature of the puys may be found in Gilles li Muisis' list, compiled in 1351, of prominent poets of the day. As I noted in chapter 2, li Muisis names Jean de le Mote third among prominent poet-musicians of his time, after Philippe de Vitry and Guillaume de Machaut. The fourth and final writer he lists is a talented illiterate who is a puy poet, probably a participant with Abbot Gilles himself in the concours at Tournai:

> Collart Hobiert n'oublieray,
> Avoec Jehan le metterai.
> S'il n'est letrés, s'est boins fasières;
> Esprouvés est par lies chières
> Es puis l'a-on l'à couronnet
> Ou l'estrivet capiel donnet.[5]

I will not forget Colard Aubert. I will put him with Jean [de le Mote]. Though he is not educated, he writes good poems; that is proven by the joyful faces in the puys where he has been crowned or awarded the contested garland.

The four poets whom Gilles mentions occupied various rungs on the social ladder: Vitry was a bishop, Machaut a canon at Reims, le Mote a clerk at Hainault, and Colard Aubert evidently an unlettered townsman, perhaps a professional minstrel. The good abbot lists these writers according to social rank, the highest first, but he nevertheless puts them all together in the world of verse. All four, together with Gilles himself, could have comfortably come together in the puy.

Prominent churchmen and distinguished citizens supported and participated in the puys. One of the few extant records of the London society records a substantial gift from Henry le Waleys, an outstanding citizen who was several times mayor, to support the chaplain of the society. The chief surviving London record is a set of regulations from the late thirteenth century, providing as complete a description as we have of a northern European puy. The rules direct that meetings be held once a year for a fine spectrum of reasons: for the honour of God, the Blessed Virgin, the saints, the king, and the barons, 'for the increasing of loyal love,' for the renown of London, 'and to the end that mirthfulness, peace, honesty, joyousness, gaiety, and good love without end may be maintained.' The pious and patriotic aspect of the purposes clearly did not rule out ardent poetic activity. While there were charitable and religious functions, the poetic and musical ends were paramount. At the meetings songs were to be submitted that praised 'the becoming pleasaunce of virtuous ladies.' The 'prince of the puy,' elected yearly, was to 'crown' the best song at the great annual feast.[6] We do not know how long the London society lasted, but if it endured a century, Chaucer and associates like Froissart and Gower, and the knight Granson too, could have belonged.[7]

The puys probably had most effect on Chaucer through their influence on the Continental poets with whom he associated. There is a good chance that Froissart began his poetic career in meetings of the puy at Valenciennes. He remained proud of his accomplishments at the concours, particularly of his victories; the manuscripts retain records of the crowning of five of his chansons: 'Canchon Amoureuse Couronnee a Valenchienes,' 'Canchon Amoureuse Couronnee a Abbeville,' 'Chançon Royale Sote Couronnee a Lille,' 'Serventois de Nostre Dame Couronnés a Valenchiennes' (twice).[8] As I have already suggested, his pastourelles probably represent adaptations of a puy genre to court purposes, providing a good example of how the court might draw strength from the presumably imitative organization. Jean de le Mote too publicized his puy experience. Towards the beginning of *Regret Guillaume*, written for Queen Philippa on the death of her father – a thoroughly courtly occasion – the dreamer muses over a poem that he wants to take to a puy;[9] no doubt le Mote had in mind a concours at Valenciennes. Even Machaut, though he came from outside the area where the puys flourished and was always associated with the courts, probably participated as a guest at more than one concours. Of his chants royaux, five have envoys addressed to 'Prince,' one requesting explicitly that his work be crowned: 'Prince, veuillez d'un chapel de soucie ... Moy et mon chant, s'il vous plaist coronner' / 'Prince, please crown me and my lyric with a wreath of marigold.'[10]

Machaut's participation seems unlikely only if we wrongly think of the puys as organizations of equivocal social status. It is true that poetic activity appropriate in the courts is sometimes distinguished from that appropriate to the puys, but this need not be taken as denigration. In the *Art de dictier*, addressed to a great lord, Deschamps refrains from describing the serventois in detail 'because this is a form which pertains to the *puis d'amours*, and noblemen do not usually compose them.'[11] A sense that Deschamps is disdainfully dismissing the puys is misleading, for elsewhere in the treatise he uses their proceedings to make an important point. In illustrating the distinction between 'musique naturelle' and 'musique artificielle,' he describes the poet's carrying his original verse to the prince at a concours, where he recites it from memory; this, Deschamps says, is known as 'en disant.' After the recitation, the poet must also sing it to the prince.[12] Thus, while we see Deschamps assuming that noblemen will not participate in the puys (a restriction that probably applied only to the highest nobility), and that certain forms are peculiar to them, his use of puy practice as example and model shows serious respect for the societies. Deschamps had good personal reason to think well of the puys. One gathers from envoys in his poems, as one might guess from his knowledgeable depiction in the *Art de dictier*, that he himself participated in the concours.[13]

Throughout the fourteenth century, puys flourished in the major French-speaking cities closest to England: Amiens, Tournai, Abbeville, Lille, Dieppe, Valenciennes. The poetic skill which Jean de le Mote and Jean Froissart brought to England no doubt reflected extensive experience in these societies which provided them opportunities to learn the conventions, to associate with the prosperous and cultivated men of the cities, and to popularize the performance and composition of the formes fixes. In the puys the forms of the crowned poems generally were five-stanza chants or related types, no longer favoured in the courts; however, the main court form, the ballade, was also popular in the societies, and all of the forms were practised there.[14] All evidence indicates that the puys were both influential and prestigious. Three unmistakable adaptations of their practices in court literature provide important evidence: an episode of le Mote's *Parfait du paon*, the court literary activity evoked in the *Cent ballades*, and the 'Charte de la Cour d'Amour.'

In Jean de le Mote's Alexander romance the *Parfait du paon* there is a long interlude, described in chapter 2, in which the court games depicted reflect two traditions: the fictive tradition that represents the posing and judging of demandes d'amour, and the social tradition by which poetic contests are held in the puys. In the interlude of the *Parfait*, after some questions of love are arbitrated, Alexander and three of his peers, together with the four daughters of the pagan King Melidus, present ballades in turn to be judged by prominent figures in their audience. After the merits of each poem are deliberated one of them is selected to be crowned. Le Mote, experienced in court ways, is not simply naïve or confused in having his fictional court imitate the puy. For him and his audience the procedures of the civic literary societies provide an attractive and wholly respectable model for the court to follow.

Another work that combines the traditions of the demande d'amour and the puy is the *Cent ballades* (c 1390),[15] which represents better than any other single text the state of formes fixes poetry at the end of the century. Froissart's long poems had incorporated increasing numbers of lyric set pieces, and Granson's *Livre Messire Ode* is preponderantly made up of them, to the point that narrative episodes are presented in the lyric pieces as well as in the connecting couplets. The *Cent ballades*, composed by Jean le Seneschal and three other noblemen, carries the poetic development to its logical end: the whole poem, both the narrative and lyric elements, is presented in a hundred sequential ballades of varying versification. The story is of a pensive young lover who goes riding; he encounters an old knight who in a long series of ballades counsels him on the necessity of loyalty in love. The second half of the work offers a contrasting lesson in a second set of ballades. A lively young lady, who is part of a group of young people that the lover encounters, argues for the delights of playing the field. Obviously, a demande d'amour is propounded here. Must a young lover remain faithful to one person, or is it preferable to divide one's amorous attentions among many?

Having listened to the arguments on both sides, the lover, a surrogate of the major author, Jean le Seneschal, returns to the château, where he consults with his three collaborators on the question whether loyalty or changeability is better in love. All four decide in favour of loyalty, but in the hundredth and last ballade they make a plea to each 'amoureux' to compose a ballade setting forth his opinion. In the thirteen ballades that follow the hundred, thirteen different noblemen offer their 're- sponses,' enunciating various solutions. In total the work involves the collaboration of seventeen Frenchmen of high rank, and it shows vividly the increasing participation by the courtiers themselves in the compo- sition of poetry. For the first sixty years of the fourteenth century, the nobility produced few of the lyrics that have come down to us. In the last forty years of the century, though, the amount of their verse in- creased: a substantial number of texts by Wenceslas of Luxembourg, Oton de Granson, and Jean de Garencières, the chamberlain of Louis d'Orléans, have survived.

The appearance of these poets, along with the seventeen noble par- ticipants in the *Cent ballades*, shows that by century's end much of the

French nobility was actively writing verse. The editor of the *Cent ballades* projects one or more 'concours poétiques' in Avignon in November 1390, when the creators of the *Cent ballades* might have presented the work and the respondents delivered their ballades.[16] Though no actual crown was offered, the call for responses in the last ballade emphasizes the competitive aspect; it is to be a contest to compose the *best* response: 'faire vëoir / ... Par vo dit, le *plus* eüreux / Conseil, dont amant main et soir / Peut *miex* manoir, / Qui *plus* le fait d'amours joieux' / 'To make clear in your poem the *most* effective counsel by which a lover can *best* maintain himself night and day, which makes him the *most* joyful in love' (c 31–6). The coming together of the *Cent ballades* poets to produce a large set of ballades on a subject of love was inspired by the practices of the puy. Instead of ignoring or patronizing the civic societies, these courtiers found a model in their practice.

The most patent courtly imitation of the puys is found in the charter of 1400 of the Cour amoureuse, attributed to Charles VI, which sets up an elaborate court with three grand conservators, eleven ordinary conservators, a 'Prince d'amour,' twenty-four ministers, and so on.[17] Ostensibly it imitates literary courts of love and governmental organizations, but the most basic model for the charter, as is amply confirmed by the prescribed procedures, is the tradition of the puys.[18] The ceremonies and feasts all partake of concours: each month there is to be a 'feste de puy d'Amours,' and on Valentine's Day a great celebration with specially composed ballades for which prizes are awarded; in May there is to be another special 'puy.' As is traditional in the puys, refrains are assigned for the ballade contests, crowns are awarded, and the feast-days of the Virgin are observed. Also following the model of the puys, a moral purpose is asserted. The court, the charter declares, is founded on the virtues of humility and loyalty to promote 'the honour, praise, and commendation of all ladies'; severe penalties are prescribed for anyone doing anything to the dispraise of womanhood. The conception of the court evidently was in part the fantasy of Isabelle of Bavaria and her entourage;[19] notwithstanding, the documents witness the strong influence of the civic puys on the literary ideas of the nobility.

The numerous membership list of the Cour amoureuse was not confined to the nobility; names from the bourgeosie, especially from the north of France, appear on the rolls.[20] Among other members are nine of the participants in the *Cent ballades*. Also named is Eustache Deschamps, 'hussier d'armes du roy et bailli de Senlis,' who is one of the 'auditeurs.' Shortly after the charter of the court appeared in 1400, Deschamps, assuming the guise of 'prince de haulte eloquence,' burlesqued it in two poems.[21] In the shorter of the two, a ballade that summarizes the longer work, he calls for a parliament to be held each May at 'Lens en Artois.' He summons several of his friends by name, the purpose being, as the refrain declares, 'Pour compte de ses bourdes rendre' / 'To give an account of one's jokes.' He who brags the best is to be 'crowned like a king' (26). At other times Deschamps freely invented strange societies and orders,[22] so we need not assign great significance to the burlesque. Whatever wry commentary on Queen Isabelle's society his poems constitute, both they and the Cour amoureuse provide further testimony of influence and seminal power flowing from puy to court rather than from court to puy.

The poetry of the courts, then, was substantially affected by the puys. Instead of disdaining the civic organizations as upstart imitators, the courts willingly adopted their customs. The professional writers active in the courts often had extensive experience in the concours and they paraded their affiliations rather than attempting to conceal them. The increasing involvement by the French nobility in the poetry, which reached its apogee in the poetry of Charles d'Orléans, thus implies their participation in an activity with origins in the guildhalls as well as in the castles. If one seeks specific effects on the lyrics themselves, the puy influence may be seen in what happens to the forms: the prescriptiveness, the tendency for the stanzaic units to become longer, the use of envoys in ballades, even the divorce of the words from the music. Or one may see it in the moral tenor of the work: the earnest ethical purposes, the absence of references to physical acts of love.

As we have traced the course of formes fixes poetry through the fourteenth century, the poets have appeared as functionaries of the court, producing verse that has its sources in the life and aspirations of the nobility. From the vantage-point of the Cent ballades and the Cour amoureuse in 1400, however, we can see that the civic puys played a part in the work. The consequences for Chaucer's poetry are important. We recognize that even the French component in his oeuvre has a non-courtly element. There is a chance that he participated in puys in London or France and learned their practices, and we know that he had important associations with poets experienced in the puys, notably le Mote and Froissart. What is more, many of the texts that he found in the courts were born in the concours or affected by poems that were. The lyrics he heard when he came into the service of the Countess of Clarence were not as foreign to his natal class as one might imagine. The civic societies that Chaucer's and Froissart's fathers and uncles might have belonged to played a part in the tradition along with the courts of the Valois and Plantagenets.

There is no evidence of imitation of the puys by the nobility in England comparable to that shown in France by the *Cent ballades* or the Cour amoureuse. To be sure, men of rank had become conspicuously involved in poetic activity; Sir Thomas Clanvowe and Sir John Montague, Earl of Salisbury, for instance, were probably composing love lyrics in the conventional forms at the end of the century. But the decline of the French language in England, the general absence of puys in the cities, and the powerful example of Chaucer's long poems dictated that as the new century opened poetic activity in England would be gradually diverted. Chaucer himself composed several ballades and ballade envoys which seem to date from the 1390s, but he was mainly busy with the *Canterbury Tales*. Nevertheless, even as there remain echoes of the Middle French lyrics in the *Tales*, so also we find in them intimations of both the court-of-love games and the puys. The demande d'amour is a feature both of the 'Knight's Tale' and the 'Franklin's Tale.' And in the Host's proposal at the end of the 'General Prologue,' which sets up a poetic competition between various citizens with the best performance to be recognized and rewarded at a dinner, the model of the concours may well have some part.[23] Nevertheless, the congruency between a concours and the assemblage of pilgrims in the *Tales* is on most counts tenuous. The major implications of puy influence are for the court poetry itself and Chaucer's stanzaic poetry. A question with a different orientation, looking not to origins but to effects, concerns the degree to which Chaucer was successful in adapting the Middle French 'natural music' to the English language, whose patterns of intonation are quite different from the French.

NATURAL MUSIC IN ENGLISH

In concluding his impressive essay 'The "Music" of the Lyric: Machaut, Deschamps, Chaucer,'[24] John Stevens applies his thoughtful understanding of the problems of rhythm and meter to the very question I want to deal with in this final section: how successful was Chaucer in translating the rhythmical character of the French lyric into English? The discussion in chapter 1 shows that Chaucer's stanzaic poetry absorbs much of the French mode, including important prosodic features, and the remainder of the book establishes a broad relationship between the formes fixes tradition and the English poet and his work; however, it has not confronted the narrower but important question of how effectively Chaucer overcame the difference between the relatively unstressed French language and the strongly stressed English in adapting the natural music to his verse. Any positive answer to the question, furthermore, evokes the broader and even more vexed question of whether this 'music' lived on after him in English poetry.

Deschamps' description of the performance of natural music gives us an idea of the qualities which the poets prized and strove for:

Et ja soit ce que ceste musique naturele se face de volunté amoureuse a la louenge des dames ... et que les faiseurs d'icelle ne saichent pas communement la musique artificiele ne donner chant par art de notes a ce qu'ilz font, toutesvoies est appellee musique ceste science naturele, pour ce que les diz et chançons par eulz faiz ou les livres metrifiez se lisent de bouche, et proferent par voix non chantable, tant que les douces paroles ainsi faictes et recordees par voix plaisent aux escoutans que les oyent, si que au *Puy d'amours* anciennement et encores est accoustemez en pluseurs villes et citez des pais et royaumes du monde.[25]

And although this natural music is made by an amorous disposition for the praise of ladies ... and although the makers of it commonly do not understand artificial music or how to compose musical notation for their verse, still this natural knowledge is called music because they read orally the dits and chansons and verse-books that they have written, presenting them without singing, so that the sweet words which they compose and recite aloud please those who hear them, as has been done of old at the puys d'amours, and still is done in many towns and cities of the countries and kingdoms of the world.

The quality of 'sweetness' or 'pleasingness' particularly characterizes both kinds of music for Deschamps. He speaks of 'la douceur tant du chant comme des paroles qui toutes sont prononcees et pointoyees par douçour de voix et ouverture de bouche' / 'the sweetness of the melody as much as of the words which are all pronounced and accented [separated ?] by the sweetness of the voice and the opening of the mouth.'[26]

Stevens offers his conclusions about Chaucer's adherence to French musique naturele only tentatively. For him the question of stress is central, though it is an aspect that Deschamps – dealing with an unstressed French language – does not consider in his discussion in the *Art de dictier*. On the one hand, Stevens finds that many of Chaucer's effects seem 'sufficiently distant from the suave norm of, say, Machaut to make us doubt whether he had the sort of *armonia* in mind that the French poets looked for.' Chaucer's effects are those of 'emphatic natural speech,' he says, while those of the French are not. In this, he believes, Chaucer breaks away from 'the ideal of *musique naturele.*' On the other hand, Stevens believes it likely that, instead of an iambic model, Chaucer 'took from the main tradition of medieval verse, in Latin, Italian and above all French, its most distinctive feature – its measurement of the line by syllables, counted and variously grouped. Concepts of a metrical foot, of regular binary stress and, I would add, of a tension between rhythm and metre belong to other systems.'[27]

In finding that Chaucer abandons the douceur of Machaut in favour of 'natural speech rhythms,' Stevens nevertheless recognizes that Deschamps' ballade praise of Chaucer's *'douce melodie'* offers a contrary indication. If, as Stevens is inclined to say, the English speech rhythms are incompatible with douceur, then the word applied to Chaucer is inaccurate. But I would offer an obvious alternative explanation, one that would save both Deschamps' 'douce melodie' and Stevens 'English speech rhythms' as accurate descriptions of Chaucer's verse. I suggest that the variations of English speech rhythms from the French intonation, in particular the strong stresses, do not vitiate the douceur that Deschamps has in mind. The single trait Stevens adduces to illustrate Chaucer's deviation from the 'sauve norm' is that of adjacent strong stresses, like 'fréssh fétures' or 'ál béaute'; however, it is mainly in the context of the iambic norm, which Stevens has excluded for Chaucer, that adjacent stresses are unmusical. One might think, then, that the douceur of the *Art de dictier* is minimally affected by stress, that it involves chiefly the features of sound that Deschamps explicitly discusses: the regular number of syllables, the regular size of lines and stanzas, and the nature of the sounds.[28] Adopting a system that takes no account of stress does not obliterate it in the language, of course, but does automatically subordinate it, and it is entirely possible to modify stress in any reading.

With the question of douceur in mind, I would like to look at three partial texts from near the end of the century. The first consists of the two initial stanzas from the eleventh response in the *Cent ballades*, a typical ballade of the 1390s. Monseigneur de La Tremoïlle argues for loyalty and against inconstancy:

De grant honneur amoureux enrichir
Ne peut, s'il n'a Loyauté en s'aÿe,
Et pour ce fay dedens mon cuer florir

Loyal Amour d'umilité garnie,
Dont doucement sans Fausseté servie
Sera la flour non pareille d'onneur,
De grant beauté, de bonté, de valeur,
Qui de mon ceur souveraine maistresse
Est et sera. S'aray dame et seignour:
En ciel un Dieu, en terre une deesse.

En ce me veul tout mon vivant tenir
Sans ressambler la fausse compaignie
De ceulx qui vont prier et requerir
Dames pluseurs, et font par tout amie
A leur pouoir; pour leur grant tricherie
Cil sont vilain, envieux et menteur
Outrecuidex, felon, fol et vanteur;
Tout leur desir a Faux Penser s'adresse.
Tel gent reny; si prens pour le milleur
En ciel un Dieu, en terre une deesse.[29]

The lover cannot grow rich in great honour if he does not have Loyalty to help him, and for this reason I cause to blossom in my heart Loyal Love adorned with Humility, with which I will sweetly serve without Falsity the unmatched flower of honour, of great beauty, of goodness, of worth, who is and will be sovereign mistress of my heart. I will have lady and lord: in Heaven a God, on earth a goddess.

In this I desire to hold fast all my life, without being like the false company of those who pray and petition many ladies, and everywhere have as many lovers as they can. Because of their great trickery they are low, envious, and liars, presumptuous, treacherous, fools, and braggarts; all their desire is directed toward False Thought. I renounce such people, and I take the best way, in heaven a God, on earth a goddess.

The final stanza elaborates the misdeeds of the followers of Faux Semblant, and the envoy returns to a commendation of loyalty.

The late-century characteristics of this ballade – the ten-line stanza form and the envoy – make it unsuited to a musical setting, but it remains a good example of natural music. In the whole poem each line has exactly ten syllables (not counting the feminine endings), and in all except one line (2) the caesura falls obviously after the fourth syllable. The four rhyme sounds alternate masculine and feminine, and their consonants are continuants only, what Deschamps calls semi-vowels. There are a substantial number of run-on lines, but the line ends occur at natural points in the syntax and the rhymes, as usual, well define the line units. The sentences are long and complex. While there are more inversions of natural word order than is common in Machaut's lyrics, on the whole these are not awkward. The diction throughout is entirely what one would expect, with numerous repetitions ('amoureux,' 'Amour'; 'Fausseté,' 'faux'; 'Loyauté,' 'loyal,' etc.). Aside from the developments in the form beyond the limits that musical notation set, one would say that the formal features are entirely consistent with the model for 'natural music' that Machaut offered.

For comparison, we might consider a sample of Chaucer's poetry from about the same time,[30] the 'Envoy de Chaucer' which the Clerk presents after his tale, identifying it as a 'song.' I quote the last three of the six stanzas:

Ye archewyves, stondeth at defense,
Syn ye be strong as is a greet camaille;
Ne suffreth nat that men yow doon offense.
And sklendre wyves, fieble as in bataille,
Beth egre as is a tygre yond in Ynde,
Ay clappeth as a mille, I yow consaille.

Ne dreed hem nat; doth hem no reverence,
For though thyn housbonde armed be in maille,
The arwes of thy crabbed eloquence
Shal perce his brest and eek his aventaille.
In jalousie I rede eek thou hym bynde,
And thou shalt make hym couche as doth a quaille.

If thou be fair, ther folk been in presence
Shewe thou thy visage and thyn apparaille;
If thou be foul, be free of thy dispense,
To gete thee freendes ay do thy travaille;
Be ay of chiere as light as leef on lynde,
And lat hym care, and wepe, and wrynge, and waille.   (E 1195–1212)

As with most of the *Canterbury Tales*, the content of the 'Clerk's Envoy' is quite different from that usual in the French lyrics, and seems far from douceur. Nevertheless, in its versification it has a close relationship to the French, and versification is the basic constituent of natural music.

The decasyllabic *ababcb* stanza form of the piece has no direct counterpart in the formes fixes, but it resembles common ballade and rondeau stanzas, and the carrying through of the same rhymes in the six strophes makes it still closer to the French forms, especially since the dominant rhymes, -*ence* and -*aille*, are characteristically French. With their feminine endings, all of the rhymes are extended, and they combine with the consistent end-stopping to emphasize the line units. A judicious sounding and muting of the final -*e's* in one's reading makes it possible to see every line as having exactly ten syllables. But the caesura is comparatively irregular. As I analyse the passage, only ten of the eighteen lines have caesuras at the standard French position, syllable 4. In six lines the caesura falls right in the middle, at syllable 5.[31] The diction, of course, is not conventional, and there are some consonant combinations in 'sklendre,' 'clappeth,' and 'crabbed' that are rough rather than douce.

In this late piece, in sum, this English verse varies substantially from the standard represented by La Tremoïlle's poem. Chaucer uses all feminine rhymes rather than an alternation of masculine and feminine; he allows more leeway in the placement of the caesura; he has a higher percentage of end-stopped lines; and he generally abandons conventional diction in favour of colourful battle and animal imagery. But in his variations, we might see Chaucer offering a compatible version of the 'natural music' rather than a rejection of the French. He retains 'the most distinctive feature' of the French, 'its measurement of the line by syllables, counted and variously grouped.'[32] Another essential feature of the French metrical effects that Chaucer uses here is the complex stanzaic unit. He most noticeably differs from Machaut in his more distinctly segmented syntax. He sets up a two-part rhythm in the successive lines of each stanza, which he varies or stretches out for firm closure in the last line: 'If thou be fair / ... if thou be foul / ... By ay of chiere / ... And lat lym care, / and wepe, and wrynge, and waille!' The flow is regularly interrupted by the breaks in the syntax and sometimes complicated by the consonant combinations and abutting stresses, but there remains a musical rhythm that justifies the Clerk's calling the envoy a 'song.'

Indeed, if one inspects the examples that Deschamps himself provides in the *Art de dictier* or in the volumes of his short verse, we do not often find the 'sauve norm' of Machaut. A rather different norm seems present, for instance, in one of the best-known and most lyrical of Deschamps' works, a virelay of unusual structure, which the editor entitles 'Portrait

of a maiden by herself.'[33] A conventional head-to-toe physical description structures the first half, quoted here:

Sui je, sui je, sui je belle?

Il me semble, à mon avis,
Que j'ay beau front et doulz vix
Et la bouche vermeillette:
Dittes moy se je suis belle.

J'ay vers yeulx, petis sourcis,
Le chief blont, le nez traitis,
Ront menton, blanche gorgette;
Sui je, sui je, sui je belle?

J'ay dur sain et hault assis,
Lons bras, gresles doys aussis
Et par le faulz sui greslette;
Dittes moy se je suis belle.

J'ay bonnes rains, ce m'est vis,
Bon dos, bon cul de Paris,
Cuisses et gambes bien faictes;
Sui ju, sui je, sui je belle?

J'ay piez rondes et petiz,
Bien chaussans, et biaux habis,
Je sui gaye et joliette;
Dittes moy se je suis belle. (1–21)

Am I, am I, am I pretty? It seems to me, I think, that I have a lovely forehead
and a sweet face and a red mouth; tell me if I am pretty.

I have grey eyes, slender eyebrows, blonde hair, straight nose, rounded chin,
white throat; am I, am I, am I pretty?

I have a firm breast set high, long arms, thin fingers also, and my waist is
slim; tell me if I am pretty.

I have good hips, I think, good back, good 'cul de Paris,' well-made thighs
and legs; am I, am I, am I pretty?

I have rounded, small feet, nice shoes, and beautiful dresses, I am gay and
graceful; tell me if I am pretty.

In the last half of the poem the girl, who is not yet fifteen, tells of her furs and clothes and brooches, and promises to guard the key of her treasure. The one who will capture her love will have to be courteous, well-bred, and brave. If he is these things, she concludes, he will win his contest (with her).

The short phrases and strong, juxtaposed monosyllables ('doulz viz,' 'vers yeulx,' 'chief blont') here make the whole quite different from what we find in Machaut. The lines are almost all end-stopped. Though they have only seven syllables, most have a strong caesura of variable position, alternating between the fourth, the third, and even the second syllable. The sentences, made up of simple phrases and clauses, are quite brief. In these matters the 'music' of the virelay is much more like the 'Clerk's Envoy' than the Machaut standard. Notwithstanding, I believe that one can still see both Chaucer's and Deschamps' poems as possessing what the Frenchman would call 'douceur.' The distinct divisions between the lines and within the lines do not make the Clerk's and the girl's lyrics less song-like. Indeed, the divisions impart a rhythmic verve to both performances that Machaut's smooth syntax cannot achieve. At the same time the regularity of the syllable count, and the organization of the lines in stanzas whose identical structure is emphasized by extended repeated rhymes, make it possible still to speak of 'sweetness' – lightness and ease – in the verse. Certainly one can say that, aside from a few isolated locutions on the 'Clerk's Envoy,' there is little that is harsh and heavy in either performance.[34]

Musique naturele is represented in the variety of styles of diverse Middle French writers. Among the contemporaries of Chaucer, the verse styles of le Mote, Machaut, and Deschamps have notable differences, but their lyrics share the basic features of the mode: a fixed number of syllables to the line with the lines bound together in uniform stanzas by a complex scheme of rhymes, often polysyllabic, and a refrain. Much of Chaucer's stanzaic poetry effectively incorporates and carries over into English the techniques and spirit of this mode, this natural music broadly conceived. All of his verse shows its effects. For the music, Machaut was his main French model, but as in the 'Clerk's Envoy' he also exploited the potential represented in the work of various authors.

It would be rash at this point to claim that Chaucer's verse participates fully in the natural music of the French mode. A consequence of such a claim would be to accept the line and the caesural segment rather than the metrical foot as the basic units of Chaucer's verse. But even if one is not prepared to go that far, it still seems clear that his versification does not accord with Old and Middle English accentual mode, and that the French syllabic model had a crucial effect on it.[35] I believe it is reasonable to maintain, in addition, that whatever conclusion one arrives at on the matter of stress, one can speak of Chaucer's having successfully created a version of the French natural music in English. I therefore want to consider very briefly the extent of the effect of his natural music on subsequent English verse.

In a 1956 essay on the relationship of word and melody – of 'lexis' and 'melos' – in the tradition of English poetry, Northrop Frye made some interesting remarks on the nature and effects of Chaucer's versification. The principle Frye enunciates for musicality in poetry is very different from Deschamps' concept; as a matter of fact, in its assumption of a stress language and variation in the number of syllables, his dictum rules out French poetry. Musicality for Frye entails 'a principle of accentual scansion, a regular recurrence of beats with a variable number of syllables between the beats.'[36] He recognizes that Chaucer did not write this kind of accentual poetry, and therefore by his standards it is unmusical,[37] but he finds that for later writers Chaucer's poetry 'began to sound more like the accentual rum-ram-ruf poets he ridiculed' and thereby became musical. Thus Spenser, in imitating Chaucer, 'begins with accentual experiments but abandons them later for an elaborate unmusical stanza.'[38] Here the opposition of Frye's concept of musical poetry to French 'natural music' is manifest. For it is Spenser's stanza, an expanded version of rime royal with ten-syllable lines and complex rhyme, that imitates the natural music of Chaucer. In using an alexandrine line to close off the stanza, Spenser provides an additional feature that emphasizes the stanzaic unit, as Chaucer, in the 'Clerk's Envoy', stretched out in other ways the last lines of the stanzas ('And lat hym care, and wepe, and wrynge, and waille'). The tradition in which Spenser is working is unbroken from Chaucer's time. Serving to connect the work of the two poets, the Ricardian poet with the Elizabethan, is the tremendous volume of poetry in rime royal and 'Monk's Tale' stanza that was produced through the fifteenth century.

Although I have conducted this discussion as if the technical features of versification are all that enter into the question of natural music, it must be acknowledged that the content of the work surely has a bearing. In his *Art de dictier* Deschamps could leave questions of content to his examples because the poetry of the formes fixes is virtually all lyric in nature. While it is not all love poetry, it is discontinuous, discursive, and reflective rather than narrative. Accordingly, the content and the treatment of content in *Troilus and Criseyde* make it possible to classify large parts as lyric. By contrast, most of the rime royal of the *Canterbury Tales* cannot be so classified. Similarly, John Lydgate's rime royal *Complaint of the Black Knight* in following Chaucer is quite in the French mode, while his *Fall of Princes*, composed in the 'Monk's Tale' stanza and equally Chaucerian, is clearly not natural music. If the influence of natural music lives in English beyond the fifteenth century, it is in the extensive lyric parts of the *Faerie Queene* and in the ensuing tradition of stanzaic poetry that Spenser fathers. Frye finds that such verse is not musical: 'Spenser and Keats belong to the tradition of unmusical opsis [visual poetry] to which Tennyson also belongs.'[39] Frye's generalizations are compelling: 'Opsis' in vivid colour is surely a quality which the work of these English poets possesses, and which the fourteenth century French poets do not strive for. In *Troilus and Criseyde*, likewise, 'melos' is dominant, at least in the lyric parts. One may question whether 'opsis' and 'melos' are mutually exclusive, as Frye seems to assume.

The complications and contradictions to which Frye's generalizations lead us are perhaps not resolvable, certainly not in brief compass. It will be better to conclude this study still in contact with a medieval authority, Eustache Deschamps, however unsteady an authority he may sometimes be. In the course of the *Art de dictier*, a treatise that seems highly quixotic and incompletely conceived, Deschamps nevertheless writes several paragraphs about the distinctive lyric poetry of his time (christening it 'natural music') which crystallize its character. His words provide profound insight into the work. At the beginning of his description of natural music, he makes an enigmatic statement which, though one could easily dismiss it as meaningless formula, has intriguing resonances: 'L'autre musique est appellee *naturele* pour ce qu'elle ne puet estre aprinse a nul, se son propre couraige naturelment ne s'i applique'[40] / 'The other music is called *natural* because it cannot be taught to anyone if his heart does not naturally devote itself to it.' The words recall Dante's explanation to Bonagiunta in *Purgatorio* 24 of the dolce stil nuovo. What differentiates our new poetry from the verse of our predecessors, Dante says, is that we listen to what Love says, and then write. His formulation and that of Deschamps suggest that the poets apply a sensibility to composing their verse that contributes an indispensable and ineffable property. Despite the frustrating vagueness of Dante's formulation, it has never been hard to accept that the ineffable enters into his work. Though it may be somewhat harder for a modern reader to accept, the fourteenth-century French poets share with Dante an authentic and profound sense of the lyrical. The natural music of their work at its best also possesses an element of lyric genius, mysterious in origin and ineffable in effect, and Chaucer's work draws an important part of its own genius from it.

Notes

PREFACE

1 Stevens '"Music" of the Lyric' 121
2 Kittredge 'Chaucer and Froissart' and 'Machaut and the *Duchess*'
3 Poirion *Le Poète et le prince*
4 Kelly *Medieval Imagination*
5 The important proceedings of the symposia have been published as *Machaut's World: Science and Art in the Fourteenth Century* edited by Cosman and Chandler and *Guillaume de Machaut, poète et compositeur*. Major recent books on Machaut and his tradition are Calin *Poet at the Fountain*; Brownlee *Poetic Identity*; Cerquiglini '*Un engin si soutil*'; and Huot *From Song to Book*.
6 Olson 'Late Medieval Court Lyric' 238. Though I disagree with his analysis of Middle French lyric, Olson's essay is based on a thoughtful and informed understanding of the culture.
7 Wood *Chaucer's 'Troilus'*; Wetherbee *Chaucer and the Poets*
8 Chaucer *Riverside Chaucer* 1028a. Quotations of Chaucer's verse herein are from this edition.
9 Boitani *Chaucer and Boccaccio* and 'Style, Iconography and Narrative' 185–99; Havely *Boccaccio*; Schless *Chaucer and Dante*; Windeatt *Troilus and Criseyde*; Wallace *Boccaccio* and 'Continental Inheritance'; and Howard *Chaucer*
10 My previous publications have varying pertinence to this study, which I will specify briefly here. Two have a general relationship to the entire work: *Chaucer and the French Love Poets* and 'Chaucer and French Poetry.' My other publications on the subject have more restricted rele-

vance. For the Machaut lyrics discussed in chapters 1 and 3, I draw on
'Guillaume de Machaut and Chaucer's Love Lyrics.' Particularly important for the background of chapter 2 is *Chaucer and the Poems of 'Ch.'*
Throughout the three chapters on Machaut (3 to 5) *Guillaume de Machaut*
(with William Kibler) supplies major materials. Also relevant to the Machaut chapters, especially chapter 4, is *The Marguerite Poetry of Guillaume
de Machaut*. For the lyric nature of Chaucer's longer poems discussed in
chapters 4 and 5, I draw on three papers: *'Anelida and Arcite,'* 'Machaut
and *Troilus and Criseyde*' and 'The French Lyric Element.' For the chapter on Froissart I have used three pieces: the treatment of several poems
in the Pennsylvania manuscript by William Kibler and myself, 'The Pastourelle in the Fourteenth Century,' *'Dit dou Bleu Chevalier,'* and 'Froissart, Chaucer, and the Pastourelles.'

CHAPTER ONE

1 Among the sometimes conflicting analyses of the *Prologue* are *Oeuvres de
Guillaume de Machaut* (Hoepffner) I, lii–lv; Kelly *Medieval Imagination*,
especially 3–12; Calin *Poet at the Fountain* 234–7; Brownlee *Poetic Identity*
especially 16–19; and Lukitsch 'Poetics of the *Prologue*.'
2 Edited in *Oeuvres* I, 1–12 (quoted herein) and in *Poésies lyriques* (Chichmaref) I, 3–13. The *Prologue* has 298 lines, including the four ballades that
open it. The fiction of the work, in which Nature and Amour appear to
Guillaume and provide him the wherewithal to write poetry, suggests
that it preceded his other work; nevertheless, it was composed late in life
(c 1370) and reflects the knowledge that a career of writing had given him.
3 See, eg, Balade notée XXXII in *Poésies*, in which the complaining lover declares, 'Je ne say mon oeuvre contrefaire' (line 19). Chaucer's Mars follows this reasoning closely in *Complaint of Mars*: 'If a wight shal pleyne
pitously / Ther mot be cause wherfore that men pleyne' (lines 156–7).
We understand that Machaut and Chaucer did not have to be suffering
to compose effective complaints, though suffering was necessary to the
poet-lovers in the fictions. Commenting on the sincerity of the earlier
French poets, Robert Guiette remarks that they write not about 'l'amour
qu'ils vivent "dans les faits" ou qu'ils ont vécu, mais l'amour idéal qu'ils
pourraient vivre et comme ils pourraient le vivre selon les suggestions de
la convention courtoise': *D'une poésie formelle* 43.
4 The opening rubric of the *Prologue* states that the goddess Nature comes
to Guillaume 'volant orendroit plus que onques mais reveler et faire es-
saucier les biens et honneurs qui sont en Amours.'

5 Thus Lukitch 'Poetics' concludes that Machaut, even though Nature makes a threefold gift to him – Rhetorique and Scens, as well as Musique – thought of poetry as a kind of music: 'All Machaut's remarks on the character of his poetry are in fact much more readily understood if we assume that he defines poetry as music' (264).

6 Staiger 'Lyrik und lyrisch' 74

7 Holman and Harmon *Handbook* sv 'lyric'

8 Frye 'Approaching the Lyric' 31–7; pages 31 and 32 are quoted here. Frye also discusses the lyric at length in *Anatomy of Criticism*, especially 246–50 and 270–81. For discontinuity as a characteristic of the long French dit see Huot *From Song to Book* 212–13, with references to Cerquiglini and Zumthor.

9 Jakobson *Language in Literature* 70. For Jakobson, at least in translation, 'emotive' and 'expressive' are synonymous (66). In this study I aim to distinguish between these adjectives.

10 Culler 'Study of Lyric' 39

11 Jakobson *Language in Literature* 70

12 Johnson *Idea of Lyric* 3

13 Machaut *Louange* nos 121, 123

14 Frye 'Approaching the Lyric' 34–5

15 Rajan 'Romanticism' 199, 203

16 Staiger 'Lyrik und Lyrisch' 76

17 Stevens 'Dante and Music' 14

18 W.R. Johnson, for instance, is interested in the ethos of the speaker, in 'praise and blame' and such matters, and very little in the sound.

19 This is Jonathan Culler's characterization of DeMan: 'Study of Lyric' 46

20 Frye 'Approaching the Lyric' 34

21 Jakobson *Language in Literature* 81–8; page 87 is quoted.

22 Ibid 66

23 Eco *Semiotics*

24 Jakobson *Language in Literature* 70

25 Ibid 451–3

26 In his analysis of the trouvère lyric, *D'une poésie formelle*, Robert Guiette makes a suggestive comparison of the medieval Romance lyric text to music, asking for a rediscovery of the 'sens formel' of the lyrics. 'One should read these chansons as one reads musical forms, in following their movements, relationships, and arrangements, but without neglecting the sense value of the theme and the expressive quality of the wordplay and the arrangements. In the chanson one must consider the number or the formula, but perceive at the same time the incantatory

power and the life, without which we would only have school exercises'
(43).

27 'Rhythmic' (ie, accentual) poetry contrasts with 'metrical' (measured)
verse. 'Rithmica species est enim musice': *Parisiana Poetria* 6. Molinet
'L'Art de Rhétorique' in Langlois *Seconde rhétorique* evidently follows
John in stating, 'Rethorique vulgaire est une espece de musique appellée
richmique,' and the anonymous author of 'L'Art de science de rhétorique' (Langlois 265) also says much the same thing.

28 *Leys d'Amours* I, 82. 'E dizem que aquesta sciensa, en quant que toca bel
ornat e bo de parlar, se fonda sobre rethorica.' The *Leys* draws much of
what it says about rhetoric from Brunetto Latini's *Trésor*, which places 'li
enseignemens de diteors' among the attributes of Rhetoric: Brunetto Latini *Livres dou Trésor* 9.

29 In *Convivio* II, xiv, 108, Dante also indirectly identifies rhetoric with poetry by associating rhetoric with the planet Venus.

30 Even the two that refer to rhymed poetry as music call it 'rhétorique vulgaire.' The notion of a 'second rhetoric' was commonplace. Depending
on the classifier's orientation, the first was either prose or Latin, and the
second was either poetry or vernacular. See Langlois *Seconde rhétorique*
i–iv.

31 Though the labels 'natural music' and 'artificial music' are not original
with Deschamps, his distinction between them – spoken text versus sung
text – evidently is new. We might nevertheless infer from the previous
treatises how Deschamps arrived at his individualistic classification. The
distinction between the two musics goes back to the ninth century, but
the older formulations envision natural music as including more than
spoken poetry. For the origins and earlier history of the concept, see
Bower 'Natural and Artificial Music.' In the view of the influential Regino of Prüm (d 915), Bower notes, 'Music exists on two levels: the natural, which embraces the music of the spheres, the harmony of the
human body and soul, and music sung to the praise of God in the eight
tones; and the artificial, music created by man, instrumental music consisting of five tones and two semitones' (22). Cassiodorus, though earlier
than Regino, is somewhat closer to Deschamps. Stevens *Words and Music*
generalizes that Cassiodorus' 'theoretical divisions apply to natural as
opposed to artificial music, music of the human voice not of instruments.
Vocal music is found both in song (sung poetry) and in speech' (378).
See also Bower 23.

32 'Et neantmoins est chascune des ces deux plaisant a ouir par soy; et se
puet l'une chanter par voix et par art, sanz parole; et aussis les diz des

chançons se puent souventefoiz recorder en pluseurs lieux ou ilz sont moult voulentiers ois, et le chant de la musique artificiele n'aroit pas tousjours lieu, comme entre seigneurs et dames estans a leur privé et secretement, ou la musique naturele se puet dire et recorder par un homme seul, de bouche, ou lire aucun livre de ces choses plaisans devant un malade, et autres cas semblables ou le chant musicant n'aroit point lieu pour la haulteur d'icellui': Deschamps *Oeuvres* VII, 272.

33 The *Art de dictier* has been the subject of substantial scholarly attention. See especially Patterson *Poetic Theory* I, 87–95; Dragonetti '"La poésie"' 49–64; Laurie 'Deschamps and the Lyric'; and Varty 'Art de Dictier.' The most recent discussion of Deschamps' concept of natural music is probably the most authoritative and provides precedent and support for important aspects of my argument: Stevens '"Music" of the Lyric.' The significance of the *Art* to Chaucer's concept of literature is treated by Olson 'Art de Dictier.' See also Olson 'Late Medieval Court Lyric,' passim, in which he credits Deschamps with more subtlety than he displays in the *Art de dictier* or elsewhere; eg, at page 235 he deduces from Deschamps' failure to talk about functions of poetry beyond what he describes as 'recreational' that Deschamps consciously excluded other functions. Considering the fragmentary system of the *Art*, Deschamps' failure to discuss a topic is minimally indicative. One might also note that Modern English 'recreation' has rather narrow connotations as compared with the medieval French cognate 'recreez' (from Latin 'recreare'), which Deschamps employs in the *Art de dictier*: *Oeuvres* VII, 269.

34 See Stevens 'Dante and Music' and *Words and Music* 19–22.

35 The change in the mimetic and emotive relationship of music to text between the Middle Ages and the Renaissance is a basic point in two books by Stevens: *Music and Poetry*, especially 33–8, and *Words and Music*, especially 300–2; and throughout his inaugral lecture, *Old Sound and New*.

36 See Stevens '"Music" of the Lyric' 111.

37 *Oeuvres* VII, 269

38 See Stevens *Words and Music* 386.

39 In *Convivio* II, xiv, 110 Dante explicates the restful effects of music by referring to its actions on the 'human spirits': 'Music draws to itself the human spirits which are, as it were, mainly vapours of the heart, so that they almost cease from any action of their own, so undivided is the soul when it listens to Music; and the virtue of all the spirits is, as it were, concentrated in the spirit of sense which receives the sound.'

40 I might cite once more the interesting parallel found in Dante; in *Convi-*

vio II xiv, 110 Dante speaks of the 'sweetness' of music found in both words and song; he says that music 'is wholly dependent on relation, as is seen in words arranged in harmony and in songs; and the harmony resulting from these is the sweeter in proportion to the beauty of the relation, which in that Science is especially beautiful, because this is its principal aim.'

41 Stevens '"Music" of the Lyric' 116 (emphasis in original)

42 Dragonetti *La Technique poétique* 545. Though Dragonetti's study, like Guiette's *D'une poésie formelle*, is based on an analysis of the Old French lyric, both works are relevant to analysis of the Middle French.

43 Machaut *Louange* no 58

44 Deschamps *Oeuvres* VII, 277: "Balade equivoque, retrograde et leonime. Et sont les plus fors balades qui se puissent faire, car il couvient que la derreniere sillabe de chascun ver soit reprinse au commencement de ver ensuient, en autre signification et en autre sens que la fin du ver precedent / 'These are the most powerful [difficult?] ballades which can be made, for it is necessary that the last syllable of each line be repeated at the beginning of the following line, with another meaning and another sense than at the end of the line preceding.' Though the meaning 'difficult' is possible for 'fortes,' I translate it according to the more common sense 'powerful' since Deschamps discusses other lyric forms, such as the lay, that were more difficult to compose. But even if one sees 'fortes' as pertaining primarily to difficulty of composition, the rationale for the effort would be the strength of the achievement.

45 I develop more fully the comparison between the French syllabic and the Middle English alliterative tradition in 'Chaucer and Deschamps' "Natural Music." '

46 Luria and Hoffman *Middle English Lyrics* 32

47 See Osberg 'Alliterative Lyric.'

48 The ballade (or ballada) stanza, to be sure, is tied more to the whole poem than are the stanzas of the chanson (or canzone). Each of the ballade stanzas has the same refrain, and the form has a fixed number of stanzas (three).

49 Dante *Literary Criticism* 51

50 Stevens *Words and Music* 21

51 Dante *Literary Criticism* 51–3

52 Ibid 49

53 Ibid 58

54 For the early development of the ballade and the related formes fixes, see Lawrence Earp's important study, 'Lyrics for Reading.'

55 Machaut *Louange* no 204 (*Poésies* CXCVI)

56 Machaut *Louange* 18

57 I follow Wilkins' introduction to *Louange*: 'The underlying musical pattern of the ballade is I I II ... Normally, the two lines rhyming a b are set to the first music section, this then being repeated with lines three and four, also rhyming a b, since it is a fundamental rule that lines of verse set to identical music must have identical rhyming and metrical structure ... When Machaut composed no music for a poem the underlying structure is, of course, theoretical but nonetheless real' (19).

58 Gieber 'Poetic Elements' 2–6

59 See ibid 6–7.

60 I assume Chaucer's 'revel' in its position at the caesura will count one syllable ('rev'l'), and that necessary elisions will be made ('mery 'nd'). One also has to assume two silent terminal *e*'s for words in the succeeding stanzas of Chaucer's poem.

61 Caesuras occur after syllables other than the fourth in *To Rosemounde* at lines 1–5, 7, 20–2; and in *Tout ensement* at lines 11 and 15.

62 Rhyme is not a major subject of discussion in Machaut's *Prologue*, though his use of rhyme there well illustrates its great importance. He does cite different types, 'serpentine,' 'equivoque,' 'leonine,' 'croisie,' 'retrograde,' 'sonant,' and 'consonant' (v 151–6). Machaut does not explain his terms, and neither Deschamps nor other writers offer consistent explanations. In general 'sonant,' 'consonant,' and 'leonine' refer to varying extensions of the rhyme ending, with 'sonant' signifying rhyme of the stressed terminal vowel only (also called 'pauvre') or of vowel and consonant (examples from 'Plourez, dames': 'pour my' and 'paly,' 'comm*ant*' and 'reman*ant*'); 'consonant,' 'riche,' and 'leonine' designate rhymes that go beyond simple vowel-consonants to full consonant-vowel-consonant syllables, or vowel-consonant-feminine ending ('*vers*,' '*divers*'; ent*ente*, 'augm*ente*'). There was no fixed label for further extensions of the rhyme ('*ce parti*,' '*departi*'). 'Riche' and 'leonine' have taken on more specific meaning in modern usage. As already discussed, for the Middle French writers 'equivoque' denotes rhyme of the same word with some change in sense ('vostre *servant*'; 'en *servant*'). 'Serpentine' perhaps signifies whole-line rhyme, very rare. Even more than with the retrograde-and-équivoque type, whole-line rhyme is more an ideal in the mind of the theoretician of natural music than a usual possibility. For definitions of the various terms, with references to the several treatises he edits, see Langlois *Receuil* 'Table des noms propres et des termes techniques' 427–73.

63 '... to me it ys a great penaunce, / Syth *rym in English hath such skarsete*,' etc. *Complaint of Venus* lines 79–80

64 The alternation was recommended in the treatises: see note 5 above.

65 J.B. Bessinger's reading of *To Rosemounde*, on the recording *The Poetry of Geoffrey Chaucer* (Caedmon TC 1226, 1967), illustrates well how the sounds of the refrain emphasize and fit in with the light spirit of the lyric.

66 Stevens 'Dante and Music' 14 (emphasis in original)

67 A good example of mimetic effects in the phonetics is found in the words of the duck and the goose in the *Parliament of Fowls*; see especially lines 498–504 and 561–7.

68 Machaut *Louange* no 276 (*Poésies* Chanson baladée XXI)

69 See Kittredge 'Antigone's Song of Love' and Wimsatt 'Machaut and *Troilus and Criseyde*' 287–9.

70 The only complaint for which Machaut provides music is that in *Remede de Fortune* lines 1193–1400. Neither he nor others followed up this musical composition.

71 In line length Chaucer's stanzas are somewhat different from Machaut's. Every fourth line in Machaut's stanza has four syllables, while the other lines uniformly have either eight or ten. The lines in Anelida's complaint more or less reverse this scheme, with his fourth lines having ten syllables and the others eight.

72 He wrote no five-stanza chansons unless, of course, they are lost or unidentified, as with the four French 'Chançons Royaux' by 'Ch' in the Pennsylvania manuscript. See Wimsatt *Poems of 'Ch'* 1–35.

73 See Deschamps *Oeuvres*, VII, 280.

74 In the *Art de dictier* Deschamps presents eight ballades, a chanson royal, three virelays, seven rondeaux, and several sections of a lay.

75 Chaucer's single ballades are *To Rosemounde*, *Truth*, *Gentilesse*, *Lak of Stedfastnesse*, *Complaint of His Purse*, *Against Women Unconstant*, and *Legend of Good Women* F 249–69 (G 203–23). His triple ballades *Fortune* and *Complaint of Venus*, as well as his triple roundeau *Merciles Beaute*, were perhaps designed for musical settings. On the polytextual technique of presenting double or triple ballades musically, see Wilkins, *One Hundred Ballades* 125; for its origins in motet practice, see Wilkins *Age of Chaucer* 10–16.

76 The near-ballades include the five 'terns' of the *Complaint of Mars* lines 164–298; the nine-stanza 'Bill of Complaint' in *Complaint unto Pity* lines 57–119, divided every third stanza by a couplet rhyming on -*eyne* lines 76–7, 97–8, 118–19); the *Envoy to Scogan* (six stanzas), the *Envoy to Bukton*, *Womanly Noblesse*, and *A Ballade of Complaint* (ascribed).

77 A single rondeau in the *Parliament of Fowls* (680–92), and a triple ron-

deau in *Merciles Beaute* (the attribution to Chaucer is safe, I believe).

78 Among studies of Chaucer's versification, only Maynard *Connection* registers a conviction that Chaucer developed the rime royal stanza from the French ballade; see especially 83–92. Maynard's study needs to be fortified by supporting data such as Wilkins and Poirion emply in their studies, and its description of the ballade is in part outdated. Baum *Chaucer's Verse* exemplifies the still current uncertainty of scholars in stating that 'no positive statement may be made' about whether Chaucer adopted rime royal from the ballade or developed it from an eight-line stanza form (48). Stevens 'Royal Stanza' is similarly unsure about the debt of Chaucer's stanzas to the French (70a). Maynard shows that the designations 'ballade and rhyme royal came to be practically synonymous,' no doubt witnessing early recognition of the French origin of Chaucer's stanzas (88). See also Stevens 'Royal Stanza' 62–6 on the name 'rime royal.'

79 *Oeuvres* II, xxxiv–liv

80 *Remede de Fortune* is quoted herein from *Guillaume de Machaut: Le Jugement du roy de Behaigne and Remede de Fortune* (Wimsatt and Kibler).

81 See Wimsatt *Marguerite Poetry* 40–59.

82 See Wimsatt and Kibler 33–5.

83 Wimsatt and Kibler 172–5.

84 I have discussed at length the connection of *Troilus* with Middle French lyric in 'The French Lyric Element.' There are specifc filiations between *Troilus* and *Remede de Fortune*. See Kittredge 'Chaucer's *Troilus*' and Wimsatt 'Machaut and *Troilus*.'

85 Robbins 'The Lyrics' thus characterizes *Troilus* (382). Comparably, in 'The Vintner's Son' he refers to *Troilus* as 'an intricate and closely worked *dit amoureux*' (161).

86 For Chaucer's knowledge of 'Plourez, dames' see Wimsatt 'Machaut and Chaucer's Love Lyrics' 74. In the refrain line of one of his two ballades on Machaut's death, Deschamps appropriately echoes 'Plourez, dames': 'Vestez vous noir, plourez tous, Champenois / La mort Machaut, le noble rhetorique': *Oeuvres* I, 244 (no 123, lines 23–4). See also Deschamps' ballade on the death of du Guesclin: II, 27–8 (no 206, lines 9–10).

87 *Louange* no 162; also *Poésies* CCXXIX, and (with its music by Leo Schrade) *Works* III, 120

88 In forms like the lay, virelay, and rondeau, in which the lines are often shorter, the refrains more extended and the rhyme endings fewer, the sound pattern is usually more obtrusive even than in the ballade.

89 For the preference for alternation of masculine and feminine rhymes, see

Deschamps' *Art de dictier* in *Oeuvres complètes* VII, 276; and the treatise of the Anonyme Lorrain in Langlois *Seconde rhétorique* 202. The principle was often ignored.

90 In Stanza 2 the first sentence carries over to the middle of line 6. While such a break in the middle of the line is unusual, the length of the sentence is not. Indeed, many ballade stanzas, especially in the rime royal form, consist of a single sentence.

91 The analysis of Chaucer's rime royal stanza in Cowling 'Note,' expressed in terms of 'pauses' and 'half-pauses,' is based on a study of all of Chaucer's stanzaic work. His conclusions suggest that the syntax of the four stanzas is typical of Chaucer's stanzas. Normally, says Cowling, the Chaucerian rime royal 'is terminated by a full pause after the seventh line,' and 'there is usually one half-pause within the stanza, dividing it most often into a quatrain followed by a tercet' (312). Also relevant to this syntactic analysis is the comparison of Chaucer's *Troilus* stanza with Boccaccio's practice in the *Filostrato* in Wallace *Chaucer and Boccaccio* chapter 6.

CHAPTER TWO

1 The term 'Machaut tradition' is employed most notably in Poirion's important *Le Poète et le prince* (1965), Poirion being the first modern scholar to treat the mode comprehensively and without condescension.

2 Though the productions of the literary societies of the towns, the predominantly bourgeois puys, have close relationships to those of the courts, particularly in lyric type, the bodies of work in many ways are independent.

3 All three types existed in the thirteenth century, but they became far better defined in the Middle French period. For the development of the formes fixes see Earp 'Lyrics for Reading.'

4 I develop this point in 'Chaucer and Deschamps' Natural Music.' For the origins of the Harley lyrics in alliterating prose, see Osberg 'Alliterative Technique.'

5 For the surviving music for English lyrics before 1400, see Dobson and Harrison *Medieval English Songs*.

6 See the *New Grove Dictionary* sv 'Adam de la Halle.' Adam spent at least some time in the service of Robert II of Artois, the first cousin of Philippe III. Robert of Artois, incidentally, built up the castle and park at Hesdin, which became a favorite stopping-place for the French kings, and was the site that Machaut chose for his long *Remede de Fortune*.

Robert's daughter, the Countess Mahaut, was also known for her encouragement of art.

7 Vitry and Jehannot Lescurel (d 1304) were especially important for the development of polyphonic music for the dance forms (ballade, rondeau, virelay); most of the surviving examples of their poetry with music are intercalated in a manuscript version of the *Roman de Fauvel*, MS Bibliothèque Nationale fonds français 146, made for the royal court – perhaps for Philippe V – in the second decade of the fourteenth century, which has interspersed in it 169 pieces of poetry with music, including a substantial number of formes fixes specimens.

8 In his *Temple d'Onnour* (lines 295–7) Froissart brags that he has met ten kings, in addition to an Emperor at Rome.

9 See Vale *Edward III*, especially 57–75.

10 Ibid 17–19; and Loomis 'Edward I'

11 Adam of Murimuth is quoted in St John Hope *Windsor Castle* I 112, 128.

12 Thomas of Walsingham, quoted ibid 128. Stowe *Annales*, quoted ibid, states that the circumference was to be 'six hundred foote and three quarters,' which agrees approximately with Walsingham's figure.

13 McKisack *Fourteenth Century* 251–3

14 See St John Hope *Windsor Castle* I, 128.

15 Scholars of the lyric commonly acknowledge, and emphasize, that Machaut was not the sole originator of the mode; but since the survival of the other early poets' verse is fragmentary, Machaut gets the lion's share of attention. And from the beginning the role of the various writers in the development has been unclear; thus, in Langlois *Seconde rhétorique* the anonymous writer says that Vitry 'trouva la maniere des motès, et des balades, et des lais, et des simples rondeaux,' but proceeds to give similar credit to Machaut, who, he says, 'commencha toutes tailles nouvelles, et les parfais lays d'amours' (12).

16 In 1332 Bonne of Luxembourg, daughter of Machaut's longtime employer and patron, King Jean of Bohemia, married Jean le Bon when he was Duke of Normandy. She obviously was instrumental in introducing and promoting the poet and his work at the royal courts. But Machaut's clear ascendancy in the wider world of French lyric poetry came only with time and the passing from the scene of Philippe de Vitry and Jean de le Mote.

17 See Thomas 'Jean de le Mote' 70.

18 For Froissart's romantic report of the courtship and marriage of Edward and Phillipe, see Coulton *Chaucer and His England* 178–81.

19 See Vale *Edward III*, especially 42–56.

20 Contemporary views of the character of Edward II are quoted and discussed in McKisack *Fourteenth Century* 1–2, 95–6. The poem attributed to Edward is edited and discussed in Studer 'Anglo-Norman Poem.' In a similarly doubtful attribution Kervyn de Lettenhove *Oeuvres de Froissart: Chroniques* I, part 1, 78–80, assigns to Edward III a poem of instruction in French octosyllabic couplets ostensibly addressed to the Black Prince (ed 541–3)

21 See McKisack *Fourteenth Century* 102, n2; Vale *Edward III* 49–50, 52.

22 See McKisack *Fourteenth Century* 97; Giffin 'Cadwalader' 116–17.

23 See Vale *Edward III* 43–5. As Vale says, 'It would ... be erroneous to conceive of Hainault as in any way parochial' (43).

24 Ouy 'French Humanism' 4

25 Denholm Young 'Richard de Bury' 160; Bury *Philobiblon*

26 Henry of Lancaster *Li Livre de seyntz medecines*

27 *Calendar of Patent Rolls* 189. See Kervyn de Lettenhove *Oeuvres de Froissart: Chroniques* I, part 1, 76n.

28 Le Mote *Regret Guillaume*. For the circumstances of composition, see lines 4554–81. Vale *Edward III* remarks that 'it is particularly interesting that ... le Mote should have chosen to address his lament ... to Philippa rather than another of his daughters' (45). It is at least another indication of le Mote's association with England.

29 See Kervyn de Lettenhove *Oeuvres de Froissart: Chroniques* and *Calendar of Patent Rolls* 203.

30 See Wilkins 'Music and Poetry' 192.

31 The motet in Pognon 'Du nouveau sur Philippe de Vitri' 49–52 is an attack on an unnamed writer in England, strictly in line with Philippe's identified ballade attack on le Mote discussed below in this chapter. Philippe is identified in rubric as the Bishop of Meaux, a position he held from 1351 till his death in 1361, so one is inclined to attribute the poem to those years.

32 Gilles le Muisis *Poésies* I, 88–9

33 Condé *Dits et contes* 'Dit des Jacobins et des Fremeneurs' lines 247–57

34 In Langlois *Seconde rhétorique* the anonymous author speaks of the illiteracy of Jean le Court, dit Brisebarre: '... et n'estoit point clers, ne ne savoit lire n'escripre' (13). Brisebarre's illiteracy, to be sure, did not deter le Mote from associating himself with his work by composing a continuation of *Restor du paon*.

35 Le Mote *Voie d'enfer*

36 Deguilleville's *ABC* is part of his *Pèlèrinage de la vie humaine*, composed in 1330. The story of le Mote's *Voie* is a dream vision in which the narra-

tor visits hell, then heaven. On his way to hell, led by Murder and Despair, he spends a night with each of the seven capital sins. When his
devotion to Mary at length merits him grace to reascend, he is escorted
to heaven by Confession and Satisfaction and given lodging on the way
by the seven virtues. Despite the obvious parallels to Dante's *Commedia*,
le Mote's mechanical handling of his narrative virtually guarantees that
he did not know the Italian work.

37 See Wimsatt, 'French Lyric Element.'

38 *Fauvel* was composed about 1310; in one great manuscript of 1316, there
are interspersed 169 lyrics with music at appropriate places in the story;
e.g., a lyric text on greed is presented in a place where papal avarice is
being denounced.

39 The distinctions I make between the types of long poem with intercalated lyric differ somewhat from the distinctions made by Huot *From
Song to Book* chapters 4 and 6. She approaches the problem from a different standpoint.

40 Jean le Court, dit Brisebarre *Le Restor du paon*

41 Longuyon *Les Voeux du paon* in *Buik of Alexander* II–IV. The *Buik of Alexander* translates Jacques' romance into Scots.

42 In the *Voeux* Longuyon transformed the narrative tradition of Alexander,
which had been more epic than romance, into something altogether
lighter and more courtly. The comment of the editor (*Buik of Alexander* I,
xxxvii) concerning the presentation of the main battle is indicative: 'The
siege of Epheson has many a pleasing interlude ... it savors more of
tournament than of war, and gives a picturesque setting for scenes of social life ... and for the love story of three damsels.' It may well be that
such works had an effect on the domestic and court scenes in *Sir Gawain
and the Green Knight*, *Troilus and Criseyde*, and the *Knight's Tale*.

43 For the part of Bishop Thiébaut in the composition of *Les Voeux du paon*,
see *Buik of Alexander* I, xxxviii–xl, and *Voeux* lines 8769–84.

44 At an assembly in 1306 Edward I presumably vowed before two swans
covered with a gold net that he would march to Scotland and punish the
Bruce; see *Buik of Alexander* I, xxxix. This story is possibly authentic and
could have provided the original inspiration for the 'vowing' motif,
though the conception seems quite literary. A more improbable tale
about Edward III is narrated as history in the 440 alexandrine lines of the
Voeux du Heron (c 1340). In this poem Edward, having been presented
with a heron, symbolizing cowardice, vows to renounce the allegiance
he has sworn (for Gascony) to Philipe VI and to invade France. See
Whiting 'Vows'; Coville 'Poèmes historiques'; and Loomis 'Edward I'

124-7. Another offspring of the *Voeux du paon*, the prose *Perceforest* (before 1340), perhaps inspired a different mingling of romance and history; a special order of knighthood instituted in this romance presumably gave Edward the idea for the founding of the Garter. See *Buik of Alexander* I, xlvii. The first part of *Le Roman de Perceforest* has been edited by Jane H.M. Taylor; the second part by Gilles Roussineau; and the lyrics of the poem by Jeanne Lods. Complete publication details are given in the bibliography.

45 The most famous literary uses of the Nine Worthies, at least in English, occur in the *Parliament of the Thre Ages* and the *Alliterative Morte Arthur*. For medieval English texts 'illustrative of the Nine Worthies, 'see *Parlement of the Thre Ages* appendix.

46 Le Mote could have been inspired to continue the Alexander story either by a personal connection with Brisebarre, who was from Douai, very near Valenciennes (the seat of Hainault), or by way of his association with the English court, in which the vowing stories flourished.

47 The 'chambre amoureuse' and the games of the *Parfait* have precedents in the Chamber of Venus and the play at 'Roy qui ne ment' in Longuyon's *Voeux du paon*, lines 1539-1882.

48 Suggestive for the procedures of the puy, which are nowhere else in literature so imaginatively dramatized, are the three stages in the contest, involving the presentation of the poem, a private meeting of the judges, and the awarding of a prize; also suggestive are the ladies' insistence that the poems must be original contributions, the provision of a golden throne for the reciters, the crownings, and the jury selected from the audience. This interlude is further analyzed in chapter 9 in a discussion of the puy.

49 See le Mote *Voie d'enfer* 9-11.

50 Though in a substantial proportion of Middle French lyrics, as here, a lady is the first-person speaker (the lyric 'je'), before Christine de Pisan (late fourteenth century) none of the formes fixes that are extant are known to have been composed by women. Notwithstanding, in all periods there were doubtless lyric poems by women. The ballades of *Parfait* are further discussed below. For more about the contest itself, see Freidrich Gennrich, 'Der Gesangswettstreit' and Kelly *Medieval Imagination* 255-6.

51 Along with numerous other romances with digressive lyrics, Froissart's Arthurian romance *Meliador* is a monumental narrative of a knight's exploits in which the intercalated pieces, composed by Wenceslas of Brabant, have mainly a decorative function.

52 The earlier *Panthère d'Amours* by Nicole de Margival and *Prise amoureuse* by Jehan Acart have in common with the *Regret* a strong lyric element partly manifested in numerous interpolations of formes fixes lyrics; nevertheless, their narratives are complex and significant in their own right. In the *Regret*, by contrast, the story serves mainly as an introduction and excuse for the lyric parts.

53 Though not as carefully worked out as Machaut's, the analysis is still of the same order. The poet asks first for Sens, Souvenir, and Mesure (Sense, Memory, and Moderation, 27–31), later for Parolle (Words), Avis (Reason), Memoire (Memory, Knowledge), and Sens again (84). As in Machaut's *Prologue*, Nature is seen as a major divine force, representing both the creative and the ordering power, to whose activity the poet's is analogous:

Ensi croi jou en mon voloir,
Que Nature vorra voloir
Que l'uevre soit bien ordenée
Et gente, non desordenée ...
Nature ne soufferoit mie,
Qui si bien fu au prince amie,
Que ses fais ne fust bien parfais.
Par sens, par raison et par fais,
Huimès mousterai le mistere
Et le valour de la matere
U j'ai m'imagination
Si bien qu'en figuration
Le voi, ce m'est vis, toute escripte,
Si bien m'en est l'uevre descripte.   (75–96)

Thus I believe in my heart that Nature will want the work well-ordered and noble, not formless ... As the beloved of this prince [William], Nature will wish his deeds to be fully displayed. According to sense, reason, and fact, I will show now the hidden power and worth in the matter to which I have so applied my imagination that I see it all written in figure, the subject being very well described to me.

The poem which he characterizes here is not narrative in kind, presenting a story from which a significance arises; instead it offers an 'imaging' of its subject, which is the procedure of the lyric. For a suggestive discussion of imagination in Middle French poetry, see Kelly *Medieval Imagination* especially 26–57. Kelly's exposition of the rhetorical device of frequentatio (42–4) is particularly apt to the *Regret*, in which the multiple virtues and exempla overlap in providing a full and various imaging of

William. A poet's use of frequentatio, as Kelly states, duplicates the manner of Nature's fecund creation: 'Just as the manifold abundance of creation could bring the beholder back to God through greater and greater abstraction, the multiplication of the manifestations of an abstract idea serve to reveal more and more of the significance of the abstraction' (42)

54 The relationship of the cycle of lyrics in the later parts of Nicole de Margival's *Panthère d'Amours* (2190–2665) to the cycle of *Remede de Fortune* suggests that Machaut also learned important lessons from Nicole, particularly about inserting lyrics in a skeletal love narrative.

55 In places I have drawn on Douglas Kelly's suggestions in *Medieval Imagination* 255–6 to translate the faults and felicities Aristé identifies.

56 One might guess that in the *Parfait* le Mote made use of ballades he had already composed and wrote new ones for the *Regret*.

57 For an analysis of the lyrics in the *Prise*, see Acart de Hesdin *Prise amoureuse* xxxix–lxii.

58 Ernest Hoepffner analyses the metrics of these ballades in detail and compares them to the lyrics of *Prise* in 'Die Balladen'; see especially 155–60.

59 'Enchaînement logique' is Poirion's description in *Le Poète et le prince* 374. He states further of the ballade, 'Les proportions triangulaires de la ballade sont en profonde harmonie avec les habitudes de la pensée médiévale. Les trois strophes identiques nous rappellent l'équilibre momentané du virelai vers le milieu du xive siècle. Mais la strophe de la ballade, plus remassée, plus simple, plus logique va assurer avec un minimum de travail dans les rimes et les rhythmes l'organisation que le virelai, aux trop grandes ambitions artistiques, n'a pas pu mener à bien. La nécessité de répartir les mots et les rimes en trois séries identiques, les images en trois volets symétriques, les idées en trois étapes logiques a fait de ce genre lyrique un moyen d'expression efficace, un langage poétique presque universel.'

60 See the table of Poirion *Le Poète et le prince* 374–5; and Hoepffner 'Die Balladen' 155–6.

61 Poirion *Le Poète et le prince* 385–6

62 Machaut *Louange* no 1 (*Poésies* CCLIV)

63 As we will discuss below, Machaut also imitated the exempla of the *Regret* in *Jugement dou roy de Navarre* (1349). For various aspects of Machaut's debt to le Mote, see Hoepffner 'Die Balladen' 163–6.

64 In his octosyllabic and decasyllabic ballades Machaut often used a short fifth line.

65 Even though no extant five-stanza works have been identified as le Mote's, we may recall that in the frame story of his *Regret* the poet is on his way to a meeting of a puy, and that the concours in his *Parfait* undoubtedly reflects such meetings. From these depictions we can confidently infer that he both composed and heard many five-stanza works, and that it would have been natural for him to adapt their fuller stanza to the ballade.

66 Bibliothèque Nationale manuscript fonds latin 3343 is a fifteenth-century collection composed of Latin prose pieces and some verse, most from the fourteenth and fifteenth centuries, several from the mid-fourteenth. The six ballades are found on folios 109r–111v, le Mote et al. 'Ballades mythologiques.'

67 Philippe de Vitry (1291–1361), secretary to Philippe VI and Bishop of Meaux (1351–61), was a friend of Petrarch. Despite his contemporary fame as musician and poet, few of his works survive except for the motets in the *Fauvel* manuscript discussed above. For his friendship with Petrarch, see Coville 'Philippe de Vitry.' Up-to-date information on Vitry, with full bibliography, may be found in the *New Grove's Dictionary* sv 'Vitry, Philippe de' (by Ernest Sanders).

68 This passage forms by far the earliest allusion to the *Commedia* in French poetry that has been identified. On Vitry's use of Dante and the question of similar use by le Mote in his response, see Wimsatt *Poems of 'Ch'* 56.

69 Vitry's ballade and the response are quoted here from the edition made from both manuscript texts in *Wimsatt Poems of 'Ch'* 52–5. Compare also Diekstra 'Poetic Exchange,' which proposes some good alternative readings and translations.

70 Very little of Vitry's extant poetry could be called love poetry, though he must have written some; he assumes an authoritative pose in scoring le Mote for his awkward love verse. None of Machaut's or Froissart's poems, ballades or otherwise, involve personal attack; Deschamps, however, used both ballade and chant for the purpose.

71 See note 31 above. The motet was probably composed later. In it, though Philippe criticizes Jean for misuse of the French tongue, he drops the charge of treason, perhaps accepting Jean's statement in his ballade that he is not French.

72 For what is known of Jean Campion see le Mote et al. 'Ballades mythologiques' 403–5; and Gilles li Muisis *Poésies* I, xxxi–xxxii; II, 259–79.

73 For the Campion–le Mote exchange, text and commentary, see Wimsatt *Poems of 'Ch'* 75–7.

74 The classical poets referred to are Homer (Maeonia), Virgil (Mantua), Ovid (Peligni), Catullus (Verona), and Horace (Flaccus).

75 Though the music does not survive, Gilles li Muisis states that le Mote composed both words and music (quoted above). Most of the thirty complainers in the *Regret* say explicitly that they will sing their ballades: 'S'en doi canter de cuer mari / Ceste tristre ballade chi' (Humelité lines 730–1), 'Em plourant me couvient canter' (Largesse 919), 'Dolentement en canterai / Une balade' (Hardiesse 1148–9) etc. Lawrence Earp has called to my attention the fact that Machaut set to music his ballade 'On ne porroit penser,' whose text imitates a ballade of le Mote. This is probably as close as one can get to le Mote's music. See Hoepffner 'Die Balladen' 63, and Gunther 'Zitate' 53–4.

76 It has been thought generally that Deschamps invented this theme around 1400. The most recent discussion of the Neuf Preuses, accepting Deschamps as the originator of the motif, is McMillan 'Men's Weapons.'

77 University of Pennslyvania Manuscript French 15, folio 23r. For analysis and enumeration of the contents of this manuscript see Wimsatt *Poems of 'Ch'*. The text used here is based on the manuscript. If written by le Mote the poem probably dates from before 1360. It is also edited by Charles Mudge in 'Pennsylvania Chansonnier' 79. Even aside from the form and the use of literary allusion there are reasons to ascribe the poem to le Mote. The theme of the Nine Worthies (Neuf Preux) is inaugurated by Jacques de Longuyon in the *Voeux du paon*, of which le Mote's *Parfait du paon* is a continuation. Furthermore, in the Pennsylvania manuscript the poem on the Neuf Preuses immediately precedes the ballade exchange between le Mote and Vitry. At the same time the work is unlike le Mote's other ballades in having a substantial number of eleven-syllable lines, including the refrain.

78 As with the longer stanzas, the envoy was imported from the five-stanza forms. Envoys appear increasingly in ballades of the last quarter of the fourteenth century.

79 The nine-line stanzas that Chaucer employs in the *Complaint of Mars* and *Anelida and Arcite* open with an *aabaab* rhyme pattern characteristic of the virelay and other forms, in contrast to the standard *abab* opening of the ballades. For an exceptional ballade stanza consisting of ten decasyllabic lines and an *aabaab* opening, see Wilkins *Armes* no. 35 (178–82).

80 See Wimsatt *Poems of 'Ch'* 1–43.

81 Machaut's first long poem, the *Dit dou Vergier*, makes no literary allusions. His next two, probably written in the 1330s, have a few, but nothing that is developed: *Jugement du roy de Behaigne* lines 421–2 (Octavian

and Galen), 1297 (Alexander and Hector); *Remede de Fortune* 109–25 (Solomon, Alexander, Hector, Godfrey of Boulogne, Absalom, Job, Judith, Socrates, Esther, Abraham), and 2317–20 (Arithmetic, Pythagoras, Music, Michalus, Milesius, Orpheus). The effect of the Nine Worthies theme is obviously important; it originates, as stated, in Longuyon's *Voeux du paon* lines 7484–7579.

82 Most of the exempla in the *Regret* are familiar: five are from the Bible, including stories of Solomon, David, Abraham, Moses, and Nebuchadnezzar; eight are classical, including Dido, Pygmalion, Paris, Alexander (twice), Jason, Caesar, and Tideus; six concern medieval epic and romance figures, including the Châtelaine de Vergy, Tristan, Arthur, Godfrey of Boulogne, Clarvus (from the Alexander romances), and Charlemagne. The origins of the remaining nine, discussed below, are not easily identified.

83 For consideration and affirmation of the relationship between the exempla of *Regret Guillaume* and Machaut's *Navarre*, see Hoepffner 'Die Balladen' 165–6.

84 Jason and the Golden Fleece, the Châtelaine de Vergy, and Dido and Aeneas appear in both the *Regret* and *Navarre*.

85 In applying her exemplum Hardemens says that just as with Tarse at Flore's death, life for her with Guillaume dead is no longer worth living; see *Regret* 995–1122. Other comparable apparent fabrications are the stories of Lurfagnons 1225–1323; Maillogres and Eglente 2112–94; Sassydoine 2314–86; Grandones 3400–56; and Malagus 3498–3531.

86 Since there is only one ballade by Vitry extant, we know little of his practice outside the motets where he makes heavy use of literary and historical reference.

87 The ballades are quoted, with some modifications of punctuation, from le Mote et al. 'Ballades mythologiques' 407–8. Some of the difficulties in sense no doubt result from defects in the ms text.

88 One might imagine that the image of Dyane and Jespé helping Clopheus to 'sacrifice his masses' involves a facetious use of a liturgical image comparable to that in the Middle English lyric in which Jankin is said to 'go Kyrie, Kyrie' with Alison (Eleison).

89 Le Mote et al. 'Ballades mythologiques' 394–5 discusses le Mote's alterations of these legends.

90 The motet is found in the same manuscript as the ballades (Bibliothèque Nationale fonds Latin 3343), though in a different part.

91 Of the three figures mentioned in the last line, Floron as well as Cerberus evidently had some status as an underworld figure. In Machaut's

Dit de la Harpe Floron is named at line 59 as one of the four kings of the Inferno, along with Pluto, Lucifer, and Cerberus. I know of no reference to 'Trible,' however.

CHAPTER THREE

1 Useful biographical reviews of Machaut's life may be found in the editions *Oeuvres* I (Hoepffner) xi–xliii and *Poésies lyriques* I (Chichmaref) vii–lxxi; and in Machabey *Guillaume de Machaut* I, 13–83. An up-to-date biography that deals even-handedly with the literary and musical production is a major desideratum, which Lawrence Earp's *Machaut Handbook* (Garland, forthcoming) will largely satisfy.

2 The *Complaint to His Purse* and 'A Toi, Hanri,' moreover, make an interesting trio with Froissart's *Dit dou Florin*, as is discussed in chapter 6.

3 Machaut *Poésies* 'Complainte III.' Though in the past there has been disagreement about the dating of this poem, the siege of 1359 no doubt is its occasion. Hoepffner *Oeuvres* I, xxxiii, supplements my analysis.

4 For the 'Evil Tax' ('maletoste') in mid-fourteenth-century France, see John Bell Henneman *Royal Taxation in Fourteenth-Century France: The Development of War Financing 1322–56* (Princeton: Princeton University Press 1971) 4.

5 Several sources have been suggested for Chaucer's *Complaint to His Purse*. Its envoy was probably composed later than the body of the poem. For the latter see Cook 'Complaint.' Cook rejects Skeat's candidates (lyrics of Machaut and Deschamps) and brings forward a chanson of the Châtelaine de Coucy. The tenuous parallels he adduces, added to Chaucer's failure to use this author's work elsewhere, make Cook's suggestion unlikely. Machaut's 'Complainte III,' as the work of a poet whose works Chaucer echoes again and again, is much more probably one of Chaucer's originals. One of Skeat's suggestions was Machaut's 'Complainte VII' (Poésies I, 261–3), which presents only a vague parallel. Skeat's reference very probably confuses 'Complainte VII' with 'Complainte III'; the works appear close together in the slim selection of Machaut's poetry that he refers to – *Les Oeuvres de Guillaume de Machaut* (Tarbé) 78–9, 89–90. In any event, of the three correspondences with 'Complainte III' that I adduce, the second and third are not matched in other suggested originals, nor in any other relevant poems I know of.

6 For Deschamps' claim, 'Il m'a nourri,' see his ballade no 447 in *Oeuvres complètes* III. For the statement in the rhetoric see Langlois *Seconde rhétorique* 14. It is not known if Deschamps and Machaut were actually re-

lated by blood. For Deschamps' description of the siege of Reims see his *Miroir de mariage* lines 11660–98 in *Oeuvres complètes* IX.

7 The Duke of Berry met his father at Boulogne on 25 October 1360; he sailed with Edward from Calais on 30 October; see Lehoux *Jean de France* I, 160–3. Chaucer carried the letter from Calais sometime between 13 October and 31 October; see Crow and Olson *Chaucer Life-Records* 19–21.

8 The poem is edited in *Oeuvres* III; Hoepffner discusses the anagram ibid xxvi–xxviii.

9 For more extensive analyses of the contents of the *Fonteinne amoureuse*, see Wimsatt *French Love Poets* 112–17; and Calin *Poet at the Fountain* 146–66.

10 *Louange* no 276 (*Poésies* Chanson Baladée no 21)

11 *Complaint unto Pity* presents Chaucer's most developed personification allegory. Though clever, the allegory is not flawlessly handled, particularly in that the distinction between Pity and the lady is not always clear in the extended 'Bill of Complaint.'

12 Machaut *Louange* no 89 (*Poésies* no 56)

13 Cruelty is not a common personification in French love poetry; it probably should not be associated with Danger, as proposed by Clemen *Chaucer's Early Poetry* 181, since Cruelty is more intractable and actively malicious than Danger. For discussion of Machaut's ballades as models for *Complaint unto Pity*, see Wimsatt 'Machaut and Chaucer's Love Lyrics' 79–81.

14 Among Machaut's works in which the lover desires to please his lady by suffering and dying are 'De desconfort, de martyre amoureus' in *Poésies* Balade notée 8 (also in *Works of Machaut* lines 15–21; 'Aus amans pour exemplaire' *Poésies* Balade notée no 43 (*Works of Machaut* III, 132–3; and Wilkins *One Hundred Ballades* 22–3) lines 18–20; and 'En desespoir, dame, de vous me part' in *Louange* no 70 (*Poésies* no 249) lines 14–16. The same masochistic desire provides the most striking theme in Chaucer's *Complaynt d'Amours*, as expressed in lines like the following:

I ne oughte to despyse my ladyes game;
It is hir pley to laughen whan men syketh,
And I assente, al that hir list and lyketh. (61–3)

See also lines 18–20 and 48–9.

15 Machaut *Louange* no 1 (*Poésies* no 254). For Chaucer's use see Wimsatt 'Machaut and Chaucer's Love Lyrics' 68–70.

16 This is the only one of Machaut's eight chants royaux to have a refrain, the usage having become common in the form only with Deschamps'

work. As Deschamps adapted the envoy to the ballade, so he adapted the refrain to the chant. The fact that the poem does not appear in the Machaut manuscripts earlier than manuscript A confirms its lateness. Machaut's other seven chants are contained in C, the earliest collection, indicating that he had virtually abandoned the form by the first years of the 1350s, coming back to it only the one time. These manuscripts are discussed below in this chapter.

17 *Louange* no 130 (*Poésies* no 219)
18 *Louange* no 114 (*Poésies* no 223)
19 *Louange* no 119 (*Poésies* no 25)
20 *Louange* no 168 (*Poésies* no 252)
21 It is not found in manuscript C, the earliest version of Machaut's 'collected works,' executed in the early 1350s.
22 For the relationship of *Scogan* to 'Puisqu'Amours faut,' see Wimsatt 'Machaut and Chaucer's Love Lyrics' 82–3.
23 That the duke is the borrower seems virtually certain; see Wimsatt 'Machaut and Chaucer's Love Lyrics' 83 and note.
24 The duke spent a total of about four years in England from late 1360 to early 1366. See Lehoux *Jean de France* I, 159–95.
25 Bibliothèque Nationale fonds français 9221; manuscript E. It is a very large late fourteenth-century codex marked by the duke's librarian and with the duke's own signature at the end.
26 For a brief summary of Pierre's efforts in the crusade, which culminated in the capture of Alexandria, with an extended discussion of Machaut's relationship with Pierre, see Wimsatt *Marguerite Poetry* 40–54.
27 Froissart *Le Joli buisson de jonece* 348–50
28 There were numerous other writers of Marguerite poems in France, the most prominent being Froissart and Deschamps. In England the poems were influential on Thomas Usk's *Testament of Love* and the Middle English *Pearl*. A standard treatment of the relationship of Chaucer's 'Prologue' to the *Legend of Good Women* to the French poems is Lowes 'Prologue to the *Legend*.' But Lowes wrote in ignorance of Machaut's seminal *Dit de la fleur de lis et de la Marguerite*, and saw Deschamps as having important influence on Chaucer and other Marguerite poets, which is doubtful. For further discussion see the chapter on Deschamps below.
29 Machaut *Poésies* I, 256–61
30 Armitage-Smith *John of Gaunt* 29. For fuller discussion of the identity of Marguerite, see Wimsatt *Marguerite Poetry* 51–9.
31 Machaut *Oeuvres* (Tarbé) 65–7; and Froissart *'Dits' et 'Débats'* 147–53. The

Dit de la Marguerite appears first in the late manuscript A, confirming that it is later than 'Complainte VI,' which appears in the earlier Vg and B as well as A. The manuscripts are discussed more fully below.

32 This is Ernest Petit's evaluation of the evidence in *Ducs de Bourgogne* I, 10–11. Froissart *Oeuvres de Froissart: Chroniques* says that Marguerite 'estoit bien dame,' whom the duke her husband would not willingly anger, especially since she brought him a great heritage and 'beaulx enffans' (XIV, 351).

33 Edited in Wimsatt *Marguerite Poetry* 15–26

34 For the occasion of *Lis et Marguerite* see Wimsatt *Marguerite Poetry* 54–7.

35 I assume that Chaucer's Marguerite poem and the other French Marguerite celebrations, following Machaut's lead in his three poems, were occasional pieces. Chaucer's reference to Queen Anne in the 'Prologue' to the *Legend* F 496–7, among other matters invites the assumption.

36 See *Louange* nos 62 and 63 (*Poésies* nos 271 and 253); cf also complaintes V, VII, VIII in *Poésies*.

37 Watriquet de Couvin and Jean de Condé, mentioned earlier, are good examples of court poets who primarily wrote moral verse, including a good deal of caustic social criticism. Both came from Hainault in the early fourteenth century.

38 *Louange* no 96 (*Poésies* no 188); music for poem in *Louange* 139–41, and *Works* III, 98–100. For an analysis of the ballade and Chaucer's use of it throughout his career see Wimsatt 'Machaut's "Il m'est avis." '

39 Bibliothèque Nationale fonds français 22545–6 is a full collection of Machaut's poetry containing several lyrics not in other manuscripts of his work. These are probably among Machaut's last works.

40 For Chaucer's use of traditional colour symbolism, see *Against Women Unconstant* refrain; *Anelida and Arcite* lines 145–6, 180, 213, 330; 'Squire's Tale' F 644–6.

41 *Louange* no 176 (*Poésies* no 272)

42 The interest in *Voir-Dit* has most recently taken the form of the book-length study by Cerquiglini *'Un engin si soutil.'*

43 Two indications of Chaucer's possible knowledge of *Voir-Dit* are pointed out in Wimsatt *French Love Poets* 82–5. The poem is edited by Paris *Le Livre du Voir-Dit*. As has been repeatedly noted, the Paris edition is quite inadequate, particularly in its excising of about five hundred lines of *Voir-Dit* that are clearly authentic.

44 Two who have written about Machaut's conception of his status as poet are Williams 'Machaut's Self-Awareness' and 'Author's Role,' and Brownlee 'Poetic *Oeuvre*' and *Poetic Identity*.

45 Some see it as an actual 'True Story,' others as a fiction. The opposing positions were argued at the conference in Reims in 1977. See, in *Guillaume de Machaut: poète et compositeur*, Musso 'Comparison statistique' (statistical evidence indicates to Musso that there were two writers; by implication a woman wrote the young lady's lyrics) and Calin 'Le *moi*' ('J'estime, moi, que dans sa totalité le *Voir Dit* est une oeuvre d'imagination pure' 249); and in the 'Débats' 215–22, 263–9 passim. See also Williams 'The Lady' for her evidence that an actual affair is involved. For broader discussions of the poem see Calin *Poet at the Fountain* 167–202 and Brownlee *Poetic Identity* 94–156. In the edition *Le Livre du Voir-dit* Paulin Paris claims to identify the lady definitively with a historical Peronelle d'Armentières. See Paris 'Notice' especially xxii–xxiii. However, as Jacqueline Cerquiglini shows, *Un engin* 223–43, Paris' working out of Machaut's anagram is far from definitive, and probably mistaken.

46 See Williams 'Author's Role,' and especially Earp 'Machaut's Role.'

47 One should be slow to ascribe to Machaut line-for-line proofreading of his manuscripts, however, or revision of the works. Full readings taken from all the manuscripts of the *Jugement du roy de Behaigne* show the text clearly deteriorating from the earliest manuscript collection to the later ones. See *Le Jugement du roy de Behaigne and Remede de Fortune of Guillaume de Machaut* 11–16. See also Wimsatt and Kibler 'Machaut's Text.'

48 A thorough and detailed account of most aspects of the Machaut manuscripts is contained in Earp 'Scribal Practice.' Even more thorough will be the section on the manuscripts in Earp's forthcoming *Guillaume de Machaut: A Guide to Research* (Garland).

49 The four manuscripts with their standard sigla (those of *Oeuvres* I, xliv–xlv, which differ from those of *Poésies* I, xxiii–xxiv), are Bibliothèque Nationale, fonds français 1584, 1585, and 1586, which are respectively A, B, and C; and New York, Wildenstein and Co., Vg.

50 Especially important has been François Avril's fixing of the date of manuscript C as between 1350–1356; see 'Manuscripts enluminés' 117–21. All poems in C, then, must have been composed before 1356. Vg and B, virtually identical, represent the next stage in the Machaut collections; they are dated about 1370. Manuscript A was made in 1371. F-G, made after Machaut's death, represents the last stage in the collections. Avril's whole essay deals valuably with the dating and style of the Machaut manuscripts from an art historical viewpoint. Other useful studies of the manuscripts in the same collection are Keitel 'Tradition manuscrite' and

Günther 'Contribution de la musicologie.' See also the 'Débat' among the participants 135–42.

51 Twenty-two of the poems set to music appear also in the *Louange des dames*. See the table in *Louange* 26–43.

CHAPTER FOUR

1 Motet XVIII 'Bone pastor Guillaume' in *Poésies*. The work evidently celebrates the enthronement of Archbishop Guillaume III of Trie in June 1324. See Machabey *Guillaume de Machault* 1, 22. For dating of Machaut's musical works see Reaney 'Chronology.'

2 From the *Book of the Duchess* alone we can see the broad range of Chaucer's reading in Machaut; see the chart of sources in Wimsatt *French Love Poets* 155–62. There are only faint indications that Chaucer knew firsthand Machaut's two late long works that are appended to the collections: the *Voir-Dit* and the chronicle of Pierre of Cyprus, the *Prise d'Alexandrie*. At the same time, he obviously was familiar with other very late works like the *Dit de la Marguerite* and the *Dit de la fleur de lis et de la Marguerite*; see Wimsatt *Marguerite Poetry* 30–9.

3 *An ABC* is related to the shorter formes fixes by way of the stanza it uses. Instead of Deguilleville's twelve-line tail rhyme verse form, Chaucer employs the eight-line 'Monk's Tale' stanza, a ballade unit.

4 The modern titles of all these 'complaints' are chosen by the editors. The various manuscript titles of each regularly include 'complaint,' but designations like 'ballade' are also found. For the title of *Anelida and Arcite* see *Riverside Chaucer* 1144b (textual notes).

5 The lines of complaintes II–V are decasyllabic in couplets; of VII, VIII, and X octosyllabic in couplets; and of IX twelve-syllable in couplets. There are also two complaints in couplets in the *Voir-Dit*, 56–7 (decasyllabic), 184–5 (octosyllabic).

6 'Complaint I' and 'Complainte VI'; *Remede de Fortune* lines 905–1480; *Dit de la fonteinne amoureuse* lines 235–1034; *Voir-Dit* pages 242–8. The stanza frequently appears in sixteen-line units, *aaabaaabbbbabbba*.

7 *Anelida and Arcite* lines 256–71, 317–32; the lines are octosyllabic except for the fourth lines, which are decasyllabic.

8 *Poésies* 'Complainte I'

9 That the use of unrepeated rhyme sounds is one of the effects that Machaut seeks in his complaints is made explicit when the lover in the *Dit*

de la fonteinne Amoureurse completes his eight-hundred-line complaint and notes with satisfaction that not one rhyme sound in the hundred that he uses is repeated (1019–22).

10 I am assuming that the four parts belong together. Though some scholars consider them unrelated fragments, they have sufficient thematic unity to satisfy one's expectations for a lover's complaint. See the headnote in *Riverside Chaucer* 1078.

11 *Lay de Confort* lay XVII *Poésies*

12 Cf Machaut's lines 164–6 with '... my owne thoght / Seyde hit were beter serve hir for noght / Than with another to be wel' (*Book of the Duchess* 843–5).

13 *La Prison amoureuse* lines 2199–2203

14 The second stanza (50–7) is defective, but it surely was intended to conform to the others.

15 *Womanly Noblesse, Complaint of Mars,* and *Anelida and Arcite* use stanzas with similar *aabaab* openings, a rhyme pattern that (as remarked in chapter 1) is typical of the virelay and lay rather than of the ballade and chant.

16 Poirion *Le Poète et le prince* 374

17 In the fifteenth century the rondeau became the great favourite.

18 Poirion *Le Poète et le prince* 404

19 Primarily 'Helas! je suis de si male heure nez' *Louange* no 89 (*Poésies* LVI)

20 The *abab* sections of rime royal become *aabaab*. Machaut uses this rhyme scheme but once in a ballade, and as with the lays and virelays that use the *aabaab* opening (and in contrast to Chaucer's stanzas) that ballade also has short lines of varying length. See *Louange* no 213 (*Poésies* XCII).

21 The Valentine poems will be discussed at more length in the chapter on Granson.

22 Clemen *Chaucer's Early Poetry* 191–2

23 *Poésies* rondel XV (page 575); and *Works* edited with music by Schrade. See the commentary of Machabey *Guillaume de Machault* I, 165–7.

24 *Dit de la harpe* 1–20

25 See Hoepffner 'Anagramme.'

26 *Louange* no 8 (*Poéseis* CCXII) lines 15–17

27 Poirion 'Le monde imaginaire' 227

28 Clemen *Chaucer's Early Poetry* 195–6

29 Two manuscripts indeed give 'The Broche of Thebes' as a title for the whole poem. See *Riverside Chaucer* 1187a.

30 I discount the theory that the last stanza of *Anelida and Arcite* (351–7),

which tells what happens subsequently, is apocryphal: see *Riverside Chaucer* 991–2. It seems Chaucerian in all respects to me.

31 Wimsatt *'Anelida and Arcite'*

32 The *Parliament of Fowls*, regularly placed just after *Anelida and Arcite* in the editions, with its 699 lines comes within a line of the length I propose for *Anelida and Arcite*.

33 For the tradition of complaint and comfort poems, see Wimsatt *French Love Poets* 103–33 and 'Machaut's *Lay de Confort*.'

34 The story of the false judge Apius is found in Livy's *History* III; *Roman de la Rose* lines 5559–5628; and Chaucer's 'Physician's Tale.' Ovid tells the story of the impious Lycaon in *Metamorphoses* I, 198–243.

35 Edited by Wimsatt as 'The Castoff Lady' in *Poems of 'Ch'* 20–1

36 There is, as a matter of fact, another poem in the Pennsylvania manuscript quite similar to 'Fauls Apyus' which has the refrain line 'Vielle me lais qui jeune m'as hussee'; edited by Wimsatt as 'The Castoff Lady II' in *Poems of 'Ch'* 44–5.

37 *Poésies* lays XIX and XX. See *Riverside Chaucer* 991a.

38 The hard heart of the chant and Anelida's image of the sword are closely associated by the mediating image in Chaucer's *Complaint to His Lady*: 'Your swete herte of stele / Is whetted now agaynes me to kene' (56–7). For fuller discussion see Wimsatt 'Machaut and Chaucer's Love Lyrics' 68–9.

39 Skeat glosses lines 304–5, '"Your demeanor may be said to flower, but it bears no seed." There is much promise, but no performance.'

40 Quoted by Clemen *Chaucer's Early Poetry* 198 n3

41 For discussion of the manuscripts and imitations, see the introduction to 'Le Jugement du roy de Behaigne' (Wimsatt and Kibler). For the detail of Chaucer's extensive line-for-line borrowing from *Behaigne*, see the explanatory notes of the edition, and also the chart of borrowings in Wimsatt *French Love Poets* 155–62.

42 For a summary and discussion of the *Altercatio Phyllidis et Florae* and other love debates, see Neilson *Court of Love*. The standard treatment of the medieval Latin debate poems is Walther *Streitgedicht*.

43 Most notably Froissart, Chistine de Pisan, and Alain Chartier wrote works in the *Behaigne* versification.

44 In his inserting lyrics in *Remede*, as Ernest Hoepffner points out in 'Dit de la Panthère,' Machaut was especially following Nicole's *Panthère*.

45 See the chart of developed lyric passages in *Remede de Fortune* in Wimsatt 'French Lyric Element' 32.

46 The content of the *Lay de Confort* and its position in the manuscripts –
which have a generally chronological ordering – indicate its occasion. It does not
appear in the early manuscript C (before 1356), but it does in the subsequent Vg
and B, being placed just before the lay composed for the *Voir-Dit* (1363–5). The
lady-narrator's speaking of her lover's 'dous nom / Qui tout veint de bon renom' (257–8), which should make it possible for him to live 'en ta prison /
Joieusement' (262–3), strongly suggests that the narrator represents Jeanne
d'Armagnac, the new wife of the Duke of Berry, addressing him in England.
Lay de Confort, then, is closely related to *Fonteinne amoureuse*, where the lover
and lady undoubtedly represent the duke and Jeanne at the time of his departure for England. See Wimsatt '*Lay de Confort* and *Book of the Duchess.*'

47 While it is commonly argued that the Black Knight attains some kind of
consolation, there is nothing explicit in the text to show this, and a comparison of him with the bereaved lady in Machaut's *Jugement du roy de
Behaigne* offers no support. The lady at the end accepts the king's kind-
ness and hospitality, but maintains a pose of inconsolability.

48 Froissart '*Dits' et 'débats'.* The *Temple d'Onnour* was originally proposed
as *the* source by Brusendorff *Chaucer Tradition* 158–65, and has recently
been pronounced the main model by Howard *Chaucer* 233–44. Nevertheless, the case for major influence is very weak; see the note below.

49 See Wimsatt *French Love Poets* 60–1; and Baugh 'Chaucer and the *Panthère d'Amours*' 50–61.

50 The main specific similarity between *Temple d'Onnour* and the *House of
Fame* that Brusendorff *Chaucer Tradition* points out (at 158) is the interest
in 'news' that both narrators manifest. Much is made of the search for
'tidings' in the *House of Fame*. In *Temple* lines 1–10 the narrator states
that there is never a day that one does not hear of 'aucune nouvelle.'
This is the last mention of 'news' of any kind; no particular point is
made of it or special attention drawn to it. Moreover, this occurrence of
'nouvelles' is hardly unique in the poetry of the time; for instance, in his
parody of the Cour amoureuse' (1400), said to be of Charles VI, Deschamps repeatedly mentions 'choses nouvelles,' specifically referring to
literary subject matter (*Oeuvres* VII, 347–60, no 1404, lines 8, 67, 85, 142,
191, etc.). Brusendorff (at 159) speaks further of the great 'similarity in
plan and construction' of *House of Fame* and *Temple d'Onnour*, but they
have only the most general resemblance. In any event *Temple d'Onnour*
may well postdate Chaucer's poem; see Wimsatt '*Dit dou Bleu Chevalier*'
394–5. Fourrier's long argument for an early date for *Temple d'Onnour* in
his edition of the '*Dits' et 'débats*' 22–37 involves substantial improbabili-
ties. He is intent on proving that the early position of *Temple d'Onnour*

in the manuscripts is consistent with a chronological ordering of Frois-sart's works in the manuscripts; for reasons presented fully in my article, the case for such ordering seems to me a lost cause.

51 Kibler and Wimsatt 'Development of the Pastourelle' 66–9

52 See Wimsatt *Poems of 'Ch'* 47–68.

53 The serventois and a number of poems in its section of the Pennsylvania manuscript indicate that the lyric poetry being written in fourteenth-century France was more diverse than we have known. Though Chaucer mainly followed Machaut, he must have been impressed and influenced at times by poets now obscure and forgotten.

54 The incident of the golden eagle probably originates in a medieval fabrication about Theseus. It is not found in the usual classical sources, but in the *Lay de franchise*, Deschamps *Oeuvres* II, no 307, line 219 speaks of 'Theseus qu'en l'aigle d'or entra,' thereby confirming a tradition involving 'the eagle of Theseus.'

55 Deschamps *Oeuvres* VII, 281 notes that the serventois form 'porte au *Puis d'amours*,' and that noblemen don't usually compose them. The special forms that individual puys adopted, specified by Langlois in *Seconde rhétorique* vi, all are five-stanza forms.

56 The puy is the subject of more extensive discussion in chapter 9.

57 *Princeton Encyclopedia* sv 'Ottava Rima' briefly discusses the form. The entry concludes that ottava rima seems 'most suited to work of a varied nature, blending serious, comic, and satiric attitudes and mingling narrative and discursive modes.' The description emphasizes the 'precarious crescendo of the third repetition of the rhyme.' The third repetition, of course, is aborted in rime royal. In W.B. Yeats's famous lyrics in ottava rima (*Sailing to Byzantium, Among School Children*, etc.), the usual effect of the stanza is affected by consistent use of slant rhyme, which mutes the 'precarious crescendo.'

58 For the analogues see, eg, Wimsatt *French Love Poets*, 53–7. The same general tradition is represented in the *Owl and the Nightingale* and other English works. For discussion of Granson's poem, see chapter 8.

59 It seems certain that Chaucer has some acquaintance with *Dit de l'alerion* (*Oeuvres* III), though he makes little specific use of it.

60 *Louange* no 56 (*Poésies* CCLXVII).

61 The thirteen-line rondeau was a particular favourite of Deschamps. For the statistics on the rondeau forms chosen by the various poets, see Poirion *Le Poète et le prince* 325, 333.

62 The rubric for the rondeau, 'Qui bien aime tard oublie,' appears in several manuscripts of the *Parliament*, probably indicating a tune to which it

might be sung. Of course in the Chaucer manuscripts there are numerous titles, subtitles, and rubrics in French, especially for the lyrics. One particularly full set of Romance rubrics is provided for the triple ballade *Fortune*.

CHAPTER FIVE

1 Burrow *Ricardian Poetry* 53. Burrow cites especially the classic article of C.S. Lewis 'What Chaucer Really Did to *Il Filostrato*,' in which Chaucer's increased attention to the Troy legend is a major subject.

2 For illustration of Chaucer's addition of circumstantial detail, see Wimsatt 'Medieval and Modern' 212–13.

3 Burrow *Ricardian Poetry* 53 (emphasis added)

4 Robbins 'Vintner's Son' 161

5 See the tables showing the developed lyric passages in *Troilus and Criseyde, Il Filostrato,* and *Remede de Fortune* in Wimsatt 'French Lyric Element' 31–2.

6 Poirion *Le Poète et le prince* 374. See 366–9, 374–7 for his further discussion.

7 'Se pour ce muir' is part of the *Louange des dames,* is among the lyrics intercalated in the *Voir-Dit,* and appears with its musical setting in Machaut's 'Balades notées.'

8 *Louange* no 193 (*Poésies* CCXLVII).

9 Though the three manuscript copies of *Against Women Unconstant* do not ascribe the poem to Chaucer, in two of the manuscripts they are associated with authentic works of his. In general, one seems well justified in seeing the poem as Chaucer's.

10 The renunciation of love allies the content of *Against Women Unconstant* more to 'Puis qu'Amours faut et Loyauté chancelle,' discussed in chapter 3.

11 The repetitive nature of the last lines of the second and third stanzas, moreover, suggest a ballade refrain.

12 *Lay* X (*Lay des dames*) *Poésies* lines 141–52. See Wimsatt 'Machaut and *Troilus and Criseyde*' 286–7.

13 I 297–8. The image that presents Troilus as making a mirror of his mind 'in which he saugh al holly *hire figure*' (I 366) also echoes *Behaigne* 411–12. Troilus' 'fixe' impression draws in addition on *Behaigne* 418: 'Dedens mon cuer se *ficha* si Plaisance.'

14 Patch 'Predestination' 405. Kirby, *Chaucer's Troilus* refines while approving Patch's statement (at 261).

15 Hoepffner (*Oeuvres de Machaut* II, xx–xxxii) analyses Machaut's use of Boethius in the *Remede*.

16 In *Lay VIII* the poet-narrator does specify that the lady's 'mercy' is nothing other than what the lover most desires, 'and if he has his desire without contradiction, then he has mercy' (*Poésies* 33–6). He elaborates that the lover doesn't have mercy unless he has sufficiency: 'I will call *souffissance* mercy / And mercy likewise *souffisance*' (41–2).

17 *Louange* no 24 (*Poésies* no 228)

18 *Lay IX* and *Lay XI* in *Poésies*. For details of Chaucer's use of these lays and ballades of Machaut for Antigone's song, see Wimsatt 'Machaut and *Troilus and Criseyde*' 287–91.

19 The name of the lady of the *Jugement dou roy de Navarre*, Bonneurté, is particularly suggestive of Bonne. See Poirion *Le Poète et le prince* 194. If she does represent Bonne, there is a certain amount of irony in her opposing the decree of her deceased father, the king of Bohemia. Of course it is possible that the offence that the ladies take in both Machaut's and Chaucer's poems is simply a literary fabrication. But probabilities are that some court ladies voiced sufficient objection, whether in earnest or in play, to give the poets occasions for their palinodes. The later related quarrel over the *Roman de la Rose*, in which Christine de Pisan was much involved, was in earnest. See Baird and Kane *La Querelle de la Rose*.

20 For the relationship between the *Regret* and the *Jugement Navarre*, and Machaut's other echoes of le Mote's work, see Hoepffner 'Die Balladen' 162–6.

21 Obvious examples are his use of Guido della Colonne's *Historia* and Benoît de Sainte Maure's *Roman de Troie*, as well as *Il Filostrato*, for *Troilus and Criseyde*; and Statius' *Thebaid* as well as the *Teseida* for the 'Knight's Tale.'

22 Machaut's complaints II–V in *Poésies*; *Panthère* lines 825–966. For Machaut's 'Complaint III' and Chaucer's use of it, see chapter 3. He also found decasyllabic lines in isolated couplets and triplets in the ballades and rondeaux, and in the triplets of Machaut's *Jugement du roy du Behaigne*. Even if Froissart's *Orloge amoureus*, a long dit in decasyllabic couplets, was composed early, there are no indications that Chaucer knew it. In his edition of *L'Orloge* (at 13–18) Dembowski proposes a date of 1368 for the poem. This is based on two assumptions: first, that manuscript B of Froissart's works places the works in chronological order (but see Wimsatt 'Dit dou Bleu Chevalier,' which poses several unanswered objections to this hypothesis); second, that it is inspired by the clock that

Charles v was having built in Paris, completed in 1370. Any discrepancy
between Charles's clock and Froissart's poetic clock would be explained
by the unfinished state of the former in 1368. The reasoning is circular,
of course.

23 For the parallel see Estrich 'Prologue to the *Legend.'*

24 Lowes 'Prologue to the *Legend'*

25 See Lossing 'Prologue to the *Legend*,' which shows that none of the correspondences between the *Lay de Franchise* and the 'Prologue' demonstrate that Chaucer used Deschamps' poem.

26 For an edition of *Lis et Marguerite* and a discussion of its influence, see
Wimsatt *Marguerite Poetry* 1–39. Machaut's *Dit de la Marguerite* and
Froissart's *Dittié de la flour de la Marguerite* are edited by Anthime Four-
rier in Froissart *'Dits' et 'débats'* 275–84, 147–53.

27 It is notable also that *Lis et Marguerite* is the only one of the French
poems that associates the Marguerite flower with a pearl (261–6) as
Chaucer does in attiring Alceste. Machaut's digression on the pearl also
serves to connect French Marguerite poetry somewhat more closely to
two other English works, Thomas Usk's *Testament of Love* and *Pearl*, in
both of which the gem is central and identified as a 'margery or 'mar-
geurite,' though the flower is not mentioned.

28 Machaut's *Dit* has sixteen-line stanzas rhyming *aaabaaabbbbabbba*; the
lines are decasyllabic, except for every fourth line, which is tetrasyllabic.
The stanzas of Froissart's *Dittié* rhyme *aaaabaaaab*; the lines have ten
syllables except for the *b* lines, which have four syllables.

29 See the discussion in the next chapter.

30 Both of these set pieces remind us of Chaucer's lengthy lyric to the Virgin, *An ABC*, which also uses one of the common formes fixes stanzas; in
that work, as already noted, Deguilleville's octosyllabic *aabaabbbabba* is
converted to the 'Monk's Tale' rhyme, decasyllabic *ababbcbc*, a common
ballade form.

31 In considering a piece like the 'Clerk's Envoy,' we may well recall the
distinction between lyric and lyrical discussed in chapter 1. Like a substantial number of formes fixes works, the envoy is not especially 'lyrical' in subject-matter, though otherwise its norms are those of Middle
French lyric poems.

32 See Wimsatt 'Machaut's "Il m'est avis" ' 124.

CHAPTER SIX

1 See Shears *Froissart* 19.

2 Dembowski *Froissart and Méliador* 28 expresses the common opinion that Froissart was a snob.

3 'Et se m'a Nature introduit / Que d'amer par amours tout chiaus / Qui aimment et chien et oisiaus': *L'Espinette amoureuse* 32–4.

4 *Joli buisson de jonece* 230–390

5 See Kibler 'Poet and Patron' 32–3; Barber 'Black Prince' 25–7.

6 *Oeuvres de Froissart: Chroniques* I, part 2, 10

7 See the prologue to book IV ibid 322; and Barber 'Black Prince' 26–7.

8 *La Prison amoureuse* 384–7

9 Ibid 398–420. In Machaut's *Remede de Fortune*, his Amant comes upon a similar carole, where 'dames, chevaliers et pucelles' were dancing happily, 'nil n'avoient la instrument' (3364–8). When Amant's turn to perform comes, he sings an original virelay a capella (3450–96).

10 The first three of his benefactors that he mentions in the *Joli buisson de jonece* (230–58) had faded from the scene. Queen Philippa and Blanche of Lancaster were dead, and Isabelle of England had married Enguerrand de Coucy (though she was in England often thereafter). Furthermore, Lionel had died and Gui of Blois had returned to France from England, while Alice Perrers had become a presence, which couldn't have pleased Froissart.

11 Froissart *Le Paradis d'Amour*

12 In the past some scholars have thought that Chaucer imitated Froissart; Normand Cartier made the most elaborate argument for this line of influence in 'Le Bleu Chevalier.' However, a great deal of evidence, both internal and external, shows that in this case Froissart follows Chaucer. See Wimsatt 'Dit dou Bleu Chevalier.'

13 See Shears *Froissart* 32.

14 In *Le Joli buisson de jonece*, Froissart memorializes Blanche, Philippa's 'fille de Lancastre' in these terms:

Haro! mettés moi un emplastre
Sur le coer. Car quant m'en souvient,
Certes souspirer me couvient,
Tant sui plains de merancolie.
Elle morut jone et jolie,
Environ de .XXII. ans,
Gaie, lie, frisce, esbatans,
Douce, simple, d'umble samblance,
La tres bonne dame eut nom Blance. (242–50)

It is curious that Froissart says she was twenty-two whereas she was a mother of six of twenty-nine years. In the *Book of the Duchess* Chaucer comparably ascribes an age of twenty-four to the Black Knight, surrogate for the twenty-nine-year-old John of Gaunt.

15 Froissart 'Lay de la Mort la Royne d'Engleterre' *Lyric Poems* 106–12

16 For the details of the historical situation represented in *Fonteinne amoureuse*, see Machaut *Oeuvres* III, xxvii–xxviii.

17 Shears *Froissart* notes the comparable use of 'avolés' by the two poets (at 13). Barber 'Black Prince' properly cautions that 'the autobiographical substance of [Froissart's] poems is thoroughly interwoven with poetic invention, and the historian can only admit that we know nothing definite of Froissart's youth and early manhood' (at 25). At the same time there are demonstrable congruencies between the fictions and Froissart's life, which indicate that the poems have value as biographical indicators.

18 The chance is not as remote as it might seem at first, since the three were all love poets writing in the restricted milieu of the French-speaking courts. With the poets' common interests and associations, their meeting in Calais certainly would seem more likely than a meeting of Chaucer with Petrarch and Boccaccio in Florence.

19 *Oeuvres de Froissart: Chroniques* XV, 140

20 Shears *Froissart* 18. Barber 'Black Prince' 25 notes that Froissart did not necessarily mean that he was in the service of King Jean and the others when he said that 'de ma jeunesse je fui .v. ans en l'ostel du roy d'Angleterre et de la royne, et si fu bien de l'ostel du roy Jehan de France et du roy Charle son filz.'

21 The relationship between the two poems is discussed more fully in Wimsatt *French Love Poets* 120–6.

22 There is also an interesting parallel between Froissart's *Joli buisson de jonece* 786–92 and the opening lines of Chaucer's *Legend* 1–6; see *Riverside Chaucer* 1061b. However, the correspondence involves a formula which the poets could have picked up independently, and the content and contexts of the passages are quite different. Chaucer elsewhere manifests no knowledge of the *Joli buisson*.

23 Even in Chichmaref's modern edition the ballade appears as Machaut's. Machaut clarifies this in *Voir-Dit*, where he presents Paien's ballade, 'Ne quier veoir' and his own 'Quant Theseus' following it, stating that Paien composed the first poem and he the second in imitation, 'par tel rime et par tel metre come il rime' (6743–4). See also the narrator's letter, page 266. The ballades are edited by Paris in *Voir-Dit*, 6753–6800, and by Chichmaref in *Poésies* as Machaut's balades notées XXXVIII and XXXIX. I follow the latter edition in quoting the poems herein.

24 'Ballade VI' *Lyric Poems* 209–10

25 This generalization does not hold for Machaut's long poems, in which lists and anaphora are not infrequent.

26 See the discussions of the correspondences in Smith 'Five Notes' 29–31 and the note to *LGW* 249–69 in the *Riverside Chaucer* 1063a.

27 'Balade I' Froissart *Lyric Poems* 205. Since Froissart's manuscripts generally observe chronological order within categories, the first ballade was probably the first the poet wrote. But chronological ordering is by no means an invariable rule; see the discussion in Wimsatt *'Dit dou Bleu Chevalier'* 393–6.

28 With Chaucer also there is a distinction between his practice in the long and the short poems. In his long poems, as with Machaut's, lists and anaphora are common; eg, the catalogues of trees in the 'Knight's Tale' lines 2921–3, part of a droll anaphoric barrage, 2920–63; or the non-humorous catalogue of trees in the *Parliament of Fowls* 176–82.

29 In contrast to the verse of poets like Machaut and Deschamps, none of Froissart's poems is extant in manuscript anthologies. As explained below, they appear only in the two manuscript collections.

30 In order to distinguish Froissart's poem from Machaut *Dit de la Marguerite*, I follow most scholarship in using the title of manuscript B, *Dittié*, rather than that of A, employed by Anthime Fourrier, whose text I quote: *Le Dit de la Marguerite 'Dits' et 'Débats'* 147–53.

31 For Froissart's various celebrations of the marguerite, see Fourrier's note to *L'Espinette amoureuse* 4179–88 (page 187).

32 For a more thorough discussion of the relationships see Wimsatt *Marguerite Poetry* especially 30–6.

33 See Shears *Froissart* 2 and note. Shears states that 1337 is the year. Barber 'Black Prince' asserts misleadingly that 1333 'is the generally accepted date' (at 25). See the discussion by McGregor in Froissart *Lyric Poems* 11–12.

34 I am assuming that Jean de le Mote has passed from the scene by this time.

35 See *Joli buisson de jonece* 85–97.

36 For insight into the poets' lives in the courts of John and Wenceslas, see Wilkins 'Pattern of Patronage.'

37 Froissart *Meliador*. For a recent treatment of the romance see Dembowski *Froissart and 'Meliador.'* Froissart's travels in England and Scotland were marked by his interest in finding traces of Arthur, who was so important to English kings. Chaucer, by contrast, as I have remarked, makes no reference to the king outside the comic tale of the Wife of Bath.

38 'Moult furent d'aultres bons ouvriers, par especial messire Jehan Froissart ... mais il fist tous ses fais a l'onneur la partie d'Engleterre.' Langlois *Sec-*

onde rhétorique 14. There seems in fact little bias for the 'partie' of England in Froissart's poetry, aside from the fact that some works were written in England for the queen. Parts of his *Chronicles,* of course, could be seen as biased, and merely a sense that he was not of the French party could have led to his poetry's exclusion from some collections.

39 Froissart's verse is preserved in Bibliothèque Nationale Paris français 830 and 831. While they do not compare in richness with the deluxe Machaut codices, they are still well written on vellum in large Gothic script with decorated and coloured initials and good texts. There is one illumination in ms 830. *Cour de May* and *Trésor amoureux,* two long poems that make up the third volume of Auguste Scheler's old edition of Froissart's poems, *Oeuvres de Froissart: Poésies* (1870–1872) are not in the two Froissart collections, and there is little reason to think that he wrote them.

40 For the general order and the notable exceptions to a chronological ordering, see Wimsatt *'Dit dou Bleu Chevalier'* 393–6. In several of Anthime Fourrier's editions of Froissart's works, the datings of the poems and the discussions of the dating are vitiated by the editor's conviction that the works are presented in the manuscripts in strict chronological order. I referred in the last chapter to his dating of the *Temple d'Onnour.*

41 *Confort d'Ami, Oeuvres* III was composed for Charles of Navarre while he was held in prison by Jean II.

42 Besides Machaut's dominating influence, there is also an important relationship between Froissart's longer dits and Jehan Acart de Hesdin's poem *Prise amoureuse,* a hunt-of-love allegory. Froissart's allegorical hunt with hounds in *Le Paradis d'Amour* seems directly inspired by the *Prise;* the notion of an *Espinette amoureuse* (a thorn-bush of love) seems to come from the bushes that effect the 'prise' (capture) in Jehan Acart's work; the closeness of the title of *Prison amoureuse* to the earlier title is obvious; and the title image of *Joli buisson de jonece* again shows a filiation to the bushes of Jehan Acart's *Prise* – indeed, that poem repeatedly uses the related images of the 'douz buisson d'Enfance' (290, 381, 485, 880) and the 'bois de Jonece' (257, 273, 281, 321).

43 See Freeman 'Froissart's *Le Joli Buisson.'*

44 Despite their narrative content the exempla are essentially lyric in their serving to support the descriptive and emotive statements.

45 For the exempla of le Mote, see chapter 2. And for the use of exempla in the dits amoureux from the *Roman de la Rose* up to Machaut, see Wimsatt *French Love Poets* 52–3 and *passim.*

46 The fact that Deschamps imitated le Mote's ballade to Vitry witnesses that the le Mote-Vitry exchange was well known, which might be as-

sumed in any event. For Deschamps' imitation see the discussion in chapter 8.

47 Froissart *'Dits' et 'débats'*

48 For these stories see *Espinette amoureuse* 2661–2737; *Prison amoureuse* 1316–1995; *Joli buisson de jonece* 2015–92 and 2102–2209.

49 See Graham 'Classical Allusion.' On Froissart's classical inventions, see also Kelly 'Les Inventions ovidiennes' and *Medieval Imagination* 156–69.

50 Kelly *Medieval Imagination* 157 cites as precedent for Froissart Machaut's imputing pregnancy to Dido in *Jugement Navarre*, and his excising Ovid's conclusions in *Confort d'Ami* (which incidentally is anticipated in the Narcissus story in the *Roman de la Rose*). These are significant but mild precedents for Froissart's exuberant inventions. Machaut more generally adhered to the inherited story, though often employing the *Ovide moralisé*, composed in the early fourteenth century.

51 Several specific connections between Chaucer's poetry and the *Chronicles* have been suggested: the naval battle in the legend of Cleopatra (*Legend of Good Women* 629–53) is compared to Froissart's accounts of Sluys and La Rochelle, the account of Theseus' victory in the 'Knight's Tale' (A 983–90) to the narration of the English assaults on Cadzant and Limoges, and the tournament in the same work (A 2491–2512) to the story of the tournament held by Richard II in 1390. The parallels, however, are general and are matched in other chronicles and reports of the day. For the details see notes to the passages in Chaucer *Works* (ed. Robinson). The 'Knight's Tale' notes are omitted in *Riverside Chaucer*.

52 *Oeuvres de Froissart: Chroniques* I, part 1, 81

53 It is interesting, though not surprising, that Froissart and Caxton in his edition of Malory express their purposes so similarly. Froissart opens his preface to book I, 'Affin que honnourables emprises et nobles aventures et faits d'armes ... soient notablement registrées et mises en mémoire perpétual, par quoy les preux aient exemple d'eulx encouragier en bien faisant, je vueil traittier et recorder hystoire et matière de grand loenge': *Oeuvres de Froissart: Chroniques* II, 4. Caxton states, 'And I, accordyng to my copye, haue doon sette in in enprynte, to the entente that noble men may see and lerne the noble actes of chyualrye, the ientyl and vertuous dedes that somme kynghtes used in tho dayes, by whyche they came to honour, and how that they that were vycious were punysshed and ofte put to shame and rebuke, etc.' *Caxton's Malory* 1, 2.

54 Froissart *Lyric Poems* 196–204. Three were crowned in Froissart's home city of Valenciennes, and one each at Lille and Abbeville. The puys did

not exclude the nobility, but they were bourgeois in origin and in the greater part of their membership.

55 The contrast between Machaut's and Froissart's stanzaic versification appears clearly in the chart showing the proportions of the ballades of the various Middle French poets in Poirion *Le Poète et le prince*, 374–5.

56 In the *Art de dictier*, *Oeuvres* VII, 271 Deschamps speaks of the poets reciting before the prince of the puy *'serventois de Nostre Dame, chançons royaulx, pastourelles, balades et rondeaulx.'* The first three in the list, five-stanza forms, are the ones most commonly associated with the puys. He explicitly states (at 281) that the serventois is a puy form. In speaking of the pastourelle form elsewhere in the treatise (at 287) he avoids giving a precise formula except to associate the pastourelle with other five-stanza works: 'Quant est aux *pastourelles* et *sotes chançons*, elles se font de semblable taille et par la maniere que font les *ballades amoureuses*, excepté tant que les materes se different selon la volunté et le sentiment du faiseur.' In the fifteenth-century treatise *Le Doctrinal de la Seconde Rhétorique* in Langlois *Seconde rhétorique* 177–8, Baudet Haurenc gives an example of a pastourelle as presented in the puy of Béthune 'chascun an, le dimenche aprèz la feste Dieu.' The example has five stanzas of eleven octosyllabic lines, with refrain and envoy, quite in accord with Froissart's practice.

57 Whiting 'Froissart as Poet'

58 Edited from the manuscript of 310 lyrics, University of Pennsylvania manuscript French 15 by Kibler and Wimsatt, 'Pastourelle in the Fourteenth Century.' The manuscript, which has significant associations with England, was discussed particularly in chapter 2.

59 For the dating see Whiting 'Froissart as Poet' 212, and Hoepffner 'La Chronologie' 39.

60 Kibler and Wimsatt 'Pastourelle in the Fourteenth Century' 38–40

61 One may compare the strictures of Chaucer's Parson 'Parson's Tale' (I 421–8) against revealing clothes such as Herman has in mind.

62 Kibler and Wimsatt 'Pastourelle in the Fourteenth Century' pastourelles VI and VII, 50–8

63 The preliminary accord of 1359 was somewhat moderated in the final Treaty of Calais (or Brétigny) of 24 October 1360, but the concessions by the French in both cases were huge.

64 Whiting 'Froissart as Poet' 210

65 Ibid 213–14

66 Froissart *Lyric Poems* 167–9

67 See Poirion Le Poète et le prince 370, 374–5.

68 Hoepffner 'La Chronologie' 38
69 Only three of his twenty deal with non-courtly subjects: the first describes the houppelande; the fifth celebrates the marriage of Poitevin and Gascon, representing the mixing of red and white wines; and the seventh describes a company of shepherds at a celebration. Assuming a roughly chronological ordering for the pastourelles in the manuscripts, Froissart soon came to devote the form entirely to court subjects.
70 Froissart 'Dits' et 'débats' 171–74
71 Ibid 175–90
72 'Je sçai françois, englois et thiés' (154). This is the florin and not the poet speaking, but it does remind us that Froissart spent long periods in Germanic-language areas (Flanders and England) and probably came to know the languages well.

CHAPTER SEVEN

1 See Edmunds 'Medieval Library' item 19, 257.
2 Braddy Chaucer and Graunson 2. Much of the medieval praise of Granson that Braddy quotes (1–21) does not apply to his poetry; he also overvalues the evidence of Oton's Continental popularity.
3 Oeuvres de Froissart: Chroniques VII, 227; IX, 136. The fact that Chaucer became, for the next century, 'flour of eloquence' (Hoccleve), 'of makeris flour' (Dunbar), and 'flour of poetes' (Lydgate) is an interesting consequence of his epithet for Granson, but does not demonstrate that Chaucer was referring primarily to the Savoyard's poetic powers. Even applied to Chaucer, the image of the flower evokes personal qualities, as when Hoccleve yokes the image with the epithet 'reverend fadir.' See Spurgeon Chaucer Criticism I xiv–xvi, 27.
4 For these poets see Garencières Le Chevalier poète; Raynaud Les Cents Ballades; and Piaget 'La Cour amoureuse' and 'Un manuscrit.' The option of writing love lyrics without musical accompaniment, which became more acceptable as the fourteenth century went along, no doubt encouraged many noblemen to compose verse.
5 For the Granson manuscripts see Oton de Grandson 107–26. This is the standard edition of his poetry, quoted herein, and also the main work on the life of Granson (11–104). As Piaget remarks (at 108), none of the manuscripts is devoted solely to Granson's work, his poems being commonly found in the manuscripts following the Livre des Cent ballades or among poems of Alain Chartier.
6 Oeuvres de Froissart: Chroniques VIII 121

7 When she speaks of Granson's serving the ladies, Christine of course is mindful of his poetry as well as his personal actions. See Christine de Pisan *Oeuvres poétiques, L'Epistre au Dieu d'Amours* lines 233–44 and *Le Débat des deux amans* lines 1610–17.

8 See Piaget's review in *Oton de Grandson* 12–20 of Granson's activities on behalf of England and Savoy from 1372 to 1390.

9 See ibid 75–7; for Philippe de Mézières see also Olson *Canterbury Tales* 7–8 and passim.

10 For an edition of Granson's five ballades, with complete variants, see Wimsatt *Poems of 'Ch'* 69–74.

11 No envoy extant of a fourteenth-century French ballade or chant resembles Chaucer's envoy to the *Complaint of Venus*. The rhymes and the rhyme scheme of the typical envoy are closely related to the lyric proper. The rhyme scheme of Chaucer's envoy is *aabaabbaab*, substantially different from the scheme of the nine stanzas of the ballades, *ababbccB*; moreover, it does not pick up any rhyme sound from the immediately preceding ballade. One might contrast the envoy of the *Complaint* with the envoy of Chaucer's other triple ballade, *Fortune*, which conforms much better to French practice (though it is still exceptionally long). Its rhyme scheme is *ababbab*, a curtailed version of the ballade stanza's *ababbcbc*, and it picks up its *a* rhyme (*-esse*) from the dominating *b* rhyme of the preceding ballade. But the very fact that *Fortune* and *Complaint of Venus*, triple ballades, have envoys is exceptional, since in French practice the envoys always belong to the individual poem, not to the sequence.

12 See Poirion *Le Poéte et le prince* 385–7.

13 The *Cinq balades* are among the poems of Granson found in the Barcelona collection; for contents see *Oton de Grandson* 116–19. Added to the consideration that composition in Spain would help account for the verse being found in a Catalan manuscript is the fact that an eight-stanza poem of Granson found in the Barcelona manuscript, *Complainte de l'an nouvel*, is accompanied by a strophe-by-strophe response by Lesparra, who shared Granson's imprisonment in Spain. For Granson's imprisonment and Lesparra see ibid 13–14, 136–7; and Braddy *Chaucer and Graunson* 27–8.

14 For the possibility that Chaucer was writing for Isabel of York, see the note in the *Riverside Chaucer* 1081a. For Granson and Isabel of York see Braddy *Chaucer and Graunson* 21, and 'Chaucer and Graunson' 362–4. She was the daughter of King Pedro of Spain, which would account for the address to 'Princes' in Chaucer's envoy. (But 'princes' also could be

the plural of 'prince.') It certainly is possible that Granson was writing for another Isabel. One candidate is Countess Isabel of Neuchâtel, with whom Granson travelled in Savoy in 1376; see *Oton de Grandson* 15–16.

15 For the musical form of the double and triple ballades, see Wilkins *One Hundred Ballades* 125, 152–5. Formal sequences of more than three poems, like Granson's *Cinq balades*, were never designed for music, and were not usual until late in the fourteenth century.

16 Chaucer's beginning with 'But' makes the connection explicit between the second and third ballade. Granson does not use conjunctions between his five ballades, making each more independent.

17 See Deschamps *Art de dictier* in *Oeuvres* VII, 276; and Anonyme Lorrain in Langlois *Seconde rhétorique* 202.

18 In the other stanzas of the poems, as in the usual ballade practice of Machaut and Granson, the end of a sentence coincides with the ending of the *abab* section of the stanza. The use of the *bb* couplet in the middle of the stanza as a syntactic unit, then, is a variation, and quite effective in this case.

19 See Robbins 'Lyrics' 389.

20 In succeeding stanzas she speaks of 'subtil Jelosie, the deceyvable' (43), then of the tormenting of jealousy (53), and finally she defies jealous people to disturb her (62). None of these has precedents in Granson's *Cinq balades*.

21 In late medieval usage, Jealousy almost always arises when a lover or other person with strong proprietary feelings senses that a personal attachment is threatened by another. In the *Roman de la Rose* Jealousy represents the parents or guardians of the Rose. Most often jealousy is attributed to husbands: thus Chaucer's Clerk, in ironically advising women to make their husband's jealous (E 1205), and the Miller, in characterizing John the carpenter (A 3224, 3294). But women can have the feeling too; the Knight attributes the problems of Thebes to Juno's jealousy of Semele (A 1329). Jealousy can even be felt by swans (*Parliament of Fowls* 342), evidently because of their strong proprietary feelings for their nests. For the various individuals in English court circles whose jealousy might be the subject of Chaucer's poem, see the discussions of *Complaint of Mars* and *Complaint of Venus* in the *Riverside Chaucer* 1079, 1081.

22 I have made the case for the priority of Chaucer's *Book of the Duchess* to Granson's poems in *French Love Poets* 143–6. Among other factors, the chronology necessitated by Braddy's claim for Granson's influence on the *Book of the Duchess* in 'Chaucer's *Book of the Duchess*' is highly im-

probable. For the case of the *Parliament of Fowls* and Granson's *Songe Saint Valentin,* in which Braddy *Chaucer and Graunson* 64–6 again sees the influence going from the French to the English, see the discussion below.

23 The rondeaux and virelay, as edited by Piaget, have unusual forms. This is perhaps due to confusing abbreviations of the texts in the manuscripts.

24 In this Granson's work is rather typical of the mode. The *Roman de la Rose* is basic to Middle French love poetry, but by Granson's time it had been thoroughly assimilated to the mode, so that much of his reference to it is obviously second-hand (mainly through Machaut). Granson's classical reference also comes by way of commonplaces of contemporary poetry.

25 For echoes of other poems, aside from Chaucer's, cf Granson's *Songe* line 29 with *Roman de la Rose* line 26; *Songe* lines 30–3 with the Middle English *Pearl* lines 9–10; *Songe* lines 302–3 with Machaut *Dit dou lyon,* in *Oeuvres* II, lines 312–13; and *Songe* with *Dit de l'alerion,* ibid, *passim.*

26 See Piaget *Oton de Grandson* 17–43.

27 If Chaucer's *Complaint of Venus* was written in the 1390s, then, it probably followed shortly after these two Granson works. When Granson returned to England in 1392, he would have provided Chaucer the opportunity of reading the works and responding to his imitations.

28 There is no question of Machaut's direct influence on Granson's narrator here. It is true that Chaucer developed his inept, comic narrator in important ways from Machaut's, but Chaucer makes his speaker more self-conscious in his desire to help lovers despite his personal awkwardness as a lover. There is no fourteenth-century French precedent for Granson's speaker's talking about his incapacity for loving. Machaut's narrator, though often comic, never declares himself unqualified for love.

29 The part quoted continues to evoke the opening of *Troilus,* and there are also definite suggestions of the *House of Fame.* Compare various lines here especially with *Troilus* I 36–9 (prayer for lovers victimized by slander), and 43–6 (prayer that lovers may please each other); and *House of Fame* 1 ('God turne us every drem to goode!) and 1884–9 (on 'newe tydynges' of love).

30 For various versions of Machaut's enigmatic devices, see Hoepffner 'Anagramme.' Granson's acrostic ISABEL suggests especially the acrostic on Pierre / Marguerite in 'Complaint VI.' See Wimsatt *Marguerite Poetry* 40–2.

31 As Chaucer has it in the *Duchess,* adapting Froissart's words,
   I have so many an ydel thoght,

Purely for defaute of slep,

That, by my trouthe, I take no kep

Of nothing ... (4–7)

32 In the justaposition of the matter of the 'anelés' (jewels or rings) with that of understanding the birds' speech, there may well be a reminiscence of the 'Squire's Tale,' where Canacee can understand the birds' language by virtue of a ring.

33 Also echoed is the original model for Chaucer's situation, the *Jugement du roy de Behaigne*, where the poet hides in the bushes and overhears the lady and the knight debating their woes. See Wimsatt *French Love Poets* especially 89–93. This evidence of Granson's recalling both poems is significant in considering the process of composition, whereby the original of the source poem is itself utilized.

34 Behind these lines in the *Duchess* is the phraseology of Machaut's *Jugement du roy de Behaigne* (88–92), but the two passages of Granson's *Livre* (1153–6, 1163–72) taken together, as well as the situation, show that the *Duchess* is Granson's major model here, though of course Granson knew and no doubt had in mind the relevant passages in both works.

35 Piaget 'Oton de Grandson.' See also *Oton de Grandson* 156–64.

36 Aside from the late date indicated by the manuscript contents and the use of *Troilus*, the two long works by Granson are associated by the common Chaucerian materials used, the similar bird allegories, and the narrative style. His two other poems that have acrostics identifying the lady addressed as 'Isabel' (*Souhait de Saint Valentin* and *Complainte de Granson*) were probably written before Granson could have known Isabel of Bavaria, and in that case would have been addressed to another woman, perhaps Isabel of York, as Braddy maintains in 'Chaucer and Graunson' 366–7. But Isabel of York is not inevitable for Chaucer or Granson; for instance, in 1376 Oton was in the company of Isabel, Countess of Neuchâtel. In any event, it would have been natural enough for Granson to redirect the Isabel poems to the queen when he came to know her in France; see Wimsatt *Poems of 'Ch'* 132 n2.

37 For Granson's imitation of the *Duchess* in *Complainte de Saint Valentin* and *Complainte de l'an nouvel*, see the discussion and references in note 21 above. Evidence of the manuscripts strongly suggests that the latter poem of Granson is early; it is found in all four collections of his poetry, including the Barcelona manuscript, which probably contains poems of Granson written before and during his captivity in Spain (1372–4), and it is among the first of the Granson poems in the Paris and Pennsylvania French 15 (formerly Florence) manuscripts, both of which tend to have a

chronological ordering. For the Granson manuscripts see *Oton de Grandson* 107–26. The Neuchâtel Manuscript is now found at Lausanne, Bibliothèque cantonale et universitaire, ms 350. The manuscripts indicate little about the dating of the *Complainte de Saint Valentin*, but on the slippery ground of the poem's contents (the narrator's youth, his lady's untimely death, his adoption of a new mistress) Piaget places it first in his edition of the poetry.

38 Kelly *Cult of Saint Valentine* and Oruch 'St Valentine.' Braddy's claim ('Chaucer and Granson' 359–60) that the poets were basing their works on 'the well-known folk belief that birds were supposed to choose their mates on Saint Valentine's' seems to have no foundation. The note in Skeat's edition (I, 516) to which Braddy refers is based on literature after the fourteenth century. There may be some justice, nevertheless, in Braddy's claim (360–1) that the vogue of Valentine poetry was 'sponsored by Granson.'

39 For the impressive body of fourteenth- and fifteenth-century Valentine poetry, see Kelly *Cult of Saint Valentine* 128–58, and Oruch 'St Valentine' 558–65.

40 The contents of the two manuscripts are printed in order in the Piaget edition at 197–280 and 283–380.

41 If Granson wrote the first Valentine poems, where did he get the idea? Kelly investigates the cult of Saint Valentine as it was practised in various places, especially Genoa, where Chaucer could have picked up local traditions connecting springtime celebrations with the saint. Granson could be perpetuating Savoyard customs.

42 *Oton de Grandson* 163n notes that the fourteenth of February occurred on Saturday in 1372, 1377 , 1383, and 1394. Since the poem is placed third in the Paris manuscript, one of the first two years would be possible for its composition. But such dating may be irrelevant; Kelly in particular makes a strong case against the Valentine's Days of the poems coming in wintry February.

43 Regarding the anaphora in this poem, Poirion *Le Poète et le prince* 226 speaks of the 'usage immoderé de la répétition.' Immoderate repetition is a frequent tendency in the later, often inferior poetry of the Machaut tradition; Machaut himself always avoided it.

44 The poem is found only in a manuscript of Alain Chartier's works; the rubric identifies it as 'Complainte amoureuse de Sainct Valentin Gransson.' For more about the manuscript see *Oton de Grandson* 121.

45 Comparably, in the *Legend of Good Women* the birds sing a song blessing Saint Valentine, 'For on this day I *chees* yow to be myn' (F 146; G 132)

46 There are three references in the *Livre Messire Ode*. Besides the lover's statement that his dream took place on Saint Valentine's Day (1974), he concludes his 'Lay de plour' with a prayer to the saint (819); and in the story of his love for a sparrow-hawk, he says he captured the bird on a Monday morning, the day after Saint Valentine's Day (1241). The reference to Monday is another of the interesting localizing features of the *Livre*, like the proper names that are mentioned in the poem. For what it is worth, the fifteenth of February occurred on a Monday in 1384, 1389, and 1395; see *Oton de Grandson* 163n. The year 1389 comes between the death of Granson's father in 1386 and his return to the king's service in England in 1392.

47 See Wimsatt *Poems of 'Ch'* 50–1, 66–7.

48 Granson's poetry, nevertheless, is better than his editor would have it. Piaget's judgment in *Oton de Grandson* 176–7 is in line with commentary about fourteenth-century French verse that was formerly fashionable: 'Les amateurs de "poetrie" et les amoureux lisaient et relisaient les vers de Grandson, en dépit de leur monotonie, de leurs pauvres rimes, de leur pauvre syntaxe et de leur pauvre vocabulaire.' The assumption seems to be that poets and readers were equally stupid.

49 It perhaps seems a major oversight on my part that John Gower is not treated in this study, since he did compose two collections of French ballades, the *Cinkante Balades* and the *Traitié*, and his friendship with Chaucer is well recognized. Nevertheless, Gower's French lyrics have but a slight relationship to those of his French contemporaries. As Fisher states in *John Gower* (at 74), 'Chaucer ... reveals a profound influence from the French court poets, whereas Gower shows little, if any, knowledge of them.' There is also no particular discernible connection between Chaucer's and Gower's lyrics. Gower's formalization of the ballade collections, and much of their composition, probably took place near and after the turn of century: see Fisher's discussion (70–88).

50 Deschamps *Oeuvres* v, 79–80 (no 893)

51 *Oton de Grandson* 177

CHAPTER EIGHT

1 Morris *Chaucer Criticism* 242–5. Many of the thirty-nine works, of course, have been discussed as sources by several scholars. The extreme example is the *Miroir de mariage*, whose relationship to Chaucer's works has been discussed in thirty-six different books and articles.

2 These are mainly figures cited by Wilkins *One Hundred Ballades* 62. Depending on acceptance of certain doubtful works, and whether certain texts are counted as one or more, the number would vary slightly.

3 Deschamps *Oeuvres*

4 Poirion *Le Poète et le prince* 229–30

5 For the biography of Deschamps see Deschamps *Oeuvres* XI, 9–99; and Hoepffner *Eustache Deschamps.*

6 See *Oeuvres* XI, 13; Hoepffner *Eustache Deschamps* 25–9.

7 *Oeuvres* V, 80, no 893, 7, 9

8 See Hoepffner *Eustache Deschamps* 41.

9 For the son-in-law see *Oeuvres* XI, 68–70; for other literary friends, see 266–7.

10 In addition to the ballade, *Oeuvres* V, 79–80, no 893, there is also a rondeau which Deschamps addresses to Granson (IV, 55, no 596) in which he describes a miserable night he spent in Calais, doubtless on the visit commemorated in the ballade.

11 *Oeuvres* VIII, 178, no 1474, 27–9. He also brackets Vitry and Machaut in V 53, no 872, 5–6. Deschamps' use of the terms 'poete,' 'poetrie,' and 'faiseur,' the first two of which were not employed before him to refer to a contemporary writer, is significant. See Brownlee *Poetic Identity* 7–14.

12 *Les règles de la seconde rhétorique*, in Langlois *Seconde rhétorique* 14: 'Aprés vint Eustace Morel [ie, Deschamps], nepveux de maistre Guillaume de Machaut.'

13 *Oeuvres* III, 259, no 447, 5

14 *Oeuvres* IX, 375, *Miroir de mariage*, 11666

15 It is true that the account of the seige is translated 'très fidelement' (*Oeuvres* XI, 198) from the *Grandes chroniques de France*, which makes Deschamps' memory very like the chronicler's.

16 Since the manuscript shows little evidence of the chronological ordering that characterizes the collections of Machaut's and Froissart's work, most of Deschamps' poems can be dated only by educated guesswork. In this case it seems to me that the subject matter and conventional treatment of the *Lay amoureux* is much more in the manner of Machaut than Deschamps' late dateable works are, and is therefore probably early.

17 *Oeuvres* II, 202, no 306 (*Lay amoureux*), lines 296–9. Robinson in *Works of Chaucer* 845a notes a similarity between these lines and the *Legend of Good Women* 412–13, where Alceste speaks of Chaucer's service to Amour 'in his makynge.'

18 Raynaud (Deschamps *Oeuvre* XI, 22) guesses 1375, while Hoepffner *Eustache Deschamps* 39 suggests the time of the marriage of Marguerite of

Flanders with Phillip of Burgundy in 1369. The poem perhaps would
have been of more current interest in the latter year.

19 *Oeuvres* I, 248–9, no 127, 1–8

20 'And I read first in the place where Fortune spoke so cruelly, how she
provides one with her goods and deprives another' (20–2). Deschamps
refers to a passage near the end of the poem in which Guillaume compares his lady to the goddess Fortune and quotes 'Titus-Livius' on the
subject. See *Le Livre du Voir-dit* 333–5. The passage on Fortune was also
a favourite with illuminators of the poem.

21 For the music, in addition to the standard edition by Schrade *The Works
of Guillaume de Machaut: Polyphonic Music* III, 124–7, see also Wilkins *One
Hundred Ballades* 152–5 and his comment 132. The texts are edited in
Oeuvres I, 243–6, nos 123 and 124, and in Wilkins *One Hundred Ballades*
67–69. I quote from Wilkins. The metrics are decasyllabic with rhyme
scheme *ababbcbC*, a favourite form of Deschamps; he also uses it in the
ballade on the delivery of the *Voir-Dit*. None of the ballades has an envoy.

22 The story of Alpheus and Arethusa, a river and a pool, is told in *Metamorphoses* V. Deschamps evidently sees them as bountiful sources of
tears for lamenting Machaut.

23 Quoted from Wilkins *One Hundred Ballades* 68–9; also edited in *Oeuvres*
III, 259–60, no 447

24 *Oeuvres* III, 318–19, no 493. The ballades to Peronne and Gauteronne are
in decasyllabic rime royal, without envoys.

25 Among numerous other poems of the sort are two in which Deschamps
extravagantly curses a number of courtiers for their mistreatment of him:
Oeuvres IV, 270–1, no 772, and IV, 316–17, no 803.

26 See, eg, Lerch 'Zu einer Stelle' 67–8, and Thundy 'Matheolus' 53–4.

27 Brusendorff *Chaucer Tradition* 489–91 evaluates Lowe's suggestions of a
date for Clifford's seeing Deschamps, and concludes (at 491) that 'the
only known opportunity Deschamps had of meeting Clifford was during
the negotiations for peace between France and England at Leulinghem in
the early spring of 1393.' Since we can only speculate on the conditions
under which Clifford might have travelled to France, Brusendorff's de-
ductions hardly provide conclusive proof that 1393 was the year. Another
ballade in which Deschamps speaks of Lewis Clifford ('l'amoureux Clif-
fort '*Oeuvres* III, 375–6, no 806, 10, 20, 30) may be dated between 1386 and
1392. See Kittredge 'Chaucer and His Friends' 7. The poem to Chaucer
may well come from the same years, though one might also make an
argument for a much earlier time.

28 The text I quote is edited by Jenkins in his article 'Deschamps' Ballade to Chaucer.' In accord with my understanding of the sense, I do not capitalize 'pandras' (9) as he does, and I alter some of the punctuation. The poem is also edited in *Oeuvres* II, 138–40, no 138. See note 32 below for 'pandras.'

29 Translations may be found in Jenkins 270–1; in Burrow *Critical Anthology* 26–8; and in Brewer *Critical Heritage* 40–2.

30 Jenkins' line-by-line commentary (271–8) clarifies a number of difficulties.

31 For 'pandras' as Pandarus, see Lerch 'Zu einer Stelle' 67–8. Jenkins 'Deschamps' Ballade' 272–3 and others found in the word Pandrasos, who was a principal foe of Brutus in Geoffrey of Monmouth's history.

32 The idea that 'pandras' is a finite verb originates in a suggestion made to me by James Atkinson. 'Pandre' would derive from the Latin 'pandere' and be cognate to OF 'espandre,' 'repandre.' All three cognates have the apt primary meaning of revealing, explaining, spreading light, etc. Supporting the identification of the word as a verb are two important facts: seven of the eight other words in the poem rhyming in *-as* are verbs; and if 'pandras' is translated as a noun, then there is no main verb for the first stanza. Incomplete sentences are very uncommon in the poetry. Assuming that the word is a verb, nevertheless, does not relieve the difficulty that 'pandre' does not appear elsewhere. One authority on the language advises that 'if *pandras* is indeed a verb, it should be second person singular future of *panr(d)re* (= *pendre*) or *pan(d)re* (= *prendre*).' Neither word fits here, however, and the existence of 'pandre' remains quite possible; the usage would have been readily created and understood.

33 *Oeuvres* VI, 251–2, no 1242. This poem to Christine has exactly the same metrics as the poem to Chaucer, but 284 other Deschamps ballades also have the same stanza form.

34 *Une Épistre à Eustace Mourel*, in Christine de Pisan *Oeuvres complètes* II, 295–301. Her letter is a rhyming tour de force, consisting of 212 lines in octosyllabic couplets, all équivoque rhymes! It begins with strong praise for Deschamps, particularly his moral poetry, and it develops into a lament about the times. The first couplets indicate the tenor of her praise:

> A trés expert, en scens apris,
> Eustace Mourel ou a pris,
> De Senlis baillif trés nottable,
> Orateur de maint vers notable.
> Ta valeur en moy a mis
> Le vouloir, chier maistre et amis ...

35 *Oeuvres* V, 229–30, no 984

36 See Wimsatt *Poems of 'Ch'* 57. The second part of Deschamps' double ballade to Machaut also notably echoes the ballade of le Mote. Cf, with the lines of le Mote quoted, Deschamps' 'O flour des flour de toute melodie' (line 1); 'Guillaume, mondains diex d'armonie' (3); and 'Le fons chierie et la fontayne helie' (9).

37 One compelling verbal parallel indicating a likely imitation by Deschamps is presented by Phillips *'Book of the Duchess.'* She points out the close correspondence between *BD* 35–44 and a ballade of Deschamps, *Oeuvres* V 93, no 902, 1–2, 9–10.

38 Brusendorff *Chaucer Tradition* 242–5, 427–9, 485–93

39 *Oeuvres* II, 140–2, nos 286 and 287

40 In general, the order of the works in the great Deschamps collection, Bibliothèque Nationale fonds français 840, does not seem significant. Beyond the very large divisions of the lyrics in classes in the first part of the manuscript – Balades de moralité, Lays, Chançons royaux, Balades amoureuse, Rondeauls et virelays – there seems to have been little attention to sequence. There are some small natural groupings like the set of four poems on the flower and the leaf, discussed below.

41 The rubric reads, 'Comment franche voulenté puet resister a tous cas.'

42 Technically, in the double and triple ballade each constituent should have the same verse form and same refrain. In Deschamps' pair the stanza form and the last half of the refrain are identical. In Chaucer's *Fortune* the form is the same, but there are different refrains for each ballade.

43 Brusendorff *Chaucer Tradition* 242–3

44 For a nearer French source for that language of *Fortune* which is not owed to Boethius or the *Roman de la Rose*, see Wimsatt 'Chaucer, Fortune, and Machaut's "Il m'est avis." '

45 This is the 'Monk's Tale' stanza, of course. According to Poirion's chart, Deschamps wrote 351 ballades with decasyllabic lines using this rhyme scheme, Granson 28, and Christine de Pisan 54. The fact of the form's popularity in the late century may be significant for the dating of Chaucer's works. We might hypothesize that Chaucer's rime royal poems, being in Machaut's favourite verse form, tend to be earlier, while the 'Monk's Tale' stanzas tend to be later.

46 *Oeuvres* II, 31–2, no 209; Brusendorff *Chaucer Tradition* 487

47 The extended flights are suitable for the hawk instead of the lowly buzzard.

48 A number of poems that treat the theme are listed in the notes to *Lak of*

Stedfastnesse in the *Riverside Chaucer* 1086a; eg *Oeuvres* I, 113, no 31 ('Contre le temps present').

49 Brusendorff *Chaucer Tradition* 487 finds that the refrain of another ballade, *Oeuvres* II, 63–4, no 234, 'almost exactly' parallels that of *Lak of Stedfastnesse*. Notwithstanding, since the poems provide radically differing contexts, the similarity (considerably less than exact) may well be fortuitous. Cf *'Tout se destruit et par default de garde'* with *'That al is lost for lak of stedfastnesse.'*

50 Kittredge *'Envoy to Bukton'* 14–15, and Brusendorff *Chaucer Tradition* 487. They cite *Oeuvres* II, 116–17, no 271; III 54–5, no 340; V 73–4, no 888; 138–9, no 929; 217–19, no 977; and IV, 343–4, no 823, quoted below.

51 Brusendorff *Chaucer Tradition* 487. He notes particularly the closeness of Deschamps' lines 8–11 to *Bukton* lines 19–20.

52 The attitude towards marriage shown in the poems no doubt is a strictly literary one. As Kittredge remarks in *'Envoy to Bukton'* 15, whatever one thinks of its taste, *Bukton* makes the kind of humorous statement that is conventionally made to a man about to be married. The poem does not constitute evidence that Chaucer was unhappily married. And Deschamps, despite his several verse warnings against marriage, seems to have been sincerely fond and admiring of his wife. For his rather brief married life, see Hoepffner *Eustache Deschamps* 52–4, who refers to the poet's edifying ballade to his daughter on her marriage, *Oeuvres* VI, 82–4, no 1150; he adjures the daughter (line 33) to make herself like her mother in goodness.

53 Poirion *Le poète et le prince* 388–9

54 As Poirion notes (ibid 389), Granson's ballade envoys have no consistent system, either. None of the ballades of Machaut and Froissart have envoys.

55 *Oeuvres* III, 382, no 541; Lowes '"Merciles Beaute"'

56 The parallels italicized by Lowes are not especially close. There are much closer parallels in expression between *Merciles Beaute* and lyrics of Machaut. See Wimsatt 'Machaut and Chaucer's Love Lyrics' 81–3.

57 See the note to line 72 of the 'F Prologue' *Riverside Chaucer* 1061b.

58 *Oeuvres* IV, 257–65, nos 764–7. The fact that these four poems come at the beginning of the large section of the Deschamps manuscript entitled 'Balade amoureuse' may imply they are of special interest.

59 *Oeuvres* IV, 259, no 765

60 Lowes 'Prologue to the *Legend*' 608–10 no doubt rightly associates this poem of Deschamps with the time when the marriage of Phillippa and Charles VI was contemplated, late 1384.

61 Among Deschamps' ballades to the marguerite, Lowes cites particularly *Oeuvres* III, 379–82, nos 539–40. None of Deschamps' poems provide likely sources for Chaucer's daisy imagery.

62 As a source for Chaucer's *Complaint to His Purse*, Skeat, in the *Oxford Chaucer* I, 88, adduced Deschamps' ballade, 'Dieux absoille le bon Roy trespassé,' *Oeuvres* II, 81–2, no 247, as 'written on a similar occasion' to Charles VI. But Cook 'Complaint of Chaucer' notes that the link Skeat finds is by way of Chaucer's envoy, which 'is quite different from the body of the poem.' The poems themselves are quite different from Chaucer's *Complaint* and similarities even to his envoy are unremarkable.

63 For an analysis of Deschamps' work by type, form, and length, see *Oeuvres* XI, 113–35.

64 See Raynaud's long chapter 'Sources de Deschamps' in *Oeuvres* XI, 143–251, and the separate entries svv 'Ovide' 231–4 and 'Virgile' 250–1.

65 Raynaud summarizes the forms of Deschamps's lays in *Oeuvres* XI, 131–2; Deschamps' own description of the lay in the *Art de dictier* is found in VII, 287–8.

66 Of Deschamps' fourteen lays, four are predominantly political, two social, three moral, one religious. Only four might be called love poems.

67 For the quotation, see page 245 above. The frame of *Lay amoureux* has general congruities with all of Chaucer's dream visions, as Sypherd points out in 'House of Fame' 5–6.

68 *Oeuvres* II, 203–14, no 307

69 See Lowes 'Prologue to the *Legend*' 601–7, 611–15; Lossing 'Prologue to the *Legend*.'

70 The notes in the *Riverside Chaucer* 1061b, following Lowes, compare 'F Prologue' 44–9 to *Lay de Franchise* 14, 27–30; and 'F Prologue' 60–5 to *Lay* 44–50.

71 See Lowes 'Prologue to the *Legend*' 604–7, and Lossing 'Prologue to the *Legend*' 32–3.

72 Lossing 'Prologue to the *Legend*' 35. Neither Lowes nor Lossing knew about Machaut's *Dit de la fleur de lis et de la Marguerite*, which presents parallels in language and structure to Chaucer's 'Prologue' beyond those offered by Machaut's and Froissart's other Marguerite poems, and further calls into question the cogency of the passages in the *Lay de franchise* adduced by Lowes (613–17). See Wimsatt *Marguerite Poetry* 30–9.

73 Lossing 'Prologue to the *Legend*' 17–18 says of Lowes's citation of the parallels in the narrators' activities, 'They reduce themselves to the following situation: both poets walked out early on a May morning; both

went to see the birds and flowers. But so did many other authors of dream poems.' However, Lossing assumes too much here. There is no other Marguerite poem, and I can think of no other dream poem, that offers a close analogy. Particularly distinctive is the fact that both poets make a point of the early time on the morning of 1 May that they set out: Cf 'whanne comen is the May ... ther daweth me no day / That I nam up and walkyng in the mede' (Prologue F 45–6) with 'Le premier jour de ce mois de plaisance ... De mon hostel me pars au point du jour ... M'acheminay pensant par une plaine' (*Lay de franchise* 14, 27, 29).

74 For the God of Love's brightness, cf Chaucer's 'His gilte heer was corowned with sonne ... Therwith me thoghte his face shoon so bryghte / That wel unnethes myghte I him beholde' ('F Prologue' 230, 232–3) with Deschamps' 'Descendre vi celle amour digne / En un char de feu sanz courtine / Tout ardant, qui fort m'espenta' (139–41). Deschamps' group of legendary lovers (146–69) who attend on the God of Love is about the same size as Chaucer's group of ladies named in the ballade (249–69), and there are some duplications in the lovers' names. The discovery of the narrator by the lovers and their words in the *Lay amoureux* 294–9 (quoted above), may be compared with 'F Prologue' 308–12, 412–16; see note 17 above.

75 To imagine that Deschamps had in hand Chaucer's 'Prologue' before May 1385 would upset a conception of the chronology of Chaucer's work that has become ingrained in scholars. It would entail a dating for *Troilus* of 1384 or before.

76 Segni *De miseria*

77 In the 'G Prologue' to the *Legend of Good Women*, in a list of works by Chaucer, Alceste says, 'He hath in prose translated Boece, / And of the Wretched Engendrynge of Mankynde, / As man may in Pope Innocent yfynde' (G 413–15). There has been much discussion of what Chaucer is referring to. Lewis, in Segni *De miseria*, weighs the various scholarly opinions and concludes that Chaucer almost certainly is referring to a prose translation, now lost, that he made of the complete *De miseria*. This is my assumption. Because the translation is not mentioned in the 'F Prologue,' it is assumed that Chaucer made it sometime after the 'Prologue,' in the late 1380s or early 1390s.

78 *Oeuvres* II, 237–305. The editor (II, 361–6) provides a description of the presentation manuscript, Bibliothèque Nationale fonds français 20029. This is the longest of Deschamps' poems which is extant in a manuscript besides the great collection; it is the only manuscript containing

Deschamps' work that would have been suitable for presentation.

79 For 'The Popularity and Influence of the *De miseria*' see Lewis in Segni *De miseria* 3–5. For its place in the widespread tradition of writings on the contempt of the world, see Howard in Segni *Misery* xxiv–xxxiii.

80 For a full enumeration of the parts of the *De miseria* that Chaucer and Deschamps use, see Lowes 'Prologue to the *Legend*' 795 n1.

81 Segni *De miseria* 114–17

82 Ibid 115

83 *Oeuvres de Guillaume de Machaut* II. Hoepffner discusses and summarizes *Dit dou lyon* II, liv–lxiii. See also Wimsatt *French Love Poets* 76–80.

84 Brusendorff *Chaucer Tradition* 429–30. Since Chaucer does not mention the *Book of the Leoun* in his other lists, Brusendorff asserts, it 'must presumably, then, be later even than the revised draft of the Prologue to the *Legend*.' The lists, however, are never said to be complete, and in fact substantial pieces like *Anelida and Arcite* and the *Complaint of Mars* appear in none of them. In the 'Retraction,' where Chaucer may be trying to be exhaustive, as in a confession of sins, he includes the catch-all phrase, 'and many another book, if they were in my remembrance' (I 1087).

85 *Oeuvres* VIII, 247–338, no 1495. Brusendorff *Chaucer Tradition* 429 n2 observes that the title *Fiction du lyon* is modern. The lion clearly is the focal figure at the beginning of the work, but the association of Chaucer's lost poem with Deschamps' work perhaps would not have been made without the correspondence in title. The title of Machaut's poem originates in the manuscripts.

86 This is the considered opinion of Raynaud. See *Oeuvres* XI, 105.

87 For the *Renart* material in *Fiction du Lyon*, see Flinn *Le Roman de Renart* 459–65. For the *Rose* see Badel *Le Roman de la Rose*. See also Raynaud's analysis of the sources in *Oeuvres* XI, 159–64.

88 Badel *Le Roman de la Rose* 107

89 See Flinn, *Le Roman de Renart* 448–59. Flinn says (at 448) that Deschamps 'semble avoir été hanté, comme Rutebeuf, par le *Roman de Renart*.'

90 See the chart of sources in Wimsatt *French Love Poets* 158 (for *BD* 388–97) and 161 (for *BD* 1024–32 and 1108–11).

91 For an exposition of Deschamps' sources of the *Miroir* section by section, see *Oeuvres* XI, 164–200.

92 Lowes 'Chaucer and the *Miroir*'

93 Thundy 'Matheolus' 24–58. Thundy notes (at 51) the demurrals by previous scholars to Lowes's claims of Deschamps' influence.

94 Actually, Thundy deals in detail only with the 'Wife of Bath's Tale,' though he promises (at 54) to show 'in future studies ... that Chaucer used Matheolus and not Deschamps in the Merchant Tale.'

95 Thundy, ibid, considers that if the marital discussions in the *Miroir* and *Tales* have a filiation, it went from Chaucer to Deschamps. Though I would agree that it is as easy to imagine the influence going that way as from Deschamps to Chaucer, in this instance the transmission from the French to the English seems to me doubtful. The discussion in the *Miroir* is more straightforward than it is in the *Tales*, where it is heavily ironized. It is easier and more natural to adapt straightforward statements to fictional and ironic contexts than to reverse the process.

96 Lowes 'Illustrations of Chaucer'

97 Ibid 116, quoting the commentary of Raynaud in Deschamps *Oeuvres* XI, 264. A much more recent example of using Deschamps' poetry to illustrate the background of Chaucer's work is Lenaghan '*Envoy to Scogan.*' Lenaghan refers to eight different Deschamps poems in fixing the poem in 'particular literary and social contexts.'

98 *Oeuvres* VII, 253–65, no 1395, 'Le dit du gieu des dez' 152–7

CHAPTER NINE

1 Poirion *Le poète et le prince* 37 finds the Cour amoureuse especially important as a reflection of the socio-political developments in France: 'Rien de plus significatif, dans cette perspective [ie, in the perspective of an evolution towards formalism and etiquette] que l'institution de la *Cour d'Amour* le 6 janvier 1400.'

2 For an excellent inclusive treatment of the Middle French poets after Machaut who continued to compose music, see Wilkins 'Post-Machaut Tradition.'

3 In the documents they are sometimes called 'puys d'amours' and sometimes 'puys-Notre Dame'; accordingly, many of the extant poems that originated in the *puy* celebrate the Virgin, and many the beloved lady. For the origin of the name 'puy' and various aspects of the organization in Arras, see Guy *Essai sur la vie* xxxiv–lviii.

4 Ibid lvi–lviii; Faral *Les Jongleurs* 139–42

5 Gilles li Muisis *Poésies* I, 89

6 Quoted from Robertson *Chaucer's London* 88

7 Fisher *John Gower* 77–84 advances the reasonable possibility that Gower could have been a member. A similar argument could be made for Chaucer and other contemporaries. Granson, though a knight, probably

would have felt no compunction at participating. One of his ballades printed in the *Jardin de Plaisance* has an envoy addressed to 'Prince du puy,' though Piaget in *Oton de Grandson* 126 thinks the envoy not authentic.

8 Froissart *Lyric Poems* 196–203

9 'En dormant melancolioie / A une cançon amoureuse, / Et par samblance grascieuse / Dis k'a .i. puis le porteroie / Pour couronner, se je pooie' (*Le Regret Guillaume* 100–3).

10 *Louange* no 7 (Poésies XLVIII) 51–3. Poems addressed simply to 'prince' may or may not be connected with a puy; often the envoy will more specifically designate 'prince du puy.' Machaut's chant royal with the refrain, 'Cuer de marbre couronné d'aymant ... (*Louange* no 1; *Poésies* CCLIV), which imitates a refrain of le Mote's (See chapter 2), could well have been designed for a concours at Valenciennes or another locale in le Mote's home area.

11 *Oeuvres* VII, 281

12 Ibid 271. Deschamps' description here is in the service of contrasting the two 'musics'; one assumes that not all presentations had both spoken and sung dimensions.

13 The envoys of a chant royal (*Oeuvres* III, 134, no 326, 46) and of a ballade (VI, 132, no 1180, 31) are addressed to the 'Prince du Pui,' and in a ballade (V, 54, no 872) directed to the 'dus de Poligieras,' who may well be the poet himself, the speaker asks that the 'duke' not depart, but rather that he remember the 'puis d'amours' (20). Many other of Deschamps' poems may be puy productions, especially the five-stanza works; there is a section of ninety-four chants royal (*Oeuvres* III, 1–205) and there are other five-stanza lyrics in other sections of his work. Envoys addressed to 'prince,' of course, may or may not indicate puy poems. Hoepffner *Deschamps* 128 n4 thinks it very unlikely that Deschamps participated in the puys, while Poirion *Le Poète et le prince* 226–7 believes as I do that he assisted, at least on occasion, at the concours.

14 The fifteenth-century rhetorical treatises that were evidently intended for the instruction of aspiring puy poets describe all the common forms. For the audiences of the treatises, see Langlois *Seconde rhétorique* vi and n2. In the *Art de dictier* Deschamps *Oeuvres* VII 271 imputes to the puy poet 'serventois de Nostre Dame, chançons royeaulx, pastourelles, balades et rondeaulx.'

15 Raynaud *Cent ballades*

16 Ibid xlviii–li

17 See Potvin 'La Cour d'Amour'; Piaget 'La Cour Amoureuse' and 'Un

Manuscrit.' For a summary of the organization of the Cour see Poirion *Le Poète et le prince* 41.

18 See ibid 38–9.

19 See Straub 'Die Gründung.'

20 In speaking of the social makeup of the court, Poirion *Le Poète et le prince* 39–40 notes, 'Sans compter les chanoines de Tournai et de Lille qui figurent parmi les *maîtres des requêtes*, on voit parmi les *substituts du procureur général* bourgeois de Tournai encore et d'Amiens.' He notes further that the prince himself presided over a kind of 'confrérie littéraire, celle du *Chapel vert*,' at Tournai and Lille.

21 *Oeuvres* VII, 347–62, nos 1404 and 1405. Poirion *Le Poète et le prince* 223–4 notes that the 'assemblée burlesque' that Deschamps envisions 'semble une exacte parodie de la *cour amoureuse*.'

22 See *Oeuvres* XI, 281–4.

23 The members of the Amiens puy who were crowned in 1389 included lawyers, prosecutors, canons, priests, mercers, tanners, goldsmiths, tavern-keepers, and other merchants. See Poirion *Le Poète et le prince* 39.

24 In Boitani and Torti *Medieval and Pseudo-Medieval Literature*

25 *Oeuvres* VII, 270–1

26 Ibid 271–2. The appeal to the example of the puys in this passage suggests once more that they had a basic role in the poetic tradition.

27 Stevens '"Music" of the Lyric' 127, 129

28 One may feel that the handling of strong stress would be a matter that the French-speaking Deschamps would not be attuned to. Nevertheless, Raynaud's glossary indicates that 'paroles ... pointoyees' in the above quotation from Deschamps signifies 'accented words.' Other glosses are possible, of course.

29 Raynaud *Cent ballades* 221–2, lines 1–20

30 The Clerk's reference to the Wife of Bath in introducing the Envoy (E 1170) indicates that it was written after Chaucer composed the 'Wife's Prologue,' generally placed in the early 1390s.

31 Of the other two lines, in one the caesura falls at the end of syllable 6, and one at the end of syllable 3. I do not believe that we should see in the frequency of the 5/5 syllable division any particular relationship to the division of lines in the English alliterative verse tradition. In English alliterative verse the first half-line tends to be heavier than the second and in any event stress is the main factor.

32 Stevens '"Music" of the Lyric' 129

33 *Oeuvres* IV, 8–10, no. 554. The text I quote is from Wilkins *One Hundred Ballades* 79–80.

34 The harshness of a few words and phrases of the clerk, like 'crabbed eloquence,' achieves a special humorous effect in part because of the generally light and easy movement of the rest of the envoy.

35 See the essays of Guthrie and Wimsatt in *Words and Music*. The discussion by Thomas Cable also has general relevance to the problem.

36 Frye 'Introduction' xvii

37 The presence or lack of musicality for Frye is descriptive; it does not involve a necessary value judgment.

38 Frye 'Introduction' xix. On Chaucer he elaborates that his 'basis is metrical rather than accentual scansion.' By 'metrical' one assumes he does not mean the quantitative standard of classical prosody.

39 Ibid xviii

40 *Oeuvres* VII, 270

Bibliography

EDITIONS

Acart de Hesdin, Jehan. *La Prise amoureuse*. Ed Ernest Hoepffner. Dresden: Gesellschaft für die romanische Literatur 1910

Alain de Lille. *The Plaint of Nature*. Trans James J. Sheridan. Toronto: Pontifical Institute 1980

Brunetto Latini. *Li Livres dou Trésor*. Ed P. Chabaille. Paris: Imprimerie Impériale 1863

The Buik of Alexander. Ed R.L. Graeme Ritchie. 4 vols. Scottish Text Society. Edinburgh: Blackwood 1921–9

Bury, Richard de. *Philobiblon*. Ed and trans E.C. Thomas. Oxford: Blackwell 1970

Cent ballades. See Jean le Seneschal

'Ch.' *Chaucer and the Poems of 'Ch' in University of Pennsylvania MS French 15*. Ed James I. Wimsatt. Chaucer Studies IX. Cambridge: Brewer 1982

Chaucer, Geoffrey. *The Complete Works of Geoffrey Chaucer: Edited from Numerous Manuscripts*. Ed Walter W. Skeat. 2d ed. 7 vols. Oxford: Clarendon Press 1899–1900

– *The Riverside Chaucer*. Ed Larry D. Benson et al. 3d ed. Boston: Houghton 1987

– *Troilus and Criseyde: A New Edition of the 'Book of Troilus'* Ed Barry A. Windeatt. London: Longman 1984

– *The Works of Geoffrey Chaucer*. Ed F.N. Robinson. 2d ed. Cambridge, Mass.: Houghton 1957

Condé, Jean de. *Dits et contes de Baudouin de Condé et de son fils Jean de Condé*. Ed Auguste Scheler. 3 vols. Brussels: Devaux 1866–7

Court, Jean le (dit Brisebarre). *Le Restor du Paon*. Ed Richard J. Carey. Geneva: Droz 1966

Dante Alighieri. *Convivio*. Trans William Walrond Jackson. Oxford: Clarendon 1909

– *Literary Criticism of Dante Alighieri*. Ed and trans Robert S. Haller. Lincoln: University of Nebraska Press 1973

– *Translation of the Latin Works*. Trans A.G. Ferrers Howell and Philip H. Wicksteed. London: Dent 1904

Deguilleville, Guillaume de. *Pélèrinage de la vie humaine*. Ed J.J. Sturzinger. London: Roxburghe Club 1893

Deschamps, Eustache. *Oeuvres complètes de Eustache Deschamps*. Ed le Marquis de Queux de Saint-Hilaire and Gaston Raynaud. 11 vols. Société des Anciens Textes Français. Paris: Firmin Didot 1878–1904

'Development of the Pastourelle in the Fourteenth Century: An Edition of Fifteen Poems with an Analysis.' Ed William W. Kibler and James I. Wimsatt. *Mediaeval Studies* 45 (1983) 22–78

Dobson, E.J., and F.L. Harrison, eds. *Medieval English Songs*. New York: Cambridge University Press 1979

Froissart, Jean. *'Dits' et 'débats' de Jean Froissart, avec en appendice quelques poèmes de Guillaume de Machaut*. Ed Anthime Fourrier. Textes Litteraires Français. Geneva: Droz 1979

– *L'Espinette amoureuse*. Ed Anthime Fourrier. Bibliothèque Français et Romane, série B, 2. Paris: Klincksieck 1974

– *Le Joli buisson de jonece*. Ed Anthime Fourrier. Textes Litteraires Français. Geneva: Droz 1975

– *The Lyric Poems of Jehan Froissart*. Ed Rob Roy McGregor Jr. University of North Carolina Studies in the Romance Languages and Literatures no 143. Chapel Hill: University of North Carolina Press 1975

– *Méliador*. Ed Auguste Longnon. 3 vols. Société des Anciens Textes Français. Paris: Firmin Didot 1886–96

– *Oeuvres de Froissart: Chroniques*. Ed Kervyn de Lettenhove. 25 vols in 26. Brussels: Devaux 1867–77

– *Oeuvres de Froissart: Poésies*. Ed Auguste Scheler. 3 vols. Brussels: Devaux 1870–2

– *Le Paradis d'Amour / L'Orloge amoureus*. Ed Peter F. Dembowski. Textes Litteraires Français. Geneva: Droz 1986

– *La Prison amoureuse*. Ed Anthime Fourrier. Paris: Klincksieck 1974

Garencières, Jean de. *Le Chevalier poète Jean de Garencières* (1372–1415). Ed Young Abernathy Neal. Paris: Nizet 1953

Gilles li Muisis. *Poésies de Gilles li Muisis.* Ed Kervyn de Lettenhove. 2 vols. Louvain: Lefever 1882

Granson, Oton de. 'Granson's Five Ballades' in *Poems of 'Ch'*. See 'Ch.'

– *Oton de Grandson: sa vie et ses poésies.* Ed Arthur Piaget. Mémoires et documents publiés par la Société de la Suisse Romande, 3d series, vol 1. Lausanne: Payot 1941

– *Oton de Granson und seine Dichtungen.* Ed G. Ludwig Schirer. Strassburg: DuMont-Schauberg 1904

Henry of Lancaster. *Le Livre de seyntz medecines.* Ed E.J. Arnould. Anglo-Norman Text Society. Oxford: Blackwell 1940

Jean le Seneschal. *Les Cent ballades: Poème du XIVe siècle composé par Jean le Seneschal avec le collaboration de ...* Ed Gaston Raynaud. Société des Ancien Textes Français. Paris: Firmin Didot 1905

John of Garland. *The Parisiana Poetria.* Ed Traugott Lawler. New Haven: Yale University Press 1974

Langlois, Ernest, ed. *Recueil d'arts de seconde rhétorique.* Paris: Imprimerie Nationale 1902

Las Leys d'Amors. Ed Joseph Anglade. Bibliothèque Méridionale. First series XVII, 4 vols. Toulouse: Edward Privat 1919–24

le Mote, Jean de. *Le Parfait du paon.* Ed Richard J. Carey. University of North Carolina Studies in the Romance Languages and Literatures no 118. Chapel Hill: University of North Carolina Press 1972

– *Le Regret Guillaume comte de Hainault.* Ed Auguste Scheler. Louvain: Lefever 1882

– *La Voie d'Enfer et de Paradis.* Ed Sr M. Aquiline Pety, OP. Washington: Catholic University of America 1940

le Mote, Jean de, et al. 'Ballades mythologiques de Jean de le Mote, Philippe de Vitry, Jean Campion.' Ed E. Pognon. *Humanisme et Renaissance* 5 (1938) 407–17

Longuyon, Jacques du. *Les Voeux du paon.* Vols 2–4 of *Buik of Alexander.* See *Buik of Alexander.*

Lorris, Guillaume de, and Jean de Meun. *Le Roman de la Rose.* Ed Félix Lecoy. 3 vols. Classiques Français du Moyen Age. Paris: Champion 1963–70

Machaut, Guillaume de. *Dit de la fleur de lis et de la Marguerite* in *The Marguerite Poetry of Guillaume de Machaut.* See Wimsatt.

– *Dit de la Harpe* in Karl Young ed *Essays in Honor of Albert Feuillerat.* New Haven: Yale University Press 1943

– *Le Jugement du roy de Behaigne and Remede de Fortune of Guillaume de*

Machaut. Ed James I. Wimsatt and William W. Kibler. Chaucer Library. Athens, Ga.: University of Georgia Press 1988

– *Le livre du Voir-dit.* Ed Paulin Paris. Paris: Société des Bibliophiles François 1875

– *La Louange des dames.* Ed Nigel Wilkins. New York: Barnes and Noble 1973

– *Oeuvres de Guillaume de Machaut.* Ed Ernest Hoepffner. 3 vols. Société des Anciens Textes Français. Paris: Firmin Didot 1908–21

– *Oeuvres.* Ed Prosper Tarbé. Collection des poètes champenois antérieurs au XVIe siècle, vol 2. Reims 1849

– *Poésies lyriques.* Ed Vladimir Chichmaref. 2 vols. 1909. Reprint Geneva: Slatkine 1973

– *La Prise d'Alexandrie.* Ed L. de Mas-Latrie. Publications de la Société de l'Orient Latin, série historique 1. Geneva: Fick 1877

– *The Works of Guillaume de Machaut: Polyphonic Music of the Fourteenth Century* vols 2–3. Ed Leo Schrade. Monaco: Editions by Lyre 1956

Malory, Thomas. *Caxton's Malory.* Ed James W. Spisak and William Matthews. 2 vols. Berkeley: University of California Press 1983

Margival, Nicole de. *Le Dit de la Panthère d'Amours.* Ed Henry A. Todd. Société des Anciens Textes Français. Paris: Firmin Didot 1883

Parlement of the Thre Ages. Ed Sir Israel Gollancz. London: Oxford University Press 1915

Pearl. Ed E.V. Gordon. Oxford: Clarendon 1953

Les Pièces lyriques du Roman de Perceforest. Ed Jeanne Lods. Publications Romanes et Françaises 36. Geneva: Droz 1953

Christine de Pisan. *Oeuvres poétiques de Christine de Pisan.* Ed Maurice Roy. 3 vols. Société des Anciens Textes Français. Paris: Firmin Didot 1886–96

Le Roman de Perceforest (part 1). Ed Jane M. Taylor. Geneva: Droz 1980

Le Roman de Perceforest (part 2). Ed Gilles Roussineau. Geneva: Droz 1987

Segni, Lotario dei (Innocent III). *De miseria conditionis humane.* Ed Robert Lewis. Chaucer Library. Athens, Ga.: University of Georgia Press 1978

– *On the Misery of the Human Condition.* Ed Donald Howard. Indianapolis: Bobbs-Merrill 1969

Voeux du Heron. Ed Thomas Wright. In *Political Poems and Songs ... from the Accession of Edward II to That of Richard III* vol 1. Rerum Brittanicarum Medii Aevi Scriptores no 14. London: Longmans 1859

Wilkins, Nigel ed. *Armes, Amours, Dames, Chevalerie: An Anthology of French Songs from the Fourteenth Century.* Cambridge: New Press 1987

– *One Hundred Ballades, Rondeaux and Virelais.* Cambridge: Cambridge University Press 1968.

HISTORY AND CRITICISM

Armitage-Smith, Sidney. *John of Gaunt*. Westminster: Constable 1904
Avril, François. 'Les Manuscrits enluminés de Guillaume de Machaut' in *Guillaume de Machaut: poète et compositeur* Actes et Colloques 23. Paris: Klincksieck 1982
– *Manuscript Painting at the Courts of France: The Fourteenth Century* (1310–1380). New York: Braziller 1978
Badel, Pierre-Yves. *Le Roman de la Rose au XIVe siècle: étude de la réception de l'oeuvre*. Geneva: Droz 1980
Baird, Joseph L., and John R. Kane, eds. *La Querelle de la Rose: Letters and Documents*. Chapel Hill: University of North Carolina Press 1978
Baltzer, Rebecca A., Thomas Cable, and James I. Wimsatt, eds. *The Union of Words and Music in Medieval Poetry*. Austin: University of Texas Press 1991
Barber, Richard. 'Jean Froissart and the Black Prince' in *Froissart: Historian*. Ed J.J.N. Palmer. Bury St Edmunds: Boydell 1981
Baugh, Albert C. 'Chaucer and the *Panthère d'Amours*' in *Britannica Festschrift für Hermann M. Flasdieck*. Ed Wolfgang Iser and Hans Schabram. Heidelberg: Winter 1960
Baum, Paull. *Chaucer's Verse*. Durham, NC: Duke University Press 1961
Boitani, Piero. *Chaucer and Boccaccio*. Oxford: Society for the Study of Medieval Languages and Literature 1977
– 'Style, Iconography and Narrative: The Lesson of the *Teseida*' in *Chaucer and the Trecento*. Ed Piero Boitani. Cambridge: Cambridge University Press 1983
Boitani, Piero, and Anna Torti, eds. *Medieval and Pseudo-Medieval Literature*. Cambridge: D.S. Brewer 1984
Bower, Calvin. 'Natural and Artificial Music: The Origins and Development of an Aesthetic Concept.' *Musica Disciplina* 25 (1971) 17–33
Braddy, Haldeen. 'Chaucer and Graunson: The Valentine Tradition.' *PMLA* 54 (1939) 362–7
– *Chaucer and the French Poet Graunson*. 1947. Reprint Port Washington, NY: Kennikat Press 1971
– 'Chaucer's *Book of the Duchess* and Two of Graunson's Complaintes.' *Modern Language Notes* 52 (1937) 487–91
Brewer, Derek, ed. *Chaucer: The Critical Heritage*. 2 vols. London: Routledge 1978
Brownlee, Kevin. *Poetic Identity in Guillaume de Machaut*. Madison: University of Wisconsin Press 1984
– 'The Poetic *Oeuvre* of Guillaume de Machaut: The Identity of Discourse

and the Discourse of Identity' in *Machaut's World*. See Cosman and Chandler.

Brusendorff, Aage. *The Chaucer Tradition*. London: Oxford University Press 1925

Burrow, John A. *Ricardian Poetry*. London: Routledge 1971

Burrow, John A., ed. *Geoffrey Chaucer: A Critical Anthology*. Harmondsworth: Penguin 1969

Calendar of the Patent Rolls, Edward III, 1327–1377. 16 vols. London: Public Records Office 1891–1916

Calin, William. 'Le *moi* chez Guillaume de Machaut' in *Guillaume de Machaut: poéte et compositeur* Actes et Colloques 23. Paris: Klincksieck 1982

– *A Poet at the Fountain: Essays on the Narrative Verse of Guillaume de Machaut*. Lexington: University Press of Kentucky 1974

Cartier, Normand. '*Le Bleu Chevalier* de Froissart et *Le Livre de la Duchesse* de Chaucer:' *Romania* 88 (1967) 232–52

Cerquiglini, Jacqueline. '*Un engin si soutil': Guillaume de Machaut et l'écriture au XIVe siècle*. Bibliothèque du XVe Siècle 47. Geneva: Slatkine 1985

Clemen, Wolfgang. *Chaucer's Early Poetry*. London: Methuen 1963

Cook, Albert S. 'The Complaint of Chaucer to His Empty Purse.' *Transactions of the Connecticut Academy of Arts and Sciences* 23 (1919–20) 33–8

Cosman, Madeleine Pelner, and Bruce Chandler eds. *Machaut's World: Science and Art in the Fourteenth Century*. Annals of the New York Academy of Sciences vol. 314. New York: New York Academy of Sciences 1977

Coulton, G.G. *Chaucer and His England*. 8th ed. London: Methuen 1963

Coville, Alfred. 'Phillippe de Vitry: notes biographiques.' *Romania* 59 (1933) 520–47

– 'Poèmes historiques de l'avènement de Philippe VI de Valois au Traité de Calais (1328–60).' *Histoire littéraire de la France* 38. Paris: Imprimerie Nationale 1941

Cowling, G.H. 'A Note on Chaucer's Stanza.' *Review of English Studies* 2 (1926) 311–27

Crépin, André. 'Chaucer and the French' in *Medieval and Pseudo-Medieval Literature*. Ed Piero Boitani and Anna Torti. Cambridge: Brewer 1984

Crow, Martin M., and Clair C. Olson eds. *Chaucer Life-Records*. Austin: University of Texas Press 1966

Dembowski, Peter. *Jean Froissart and His 'Meliador': Context, Craft, and Sense*. Edward C. Armstrong Monographs on Medieval Literature 2. Lexington, Ky.: French Forum 1983

Denholm-Young, N. 'Richard de Bury (1287–1345).' *Transactions of the Royal Historical Society* 20 (1937) 135–68

Diekstra, F.N.M. 'The Poetic Exchange Between Philippe de Vitry and Jean de le Mote: A New Edition.' *Neophilologus* 70 (1986) 504–19

Dragonetti, Roger. '"La Poésie ... ceste musique naturele," Essai d'exégèse d'un passage de l'*Art de dictier* d'Eustache Deschamps.' In *Fin du Moyen Age et Renaissance* Mélanges ... Robert Guiette. Antwerp: Nederlandische Boekhandel 1961

– *La Technique poétique des trouvères dans la chanson courtoise*. Bruges: De-Tempel 1960

Earp, Lawrence, 'Lyrics for Reading and Lyrics for Singing in Late Medieval France' in *The Union of Words and Music in Medieval Poetry*. *See* Baltzer et al.

– 'Machaut's Role in the Production of Manuscripts of His Works.' *Journal of the American Musicological Society* 42 (1989) 461–502

– 'Scribal Practice, Manuscript Production and the Transmission of Music in Late Medieval France: The Manuscripts of Guillaume de Machaut.' PHD dissertation, Princeton University 1983

Eco, Umberto. *A Theory of Semiotics*. Bloomington: Indiana University Press 1976

Edmunds, Sheila. 'The Medieval Library of Savoy (II): Documents.' *Scriptorium* 25 (1971) 253–84

Estrich, Robert M. 'Chaucer's Prologue to the *Legend of Good Women* and Machaut's *Le Jugement dou Roy de Navarre*.' *Studies in Philology* 25 (1939) 20–39

Faral, Edmond. *Les Jongleurs en France au Moyen Age*. Paris: Champion 1910

Fisher, John H. *John Gower: Moral Philosopher and Friend of Chaucer*. New York: New York University Press 1964

Flinn, John. *Le Roman de Renart dans la littérature française et dans les littératures étrangères au Moyen Age*. Toronto: University of Toronto Press 1963

Freeman, Michelle A. 'Froissart's *Le Joli Buisson de Jonece*: A Farewell to Poetry?' in *Machaut's World*. *See* Cosman and Chandler.

Frye, Northrop. *Anatomy of Criticism*. Princeton: Princeton University Press 1957

– 'Approaching the Lyric' in *Lyric Poetry: Beyond New Criticism*. *See* Hošek and Parker.

– 'Introduction' in *Sound and Poetry*. Ed Northrop Frye. English Institute Essays 1956. New York: Columbia University Press 1957

Gennrich, Friedrich. 'Der Gesangswettstreit im *Parfait du Paon*.' *Romanische Forschungen* 58/59 (1947) 208–32

Gieber, Robert L. 'Poetic Elements of Rhythm in the Ballades, Rondeaux and Virelays of Guillaume de Machaut.' *Romanic Review* 73 (1982) 1–9

Giffin, Mary E. 'Cadwalader, Arthur, and Brutus in the Wigmore Manuscript.' *Speculum* 16 (1941) 109–20

Graham, Audrey. 'Froissart's Use of Classical Allusion in His Poems.' *Medium Aevum* 33 (1963) 24–33

Guiette, Robert. *D'une poésie formelle en France au Moyen Age.* Paris: Nizet 1972

Guillaume de Machaut: poète et compositeur. Actes et Colloques 23. Paris: Klincksieck 1982

Günther, Ursula. 'Contribution de la musicologie à la biographie et è la chronologie de Guillaume de Machaut.' In *Guillaume de Machaut: poète et compositeur.* Actes et Colloques 23. Paris: Klincksieck 1982

– 'Zitate in französischen Liedsätzen der Ars Nova und Ars Subtilior.' *Musica Disciplina* 26 (1972) 53–68

Guthrie, Steven. 'Meter and Performance in Machaut and Chancer.' In *The Union of Words and Music in Medieval Poetry.* See Baltzer et al.

Guy, Henry. *Essai sur la vie et les oeuvres du trouvère Adam de la Hale.* Paris: Hachette 1898

Havely, Nicholas, ed and trans. *Chaucer's Boccaccio: Sources of 'Troilus' and the 'Knight's' and 'Franklin's Tales.'* Chaucer Studies V. Woodbridge: Brewer 1980

Hoepffner, Ernest. 'Anagramme und Rätselgedichte bei Guillaume de Machaut.' *Zeitschrift für romanische Philologie* 30 (1906) 401–13

– 'Die Balladen des Dichters Jehan de le Mote.' *Zeitschrift für romanische Philologie* 35 (1911) 153–66

– 'La Chronologie des Pastourelles de Froissart.' *Mélanges offerts à M. Émile Picot* vol. 2. Paris: Société des Bibliophiles François 1913

– *Eustache Deschamps: Leben und Werke.* Strassburg: Trübner 1904

– 'Les Poésies lyriques du *Dit de la Panthére*.' *Romania* 46 (1920) 204–30

Holman, C. Hugh, and William Harmon eds. *Handbook to Literature.* 5th ed. New York: Macmillan 1986

Hošek, Chaviva, and Patricia Parker, eds. *Lyric Poetry: Beyond New Criticism.* Ithaca: Cornell University Press 1985.

Howard, Donald. *Chaucer: His Life, His Works, His World.* New York: Dutton 1987

Huot, Sylvia. *From Song to Book: The Poetics of Writing in Old French Lyric and Lyrical Narrative Poetry.* Ithaca: Cornell University Press 1987

Jakobson, Roman. *Language in Literature.* Ed Krystyna Pomorska and Stephen Rudy. Cambridge: Harvard University Press 1987

Jenkins, T. Atkinson. 'Deschamps' Ballade to Chaucer.' *Modern Language Notes* 33 (1918) 268–78

Johnson, W.R. *The Idea of Lyric: Lyric Modes in Ancient and Modern Poetry.* Berkeley: University of California Press 1982

Keitel, Elizabeth. 'La Tradition manuscrite de Guillaume de Machaut.' In *Guillaume de Machaut: poète et compositeur.* Actes et Colloques 23. Paris: Klincksieck 1982

Kelly, Douglas. 'Les Inventions ovidennes de Froissart: réflexions intertextuelles comme imagination.' *Littérature* 41 (1981) 82–92

– *Medieval Imagination: Rhetoric and the Poetry of Courtly Love.* Madison: University of Wisconsin Press 1978

Kelly, Henry A. *Chaucer and the Cult of Saint Valentine.* Davis Medieval Texts and Studies v. Leiden: Brill 1986

Kibler, William W. 'Poet and Patron: Froissart's *Prison amoureuse.' Esprit Créateur* 18 (1978): 32–46.

Kibler, William W., and James I. Wimsatt. 'The Development of the Pastourelle in the Fourteenth Century: An Edition of Fifteen Poems with an Analysis.' *Mediaeval Studies* 45 (1983) 22–78

Kirby, Thomas A. *Chaucer's Troilus: A Study in Courtly Love.* University, La: Louisiana State University Press 1940

Kittredge, George L. 'Antigone's Song of Love.' *Modern Language Notes* 25 (1910) 158

– 'Chaucer and Froissart.' *English Studies* 26 (1899) 321–36

– 'Chaucer and Some of His Friends.' *Modern Philology* 1 (1903) 1–18

– 'Chaucer's *Envoy to Bukton.' Modern Language Notes* 24 (1910) 14–15

– 'Chaucer's *Troilus* and Guillaume de Machaut.' *Modern Language Notes* 30 (1915) 69

– 'Guillaume de Machaut and the *Book of the Duchess.' PMLA* 30 (1915) 1–24

Laurie, I.S. 'Deschamps and the Lyric as Natural Music.' *Modern Language Review* 59 (1964) 561–70

Lehoux, Françoise. *Jean de France, duc de Berri: sa vie, son action politique (1340–1416).* 4 vols. Paris: Picard 1968

Lenaghan, R.T. 'Chaucer's *Envoy to Scogan*: The Uses of Literary Conventions.' *Chaucer Review* 10 (1975) 46–61

Lerch, Eugen. 'Zu einer Stelle bei Eustache Deschamps.' *Romanische Forschungen* 62 (1950) 67–8

Lewis, C.S. 'What Chaucer Really Did to *Il Filostrato.' Essays and Studies* 17 (1952) 56–76

Loomis, Roger Sherman. 'Edward I, Arthurian Enthusiast.' *Speculum* 38 (1953) 114–27

Lossing, Marian. 'The Prologue to the *Legend of Good Women* and the *Lai de Franchise.' Studies in Philology* 39 (1942) 15–35

Lowes, John L. 'Chaucer and the *Miroir de Mariage.*' *Modern Philology* 8 (1911) 165–86, 305–34
– 'The Chaucerian "Merciles Beaute" and Three Poems of Deschamps.' *Modern Language Review* 5 (1910) 33–9
– 'Illustrations of Chaucer, Drawn Chiefly from Deschamps.' *Romanic Review* 2 (1911) 113–28
– 'The Prologue to the *Legend of Good Women* as Related to the French *Marguerite* Poems and the *Filostrato.*' *PMLA* 19 (1904) 593–683
– 'The Prologue to the *Legend of Good Women* Considered in Its Chronological Relations.' *PMLA* 20 (1905) 749–864
Luria, Maxwell S., and Richard L. Hoffman eds. *Middle English Lyrics.* New York: Norton 1974
Lukitsch, Shirley. 'The Poetics of the *Prologue*: Machaut's Conception of the Purpose of His Art.' *Medium Aevum* 52 (1983) 258–71
Machabey, Armand. *Guillaume de Machault 130?–1377: la vie et l'oeuvre musicale.* 2 vols. Paris: Richard-Masse 1955
McKisack, May. *The Fourteenth Century, 1307–99.* Oxford History of England vol. 5. Oxford: Clarendon Press 1959
McMillan, Ann. 'Men's Weapons, Women's War: The Nine Female Worthies, 1400–1640.' *Medievalia* 5 (1979) 113–39
Maynard, Theodore. *The Connection between the Balade, Chaucer's Modification of It, Rime Royal, and the Spenserian Stanza.* Washington: Catholic University of America 1934
Morris, Lynn King. *Chaucer Source and Analogue Criticism.* New York: Garland 1985
Mudge, Charles. 'The Pennsylvania Chansonnier.' PHD dissertation, University of Indiana 1972
Muscatine, Charles. *Chaucer and the French Tradition: A Study in Style and Meaning.* Berkeley: University of California Press 1957
Musso, Nöel. 'Comparison statistique des lettres de Guillaume de Machaut et de Peronne d'Armentières dans le *Voir-Dit*' in *Guillaume de Machaut: poète et compositeur.* Actes et Colloques 23. Paris: Klincksieck 1982
Neilson, William A. *Origins and Sources of the Court of Love.* Harvard Studies and Notes in Philology and Literature VI. Cambridge: Harvard University Press 1899. Reprint 1967.
New Grove Dictionary of Music and Musicians. Ed Stanley Sadie. 20 vols. London: Macmillan 1980
Olson, Glending. 'Deschamps' *Art de Dictier* and Chaucer's Literary Environment.' *Speculum* 48 (1973) 714–23
– 'Toward a Poetics of the Late Medieval Court Lyric' in *Vernacular Poetics of*

the Middle Ages. Ed. Lois Ebin. Studies in Medieval Culture XVI. Kalamazoo: Medieval Institute Publications 1984

Olson, Paul. *The Canterbury Tales and the Good Society*. Princeton: Princeton University Press 1986

Oruch, Jack B. 'St Valentine, Chaucer, and Spring in February.' *Speculum* 56 (1981) 534–65

Osberg, Richard H. 'The Alliterative Lyric and Thirteenth-Century Devotional Prose.' *JEGP* 76 (1977) 40–54

– 'Alliterative Technique in the Lyrics of MS Harley 2253.' *Modern Philology* 82 (1984) 125–55

Ouy, Gilbert. 'In Search of the Earliest Traces of French Humanism: The Evidence from Codicology.' *Library Chronicle* 43 (1970) 1–38

Patch, Howard R. 'Troilus on Predestination.' *Journal of English and Germanic Philology* 17 (1918) 399–422

Patterson, Warner F. *Three Centuries of French Poetic Theory*. 3 vols. University of Michigan Publications in Language and Literature. Ann Arbor: University of Michigan Press 1935

Petit, Ernest. *Les ducs de Bourgogne de la maison de Valois* vol. 1. Paris: Picard 1910

Phillips, Helen. '*The Book of the Duchess*, ll. 31–96: Are They a Forgery?' *English Studies* 67 (1986) 113–21

Piaget, Arthur. 'La Cour amoureuse, dite de Charles VI.' *Romania* 20 (1891) 417–54

– 'Oton de Grandson: amoureux de la reine.' *Romania* 61 (1935) 72–82

– 'Un manuscrit de la *Cour amoureuse de Charles VI*.' *Romania* 31 (1902) 597–603

Pognon, E. 'Du nouveau sur Philippe de Vitri et ses amis.' *Humanisme et Renaissance* 6 (1939) 48–55

Poirion, Daniel. 'Le monde imaginaire de Guillaume de Machaut' in *Guillaume de Machaut: poète et compositeur*. Actes et Colloques 23. Paris: Klincksieck 1982

– *Le Poète et le prince: l'évolution du lyrisme courtois de Guillaume de Machaut à Charles d'Orléans*. Université de Grenoble Publications de la Faculté des Lettres et Sciences Humaines 35. Paris: Presses Universitaires de France 1965

Potvin, Charles ed. 'La Charte de la Cour d'Amour de l'année 1401.' *Bulletin de l'Académie Royale des Sciences, des Lettres, et des Beaux-Arts de Belgique* 3d Series, vol. 12 (1886) 191–220

Princeton Encyclopedia of Poetry and Poetics. Ed. Alex Preminger. Princeton: Princeton University Press 1965

Rajan, Tilottama. 'Romanticism and the Death of Lyric Consciousness' in *Lyric Poetry: Beyond New Criticism. See* Hošek and Parker.

Reaney, Gilbert. 'Towards a Chronology of Machaut's Musical Works.' *Musica Disciplina* 21 (1967) 87–96

Robbins, Rossell Hope. 'The Lyrics' in *Companion to Chaucer Studies.* Ed Beryl Rowland. Rev. ed. New York: Oxford University Press 1979

– 'The Vintner's Son:' French Wine in English Bottles' in *Eleanor of Aquitaine: Patron and Politician.* Ed William W. Kibler. Austin: University of Texas Press 1979

Robertson, D.W. Jr. *Chaucer's London.* New York: Wiley 1968

St John Hope, William H. *Windsor Castle: An Architectural History* 3 vols. London: Country Life 1913

Schless, Howard. *Chaucer and Dante: A Revaluation.* Norman, Okla.: Pilgrim Press 1984

Shears, F.S. *Froissart: Chronicler and Poet.* London: Routledge 1930

Smith, R.M. 'Five Notes on Chaucer and Froissart.' *Modern Language Notes* 66 (1966) 27–32

Spurgeon, Caroline F.E. *Five Hundred Years of Chaucer Criticism and Allusion, 1357–1900.* Chaucer Society, 2d ser. 40–50, 52–6. London: 1914–25 for 1908–17. Reprint New York: Russell and Russell 1960

Staiger, Emil. 'Lyrik und lyrisch' in *Zur Lyrik Diskussion.* Ed Reinhold Grimm. Wege der Forschung CXI. Darmstadt: Wissenschaftliche Buchgesellschaft 1974

Stevens, John. 'Dante and Music.' *Italian Studies* 23 (1968) 1–18

– *Music and Poetry in the Early Tudor Court.* London: Methuen 1961

– 'The "Music" of the Lyric: Machaut, Deschamps, Chaucer' in *Medieval and Pseudo-Medieval Literature. See* Boitani and Torti.

– *The Old Sound and the New.* Inaugural lecture. Cambridge: Cambridge University Press 1982

– *Words and Music in the Middle Ages: Song, Narrative, Dance and Drama, 1050–1350.* Cambridge: Cambridge University Press 1986

Stevens, Martin. 'The Royal Stanza in Early English Literature.' PMLA 94 (1979) 62–76

Straub, Theodor. 'Die Gründung des Pariser Minnehofs von 1400.' *Zeitschrift für romanische Philologie* 77 (1961) 1–14

Studer, P. 'An Anglo-Norman Poem by Edward II, King of England.' *Modern Language Review* 16 (1921) 34–46

Sypherd, Wilbur O. *Studies in Chaucer's 'House of Fame.'* Chaucer Society, 2d series 39. London: Haskell House 1907

Thomas, Antoine. 'Jean de le Mote, trouvère.' *Histoire littéraire de la France* 36. Paris: Imprimerie Nationale 1926

Thundy, Zacharias P. 'Matheolus, Chaucer, and the Wife of Bath' in *Chaucerian Problems and Prespectives: Essays Presented to Paul E. Beichner, csc.* Ed Edward Vasta and Zacharias P. Thundy. Notre Dame: Notre Dame University Press 1979

Vale, Juliet. *Edward III and Chivalry: Chivalric Society and Its Context 1270–1350.* Woodbridge: Boydell 1982

Varty, Kenneth. 'Deschamps' *Art de Dictier.*' *French Studies* 19 (1965) 164–8

Wallace, David. *Chaucer and the Early Writings of Boccaccio.* Chaucer Studies XII. Woodbridge: Brewer 1985

– 'Chaucer's Continental Inheritance' in *The Cambridge Chaucer Companion.* Ed Piero Boitani and Jill Mann. Cambridge: Cambridge University Press 1986

Walther, Hans. *Das Streitgedicht in der lateinischen Literatur des Mittelalters.* Munich: Beck 1920

Wetherbee, Winthrop. *Chaucer and the Poets: An Essay on 'Troilus and Criseyde.'* Ithaca: Cornell University Press 1984

Whiting, Bartlett J. 'Froissart as Poet.' *Mediaeval Studies* 8 (1946) 189–216

– 'The Vows of the Heron.' *Speculum* 20 (1945) 261–78

Wilkins, Nigel. 'Music and Poetry at Court: England and France in the Late Middle Ages' in *English Court Culture in the Later Middle Ages.* Ed V.J. Scattergood. London: Duckworth 1983

– *Music in the Age of Chaucer.* Cambridge: Brewer 1979

– 'A Pattern of Patronage: Machaut, Froissart and the Houses of Luxembourg and Bohemia in the Fourteenth Century.' *French Studies* 37 (1983) 257–84

– 'The Post-Machaut Tradition of Poet-Musicians.' *Nottingham Medieval Studies* 12 (1968) 40–84

Williams, Sarah Jane Manley. 'An Author's Role in Fourteenth-Century Book Production: Guillaume de Machaut's "Livre ou je met toutes mes choses." ' *Romania* 90 (1969) 433–54

– 'The Lady, the Lyrics, and the Letters.' *Early Music* 5 (1977) 462–8

– 'Machaut's Self-Awareness as Author and Producer' in *Machaut's World: Science and Art in the Fourteenth Century. See* Cosman and Chandler.

Wimsatt, James I. '*Anelida and Arcite*: A Narrative of Complaint and Comfort.' *Chaucer Review* 5 (1970): 1–8

– 'Chaucer and Deschamps' "Natural Music" ' in *The Union of Words and Music in Medieval Poetry. See* Baltzer et al.

– 'Chaucer and French Poetry' in *Geoffrey Chaucer.* Ed Derek Brewer. London: Bell 1974

- *Chaucer and the French Love Poets: The French Background of the 'Book of the Duchess.'* University of North Carolina Studies in Comparative Literature no 43. Chapel Hill: University of North Carolina Press 1968
- *Chaucer and the Poems of 'Ch' in University of Pennsylvania* MS *French 15.* Chaucer Studies IX. Cambridge: Brewer 1982
- 'Chaucer, Fortune, and Machaut's "Il m'est avis" ' in *Chaucerian Problems and Perspectives: Essays Presented to Paul E. Beichner, CSC.* Ed Edward Vasta and Zacharias P. Thundy. Notre Dame: University of Notre Dame Press 1979
- 'The *Dit dou Bleu Chevalier*: Froissart's Imitation of Chaucer.' *Mediaeval Studies* 34 (1972) 388–400
- 'The French Lyric Element in *Troilus and Criseyde*' *Yearbook of English Studies* 15 (1985) 18–32
- 'Froissart, Chaucer, and the Pastourelles of the Pennsylvania Manuscript.' *Studies in the Age of Chaucer* proceedings I (1984) 69–79
- 'Guillaume de Machaut and Chaucer's Love Lyrics.' *Medium Aevum* 47 (1978) 68–87
- 'Guillaume de Machaut and Chaucer's *Troilus and Criseyde*.' *Medium Aevum* 45 (1976) 277–93
- 'Machaut's *Lay de Confort* and Chaucer's *Book of the Duchess*' in *Chaucer at Albany.* Ed Rossell Hope Robbins. New York: Burt Franklin 1975
- *The Marguerite Poetry of Guillaume de Machaut.* University of North Carolina Studies in the Romance Language and Literatures, no 87. Chapel Hill: University of North Carolina Press 1970
- 'Medieval and Modern in Chaucer's *Troilus and Criseyde*.' PMLA 92 (1977) 203–15
Wimsatt, James I., and William Kibler. 'Machaut's Text and the Question of His Personal Supervision.' *Studies in the Literary Imagination* 20 (1987) 41–53
Wood, Chauncey. *The Elements of Chaucer's 'Troilus.'* Durham: Duke University Press 1984
Zumthor, Paul. *Le Masque et la lumière: la poétique des grands rhétoriqueurs.* Paris: Seuil 1972

Index

The italicized numbers signify extended quotations of text with analysis.